SP
ALLE ZEIT WACH
1842

Satya R. Chakravarty

Ethical Social Index Numbers

With 14 Figures

Springer-Verlag Berlin Heidelberg New York
London Paris Tokyo Hong Kong

Professor Satya R. Chakravarty
Institut für Wirtschaftstheorie und OR
Universität Karlsruhe
Kaiserstraße 12
D-7500 Karlsruhe, FRG

Economic Research Unit
Indian Statistical Institute
203 B.T.Road
Calcutta, 700 035
India

ISBN-13: 978-3-642-75504-0 e-ISNB-13: 978-3-642-75502-6
DOI: 10.1007/978-3-642-75502-6

Softcover reprint of the hardcover 1st edition 1990

Printing: Schmidt & Sohn GmbH, Mannheim 61
Bookbinding: T. Gansert GmbH, Weinheim-Sulzbach
2142/7130-543210

To my son **Ananyo**
and
nephews **Gaurav** and **Saurav**

Preface

In this book we are concerned with income profile based ethical social index numbers. An ethical index is designed from an explicit social evaluation function with a specific purpose in mind. For example, an ethical relative inequality index determines the fraction of total income that could be saved without any welfare loss if society distributed incomes equally. Ethical indices contrast with descriptive indices which are derived without using any concept of social welfare. Needless to say, ethical indices are not meant to supplant descriptive indices, rather they are constructed with different aims.

We begin Chapter 1 with a formal discussion on the concept of a social evaluation function. In the main body of this chapter we consider the problem of ranking income profiles using a social evaluation function. In Chapter 2 we set about analyzing alternative approaches to the measurement of inequality. In Chapter 3 we focus our attention on the Gini index, the most frequently used index of inequality, and its extensions.

In Chapter 4 we formulate the notion of an ethical distance function that measures welfare of one population relative to another. Chapter 5 is devoted to quantifications and discussions of alternative definitions of relative deprivation put forward by Runciman(1966).

In Chapter 6 we discuss alternative approaches to the measurement of poverty. Chapter 7 makes a detailed discussion on poverty indices which possess an attractive aggregation property. Such indices are helpful in identifying causal factors of poverty and in formulating poverty alleviation policies.

Chapter 8 provides a synthesis of point and overall measures of tax progressivity. This chapter also makes a discussion on ethical horizontal inequity indices which measure the size of welfare loss resulting from changes in the before–tax rankings of individuals caused by a fiscal system. Finally, in Chapter 9 we discuss ethical mobility indices which are measures of the change in welfare resulting from mobility.

This book was started at Calcutta; but substantial portions of the work took shape during my visit to the University of Karlsruhe, Federal Republic of Germany, in 1988–89. My work at the University of Karlsruhe was made possible through a grant from the German Research Foundation.

In preparing this book I derived much benefit from comments and suggestions made by many persons including Nikhiles Bhattacharya, Walter Bossert, Dipankar Coondoo, Bhaskar Dutta, Udo Ebert, Wolfgang Eichhorn, Gustav Fleig, Jan de V. Graaff, Robin Mukherjee, Andreas Pfingsten, Rainer Rothermel, Hirendra Nath Roy, Amartya K. Sen, Jacques Silber, Frank Stehling, Christof Weinhardt, John A. Weymark and Shlomo Yitzhaki. I wish to express my gratitude to all of them. However, none of these gentlemen should be held responsible for the errors and shortcomings of this work.

The first draft of this manuscript was typed by Samir Chakraborty, Subhas Dutta and Ingeborg Kast. Buddhadev Ghosh, Chiranjib Neogy and Padmaja Pal did all the numerical computations. The figures were drawn by Wolfgang Rack. I am grateful to all of them for their cooperation. I offer special thanks to Jochen Schneider who, in addition to providing helpful comments, spent many weeks on the word processor preparing the final draft of the book.

Finally, my wife, Sumita, made it all worthwhile.

CONTENTS

Glossary of Notation

$\mathbb{N}$: Set of positive integers.

1^n: n–coordinated vector of ones.

$\mathbb{R}^n_+$: Non–negative orthant of the Euclidean n–space $\mathbb{R}^n$.

D^n: $\mathbb{R}^n_+ \backslash \{0 \cdot 1^n\}$.

$\mathbb{R}_+$: $\bigcup_{n \in \mathbb{N}} \mathbb{R}^n_+$.

D: $\bigcup_{n \in \mathbb{N}} D^n$.

W^n: Restriction of the function W: $\mathbb{R}_+(D) \longrightarrow \mathbb{R}^1$ on $\mathbb{R}^n_+(D^n)$.

$E^n(x)$: Atkinson–Kolm–Sen (AKS) equally distributed equivalent (EDE) income associated with the income profile $x = (x_1, x_2, ..., x_n)$.

$\lambda(x)$: Mean of the profile x.

$\bar{x}$: Illfare ranked permutation of the profile x.

$\overset{\circ}{x}$: Welfare ranked permutation of the profile x.

x^*: Censored income profile corresponding to the profile x.

$x \gtrsim_L y$: x strictly Lorenz dominates y.

$x \gtrsim_{GL} y$: x strictly dominates y in the generalised Lorenz sense.

I_3: AKS inequality index.

A_1: Blackorby–Donaldson–Kolm (BDK) inequality index.

π: Poverty line.

$\pi(x)$: Set of poor persons in the profile x.

$P_1 = q/n$: Head–count ratio.

P_2: Income gap ratio.

P_3: Sen poverty index.

CHAPTER I

ON QUASI–ORDERINGS OF INCOME PROFILES

1.1 Introduction

In income distributions theory quite often we become interested in developing a criterion that can rank alternative profiles of income. Income profiles cannot be socially ordered if we do not make some prior value judgements. Value judgements, which are generally regarded as ethical statements, cannot be ascertained to be true or false on the basis of factual evidence. In the context of income profile ranking it is a convention to make the following value judgements: social preference for a more 'equitable' profile and higher incomes, ceteris paribus. These value judgements are referred to as 'equity preference' and 'efficiency preference' respectively.

In his seminal article drawing on works on uncertainty theory, Atkinson(1970) showed that many seemingly unrelated procedures for evaluating alternative income profiles are equivalent. The attractive feature of the Atkinson approach is that it is built upon the Lorenz curve (LC), which indicates the share of total income enjoyed by the bottom t proportion ($0 \leqq t \leqq 1$) of the population. To illustrate the Atkinson result, let us consider two income profiles x and y of a given total income over a fixed population size. Suppose that x strictly Lorenz dominates y (that is, the LC of y is nowhere inside that of x and at some places (at least) strictly outside the former). Then Atkinson's result says that a social evaluation function (SEF), which is taken as the sum of identical individual strictly concave utility functions, will make x socially better than y regardless of the form of the utility function. Furthermore, the converse is also true. This condition of Lorenz domination is also equivalent to the condition that the profile x can be obtained from the profile y by a finite sequence of rank preserving transformations transferring income from the rich to the poor.

However, if the two LCs cross, we can get two different strictly concave utility functions that will rank the two income profiles differently in regard to the level of social welfare. This means that the Lorenz criterion of ranking income profiles is not a com–

plete relation, that is, as a decisive criterion it is free to withhold judgements over some pairs of social states. Thus, the ordering of income profiles generated by the LC comparison is a quasi–ordering – it is transitive but not complete[1]. This quasi–ordering of income profiles should not be considered as a shortcoming of the Lorenz criterion. According to Sen(1973) equality is a manyfaceted phenomenon and is therefore essentially a question of quasi–ranking.

But the additivity assumption imposed on the SEF in the Atkinson theorem is highly restrictive. Dasgupta, Sen and Starrett(1973) and Rothschild and Stiglitz(1973) showed that the quasi–ordering of income profiles according to the LC is identical with the ordering implied by any symmetric SEF which exhibits a clear preference for equality (in the sense of being strictly quasi–concave). Dasgupta, Sen and Starrett also considered the problem of ranking income profiles over different population sizes.

The LC makes distributional judgements independently of the size of the profiles, that is, over profiles with a fixed mean. Thus, in LC comparison efficiency considerations are absent. In most circumstances in which we make distributional comparisons mean income is likely to vary. This is certainly true of intertemporal and intercountry comparisons. Shorrocks(1983) developed a criterion which would rank any two income profiles with different means. The new criterion, which is called the generalised Lorenz curve (GLC), is produced by scaling up the LC by the mean income. Shorrocks showed that if the GLC of one profile strictly dominates that of another, then the former is regarded as socially better than the latter by any SEF which is symmetric, equality preferring and increasing in its arguments. Thus, the generalised Lorenz domination reflects both a desire for greater equality and higher incomes. But the welfare judgements embodied in the generalised Lorenz domination may come into conflict with the social desire for more equal profile; a large increase in the income of the richest individual would usually be regarded as representing an increase in inequality. In order to avoid such a conflict between efficiency and equality, Shorrocks made two alternative suggestions to restrict the classes of admissible evaluation functions by weakening efficiency preference

[1] Formally, let $\{z_1,z_2,z_3,...\}$ be the set of alternatives on which a ranking relation R is defined. Then R is said to be complete if for any pair of alternatives z_1 and z_2, either $z_1 R z_2$ holds or $z_2 R z_1$ holds, or both. According to transitivity for any three alternatives z_1, z_2, z_3, if we have $z_1 R z_2$ and $z_2 R z_3$, then we must have $z_1 R z_3$. R is called an ordering if it is reflexive, transitive and complete. Reflexivity of R requires that for any $z \in \{z_1, z_2,...\}$, $z R z$. If a relation R is interpreted as 'at least as good as' and if we have $z_1 R z_2$ but not $z_2 R z_1$, then we say that z_1 is better than z_2. But if we have both $z_1 R z_2$ and $z_2 R z_1$, then z_1 and z_2 can be treated as indifferent.

so that they would make them compatible with greater equality. He derived results on generalised Lorenz domination under these frameworks.

In Section 4 of this chapter we make a detailed discussion on the Lorenz quasi–ordering. Section 5 presents the alternative quasi–orderings based on the GLC. SEFs have conceptual links with individual utility functions. These ideas will be explored in Section 2 of this chapter. Section 3 presents some definitions and Section 6 makes some concluding remarks including a discussion on the problem of ranking social states when LCs cross.

1.2 Social Evaluation (Welfare) Functions and their Arguments

One of the main objectives of welfare economics is to construct an ordering (that is, a reflexive, transitive, complete relation) that can rank all possible social states in a community. The term social state can be interpreted as 'a complete description of the amount of each type of commodity in the hand of each individual, the amount of each productive resource invested in each type of productive activity and the various types of collective activity' (Arrow(1951)). A reflexive, complete, transitive ranking of alternative social states is usually reffered to as social welfare ordering (SWO). If an SWO is assumed to be continuous[2], then it can be represented by a social welfare function (SWF) that assigns a real number to each social state. An SWF is continuous and order–preserving. The aim of this section is to make a brief discussion on SWFs. The discussion is based mainly on the works of Arrow(1951, 1963), Sen(1970, 1976, 1977, 1977a, 1979, 1986), Hammond(1976, 1979), D'Aspremont and Gevers(1977), Gevers(1979), Roberts(1980, 1980a), Blackorby, Donaldson and Weymark(1984) and Boadway and Bruce(1984).

Social states cannot be ranked if we do not make certain value judgements. A natural value judgement here is to require that the rankings of social states depend only on the personal utility levels, so that two arbitrary social states are ranked entirely on the basis of personal utilities in the respective states. To make this notion explicit let $X = \{z_1, z_2, ...\}$ stand for the set of all social states in a community of n individuals. We assume that preferences of individual i over the social states can be represented by a utility

[2] Continuity of a ranking relation R defined on the set of alternatives X requires that for all $z \in X$, the sets $\{z_1 \in X | z_1 \, R \, z\}$ and $\{z_1 \in X | z \, R \, z_1\}$ be closed.

function U_i over the space of social states. That is, preferences of the individuals are represented by a list of functions U_1, U_2,...,U_n. Our objective now is to derive an SWO over social states from the individual orderings of social states. Thus, technically we can now regard an SWO as a reflexive, complete, transitive relation on the set of all utility profiles of the form (U_1, U_2,...,U_n).

The value judgement that an SWO should ignore all nonutility features has been referred to as welfarism by Sen(1977). This is a strong requirement because it demands that an SWO will depend only on the individual utilities without providing any information on how the individual utilities are determined. Sen(1977) demonstrated that three conditions are sufficient for welfarism. These three conditions are unrestricted domain (UD), independance of irrelevant alternatives (IIA) and Pareto indifference (PI). UD requires that any logically possible n–coordinated utility profile should work in determining an SWO. IIA requires that if people's feelings change about some set of irrelevant alternatives, but do not change about the pair of alternatives z_1 and z_2, then the social ranking of z_1 and z_2 must remain the same. According to PI if all individuals are indifferent between two alternatives z_1 and z_2, then the society will also be indifferent between these two alternatives.

The next step is to specify the assumptions about measurability and comparability of individual utility functions. A measurability assumption regarding a particular utility function will determine the set of transformations that can be applied to the utility function without altering the usuable information. A comparability assumption shows to what extent the utility function of an individual is comparable with that of another individual. Alternative measurability and comparability assumptions can be made explicit by considering the set of transformations Ψ_i that can be applied to different utility functions without altering the SWO. Following D'Aspremont and Gevers(1977), Roberts(1980a), Sen(1977a, 1986), Blackorby, Donaldson and Weymark(1984) and Boadway and Bruce(1984), we write $\Psi(\underline{U}(z))$ for a vector of transformation functions $[\Psi_1(U_1(z)),\Psi_2(U_2(z)),...,\Psi_n(U_n(z))]$, where $\underline{U}(z)$ stands for the utility profile $(U_1(z),U_2(z),...,U_n(z))$ and z is any arbitrary social state. Measurability and comparability assumptions can now be formally stated by imposing restrictions on the transformations Ψ_i. We mention below some of the very important candidates.

(i) Ordinally Measurable, Noncomparable Utilities (OM – NC):
For all i, Ψ_i is increasing in its argument.

(ii) Ordinally Measurable, Fully Comparable Utilities (OM – FC):
For all i, $\Psi_i = \Psi$, with Ψ being increasing in its argument.

(iii) Cardinally Measurable, Noncomparable Utilities (CM – NC):
$\Psi_i(t) = a_i + b_i t$, $b_i > 0$, for all i.

(iv) Cardinally Measurable, Unit Comparable Utilities (CM – UC):
$\Psi_i(t) = a_i + bt$, $b > 0$, for all i.

(v) Cardinally Measurable, Fully Comparable Utilities (CM – FC):
$\Psi_i(t) = a + bt$, $b > 0$, for all i.

(vi) Perfectly Measurable, Fully Comparable Utilities (PM – FC):
Ψ_i is the identity mapping for all i.

In (i) and (ii) we have the same assumption of measurability. If a utility function is ordinally measurable, then the associated indifference curves can be numbered in an arbitrary manner. But the numbering must preserve the ranking of indifference curves – a higher number must be attached to a higher indifference curve. We, however, note that while (ii) allows interpersonal comparisons of utilities, (i) does not allow this. (iii) is analogous to (i) with the only exception that the concept of utility is cardinal in (iii). If a utility function U_i is cardinally measurable, then an affine transformation of U_i, that is, a transformation of the form $a + b \cdot U_i$, $b > 0$, gives us the same information as U_i. In (iv) and (v) utilities are cardinally measurable and (iv) allows comparisons of utility differences but does not allow comparison of utility levels. On the other hand with (v) we can compare both utility levels and utility differences. (vi) shows that all utility numbers have complete numerical significance. In this case each indifference curve of an individual has to be identified by a unique real number.

To investigate whether welfarism along with some specific assumption about the measurability and comparability of utilities leads to an explicit form of the SWF, we need to impose some more restrictions on SWO. One such restriction is the strong Pareto condition (SPC). According to this condition between two social states z_1 and z_2, z_1 is socially better than z_2 if none prefers z_2 to z_1 and at least one individual strictly prefers z_1 to z_2. A weaker version of this principle, the weak Pareto condition (WPC), demands that a social state z_1 is better than z_2 if every individual strictly prefers z_1 to z_2. Another restriction is symmetry, which requires that if U is a utility profile associated a social state z and U^* is any permutation of U, then the rankings of U and U^* generated by the SWO with respect to other utility profiles must be the same. Thus, according to symmetry the names of individuals are completely irrelevant to the social decision process.

We are now ready to state Arrow's(1951, 1963) fundamental theorem, a result on which almost all of the collective choice theory is based. Arrow's theorem says that welfarism, OM – NC and WPC imply that the only SWO is a dictatorship. That is, the SWO ordering must coincide with the preference of some individual irrespective of the preferences of the remaining individuals in the community. Arrow's theorem is usually stated as an impossibility theorem. This can be done by assuming directly a non–dictatorship requirement. According to the condition of non–dictatorship there should be no individual such that whenever he strictly prefers a social state z_1 to another state z_2, then invariably z_1 is regarded as socially better than z_2. We can state Arrow's result as an impossibility theorem also by imposing symmetry which rules out dictatorship automatically. Sen(1970) showed that Arrow's theorem remains valid if OM – NC is replaced by CM – NC. Another type of dictatorship that can emerge as an SWO is a positional dictatorship. In this case the decision making power is alloted to a particular rank or position, not to a particular person. An example of a positional dictatorship is the Rawlsian maximin criterion (Rawls(1971)), where the SWO is dictated by the preference of the individual with the minimum utility position. It has been shown that under welfarism, OM – FC, WPC and symmetry are necessary and sufficient for positional dictatorship (Gevers(1979), Roberts(1980) and Blackorby, Donaldson and Weymark(1984)). By adding an equity postulate of some type we can reduce the positional dictatorship to the maximin criterion.

So far we have discussed some forms of dictatorship as possible SWOs. It will certainly be interesting to consider some non–dictatorial SWOs or SWFs also. One such SWF is the generalised utilitarian rule $\sum_{i=1}^{n} a_i U_i$, where a_i's are positive scalars. Generealised utilitarian rule emerges as the only SWF under welfarism if we combine CM – UC with WPC and continuity (Blackorby, Donaldson and Weymark(1984)). By adding symmetry to the above list of axioms, an axiomatisation of utilitarianism is obtained, that is, the SWF is given by $\sum_{i=1}^{n} U_i$ (Gevers(1979)).

Before we conclude this discussion we may mention that 'with perfectly measurable, fully comparable utilities, any continuous SWF is compatible with the welfarism axioms and continuity' (Blackorby, Donaldson, Weymark(1984)). That is, the SWF in this case is the general Bergson(1938) – Samuelson(1947) form $B(U_1(x), U_2(x),..., U_n(x))$, where the function B is continuous. Thus, we observe that welfarism along with alternative assumptions about measurability and comparability of individual utility functions will lead to different forms of SWFs depending on further ethical judgement(s). The choice of a particular form from the set of possible SWFs will mean that for ranking alternative social states we have decided to make the value judgements that will completely characterise the chosen form of the SWF. For further discussions the reader is referred to the articles cited in the beginning of this section.

In subsequent discussions by a social state in a community of n–persons, we will mean an income profile $y = (y_1, y_2, \quad ,y_n)$, where $y_i \geq 0$ is the income earned by individual i. We assume that no ambiguity arises in connection with the definitions of income, the income earning unit (here individual) and the reference period over which income is observed. The conceptual problems connected with these definitions can be found in Atkinson(1974, 1983a) and Tinbergen(1975). For a fixed $n \geq 1$, the set of all income profiles is D^n, the non–negative orthant of the Euclidean n–space $\mathbb{R}^n$ with the origin deleted. The set of all possible income profiles is $D = \bigcup_{n \in \mathbb{N}} D^n$, where $\mathbb{N}$ is the set of all positive integers[3].

The following notation will also be adopted in this book. For any function $f: D \longrightarrow \mathbb{R}^1$ we denote the restriction of f on D^n by f^n, where $n \in \mathbb{N}$. For all $n \in \mathbb{N}$, for all $y \in D^n$, we write $\lambda(y) = \frac{1}{n} \cdot \sum_{i=1}^{n} y_i$ for the mean of y. For all $n \in \mathbb{N}$ and $y \in D^n$, $\bar{y}$ and $\mathring{y}$ represent respectively the illfare and welfare ranked permutations of y, that is, $\bar{y}_1 \leq \bar{y}_2 \leq ... \leq \bar{y}_n$ and $\mathring{y}_1 \geq \mathring{y}_2 \geq ... \geq \mathring{y}_n$. An n–coordinated vector of ones is denoted by 1^n, $n \in \mathbb{N}$.

---

[3]However, in some cases $\mathbb{R}^n_+$, the non–negative orthant of $\mathbb{R}^n$, will be taken as the set of income profiles over a population size n. Consequently, the set of all possible income profiles will be $\mathbb{R}_+ = \bigcup_{n \in \mathbb{N}} \mathbb{R}^n_+$.

In order to use income distribution statistics for ranking alternative profiles of income, we assume that individual i's utility function depends only on his income, that is, U_i depends only on y_i. It is also necessary to assume that these utilities are comparable between persons. We know that one way of ensuring that this is the case is to assume that all individuals have the same utility function, that is, for all i, $U_i(\cdot) = U(\cdot)$. Then we assume that the SWF $B(U(y_1), U(y_2), \ldots ,U(y_n))$ can be rewritten as $F(y_1, y_2, \ldots , y_n)$. The function F can now be regarded as the restriction W^n of $W: D \longrightarrow \mathbb{R}^1$ on D^n, $n \in \mathbb{N}$. Blackorby and Donaldson(1980) suggested that the term social evaluation function (SEF) would be more appropriate for W since it is defined on the distributions of incomes.

1.3 Some Definitions

In this section we present some definitions which relate to the concavity, quasi–concavity and Schur–concavity of a function. Functions possessing such properties will be used extensively in subsequent discussions.

Definition 1.1

A function $f^n: D^n \longrightarrow \mathbb{R}^1$ is concave if

$$f^n(\Theta\cdot x + (1-\Theta)\cdot y) \geq \Theta\cdot f^n(x) + (1-\Theta)\cdot f^n(y) , \tag{1.1}$$

for all $\Theta \in [0,1]$ and for all $x, y \in D^n$.

For a strictly concave function the defining inequality is

$$f^n(\Theta\cdot x + (1-\Theta)\cdot y) > \Theta\cdot f^n(x) + (1-\Theta)\cdot f^n(y) , \tag{1.2}$$

for all $\Theta \in (0,1)$ and for all $x, y \in D^n$ with $x \neq y$.

The above definition shows that a strictly concave function is necessarily concave, but the converse is not true. For example, an affine map is concave but not strictly so. If we draw the graph of a (strictly concave) concave function, we find that this graph possesses the following geometric feature: The straight line joining any two points on the graph lies (entirely below) on or below the graph.

Definition 1.2

A function $f^n: D^n \longrightarrow \mathbb{R}^1$ is (strictly) convex if $-f^n$ is (strictly) concave.

Definition 1.3

A function $f^n: D^n \longrightarrow \mathbb{R}^1$ is quasi–concave if

$$f^n(\Theta \cdot x + (1-\Theta) \cdot y) \geq \min \{f^n(x), f^n(y)\} , \qquad (1.3)$$

for all $\Theta \in [0,1]$ and for all $x, y \in D^n$.

For a strictly quasi–concave function f^n the defining inequality is

$$f^n(\Theta \cdot x + (1-\Theta) \cdot y) > \min \{f^n(x), f^n(y)\} , \qquad (1.4)$$

for all $\Theta \in (0,1)$ and for all $x, y \in D^n$ where $x \neq y$.

Note that quasi–concavity is a weaker condition than concavity. Any (strictly) concave function will be (strictly) quasi–concave, but not of course, vice–versa. For instance, $f^1: D^1 \longrightarrow \mathbb{R}^1$ defined by $f^1(z) = z^3$ is quasi–concave but not concave. For a two–coordinated strictly quasi–concave function, definition 1.3 tells us that if $f^2(x) = f^2(y)$ and $x \neq y$ so that x and y are on the same contour, then

$$f^2(\Theta \cdot x + (1-\Theta) \cdot y) > f^2(x) = f^2(y) , \Theta \in (0,1) . \qquad (1.5)$$

That is, the line joining x and y lies entirely above the contour containing x and y. Thus, strictly quasi–concave functions are those quasi–concave functions whose contours do not contain any flat section. On the other hand, strictly concave functions are those concave functions whose graphs do not contain any flat section (Madden(1986)).

Definition 1.4

A function $f^n: D^n \longrightarrow \mathbb{R}^1$ is (strictly) quasi–convex if $-f^n$ is (strictly) quasi–concave.

To define Schur–concavity, what we write S–concavity, we need to define a permutation matrix.

Definition 1.5

A square matrix of order n is said to be a bistochastic marix if all of its entries are non–negative and each of its rows and columns sums to one; a matrix is a permutation marix if it is bistochastic and has exactly one positive entry in each row and each column.

We can now express symmetry of an n–coordinated function using a permutation matrix:

Definition 1.6

A function $f^n: D^n \longrightarrow \mathbb{R}^1$ is said to be symmetric if $f^n(P\,x) = f^n(x)$ for all $x \in D^n$, where P is any permutation matrix of order n.

Definition 1.7

A function $f^n: D^n \longrightarrow \mathbb{R}^1$ is S–concave if $f^n(B\,x) \geq f^n(x)$ for all $x \in D^n$, where B is any bistochastic matrix of order n.

For strict S–concavity of f^n, the weak inequality is to be replaced by a strict inequality whenever B x is not a permutation of x.

Definition 1.8

A function $f^n: D^n \longrightarrow \mathbb{R}^1$ is said to be (strictly) S–convex if $-f^n$ is (strictly) S–concave.

All S–concave and S–convex functions are symmetric. Symmetry and quasi–concavity of a numerical function implies S–concavity, but the converse is not true (Berge(1961)). Thus, for a symmetric function, the idea of S–concavity is a generalisation of the idea of quasi–concavity.

The definitions that have been presented in this section assumed that n, the dimension of domain D^n of the function f^n, is fixed. However, quite often we become interested in studying the properties of a function defined on the general domain D. A function h: $D \longrightarrow \mathbb{R}^1$ will be called (strictly) concave if for all $n \in \mathbb{N}$, h^n is (strictly) concave. Similarly, we can define quasi–concavity and S–concavity of a function on D. A function h: $D \longrightarrow \mathbb{R}^1$ will be called symmetric if for all $n \in \mathbb{N}$, h^n is invariant to permutations of its arguments, that is, h^n is symmetric.

1.4 The Lorenz Quasi–Ordering

Income distribution data can be presented in an illuminating way through what is called a Lorenz curve (LC) due to Lorenz(1905). An LC indicates the share of total income which is received by the bottom t proportion ($0 \leq t \leq 1$) of the population. Formally, in terms of the illfare ranked permutation $\bar{x}$ of a given profile of income x over a population size n, the LC $L(x,i/n)$ is a plot of $\sum_{j=1}^{i} \bar{x}_j / n\lambda(x)$ against i/n, as i goes from 0 to n, where $L(x,0) = 0$. Obviously 0% of the population possesses 0% of the total income and 100% of the population possesses the entire income. So an LC runs from the south–west corner of the unit square to the diametrically opposite corner, that is, the north–east corner. The LC is extremely useful because it gives a diagrammatic exposition of the degree of dispersion of incomes. If all the incomes are equal, so that every

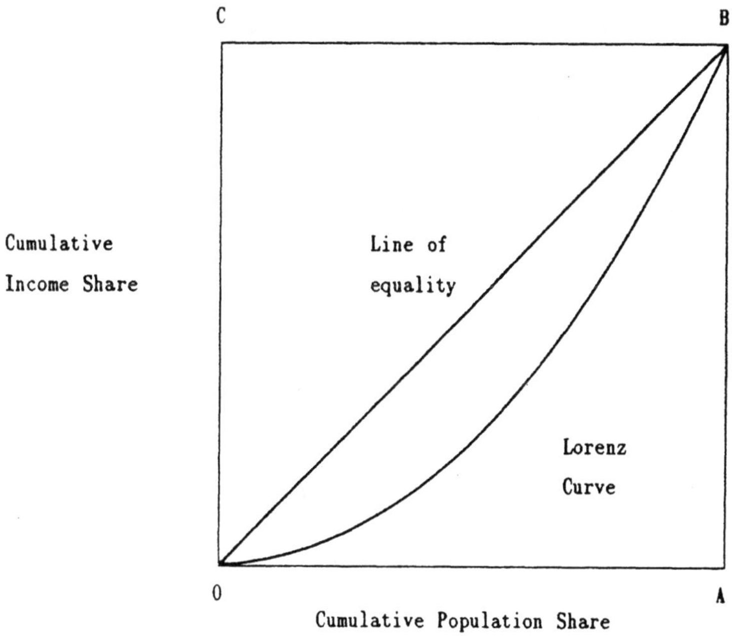

Figure 1.1

t% of the population possesses t% of the total income, the LC coincides with the diagonal 'line of income equality' or the 'egalitarian line'. If the bottom t% of the population possesses less than t% of the total income, then the LC lies below the egalitarian line. In the extreme case where only one person receives the entire income, the LC runs through the horizontal axis until we reach the richest person and it then rises perpendicularly. Therefore, the divergence of the LC from the egalitarian line is one way of assessing the extent of income differences within a given population[4].

For discussing the role of LCs in ranking alternative profiles of income, we need to define the Lorenz domination relation. For simplicity, we initially restrict our attention on distributions of income over a given population size n. The variable population case will

[4] A rigorous discussion on the properties of the LC can be found in Chapter 3.

be discussed later on. An income profile $x \in D^n$ is said to Lorenz dominate another profile $y \in D^n$ in the weak sense if the LC of x lies nowhere below the LC of y. Formally, x weakly Lorenz dominates y if

$$\frac{1}{n\lambda(x)} \sum_{j=1}^{i} \bar{x}_j \geq \frac{1}{n\lambda(y)} \sum_{j=1}^{i} \bar{y}_j , \tag{1.6}$$

for all i = 0, 1, 2, ... ,n. We say that x strictly Lorenz dominates y, what we write $x \succsim_L y$, if (1.6) holds with the additional restriction that there will be strict inequality for at least one i < n. That is, x strictly Lorenz dominates y if the LC of x is nowhere below and at some places (at least) above the LC of y. Thus, in figure 1.2

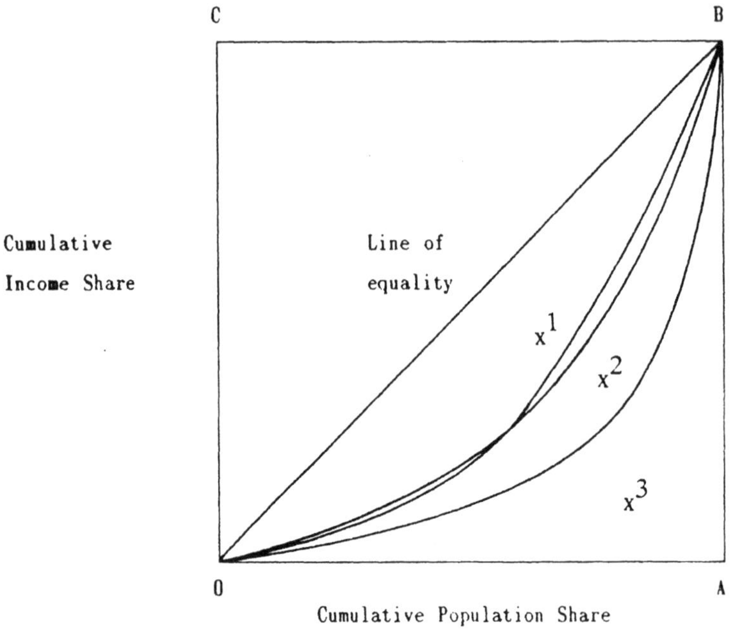

Figure 1.2

both the profiles x^1 and x^2 strictly Lorenz dominate x^3. On the other hand, the ordering of income profiles generated by the LC comparison is a quasi–ordering, since if the LCs intersect neither can be said to be preferred by the Lorenz domination criterion. We cannot rank the profiles x^1 and x^2 by this criterion. Clearly, while the weak Lorenz criterion satisfies both reflexivity and transitivity, the strict criterion meets only transitivity.

A remarkable consequence of the strict Lorenz domination relation, which will also be referred to as the Lorenz superiority relation, was proved by Atkinson(1970). This we state below.

Theorem 1.1 (Atkinson 1970)

Suppose that the SEF is utilitarian symmetric in incomes, so $W^n(x) = \sum_{i=1}^{n} U(x_i)$.

Then for x, y $\in D^n$ where $\lambda(x) = \lambda(y)$, the following conditions are equivalent:

(i) $x \gtrapprox_L y$.

(ii) $W^n(x) > W^n(y)$ for any strictly concave real valued utility function U.

The intuition behind the Atkinson result is fairly straightforward. Since x and y are two distributions of income of a given total over a given population size, it can be shown that we can obtain the profile x from the profile y by redistributing incomes from the rich to the poor. These redistributions will increase social welfare, since with a strictly decreasing marginal utility function the gain to the poor person will be greater than the loss incurred by the rich person. Thus, if we add up all the changes together, social welfare must increase (Boadway and Bruce(1984)).

But as mentioned earlier, the utilitarian SEF is not the only SEF that can be consistent with Lorenz domination. Dasgupta, Sen and Starrett(1973) and Rothschild and Stiglitz(1973) generalised the Atkinson theorem by weakening the concavity and the additivity assumptions sufficiently.

Theorem 1.2 (Dasgupta, Sen and Starrett 1973)

Let x, y be two profiles of the same amount of total income over a given population size n; that is, x, y $\in D^n$ where $\lambda(x) = \lambda(y)$. Then the following statements are equivalent:

(i) $x \gtrapprox_L y$.

(ii) $W^n(x) > W^n(y)$ for all strictly S–concave SEFs $W^n: D^n \rightarrow \mathbb{R}^1$.

What Theorem 1.2 tells is that if the LCs of the profiles x and y with the same mean do not cross, then the profile associated with the LC closer to the line of equality will represent higher social welfare for any SEF provided that it is strictly S–concave. However, the theorem also warns that if the two LCs intersect the ranking of the profiles cannot be unambiguous by SEFs: We can get two strictly S–concave SEFs that will rank the profiles in different directions.

The proof of Theorem 1.2 proceeds by using certain well-known results of Hardy, Littlewood and Polya(1934) on mathematical inequalities. For x, y $\in D^n$, where $\lambda(x) = \lambda(y)$, they show that the following conditions are equivalent:

(a) For all $k \leqq n$, $\sum_{i=1}^{k} \bar{x}_i \geqq \sum_{i=1}^{k} \bar{y}_i$, with at least one $k < n$ such that $\sum_{i=1}^{k} \bar{x}_i > \sum_{i=1}^{k} \bar{y}_i$.

(b) If $\bar{x}$ is not a permutation of $\bar{y}$, there exists a bistochastic matrix Q such that $\bar{x} = Q\bar{y}$.

(c) $\bar{y}$ can be transformed into $\bar{x}$ by a finite sequence of transformations of the form

$$\bar{y}_i^{\alpha+1} = \bar{y}_i^{\alpha} + c^{\alpha} \leqq \bar{y}_j^{\alpha}$$
$$\bar{y}_j^{\alpha+1} = \bar{y}_j^{\alpha} - c^{\alpha} \geqq \bar{y}_i^{\alpha}$$

for $i < j$ and $c^{\alpha} > 0$, with $\bar{y}_k^{\alpha+1} = \bar{y}_k^{\alpha}$ if $k \neq i, j$.

(d) For any strictly concave real valued U, $\sum_{i=1}^{n} U(x_i) > \sum_{i=1}^{n} U(y_i)$.

Given that the means of the profiles x and y are the same, the first condition in the Hardy–Littlewood–Polya theorem says that the LC of x is closer to the line of equality than the LC of y. Since a bistochastic matrix is a matrix with non-negative entries whose row and column sums are all one, condition (b) means that each income in the vector $\bar{x}$ is a weighted average of the incomes of $\bar{y}$, where the non-negative weights sum to one. By the third condition we mean that the profile $\bar{x}$ is obtained from the profile $\bar{y}$ by a finite sequence of rank preserving transformations $\{ c^{\alpha} \}$ transferring income from the rich to the poor. Finally, condition (d) means that x is regarded as more equal than y by the symmetric utilitarian SEF as long as the identical utility function U is strictly concave.

Proof of Theorem 1.2

(i) $\Rightarrow$ (ii):

Suppose $x \geqq_L y$. Now by the Hardy–Littlewood–Polya theorem $x \geqq_L y$ implies that there must be a bistochastic matrix Q such that $\bar{x} = Q\bar{y}$. It follows immediately that for any strictly S-concave $W^n: D^n \to \mathbb{R}^1$, $W^n(\bar{x}) = W^n(Q\bar{y}) > W^n(\bar{y})$. Since an S-concave function is symmetric, we have $W^n(\bar{x}) = W^n(x)$ and $W^n(\bar{y}) = W^n(y)$. Thus, $x \geqq_L y$ implies that for all strictly S-concave $W^n: D^n \to \mathbb{R}^1$, $W^n(x) > W^n(y)$.

(ii) $\Longrightarrow$ (i):

Since in the Hardy–Littlewood–Polya theorem conditions (a) and (d) are equivalent, it implies that not (a) implies not (d). That is, if not $x \geq_L y$, then for some strictly concave U, $\sum_{i=1}^{n} U(x_i) \leq \sum_{i=1}^{n} U(y_i)$. Now, given strict concavity of U, we can regard $\sum_{i=1}^{n} U(x_i)$ as a strictly S–concave function (Marshall and Olkin(1979), p. 64). Therefore, it now follows that if not $x \geq_L y$, then for some strictly S–concave real valued W^n, $W^n(x) \leq W^n(y)$. That is, not (i) implies not (ii). Hence (ii) $\Longrightarrow$ (i). ∎

Theorem 1.2 is very valuable since it provides a strong justification to accept strict S–concavity as an egalitarian principle – strict S–concavity of an SEF is equivalent to the requirement that a rank preserving transfer of income from a rich person to a poor person increases social welfare. Thus, strict S–concavity is a sufficient condition to incorporate egalitarian bias into distributional judgements.

Rothschild and Stiglitz(1973) established that the quasi–ordering of income profiles according to the Lorenz criterion is identical with the ordering generated by any symmetric, strictly quasi–concave SEF. Since strict quasi–concavity and symmetry imply strict S–concavity, the restriction imposed on the SEF in the Dasgupta–Sen–Starrett theorem can be regarded as weaker than that in the Rothschild–Stiglitz theorem. In view of this, we will not go for further discussion of the Rothschild–Stiglitz theorem.

We know that Theorem 1.2 is applicable to comparison of income profiles of a given total over the same population size. However, international comparisons usually involve different population sizes and different means, as do intertemporal comparisons for the same country. The problem of ranking profiles with different means will be discussed in the next section. For ranking profiles with the same mean over different population sizes, Dasgupta, Sen and Starrett(1973) proposed a postulate for the SEF, which they called the symmetry axiom for population (SAP). According to SAP, if an income profile is replicated k times, then the aggregate welfare of the replicated profile is simply k times the welfare of the actual profile.

Symmetry Axiom for Population (SAP)

For all $n \in \mathbb{N}$, for all $x \in D^n$, $W^{nk}(y) = k \cdot W^n(x)$, where $y = (x^{(1)}, x^{(2)}, \ldots, x^{(k)})$, each $x^{(i)} = x$ and $W: D \longrightarrow \mathbb{R}^1$.

Thus, SAP reflects that average (community) welfare is population replication invariant.

Theorem 1.3 (Dasgupta, Sen and Starrett 1973)

Let y^1 and y^2 be two profiles of income with the same mean over the population sizes n_1 and n_2 respectively. That is, $y_1 \in D^{n_1}$ and $y^2 \in D^{n_2}$ where $\lambda(y^1) = \lambda(y^2)$. Then the following statements are equivalent:

(i) $y^1 \geq_L y^2$.

(ii) $W^{n_1}(y^1)/n_1 > W^{n_2}(y^2)/n_2$ for all SEFs $W: D \longrightarrow \mathbb{R}^1$ that satisfy strict S–concavity and SAP.

Proof

(i) ⟹ (ii):

Let $y^3(y^4)$ denote the $n_2(n_1)$ fold replication of $y^1(y^2)$. Clearly $y^3, y^4 \in D^{n_1 n_2}$ and $\lambda(y^3) = \lambda(y^4)$. Now, the LC is population replication invariant. Consequently, y^3 and y^4 have the same LCs as y^1 and y^2 respectively. Therefore, $y^1 \geq_L y^2$ implies that $y^3 \geq_L y^4$. Hence by Theorem 1.2 for all strictly S–concave SEFs $W^{n_1 n_2}: D^{n_1 n_2} \longrightarrow \mathbb{R}^1$, $W^{n_1 n_2}(y^3) > W^{n_1 n_2}(y^4)$. But the SEF satisfies SAP. Therefore, $W^{n_1 n_2}(y^3) = n_2 W^{n_1}(y^1)$ and $W^{n_1 n_2}(y^4) = n_1 \cdot W^{n_2}(y^2)$. Hence $W^{n_1}(y^1)/n_1 > W^{n_2}(y^2)/n_2$.

(ii) ⟹ (i):

This part of the theorem follows from a construction similar to the above, again using Theorem 1.2. ■

Thus, Theorem 1.3 suggests that under symmetry axiom for population and strict S–concavity, Lorenz domination with the same mean income implies a higher mean welfare level even for the case of variable population sizes.

1.5 Some Alternative Quasi–Orderings

In this section we discuss some extensions of the results presented in the previous section to the case of variable mean incomes. It would be reasonable to assume that if one profile $x \in D^n$ has both a higher mean and a higher LC than another profile $y \in D^n$, then social welfare under x is also higher than social welfare under y. Shorrocks(1983) argued that this will be true if the SEF $W^n: D^n \to \mathbb{R}^1$ is strictly S–concave and increasing (see also Rothschild and Stiglitz(1973)). But even now the ranking of income profiles with differing means is limited because we need both a higher LC and a higher mean for a clear verdict.

The ability of LCs to provide unambiguous ranking of income profiles with differing means improves substantially if we extend the concept of LC to what Shorrocks(1983) has referred to as generalised Lorenz curve (GLC). The GLC is constructed by scaling up the LC by the mean income. Formally, in terms of the illfare ranked permutation $\bar{x}$ of a given profile $x \in D^n$ the GLC GL(x, i/n) is a plot of $\sum_{j=1}^{i} \bar{x}_j/n$ against i/n as i goes from 0 to n where GL(x,0) = 0. We say that an income profile $x \in D^n$ weakly dominates another profile $y \in D^n$ in the generalised Lorenz sense if

$$\frac{1}{n}\sum_{j=1}^{i} \bar{x}_j \geq \frac{1}{n}\sum_{j=1}^{i} \bar{y}_j \tag{1.7}$$

for all i = 0, 1, ..., n. x strictly dominates y in the generalised Lorenz sense, what we write $x \gtrsim_{GL} y$, if (1.7) holds with the additional restriction that there will be strict inequality for at least one $i \leq n$. That is, by $x \gtrsim_{GL} y$ we mean that the GLC of x is nowhere below and at some places (at least) inside the GLC of y.

The following theorem explains the role of GLCs in ranking income profiles with different means:

Theorem 1.4 (Shorrocks 1983)

Let x and y be two profiles of income over a given population size n, that is, x, y $\in D^n$. Then the following statements are equivalent:

(i) $x \gtrsim_{GL} y$.

(ii) $W^n(x) > W^n(y)$ for all increasing, strictly S–concave SEFs $W^n: D^n \to \mathbb{R}^1$.

Thus, unlike the Lorenz criterion, the generalised Lorenz domination takes explicitly into account the sizes of the income profiles under comparison. Clearly, the ranking of income profiles according to the generalised Lorenz domination agrees with the strong

Pareto principle.

The proof of Theorem 1.4 relies on a result of Marshall and Olkin(1979). For x, y $\in$ D^n they show that the following conditions are equivalent:

(a) $\sum_{i=1}^{k} \bar{x}_i \geq \sum_{i=1}^{k} \bar{y}_i$ for all $k \leq n$, with strict inequality for at least one k.

(b) For any strictly concave, increasing real valued U, $\sum_{i=1}^{n} U(x_i) > \sum_{i=1}^{n} U(y_i)$.

(c) There exists a bistochastic matrix Q such that $\bar{x} \geq Q\bar{y}$[5].

The first condition in the Marshall–Olkin theorem is simply the statement that the GLC of x lies everywhere on and at some places (at least) above the GLC of y. That is, x is superior to y in the generalised Lorenz sense – $x \geq_{GL} y$. According to condition (b) the profile x is regarded as socially better than the profile y by the utilitarian SEF, where the utility function is increasing and strictly concave. Assuming that an individual prefers more income to less, the requirement $Q\bar{y} \leq \bar{x}$ means that some individuals may be indifferent between $Q\bar{y}$ and $\bar{x}$, at least one individual strictly prefers $\bar{x}$ to $Q\bar{y}$ and no individual prefers $Q\bar{y}$ to $\bar{x}$. That is, $Q\bar{y} \leq \bar{x}$ is consistent with the strong Pareto rule.

Proof of Theorem 1.4

(i) $\Rightarrow$ (ii):

Suppose $x \geq_{GL} y$. Now by the Marshall–Olkin theorem $x \geq_{GL} y$ implies that there must be a bistochastic matrix Q such that $Q\bar{y} \leq \bar{x}$. Let W^n: $D^n \rightarrow \mathbb{R}^1$ be increasing and strictly S–concave. Then by increasingness of W^n, $W^n(\bar{x}) > W^n(Q\bar{y})$. Again, strict S–concavity of W^n implies that $W^n(Q\bar{y}) > W^n(\bar{y})$. By symmetry of W^n, we have $W^n(\bar{x}) = W^n(x)$ and $W^n(\bar{y}) = W^n(y)$. Thus, $x \geq_{GL} y$ implies that $W^n(x) > W^n(y)$.

(ii) $\Rightarrow$ (i):

Since in the Marshall–Olkin theorem conditions (a) and (b) are equivalent, it implies that not (a) implies not (b). That is, if not $x \geq_{GL} y$, then for some in-

[5] The inequality $\bar{x} \geq Q\bar{y}$ means that for all $i \leq n$, the ith coordinate of $Q\bar{y}$ is less than or equal to the ith coordinate of $\bar{x}$, with strict inequality for at least one i.

creasing, strictly concave U, $\sum_{i=1}^{n} U(x_i) \leq \sum_{i=1}^{n} U(y_i)$. Now, given increasingness and strict concavity of U, we can regard $\sum_{i=1}^{n} U(x_i)$ as an increasing, strictly S–concave function (Marshall and Olkin(1979), p. 64). Thus, it now follows that if not $x \geq_{GL} y$, then for some increasing, strictly S–concave real valued W^n, $W^n(x) \leq W^n(y)$. That is, not (i) implies not (ii). Hence (ii) implies (i). ■

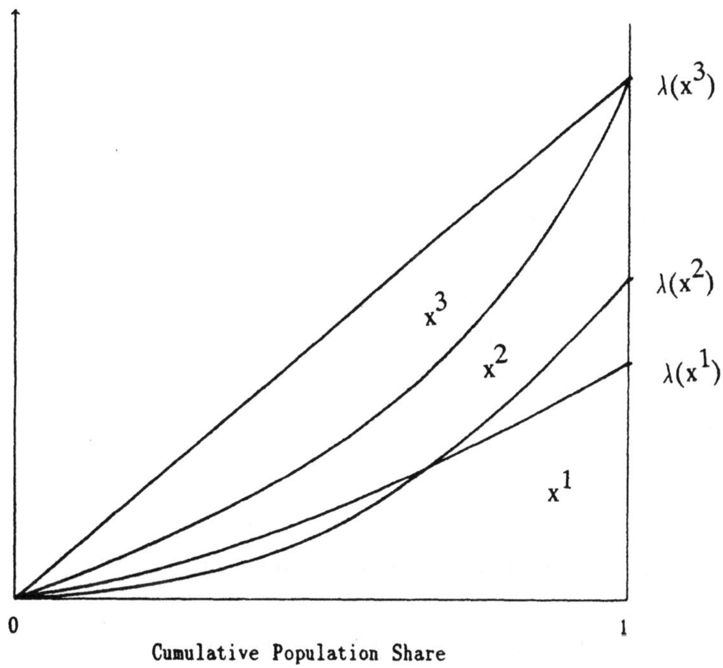

Figure 1.3

Theorem 1.4 indicates that an unambiguous ranking of income profiles by all increasing, strictly S–concave SEFs can be obtained if and only if the the GLCs do not intersect. 'Clearly this latter condition will apply if one of the distributions has both a higher mean and a higher LC. But it will also be satisfied in other cases if the higher mean is sufficient to offset the lower part of the LC. This is likely to be true in many important practical situations, since differences between LCs tend to be relatively small compared with variations in mean incomes' (Shorrocks(1983)). Thus, the GLCs are likely to intersect less often than the LCs. In figure 1.3, x^3 is preferred to both x^1 and x^2. The larger mean of x^3 is sufficient to compensate for whatever differences in the income distribution may exist. Obviously, the ordering generated by the comparison of GLCs remains a partial one[6].

As a particular case let us now suppose that the society has adopted the policy of maximising the income of the worst–off individual. Since the Rawlsian maximin SEF $\min_i \{x_i\}$ is non–decreasing and S–concave, the following result drops out as an interesting corollary to Theorem 1.4.

<u>Corollary 1.1</u>

Suppose that the SEF W is of the Rawlsian maximin type. Then for arbitrary x, y $\in D^n$ the following statements are equivalent:

(i) $W^n(x) \geqq W^n(y)$.

(ii) x weakly dominates y in the generalised Lorenz sense.

Rothschild and Stiglitz(1973) defined an inefficient regressive transfer (IRT) as a redistribution of income in which a poor person i gives up d while a richer man j receives less than d. Formally, the profile $y \in D^n$ results from the profile x by means of an IRT if (a) $x_k = y_k$ for all $k \neq i,j$, (b) $x_i - y_i > y_j - x_j$ and (c) $y_i < x_i \leqq x_j < y_j$. Marshall and Olkin(1979) showed that $x \geqq_{GL} y$ is equivalent to the condition that y is obtained from x by a finite sequence of rank preserving IRTs. Thus, the concept of IRT provides grounds to assess relative desirability of profiles with unequal means.

We can now extend Theorem 1.4 to the case of populations with different sizes. For this it is sufficient to assume that the SEF satisfies SAP. We will say that an SEF $W: D \longrightarrow \mathbb{R}^1$ is increasing if for all $n \in \mathbb{N}$, W^n is increasing. Since population replication leaves GLCs unchanged we can now state the following theorem:

---

6 Strictly speaking, Shorrocks proved the weak version of Theorem 1.4 and its extension to the variable population case, Theorem 1.5. For instance, the weak version of Theorem 1.4 will require that the ranking of income profiles by the weak generalised Lorenz criterion should agree with the ranking generated by any non–decreasing, S–concave SEF. It should also be clear that all the theorems presented in Section 1.4 have got corresponding weak versions. We may mention that our proof of Theorem 1.4 does not proceed along the line suggested by Shorrocks. We will, however, prove Theorems 1.6 and 1.7, the subsequent theorems of this section, in their weak form.

Theorem 1.5 (Shorrocks 1983)

Let y^1 and y^2 be two income profiles over population sizes n_1 and n_2 respectively, that is, $y^1 \in D^{n_1}$ and $y^2 \in D^{n_2}$. Then the following statements are equivalent:

(i) $y^1 \geq_{GL} y^2$.

(ii) $W^{n_1}(y^1)/n_1 > W^{n_2}(y^2)/n_2$ for all SEFs $W: D \rightarrow \mathbb{R}^1$ that satisfy increasingness, strict S–concavity and SAP.

However, the welfare judgements captured by the generalised Lorenz domination may come into conflict with the social desire for more equally distributed income. This can be easily demonstrated if we increase the income of the richest individual keeping all other incomes fixed. Clearly, in this case the total income increases, as does income inequality. Hence there is a conflict between efficiency gain and equity loss. As Shorrocks pointed out, in the case of the utilitarian SEF, the possible conflict between efficiency gain and equity loss is always resolved on the efficiency side. Thus, a welfare improvement according to the generalised Lorenz domination rule may be compatible with an increase in inequality.

Therefore, the question that now arises is: can we have some alternative efficiency preference concept that will avoid the above difficulty and to what extent this alternative efficiency preference rule is helpful in distributional ranking? In this context Shorrocks made two alternative suggestions. According to his first suggestion welfare should improve if the incomes are raised equiproportionally. Formally, an SEF $W^n: D^n \rightarrow \mathbb{R}^1$ is said to satisfy the 'scale improvement' efficiency condition if for all $x \in D^n$ and for all $k \geq 1$,

$$W^n(k \cdot x) \geq W^n(x) \ . \tag{1.8}$$

In (1.8) the increase in efficiency is associated with a higher value of k keeping the same distribution of relative incomes, that is, keeping the ratios x_i/x_j constant. The scale improvement efficiency condition corresponds to a preference for higher incomes keeping relative inequality[7] unaltered. Obviously, the assumption (1.8) is weaker than the increasingness assumption and consequently, the ordering generated by SEFs satisfying (1.8) will be weaker than the ordering induced by increasing SEFs. Shorrocks showed that the ranking of income profiles by SEFs satisfying S–concavity and scale improve-

[7] Alternative concepts of inequality are defined rigorously in Chapter 2.

ment condition is equivalent to the common practice of ranking profiles on the basis of the mean income λ and the LC.

Theorem 1.6 (Shorrocks 1983)

For $x,y \in D^n$, the following conditions are equivalent:

(i) $\lambda(x) \geq \lambda(y)$ and x weakly Lorenz dominates y ($x \geq_{WL} y$ for short).

(ii) $W^n(x) \geq W^n(y)$ for all SEFs W^n: $D^n \longrightarrow \mathbb{R}^1$ satisfying the scale improvement condition and S–concavity.

Proof

(i) $\Rightarrow$ (ii):

Suppose $\lambda(x) \geq \lambda(y)$ and $x \geq_{WL} y$. Define $y^1 := \lambda(x) \cdot y/\lambda(y)$. Since W^n satisfies the scale improvement condition, we have $W^n(y^1) \geq W^n(y)$. By construction of y^1, $L(y^1, i/n) = L(y, i/n)$. Hence $x \geq_{WL} y$ implies $x \geq_{WL} y^1$. But we also have $\lambda(y^1) = \lambda(x)$. Therefore, by S–concavity of W^n we have $W^n(x) \geq W^n(y^1)$. Thus, $W^n(x) \geq W^n(y)$.

(ii) $\Rightarrow$ (i):

Let us define W^n: $D^n \longrightarrow \mathbb{R}^1$ by $(\lambda(y))^m f(y/\lambda(y))$, where $m \geq 0$ and f is S–concave on D^n. Clearly, W^n satisfies (1.8) and S–concavity. Now for $x,y \in D^n$, $W^n(x) \geq W^n(y)$ implies $(\lambda(x))^m f(x/\lambda(x)) \geq (\lambda(y))^m f(y/\lambda(y))$. By choosing $f(z) \equiv 1$, $W^n(x) \geq W^n(y)$ implies $(\lambda(x))^m \geq (\lambda(y))^m$. Hence $\lambda(x) \geq \lambda(y)$. Alternatively, by choosing $m = 0$, we have $f(x/\lambda(x)) \geq f(y/\lambda(y))$. But f is an arbitrary S–concave function and the profiles $x/\lambda(x)$ and $y/\lambda(y)$ have the same mean (= 1). Hence by the weak version of Theorem 1.2, $\frac{x}{\lambda(x)} \geq_{WL} \frac{y}{\lambda(y)}$, from which we have $x \geq_{WL} y$. ■

Theorem 1.6 gives the implications of replacing the increasingness assumption, which is one interpretation of efficiency preference, with the weaker one of scale improvement. However, the value judgement given by (1.8) may be too strong to be acceptable. Because if one adopts (1.8), while relative incomes remain unchanged, absolute differences of the form $x_i - x_j$ get widened. This motivated Shorrocks(1983) to suggest another type of efficiency preference, namely the 'incremental improvement' condition. Formally, W^n: $D^n \longrightarrow \mathbb{R}^1$ satisfies the incremental improvement condition if for all $x \in D^n$, for all $k \geq 0$,

$$W^n(x + k \cdot 1^n) \geq W^n(x) \ . \tag{1.9}$$

In (1.9) the increase in efficiency is associated with a higher value of k keeping the absolute income differentials constant. Equivalently, the incremental efficiency condition corresponds to a preference for higher incomes keeping absolute income inequality constant. Assuming that S–concavity is a common property for the two classes of SEFs that verify properties (1.8) and (1.9) respectively, the ordering induced by the former class is weaker than the ordering induced by the latter. This follows from the observation that an incremental improvement in all incomes can be achieved first by increasing the incomes proportionally and then transferring incomes from the rich to the poor. The following interesting implication of the alternative efficiency preference in (1.9) was proved by Shorrocks.

Theorem 1.7 (Shorrocks 1983)

For $x, y \in D^n$, the following conditions are equivalent:

(i) $\lambda(x) \geq \lambda(y)$ and $GL(x, i/n) - \lambda(x)\cdot i/n \geq GL(y, i/n) - \lambda(y)\cdot i/n$ for all $i \leq n$.

(ii) $W^n(x) \geq W^n(y)$ for all SEFs W^n: $D^n \rightarrow \mathbb{R}^1$ that satisfy S–concavity and the incremental improvement condition.

Proof

(i) $\Rightarrow$ (ii):

Define $y^1 = y + (\lambda(x) - \lambda(y))\cdot 1^n$. Since W^n satisfies the incremental improvement condition, $W^n(y^1) \geq W^n(y)$. Furthermore, $\lambda(y^1) = \lambda(x)$ and $GL(y^1, i/n) = GL(y, i/n) + i/n\cdot(\lambda(x) - \lambda(y)) \leq GL(x, i/n)$ for all $i \leq n$. This shows that $L(y^1, i/n) \leq L(x, i/n)$ for all $i \leq n$. Hence by S–concavity of W^n, $W^n(y^1) \leq W^n(x)$, which shows that $W^n(x) \geq W^n(y)$.

(ii) $\Rightarrow$ (i):

Suppose that W^n: $D^n \rightarrow \mathbb{R}^1$ is given by $(\lambda(y))^m\cdot f(y + (\Theta - \lambda(y))1^n)$, where $m \geq 0$, f is S–concave on D^n and $\Theta > 0$ is such that $y + (\Theta - \lambda(y))1^n \in D^n$. Clearly, W^n defined above is S–concave and meets the incremental improvement condition. Now for $x, y \in D^n$, $W^n(x) \geq W^n(y)$ implies $(\lambda(x)/\lambda(y))^m f(x + (\Theta - \lambda(x))1^n) \geq f(y + (\Theta - \lambda(y))1^n)$. By choosing $f(z) \equiv 1$, $W^n(x) \geq W^n(y)$ implies $(\lambda(x))^m \geq (\lambda(y))^m$. By non–negativity of m, we conclude that $\lambda(x) \geq \lambda(y)$. Alternatively, by choosing $m = 0$, we obtain $f(x + (\Theta - \lambda(x))1^n) \geq f(y + (\Theta - \lambda(y))1^n)$. Since the profile $x + (\Theta - \lambda(x))1^n$ and $y + (\Theta - \lambda(y))1^n$ have the same mean ($= \Theta$) and f is any S–concave function, we can conclude that $L(y + (\Theta - \lambda(y))1^n, i/n) \leq L(x + (\Theta - \lambda(x))1^n, i/n)$ for all $i \leq n$. Now, in the case of distributions with common mean the generalised Lorenz ranking coincides with the Lorenz ranking. The above inequality, therefore, is equivalent to $GL(y, i/n) + (\Theta - \lambda(y))i/n \leq GL(x, i/n) + (\Theta - \lambda(x))i/n$ for all $i \leq n$. The result now follows from the last inequality. ■

Thus, Theorem 1.7 can be used to test whether any pair of income profiles y and y^1 can be ranked using SEFs satisfying (1.9) and S–concavity. One way of doing the comparison is to calculate $GL(\cdot, i/n) - \lambda(\ )i/n$ for each of the profiles and make pairwise comparison of these values and the mean incomes.

Moyes(1987) offered an alternative interpretation of Theorem 1.7. He referred to the GLC of the profile $x - \lambda(x)\cdot 1^n$ as the absolute LC of x. The absolute LC $LA(x, i/n)$ coincides with the horizontal axis when incomes are equal. It is decreasing with i for $0 \leq i \leq i^*$ and increasing for $i^* < i \leq n$ where i^* is such that $\bar{x}_{i^*} < \lambda(x) \leq \bar{x}_{i^*+1}$. It is easy to see that $-LA(x, i/n)$ measures the vertical distance evaluated at i/n between the line of equality and the GLC $GL(x, i/n)$. That is, it represents the average income shortfall of the $\frac{i}{n}\cdot 100\%$ poorest individuals from the equal distribution $\lambda(x)\cdot 1^n$. Thus, $-i\cdot LA(x, i/n)$ determines the total amount of income necessary to make everyone's (among bottom i persons) income equal to $\lambda(x)$. Theorem 1.7 can now be restated as: For all $x, y \in D^n$, the following conditions are equivalent:

(i) $W^n(x) \geq W^n(y)$ for all W^n which are S–concave and satisfy the incremental improvement condition.

(ii) $\lambda(x) \geq \lambda(y)$ and $LA(x, i/n) \geq LA(y, i/n)$ for all $i = 0, 1,..., n$.

1.6 Concluding Remarks

We began this chapter with a discussion on the relationship between utility functions and a social evaluation function. We then discussed the problem of ranking income profiles using a social evaluation function (SEF). As a first step it has been observed that the ranking of income profiles of a given total income with an equity conscious (in the sense of being strictly S–concave) SEF can be implemented by seeking a dominance relation in terms of the Lorenz curve (LC) (Atkinson(1970), Dasgupta, Sen and Starrett (1973), Rothschild and Stiglitz(1973)). On the other hand, for ranking profiles with differing means we need equity orientation as well as increasingness of the SEF. In this case the ordering can be implemented by seeking a dominance relation involving the generalised Lorenz curve (GLC), obtained by scaling up the LC by the mean (Shorrocks(1983)). However, the increasingness assumption may come into conflict with the desire for greater equality. Replacing the increasingness assumption by alternative efficiency preferences, which avoid this conflict, it is possible to generate orderings in terms of the LC or the GLC (Shorrocks(1983)).

Marshall and Olkin(1979) studied the interesting problem of identifying the class of functions that preserve the Lorenz ranking of income profiles. They showed that the only functions with this property are affine functions. Their result is formally stated as:

Theorem (Marshall and Olkin 1979)

Let f: $D^1 \rightarrow D^1$ be continuous. Then for x, y $\in D^n$, where $\lambda(x) = \lambda(y)$, $x \geq_L y$ implies $(f(x_1), f(x_2), \ldots, f(x_n)) \geq_L (f(y_1), f(y_2), \ldots, f(y_n))$ if and only if f is affine.

What the theorem says is the following: If an income profile x is judged to be better than another profile y by the Lorenz criterion, then the profiles that emerge from x and y after some process has been effective (here the function f) will be similarly related as x and y if and only if the process is affine. Marshall and Olkin(1979) and Moyes(1989) recognised the fact that increasing and strictly concave functions preserve the generalised Lorenz ranking of income profiles.

We have noted that scaling up the LCs to form the GLCs may reveal a dominance relationship which may not be achieved by comparing the mean incomes and the LCs. A problem, however, remains when the GLCs cross. Shorrocks'(1983) empirical study shows that in a comparison between income profiles in 20 countries conclusive results were obtained in 84 percent of the pairwise comparisons of the GLCs. Kakwani(1984) used income data for 72 countries to perform a comparison of welfare using the generalised Lorenz criterion. In about 80% of all pairwise comparisons it was possible to draw unambiguous conclusions. The LCs, on the other hand, crossed in more than 30% of all such pairwise comparisons.

We will now make a discussion on what can be said about unambigous ranking of income profiles when GLCs cross. Shorrocks and Foster(1987) and Dardanoni and Lambert(1988) made some interesting investigations in this direction. Following Shorrocks and Foster(1987) we say that the LC of $x \in D^n$ intersects that of $y \in D^n$ once, from above, if and only if there exists an integer i^*, $1 \leq i^* < n$, such that

$$L(x, i/n) \geq L(y, i/n) \text{ for all } i \leq i^* \text{ and } > \text{ for some } i,$$
$$L(x, i/n) \leq L(y, i/n) \text{ for all } i \geq i^* \text{ and } < \text{ for some } i. \qquad (1.10)$$

That is, the proportion of aggregate income enjoyed by earners below a certain income level will be greater under x than under y. We observe that in figure 1.2, the LC of x^2 intersects that of x^1 once, from above. Similarly in figure 1.3, the GLC of x^1 crosses that of x^2 once, from above. Dardanoni and Lambert showed that in the simplest situation where the GLCs cross once, a ranking relation in terms of the mean, the Rawlsian criterion and the variance, the average squared deviations of individual incomes from the mean, can be obtained. More precisely, suppose that x and y are two income profiles over a given population size n and the GLC of x crosses that of y once, from above. Then x is considered to be at least as good as y by any symmetric utilitarian SEF, where the utility function is increasing, strictly concave with a strictly convex marginal, if and only if the following conditions hold: (a) x is preferred to y by the Rawlsian criterion, (b) the variance of x does not exceed that of y and (c) the mean of x equals that of y. Strict convexity of the marginal utility function means that more weight is attached to transfers of income if they take place at the lower end of the profile[8]. The above result, which is a generalisation of a theorem of Shorrocks and Foster(1987), shows that in equal mean comparisons for which LCs cross once, the variance is the appropriate, ethically supported income distribution statistic. In the unequal mean income case of a single GLC crossing, the variance, once again, plays the role to resolve the equity–efficiency trade–off faced (see Dardanoni and Lambert(1988)). These results, therefore, indicate the importance of intersecting LCs/GLCs in ranking alternative profiles of income.

---

8 See Chapter 2, Section 2.2, for a detailed discussion.

CHAPTER 2

ETHICAL INDICES OF INEQUALITY

2.1 Introduction

While the Lorenz criterion provides only a quasi–ordering of income profiles, an alternative statistic that completely orders the set of all income profiles is an inequality index. An inequality index is a scalar representation of interpersonal income differences within a given population. Quite often indices of inequality are used in the public finance and development studies to evaluate a paricular profile of income or to examine the distributional effects of a particular economic policy. The standard questions that arise in these studies are: (i) Is the income profile in region A more equal now than it was in the past? (ii) Is income inequality in region B less than that in region C? (iii) Is post–tax income profile more equal than the pre–tax income profile? (iv) What are the contributions of different income sources to the aggregate inequality in region A?

Inequality indices may be relative, absolute or intermediate. Relative indices are homogeneuous of degree zero in their arguments, while absolute indices are translation invariant functions. Intermediate inequality is defined to be a mix of the concepts of relative and absolute inequality. It is well–known that alternative indices of inequality do not provide the same ranking of different income profiles (Yntema(1933), Atkinson (1970)). This happens because there are several aspects of income inequality and some indices are suited to reflect one aspect and some another (Sen(1973), Champernowne (1974)).

In his pioneering article, Dalton(1920) pointed out that 'the degree of inequality cannot, in general, be measured without introducing social judgements'. He then argued that the social judgements concerning indices of inequality should be made explicit through the use of a social evaluation function (SEF), which simply ranks alternative income profiles in the order of society's preference. It then becomes clear what distributional objectives are being incorporated as a result of adopting a certain index of inequality. Assuming that the SEF is given by the sum of identical individual utility functions, Dalton proposed an inequality index based on the idea of proportional welfare loss resulting from unequal distribution. Atkinson(1970) criticised the Dalton formula on the ground that it is variant with respect to affine transformations of the utility function, and proposed an alternative index retaining the form of the SEF considered by Dalton. Atkinson's index is the ratio of the 'equally distributed equivalent' or 'representative' income to the mean income. This representative income is an inequality or welfare adjusted per capita income, that is, the level of income which, if given to each individual would prove socially equivalent to the current profile of income. Sen(1973) proposed a generalised version of the Atkinson formula using more general assumptions about the SEF than those considered by Dalton and Atkinson. Blackorby and Donaldson(1978, 1980) established (ordinal) SEFs that imply and are implied by various commonly used (cardinally significant) relative and absolute inequality indices. In Sections 3 and 4 of this chapter we discuss alternative approaches to the construction of cardinally significant inequality indices. Simple proofs of the theorems of Atkinson, and Blackorby and Donaldson are provided in these sections.

However, according to the Blackorby–Donaldson procedure an ordinal transform of a given inequality index may lead to an SEF which need not be ordinally related to the SEF consistent with the given index. That is, if the concept of inequality is assumed to be a purely ordinal one, then the Blackorby–Donaldson method is an inappropriate procedure. Ebert(1987) proposed a procedure which avoids this difficulty. He derives an ordering in terms of social welfare which is based on the explicit value judgements about the size and distribution of incomes. The SEFs representing this ordering allow a size distribution split up. This procedure can be reversed. We discuss Ebert's suggestion in Section 5 of this chapter.

Section 2 sets out the different postulates by which indices of inequality can be selected and discusses implications of these postulates. Consequently, the class of inequality indices consistent with the Lorenz criterion is identified. In Section 6 we outline different procedures suggested in the literature for measuring inequality among and within subgroups of a population partitioned with respect to some homogeneous characteristic (age, sex, geographical region etc.). This type of analysis helps us to calculate contributions of different groups to overall inequality and hence to identify the major sources of inequality. The section also highlights the problem of decomposing an inequality index when the income of each individual is disaggregated into the amounts received from a variety of sources (employment, capital, pension schemes etc.). This helps us to assess the impact of each of these sources. Section 7 makes some concluding remarks and discusses some indices of inequality which possibly cannot be interpreted in the frameworks considered in Sections 3, 4 and 5.

2.2 Postulates for the Selection of an Index of Inequality

We begin this section with the widest possible definition of an inequality index, allowing both population size and total income to be variable. The term inequality index is used to indicate a function $I: D \longrightarrow \mathbb{R}^1$, which offers comparisons of inequality across populations. The restriction I^n of I on D^n gives comparisons of inequality for a fixed level of population. Thus, each inequality index I on D is uniquely associated with a class of indices $\{I^n\}$, one for each population size. For $n = 1$ the definition of an inequality index is vacuous. We, therefore, assume that $n \geq 2$.

An inequality index will be called ordinally significant if it is unique up to an increasing transformation. That is, if a function is a suitable representation of an inequality ordering, then any other increasing transform of the function will be as well. On the other hand, an inequality index will be cardinally significant if it is unique up to an affine transformation. That is, the inequality index and an affine transformation of the index convey the same information. Thus, while with ordinal scale measurability we are interested in ranking income profiles in terms of inequality, with cardinal scale measurability we look at inequality levels and inequality differences.

Whether a particular type of change in incomes will keep the inequality of incomes unchanged is a matter of subjective evaluation. That is, this depends on evaluator's judgement on inequality equivalence. An inequality index I_R corresponds to a concept of relative inequality if proportional changes in all incomes do not change inequality, that is, for all $n \in \mathbb{N}$, $x \in D^n$,

$$I_R^n(c \cdot x) = I_R^n(x) , \tag{2.1}$$

where $c > 0$ is any scalar. In contrast, an inequality index I_A corresponds to a concept of absolute inequality if it is invariant to equal absolute changes in all incomes: for all $n \in \mathbb{N}$, $x \in D^n$,

$$I_A^n(x + c\cdot 1^n) = I_A^n(x) , \tag{2.2}$$

where c is any scalar such that $x + c\cdot 1^n \in D^n$.

Research to date has not produced satisfactory conclusions about acceptability of axioms (2.1) and (2.2). Clearly, a relative index has the convenient property of being invariant to changes in the unit of money. That is, relative inequality of a profile remains unaltered if incomes are measured in dollars instead of in rupees. Obviously, an absolute index does not possess this property. But Dalton(1920) argued that if money units in two different cases are to be compared, then they must have the same purchasing power.

Taussig(1939) and Blau(1977) felt that a variation of incomes in the same proportion should not change inequality. Kolm(1976), on the other hand, argued that proportionate additions to all incomes represent an increase in inequality. Taking the opposite point of view, Dalton(1920) suggested that inequality should decrease when incomes are increased proportionally[1] (see also Sen(1973)). While Kolm(1976) argued that an inequality index should be invariant under equal absolute changes in its arguments, Dalton(1920), however, felt that an equal addition to all incomes decreases inequality[2] (see also Cannan(1930)). Bossert and Pfingsten(1989) (also Pfingsten(1986)) noted that a natural generalisation of (2.1) and (2.2) is an intermediate condition, which states that a convex combination of relative and absolute variations in incomes should leave inequality unchanged. That is, an inequality index I_μ represents an intermediate concept of inequality if for all $n \in \mathbb{N}$, $x \in D^n$,

$$I_\mu^n(x + c\cdot(\mu\cdot x + (1-\mu)\cdot 1^n)) = I_\mu^n(x) , \tag{2.3}$$

where $0 \leq \mu \leq 1$ and c is a scalar such that $x + c\cdot(\mu\cdot x + (1-\mu)\cdot 1^n) \in D^n$. μ is a parameter which reflects an evaluator's value judgement on inequality equivalence. μ and $(1-\mu)$ can be interpreted as the weights attached to variations in income along the relative and absolute scales respectively. If $\mu = 1$, only relative variations matter and (2.3) coincides with (2.1). On the other hand, if $\mu = 0$, we become interested in absolute variations only and (2.3) coincides with (2.2). Thus, the closer μ is to unity (zero), the greater is the concern for relative (absolute) inequality concept. A value of $\mu = 1/2$ means that we

---

[1] This is popularly known as the Daltonian principle of proportionate additions to incomes.

[2] This suggestion of Dalton is called the principle of equal additions to incomes.

have some sort of centrist position (also see Eichhorn(1988 a) for a discussion on this matter).

When n = 2, the three concepts of inequality can be explained graphically (Pfingsten (1986)):

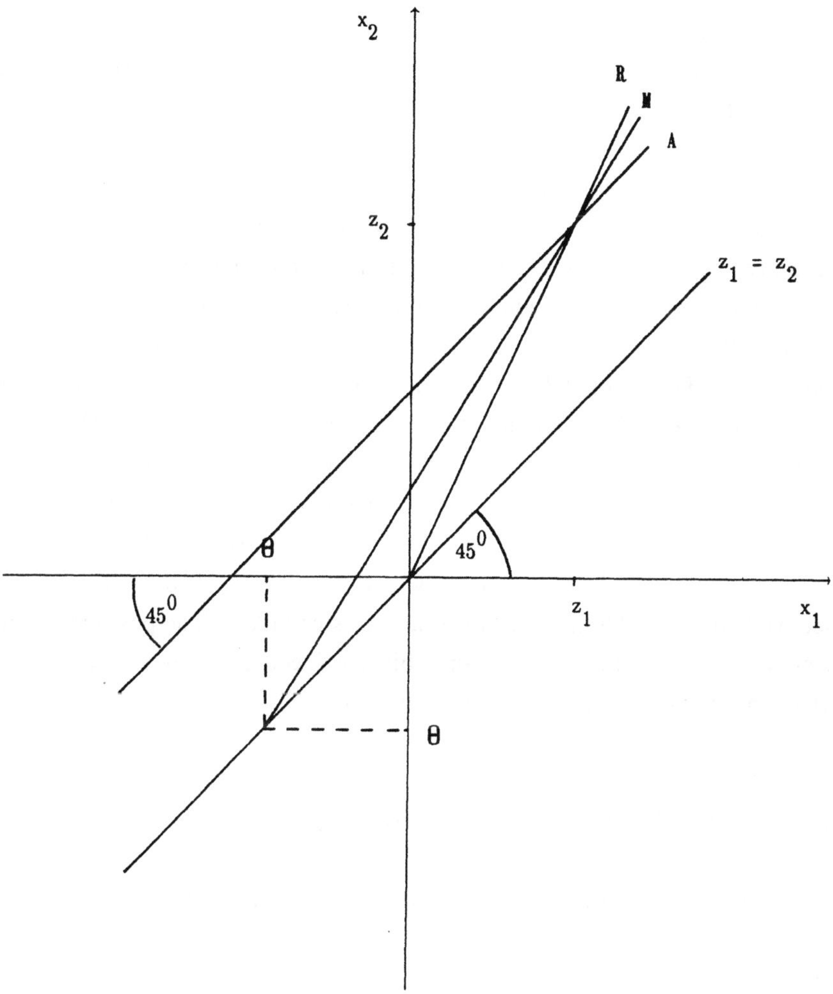

Figure 2.1

For an initial profile $z = (z_1, z_2)$, the straight lines denoted by R, A and M represent the sets of the profiles in D^2 which are inequality equivalent to z according to equations (2.1), (2.2) and (2.3) respectively. As $\Theta = -\frac{(1-\mu)}{\mu} \longrightarrow 0$, M coincides with R and as $\Theta \longrightarrow -\infty$, M coincides with A. Thus, we can say that according to absolute inequality, income profiles with the same inequality as the initial profile z will lie on a ray (through z) intersecting the 45° line through the origin at minus infinity. Correspondingly, the line showing profiles with the same relative inequality as z will pass through the origin and z. For an intermediate inequality concept such a line will intersect the 45° line through the origin at (Θ, Θ).

The classes of all possible inequality indices satisfying (2.1), (2.2) and (2.3) respectively may be rather large. A number of properties which can be regarded as being intrinsic to the concept of inequality can reduce the number of allowable indices. Discussions on alternative properties of inequality indices have been made by Dalton(1920, 1922), Atkinson(1970), Bentzel(1970), Hirschman(1973), Sen(1973), Champernowne (1974), Kondor(1975), Hammond(1976 a), Kolm(1976), Cowell(1977), Hansson(1977), Kurabayashi and Yatsuka(1977), Allison(1978), Blackorby and Donaldson(1978, 1980, 1984), Bürk and Gehrig(1978), Fields and Fei(1978), Schwartz and Winship(1979), Kakwani(1980), Cowell and Kuga(1981, 1981 a), Weymark(1981), Eichhorn and Gehrig (1982), Jasso(1982), Kanbur(1984), Fine(1985), Foster(1985), Morris and Preston(1986), Le Breton and Trannoy(1987), Moyes(1987), Ebert(1988, 1988 a, 1988 b), Foster and Shorrocks(1988 b), Shorrocks(1988), Yaari(1988) and Bossert(1989). The postulates that have been suggested in the literature for an arbitrary inequality index $I: D \longrightarrow \mathbb{R}^1$, whether relative, absolute or intermediate are listed below.

<u>Normalisation (NM)</u>

For all $n \in \mathbb{N}$, $I^n(c \cdot 1^n) = 0$, where $c > 0$ is any scalar.

Condition NM says that when all incomes are equal, the inequality index takes the value zero.

<u>Impartiality (IM)</u>

For all $n \in \mathbb{N}$, $x \in D^n$, $I^n(Px) = I^n(x)$, where P is any permutation matrix of order n.

Condition IM means that the inequality index I is symmetric – inequality remains unchanged when individuals exchange places. IM is unavoidable as long as individuals are not distinguished by anything other than income.

A third property which can be regarded as the central property of inequality indices is the Pigou(1912) – Dalton(1920) transfers principle. According to the Pigou–Dalton transfers principle inequality should increase (decrease) when income is transferred from one person to someone richer (poorer). Following Rothschild and Stiglitz(1973) we say that y is obtained from $x \in D^n$ by a regressive transfer if for some i, j: (i) $x_j \leq x_i$, (ii) $y_i - x_i = x_j - y_j > 0$, and (iii) $y_k = x_k$ for all $k \neq i, j$. That is, x and y are identical except for a positive transfer of income from the poor person j to the rich person i. Equivalently, we may say that x is obtained from y through a progressive transfer.

Pigou–Dalton Transfers Principle (PD)

For all $n \in \mathbb{N}$, $x \in D^n$ if y is obtained from x by a regressive transfer, then $I^n(y) > I^n(x)$.

Thus, PD implies that a regressive income transfer increases inequality. Equivalently, a progressive transfer decreases inequality. If I treats individuals symmetrically, that is, if I satisfies IM, then PD only allows those transfers that do not alter rank order of individuals.

A stronger version of PD is the diminishing transfers principle, which demands that the inequality index should give more weight to transfers of income at the lower end of the profile than at upper ends (Atkinson(1970), Sen(1973), Kolm(1976, 1976 a), Fishburn and Willig(1984), Shorrocks and Foster(1987)).

Diminishing Transfers Principle (DT)

For all $n \in \mathbb{N}$, $x \in D^n$, if y is obtained from x through a progressive transfer of income from the person with income $x_i + h$ to a person with income x_i, then for a given $h > 0$, the magnitude of decrease in inequality $I^n(x) - I^n(y)$ increases as x_i decreases. More precisely, for all $x \in D^n$ and all t, u satisfying: (a) $t = \Delta(e_i - e_j)$, (b) $u = \delta(e_k - e_l)$, (c) $\Delta = \delta > 0$, (d) $x_j - x_i = x_l - x_k > \Delta$, (e) $x_k > x_i$, where e_i is the n–tuple (0, 0, ..., 0, 1, 0, ...,0) whose only non–zero element occurs in the ith position, $I^n(x) - I^n(x + t) > I^n(x) - I^n(x + u)$.

Thus, under DT, the progressive transfers of a fixed size between donors and recipients at a fixed income distance apart have a greater impact on inequality if they take place at lower income levels. For example, a transfer of income from a person who earns 900 pounds a month to another who earns 500 pounds is considered to be more weighty than an equal amount of transfer from a 1400 pounds earner to someone who earns 1000 pounds. An interesting implication of DT is that the variance of $x + t$ equals that of $x + u$.

Postulates (2.1), (2.2) and (2.3) allow us to deal with income profiles having different means over a given population size. Quite often we become interested in cross population comparisons. The following postulate, suggested by Dalton(1920), helps us to compare income profiles over different population sizes.

Dalton Population Principle (PP)

For all $n \in \mathbb{N}$, $x \in D^n$, $I^{nk}(y) = I^n(x)$, where y is the k–fold replication of x, that is, $y = (y^{(1)}, y^{(2)}, ..., y^{(k)})$ and each $y^{(i)} = x$.

Thus, under PP, if a particular income profile is pooled several times, then the inequality of the original profile and the inequality of the pooled profile are the same. Clearly, PP leads us to view inequality in average terms. Obviously, PP is parallel to the symmetry axiom for population considered by Dasgupta, Sen and Starrett(1973).

The next postulate, we consider, is continuity. Given the difficulties in measuring incomes accurately, it seems reasonable to require an inequality index to vary continuously with income.

Continuity (CON)

For all $n \in \mathbb{N}$, I^n is a continuous function.

In addition to the above a few authors like Champernowne(1974) have laid down some stipulations regarding the upper bound of an inequality index. An inequality index should take the maximum value when the richest individual monopolises the whole income and all others have zero income. Champernowne stipulated that in the limit as the number of incomes n increases while one individual gets all the income, a relative inequality index should tend to the value one. But for some of the widely used indices of inequality the upper bound tends to infinity in the limit as $n \rightarrow \infty$. However, the upper bound need not to be a criterion for preferring one inequality index to another, because, simple transformations can produce any desired upper bound. If we want to make the upper bound of an inequality index independent of n, we can do so by dividing the index by its maximum attainable value. But such normalisation of an inequality index that satisfies PD is obtained at the cost of PP.

We now discuss some implications of the above properties. We begin with the following obvious observation: An implication of NM and PD is 'positivity out of equality', which states that for all $n \in \mathbb{N}$, $I^n(x) > 0$ whenever $x \in D^n$ is not of the form $c \cdot 1^n$, where $c > 0$ is any scalar. That is, an inequality index satisfying normalisation and the Pigou–Dalton transfers principle takes a positive value for an unequal distribution of income. Clearly, if in addition to the above two properties, the index verifies IM and (2.1) also, then it is bounded where the bounds are given respectively by 0 and $I^n(1, 0, ..., 0)$, $n \in \mathbb{N}$.

The following theorem of Foster(1985) identifies the class of inequality indices that implies and is implied by the Lorenz quasi-ordering. Closely related results have been proved by Kurabayashi and Yatsuka(1977), Fields and Fei(1978) and Eichhorn and Gehrig(1982).

Theorem 2.1 (Foster 1985)

Let $x^1, x^2 \in D$ be arbitrary. Then the following statements are equivalent:

(i) $I(x^1) > I(x^2)$ for all relative inequality indices $I: D \longrightarrow \mathbb{R}^1$ that satisfy IM, PD and PP.

(ii) $x^2 \geq_L x^1$, that is, x^2 is Lorenz superior to x^1.

Proof

(i) $\Longrightarrow$ (ii):

Let $x^1 \in D^m$ and $x^2 \in D^n$ and $I^m(x^1) > I^n(x^2)$. Denote the n–fold and m–fold replications of x^1 and x^2 by x^3 and x^4 respectively, so that $x^3, x^4 \in D^{mn}$. Since I satisfies PP, $I^{mn}(x^3) = I^m(x^1)$ and $I^{mn}(x^4) = I^n(x^2)$. The mean income λ is also population replication invariant, hence we have $\lambda(x^1) = \lambda(x^3)$ and $\lambda(x^2) = \lambda(x^4)$. Now, let $\alpha = \lambda(x^1)/\lambda(x^2) = \lambda(x^3)/\lambda(x^4)$. Define $x^5 = \alpha \cdot x^4$. Since I is a relative index, $I^{mn}(x^5) = I^{mn}(x^4)$. Also observe that $\lambda(x^5) = \alpha \cdot \lambda(x^4) = \alpha \cdot \lambda(x^2) = \lambda(x^1)$. Thus, x^3 and x^5 are two distributions of the same total income $m \cdot n \cdot \lambda(x^1)$ over the population size mn. Since $I^{mn}(x^3) > I^{mn}(x^5)$ and I satisfies PD and IM, we can say that x^5 can be obtained from x^3 by a sequence of rank preserving transfers transferring income from the rich to the poor. Thus, by Theorem 1.2, $x^5 \geq_L$

x^3. Since the LC is population replication and scale transformation invariant, $x^5 \geq_L x^3$ implies $x^2 \geq_L x^1$.

(ii) $\Rightarrow$ (i):

This part of the theorem follows from a construction similar to the above, again using Theorem 1.2. ■

Theorem 2.1 shows that an unanimous ranking of income profiles by relative inequality indices can be obtained through the pairwise comparisons of LCs of the profiles. A similar result for absolute indices can be established using a dominance relation involving the absolute LC (Moyes(1987) and Chakravarty(1989)).

We can also focus our attention on fixed population, arbitrary mean income case. In such a case the domain of definition of the inequality index is D^n, where $n \in \mathbb{N}$ is fixed. We then have

<u>Theorem 2.2</u> (Fields and Fei 1978, Foster 1985)

Let x and y be two distributions of income over a given population size n, that is $x, y \in D^n$. Then the following statements are equivalent:

(i) $I^n(x) > I^n(y)$ for all relative inequality indices $I^n: D^n \to \mathbb{R}^1$ that satisfy PD and IM.

(ii) $y \geq_L x$.

If the mean income λ is fixed and population size is a variable, the domain of definition of the inequality index is an appropriate subset D_c of D, where $D_c = \{x \in D | \lambda(x) = c\}$. For indices that are consistent with the Lorenz criterion on a given D_c, we have the following theorem.

<u>Theorem 2.3</u> (Foster 1985)

Let $x, y \in D_c$ be arbitrary. Then the following statements are equivalent:

(i) $I(x) > I(y)$ where $I: D_c \to \mathbb{R}^1$ is any inequality index that satisfies IM, PD and PP.

(ii) $y \geq_L x$.

The proofs of Theorems 2.2 and 2.3 are similar to the proof of Theorem 2.1 and hence omitted. It is now evident that for any two income profiles x and y of a given total over a given population size, $x \geq_L y$ if and only if x is regarded as less unequal than y by any inequality index satisfying IM and PD. But by Theorem 1.2 the former is also equivalent to the requirement that x is regarded as better than y by any strictly S–concave SEF. This equivalence holds on any simplex D^n_c in D^n. We, therefore, have the following:

Theorem 2.4

The following statements are equivalent:

(i) $I^n: D^n_c \longrightarrow \mathbb{R}^1$ is strictly S–convex.

(ii) $I^n: D^n_c \longrightarrow \mathbb{R}^1$ satisfies IM and PD.

Given that we have identified the inequality indices satisfying PD and IM as strictly S–convex functions, the next step can be a search for indices that meet the diminishing transfers principle. Suppose that an inequality index $I^n: D^n \longrightarrow \mathbb{R}^1$ corresponds to the utilitarian SEF $\sum_{i=1}^{n} U(x_i)$ in a negative monotonic way, where the utility function is increasing and strictly concave. Then I^n meets DT if and only if the marginal utility function is strictly convex (Fishburn and Willig(1984), Shorrocks and Foster(1987)). Given that marginal utility is a decreasing function of incomes, we can say that if two people have different incomes, then adding the same fixed amount to each of their incomes narrows the gap between their marginal utilities. Strict convexity of marginal utility implies that if person i has an income level b and person j has income level $b + c > b$, then a regressive transfer from i to j results in a decrease (increase) in welfare (inequality) which is decreasing in b. That is, strict convexity of marginal utility implies that a given regressive transfer has a greater impact if it takes place at lower income levels.

It will now be interesting to look at the behaviour of an absolute inequality index to equiproportionate variations in incomes or of a relative index to equal absolute changes in incomes. The investigation can as well be carried out for an intermediate inequality index. The following theorem can be regarded as a step in this direction.

Theorem 2.5

Let $I: D \longrightarrow \mathbb{R}^1$ be any inequality index that satisfies PD.

(a) If I satisfies the intermediate inequality equivalence concept in (2.3), where $0 \leq \mu < 1$, then for all $n \in \mathbb{N}$, $\Theta > 0$,

$$I^n(x + \Theta \cdot x) > I^n(x) . \tag{2.4}$$

(b) If I satisfies the intermediate inequality equivalence concept in (2.3), where $0 < \mu \leqq 1$, then for all $n \in \mathbb{N}$, $\delta > 0$,

$$I^n(x + \delta \cdot 1^n) < I^n(x) \ . \tag{2.5}$$

Proof[3]

(a): For any $n \in \mathbb{N}$, let us take $x \in D^n$ such that $I^n(x) \neq 0$. For a given $\Theta > 0$, we determine c_Θ as a function of the mean income $\lambda(x)$ such that

$$\lambda(x)\cdot(1 + \Theta) = \lambda(x) + c_\Theta \cdot (\mu \cdot \lambda(x) + 1 - \mu) \ , \tag{2.6}$$

which implies

$$c_\Theta = \Theta \cdot \lambda(x)/[\mu \cdot \lambda(x) + 1 - \mu] \ . \tag{2.7}$$

Then the profiles $x \cdot (1 + \Theta)$ and x_Θ defined by

$$x_\Theta = x + c_\Theta \cdot (\mu \cdot x + (1 - \mu) \cdot 1^n) \tag{2.8}$$

have the same mean $(= \lambda(x)\cdot(1 + \Theta))$. Furthermore, since I is an intermediate index, we have $I^n(x) = I^n(x_\Theta)$.

Now, $\quad (\Theta + 1) \cdot x - x_\Theta$

$$= \Theta \cdot [x - \frac{\lambda(x) \cdot [\mu \cdot x + (1 - \mu) \cdot 1^n]}{\mu \cdot \lambda(x) + 1 - \mu}]$$

$$= \Theta \cdot (1 - \mu) \cdot [x - \lambda(x) \cdot 1^n]/[\mu \cdot \lambda(x) + 1 - \mu] \ . \tag{2.9}$$

(2.9) shows that we can move from $(\Theta + 1) \cdot x$ to x_Θ by decreasing (increasing) all incomes which are greater (less) than the mean $\lambda(x)$. That is, starting from $(\Theta + 1) \cdot x$ transfers yielding x_Θ decrease inequality according to the transfers principle. Thus, $I^n((\Theta + 1) \cdot x) > I^n(x_\Theta) = I^n(x)$.

(b): For any $N \in \mathbb{N}$, we take $x \in D^n$ such that $I^n(x) \neq 0$, we determine c_δ such that

$$\lambda(x) + \delta = \lambda(x) + c_\delta \cdot (\mu \cdot \lambda(x) + 1 - \mu), \tag{2.10}$$

which implies

$$c_\delta = \delta/[\mu \cdot \lambda(x) + 1 - \mu]. \tag{2.11}$$

[3] Bossert and Pfingsten(1989) proved Theorem 2.5 when $\mu \in (0,1)$. Clearly, (2.4) and (2.5) will hold for all intermediate indices when $\mu \in (0,1)$. In proving Theorem 2.5 we will follow Bossert and Pfingsten.

Then the profiles $x + \delta\cdot 1^n$ and x_δ defined by

$$x_\delta = x + c_\delta\cdot(\mu\cdot x + (1-\mu)\cdot 1^n) \qquad (2.12)$$

have the same mean ($= \lambda(x) + \delta$). Also we have $I^n(x) = I^n(x_\delta)$. Noting that the difference $x + \delta\cdot 1^n - x_\delta$ can be written as $\delta\cdot\mu\cdot[\lambda(x)1^n - x]/[\mu\lambda(x) + 1 - \mu]$, it can be concluded that we can move from $x + \delta 1^n$ to x_δ by increasing (decreasing) all incomes which are greater (less) than the mean income $\lambda(x)$. Thus, by the transfers principle, $I^n(x + \delta 1^n) < I^n(x_\delta) = I^n(x)$. ∎

Theorem 2.5 says that all intermediate inequality indices, of which relative indices are a special case, satisfying the Pigou–Dalton transfers principle meet the Daltonian principle of equal additions to incomes. On the other hand, all intermediate indices, of which absolute indices are a special case, increase under equiproportionate additions to all incomes, instead of decreasing,as suggested by the Daltonian principle of equiproportionate additions to incomes.

Before we conclude this section we may mention that properties NM, IM, DT (hence PD), PP and CON are consistent in the sense that there exists a function that will meet these properties. Examples of such a function are discussed in the next section.

2.3 Cardinally Significant Ethical Indices of Relative Inequality

We start out with a discussion of the inequality index of Dalton(1920), who pioneered the idea that the choice of an inequality index involves some implicit normative judgement.

2.3.1 Dalton's Index

Dalton(1920) chose the symmetric utilitarian form of the SEF, where the identical individual utility function U is assumed to be increasing and strictly concave in its argument. Therefore, the welfare value of $x \in D^n$ is given by

$$W^n(x) = \sum_{i=1}^{n} U(x_i)\ . \qquad (2.13)$$

Since U is strictly concave by Jensen's inequality (Marshall and Olkin(1979, p. 454)) we have $W^n(\lambda(x)1^n \geq W^n(x)$, where equality holds only when $x = \lambda(x)\cdot 1^n$, that is, when everybody enjoys the mean income $\lambda(x)$. Assume positivity of the utility function U. The Dalton inequality index is then defined by $I_1: D \longrightarrow \mathbb{R}^1$, where for all $n \in \mathbb{N}$, $x \in D^n$

$$I_1^n(x) = 1 - \frac{W^n(x)}{W^n(\lambda(x)\cdot 1^n)} . \tag{2.14}$$

I_1 is bounded between zero and one, where the lower bound is achieved whenever incomes are equal. I_1 tells us by how much (in relative terms) we can increase social welfare by distributing incomes equally. I_1 is symmetric and sensitive to transfers of income. But I_1 need not be a relative index for an arbitrary increasing, strictly concave utility function.

The Dalton approach to the measurement of inequality was largely ignored by later researchers until Aigner and Heins(1967) propossed some alternative forms of U and derived corresponding indices of inequality. From discussions carried out in Section 1.2 we know that the welfare ordering corresponding to the SEF in (2.13) satisfies information invariance with cardinally measurable, fully comparable utilities. Therefore, any index which is constructed using the SEF in (2.13) should remain invariant under affine transformations of the utility function. Atkinson(1970) rightly pointed out that the formula I_1^n does not meet this property. He modified Dalton's index to remedy this defect.

2.3.2 Atkinson's Index

Atkinson(1970) assumed that the SEF is given by (2.13) and defined what he called the 'equally distributed equivalent' (EDE) income of a given profile of a total income as that level of income which if enjoyed by every individual would make the total welfare exactly equal to the total welfare genereated by the actual profile[4]. Denoting the EDE

[4] An earlier use of the concept of the EDE income can be found in Champernowne (1952), where one of the measures was 'the proportion of total income that is absorbed in compensating for the loss of aggregate satisfaction due to inequality' (op. cit., p. 610). Kolm(1969) referred to the EDE income as 'the equal equivalent income'.

income associated with $x \in D^n$ by x_e, we have $n \cdot U(x_e) = \sum_{i=1}^{n} U(x_i)$. By strict concavity of U, $x_e < \lambda(x)$, the mean income. Atkinson replaced the Dalton index by $I_2 \colon D \longrightarrow \mathbb{R}^1$, where for all $n \in \mathbb{N}$, $x \in D^n$

$$I_2^n(x) = 1 - \frac{x_e}{\lambda(x)} \,. \tag{2.15}$$

I_2 is bounded between zero and one. Furthermore, it is cardinally significant and remains invariant under affine transformations of U.

Theorem 2.6

Suppose that the utility function U in (2.13) is continously differentiable. Then I_2^n is a relative index if and only if

$$U(x_i) = \begin{cases} A + B \cdot \dfrac{x_i^r}{r} \,, & r < 1, r \neq 0 \\ A + B \cdot \log x_i, & r = 0 \end{cases} \,, \tag{2.16}$$

where $B > 0$ and A are constants[5].

Proof

We require that $I_2^n(c \cdot x)$ be same as $I_2^n(x)$ for all $c > 0$ and $x \in D^n$. Since $\lambda(c \cdot x) = c \cdot \lambda(x)$, I_2^n will be a relative index if and only if the EDE income of the distribution $c \cdot x$ is given by $c \cdot x_e$. That is, given

$$\sum_{i=1}^{n} U(x_i) = n \cdot U(x_e) \,, \tag{2.17}$$

we must have

[5] Atkinson(1970) stated that this theorem can be proved by applying results of Arrow (1971) and Pratt(1964) in the theory of choice under uncertainty. Here we give a simple proof using functional equations.

$$\sum_{i=1}^{n} U(c \cdot x_i) = n \cdot U(c \cdot x_e) . \tag{2.18}$$

From (2.17) and (2.18) we get

$$\frac{d\, U(x_i)}{d\, x_i} = n \cdot \frac{d\, U(x_e)}{d\, x_e} \cdot \frac{\delta\, x_e}{\delta\, x_i} \tag{2.19}$$

and

$$\frac{d\, U(c \cdot x_i)}{d\, (c \cdot x_i)} \cdot \frac{d(c \cdot x_i)}{d\, x_i} = n \cdot \frac{d\, U(cx_e)}{d\, (cx_e)} \cdot \frac{d(cx_e)}{dx_e} \cdot \frac{\delta x_e}{\delta x_i} . \tag{2.20}$$

Dividing the left (right) hand side of (2.20) by the left (right) hand side of (2.19), we get

$$\frac{dU(cx_i)/d(cx_i)}{dU(x_i)/dx_i} = \frac{dU(cx_e)/d(cx_e)}{dU(x_e)/dx_e} \tag{2.21}$$

Thus, the left hand side of (2.21) is independent of i. This shows that $U'(x_j)/U'(x_i)$ is homogeneous of degree zero in (x_j, x_i)[6], where U' stands for the derivative of U. That is, $U'(x_i)/U'(x_j)$ is of the form $g(x_i/x_j)$ for some continuous function g. Hence $U'(x_i) = Bx_i^{r-1}$, where increasingness and strict concavity of U require that $B > 0$ and $r < 1$ (Aczél(1966), p. 144). Integrating $U'(x_i)$ with respect to x_i we get the form of U given by (2.16). This establishes the necessity part of the theorem. The sufficiency can be verified easily. ■

Using the form of U given by (2.16), we get the explicit form of the Atkinson index

---

6 A function $f^n: D^n \longrightarrow \mathbb{R}^1$ is homogeneous of degree r if for all $x \in D^n$, $f^n(cx) = c^r \cdot f^n(x)$, where $c > 0$ is any scalar. If $r = 1$, then f^n is called linearly homogeneous. $f: D \longrightarrow \mathbb{R}^1$ is called homogeneous of degree r, if for all $n \in \mathbb{N}$, f^n is homogeneous of degree r.

$$I_2^n(x) = \begin{cases} 1 - [\frac{1}{n} \cdot \sum_{i=1}^{n} (\frac{x_i}{\lambda(x)})^r]^{1/r} & , r < 1, r \neq 0 \\ 1 - \prod_{i=1}^{n} (\frac{x_i}{\lambda(x)})^{1/n} & , r = 0 \end{cases} \quad . \tag{2.22}$$

The parameter r is said to represent the degree of inequality aversion or the relative sensitivity of I_2^n to transfers of income at different income levels. For a given $x \in D^n$, I_2^n is monotonically decreasing in r. As r decreases, greater weight is attached to transfers at the lower end of the profile and less to transfers at the top. As $r \to -\infty$, $I_2^n \to 1 - \min_i\{x_i\}/\lambda(x)$, the relative maximin index, which corresponds to the Rawlsian maximin criterion that ranks income profiles in terms of the income of the worst off individual. On the other hand, if $r = 1$ the utility function in (2.16) becomes linear and the distributions are ranked on the basis of the total income only.

Atkinson in the same paper made an extremely interesting application of his measure to intercountry comparisons of inequality. His results indicate that the ranking of countries changes considerably with changes in the values of r. Some other interesting applications of Atkinson's index can be found in Allingham(1972), Bruno(1974), Muellbauer(1974, 1974 a), Hammond(1975), Harrison(1975), Bartels and Nijkamp(1976), Bruno and Habib(1976), Williamson(1977), Ulph(1978), von Weizsäcker(1978), Birchenhall and Grout(1978), Kanbur(1979), Blackorby and Donaldson(1984 a) and Kakwani (1988).

However, the form of the SEF assumed by Atkinson seems to be unnecessarily restrictive. It can be substantially generalised and this would lead to a more general normative index of inequality based on the EDE income approach. This is discussed in the next subsection.

2.3.3 A General Index

Following Sen(1973) we assume that ethical judgements on alternative profiles of income can be summarised by an SEF $W: D \to \mathbb{R}^1$, where W is ordinally significant. Furthermore, it is supposed that W satisfies a number of regularity conditions:

(i) for all $n \in \mathbb{N}$, W^n is continuous,

(ii) for all $n \in \mathbb{N}$, W^n is increasing along the ray of equality (minimal increasingness),

(iii) each level surface of W^n, $n \in \mathbb{N}$, crosses the ray of equality.

Clearly, by assuming continuity we are able to exclude all discontinuous SEFs like the lexicographic extension of the maximin criterion (Sen(1970), Hammond(1976)) from the outset. According to the lexicographic rule if the worst–off persons in two social states are equally badly off, then we compare the second worst–off, and so on. Minimal increasingness means that if all individuals enjoy the same income level, more income is preferred to less. Increases in the income of an individual, other individuals' incomes remaining fixed, may or may not be preferred. This means that the increase in inequality which results when the income of one individual is raised, all other incomes remaining fixed, may or may not be balanced by the increase in the efficiency measure (the aggregate income). Minimal increasingness is weaker than any of the Pareto preference conditions. (The term minimal increasingness is due to Blackorby and Donaldson (1984a).) Condition (iii) means that each income profile is indifferent to some perfectly equal distribution of income. An evaluation function W satisfying conditions (i) – (iii) will be called regular.

The Atkinson(1970) – Kolm(1969) – Sen(1973) (AKS) EDE income x_f associated with $x \in D^n$ is defined as that level of income which if given to each individual will make the existing profile x socially indifferent. Thus, x_f is implicitly defined by

$$W^n(x_f \cdot 1^n) = W^n(x) . \tag{2.23}$$

Since W satisfies regularity conditions (ii) and (iii), we can solve (2.23) for the unique EDE income

$$x_f = E^n(x) . \tag{2.24}$$

By continuity of W^n, E^n is a continuous function. Furthermore, E^n is a specific cardinalisation of W^n, that is

$$W^n(x) \gtrless W^n(y) \Leftrightarrow E^n(x) \gtrless E^n(y) \Leftrightarrow x_f \gtrless y_f . \tag{2.25}$$

Thus, one profile is preferred to another with the same population size if and only if its EDE income is higher. The indifference surfaces of E^n are numbered so that

$$E^n(c \cdot 1^n) = c, c > 0. \quad (2.26)$$

x_f is an inequality adjusted per capita income. If W is strictly S–concave, $x_f < \lambda(x)$, the mean income.

The AKS index of inequality is defined by I_3: $D \longrightarrow \mathbb{R}^1$, where for all $n \in \mathbb{N}$, $x \in D^n$,

$$I_3^n(x) = 1 - \frac{E^n(x)}{\lambda(x)} . \quad (2.27)$$

For a regular and strictly S–concave W, I_3 is continuous, strictly S–convex and bounded between zero and one, where the lower bound is achieved in the case of perfect equality. I_3 gives the fraction of national income that could be saved without any welfare loss if society distributed incomes equally. It satisfies the Daltonian population principle, if E satisfies the same. Given a functional form for I_3^n, we can recover E^n (hence W^n) using (2.27), (2.24) and (2.23). I_3 is cardinally significant in contrast to W, which is an ordinal indicator. Since contours of E are numbered, we can write the denominator of I_3^n as $E^n(\lambda(x) \cdot 1^n)$. Hence I_3 can also be interpreted as the proportional welfare loss generated by the existence of inequality.

For $n = 2$, I_3^n can be presented diagramatically as follows.

QAD is the social indifference curve. Strict S–concavity of W ensures that the indifference curve is convex to the origin. Symmetry of W implies symmetry of QAD about the ray of equality $x_1 = x_2$. Thus, the points Q and D represent two distributions of the total income $2 \cdot \lambda(x)$ (denoted by OM = ON). By similarity of triangles OAx_f and $OB\lambda(x)$, the AKS index now becomes 1 – OA/OB.

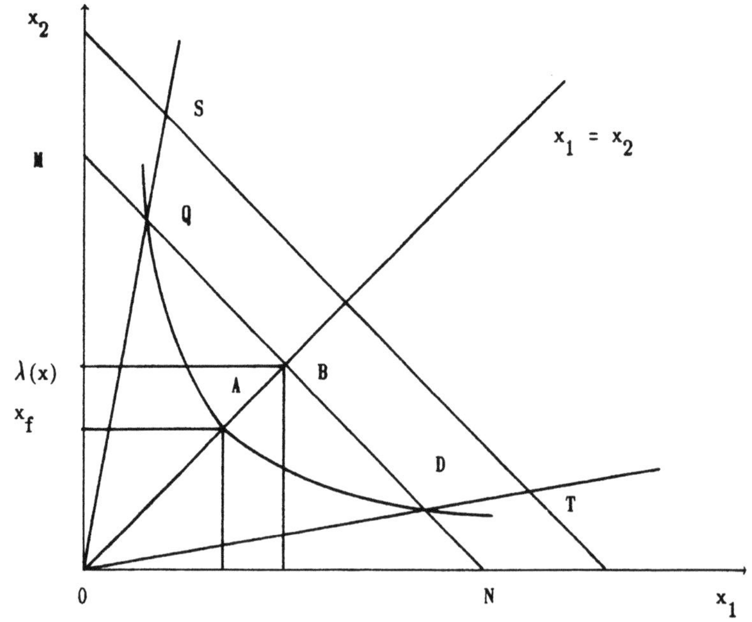

Figure 2.2

Since in (2.27) two functions of incomes appear in a ratio form, it is intuitively reasonable to interpret I_3 as a relative index. However, in general, I_3 is not a relative index. In terms of figure 2.2, suppose that the distribution $y = (cx_1, cx_2)$, where $c > 0$, is obtained from the distribution $x = (x_1, x_2)$ denoted by Q by raising or decreasing incomes proportionally. Clearly, y lies on the ray OS. Then for I_3^2 to be a relative index it is necessary that $E^2(x_1, x_2)/\lambda(x_1, x_2) = E^2(cx_1, cx_2)/\lambda(cx_1, cx_2)$, which means $E^2(cx_1, cx_2) = c \cdot E^2(x_1, x_2)$. That is, 'the whole set of indifference curves can be generated by radial expansion or contraction (by means of rays emanating from the origin) of a single curve' (Graaff(1977)). Thus, the SEF should be an ordinal transform of a linearly homogeneous function. All such SEFs are called homothetic. Formally, $W^n: D^n \to \mathbb{R}^1$ is homothetic if for all $x \in D^n$,

$$W^n(x) = \phi(\bar{W}^n(x)) \tag{2.28}$$

where $\bar{W}^n$ is linearly homogeneous and ϕ is increasing in its argument. An SEF $W: D \longrightarrow \mathbb{R}^1$ is homothetic if for all $n \in \mathbb{N}$, W^n is homothetic. The above observation can be formalised rigorously as

Theorem 2.7 (Blackorby and Donaldson 1978)

The Atkinson–Kolm–Sen inequality index I_3 is a relative index if and only if W is homothetic.

Proof[7]

Necessity:

Suppose that I_3^n is a relative index. Now, from (2.27) we have

$$E^n(x) = \lambda(x) \cdot (1 - I_3^n(x)) \ . \tag{2.29}$$

Since I_3^n is homogeneous of degree zero, linear homogeneity of $\lambda(x)$ implies linear homogeneity of $E^n(x)$. From(2.23) we have

$$\begin{aligned} W^n(x) &= W^n(x_f \cdot 1^n) \\ &= \Psi(x_f) \\ &= \Psi(E^n(x)) \ , \end{aligned} \tag{2.30}$$

where Ψ is increasing in its argument (since W^n is ordinal). Hence W^n is homothetic.

Sufficiency:

To demonstrate the sufficiency part of the theorem, suppose that W^n is homothetic. Then

$$W^n(x) = \phi(\bar{W}^n(x)) \ , \tag{2.31}$$

where $\bar{W}^n$ is linearly homogeneous and ϕ is increasing in its argument. Since $\bar{W}^n$ is linearly homogeneous, we have

[7] The proof given here is much simpler than the Blackorby–Donaldson proof.

$$x_f = E^n(x) = \frac{\bar{W}^n(x)}{\bar{W}^n(1^n)} . \tag{2.32}$$

By linear homogeneity of $\bar{W}^n$, E^n is linearly homogeneous. Since $\lambda(x)$ is also linearly homogeneous, I_3^n given by (2.27) becomes homogeneous of degree zero. Thus, I_3^n is a relative index. Clearly, our proof holds for all $n \in \mathbb{N}$. Hence I_3 is a relative index if and only if W is homothetic. ■

Thus, all relative inequality indices imply and are implied by homothetic SEFs. Blackorby and Donaldson(1978) investigated the properties of the SEFs that are consistent with the following strictly S–convex, population replication invariant indices of relative inequality:

Theil's(1967) entropy index:

$$T^n(x) = \frac{1}{n} \cdot \sum_{i=1}^{n} \frac{x_i}{\lambda(x)} \cdot \log \frac{x_i}{\lambda(x)} . \tag{2.33}$$

The coefficient of variation:

$$C^n(x) = \frac{\sigma_n}{\lambda(x)} = \frac{\left[\frac{1}{n} \cdot \sum_{i=1}^{n} (x_i - \lambda(x))^2\right]^{1/2}}{\lambda(x)} , \tag{2.34}$$

where σ_n is the standard deviation, the positive square root of the variance of the distribution $x \in D^n$.

The Gini(1912) index:

$$G^n(x) = \frac{\frac{1}{n^2} \cdot \sum_{i=1}^{n} \sum_{j=1}^{n} |x_i - x_j|}{2\,\lambda(x)} . \tag{2.35}$$

The Theil index takes a maximum value of log n when the richest person monopolises the entire income. For this index the effect of a transfer of income between two individuals i and j will depend on the ratio x_j/x_i, and hence the index attaches more wieght to transfers at lower income levels. The EDE income function associated with the normalised Theil index $T^n(x)/\log n$ can be written as

$$E_T^n(x) = \frac{1}{n \cdot \log n} \cdot [n \cdot \lambda(x) \cdot \log n \cdot \lambda(x) - \sum_{i=1}^{n} x_i \cdot \log x_i] . \tag{2.36}$$

The coefficient of variation achieves its upper bound $\sqrt{n-1}$ in the case of perfect inequality. For this index the effect of a transfer between two incomes depends on the difference between the incomes concerned and hence the index attaches equal weight to transfers at all income positions. The EDE income of the normalised index $C^n(x)/\sqrt{n-1}$ is given by

$$E_C^n(x) = \lambda(x) - \frac{[\frac{1}{n} \cdot \sum_{i=1}^{n} (x_i - \lambda(x))^2]^{1/2}}{\sqrt{n-1}} . \tag{2.37}$$

The Gini coefficient which is the most widely used index of inequality, can be interpreted and reformulated in many ways. The numerator of the expression (2.35) is called the Gini mean difference. If divided by the mean $\lambda(x)$, this difference gives the relative mean difference. Since $|x_i - x_j|$ can be written as $\max(0, x_j - x_i) + \max(0, x_i - x_j)$, the Gini index in (2.35) can be interpreted as 'the average gain to be expected, if each individual has the choice of being himself or some other member of the population drawn at random, expressed as a proportion of the average level of income' (Pyatt(1976))[8]. The observation

$$\min(x_i, x_j) = \frac{x_i + x_j - |x_i - x_j|}{2} \tag{2.38}$$

helps us to rewrite the Gini index in terms of $\mathring{x}(\bar{x})$, the welfare (illfare) ranked permutation of x, as follows (Sen(1973)):

[8] The Gini index has been interpreted as an index of relative deprivation by Sen(1973), Yitzhaki(1979, 1982) and Chakravarty and Chakraborty(1984). This issue is discussed in detail in Chapter 5.

$$G^n(x) = 1 - \frac{1}{n^2\lambda(x)} \cdot \sum_{i=1}^{n} \sum_{j=1}^{n} \min(x_i, x_j) \tag{2.39}$$

$$= 1 - \frac{1}{n^2\lambda(x)} \cdot \sum_{i=1}^{n} (2i - 1) \cdot \mathring{x}_i \tag{2.40}$$

$$= 1 - \frac{1}{n^2\lambda(x)} \cdot \sum_{i=1}^{n} [2 \cdot (n - i) + 1] \cdot \bar{x}_i \; . \tag{2.41}$$

Formula (2.39) shows that the Gini index is a continuous but non–differentiable function on D^n. However, all the first order partial derivatives of the Gini index exist if incomes are arranged in ascending or descending order. From (2.40) and (2.41) it is clear that for the Gini index the effect of a transfer of income between two individuals i and j will depend on their rank difference $(i - j)$. Thus, for a typically shaped income profile where a substantial number of incomes are concentrated around the modal value, the Gini index tends to be most sensitive to transfers around the middle of the distribution and least sensitive among the very rich or very poor.

In view of formulations (2.40) and (2.41) we can write the Gini SEF as

$$E_G^n(x) = \frac{1}{n^2} \cdot \sum_{i=1}^{n} (2i - 1) \cdot \mathring{x}_i \tag{2.42}$$

$$= \frac{1}{n^2} \cdot \sum_{i=1}^{n} [2(n - i) + 1] \cdot \bar{x}_i \; . \tag{2.43}$$

Thus, the Gini SEF is a rank order weighted average of individual incomes, where the weight attached to the ith ranked income is independent of the income profile. For $x, y \in D^n$ and for $0 < \otimes < 1$, we have

$$E_G^n(\Theta \cdot x + (1 - \Theta) \cdot y) = \Theta \cdot E_G^n(x) + (1 - \Theta) \cdot E_G^n(y) \; , \tag{2.44}$$

where it has been assumed that the ranks of individuals in the profiles x and y are the same. (2.44) shows that with a given rank order of incomes, the Gini SEF is linear. This proves the statement that the Gini index does not correspond to a strictly quasi–concave group welfare function (Newbery(1970), Kats(1972), Sheshinski(1972), Dasgupta, Sen and Starrett(1973) and Rothschild and Stiglitz(1973)). Moreover, the SEF E_G^n is not additively separable. Lambert (1985) attempted to overcome the problem of non-separability by defining the individual utility function as a function of the individual's position in the distribution as well as his income level. Thus, preferences depend not only on the individual's income level per se, but also on his sense of deprivation, that is, on the number of all better off individuals. The utility of the ith ranked income $\bar{x}_i$ is now given by $(2(n - i) + 1) \cdot \bar{x}_i)$. Obviously, with this restricted definition of utility the Gini SEF in (2.43) becomes additively separable. But by overcoming the problem of non-additivity we do not gain anything so far as the problem of non strict quasi-concavity of the Gini SEF is concerned[9].

Blackorby and Donaldson(1978) drew three dimensional welfare contours to investigate further properties of the SEFs. For a fixed mean income and letting $n = 3$, the set of all income profiles in the appropriate simplex forms a plane. The welfare contours of the Gini SEF constitute symmetrical hexagons in this plane, centered at the point of equality. Figure 2.3(a) illustrates this situation, while the conical structure, for $n = 2$ is depicted in figure 2.4(a). 2.3(b) and 2.4(b) show the corresponding diagrams for the coefficient of variation.

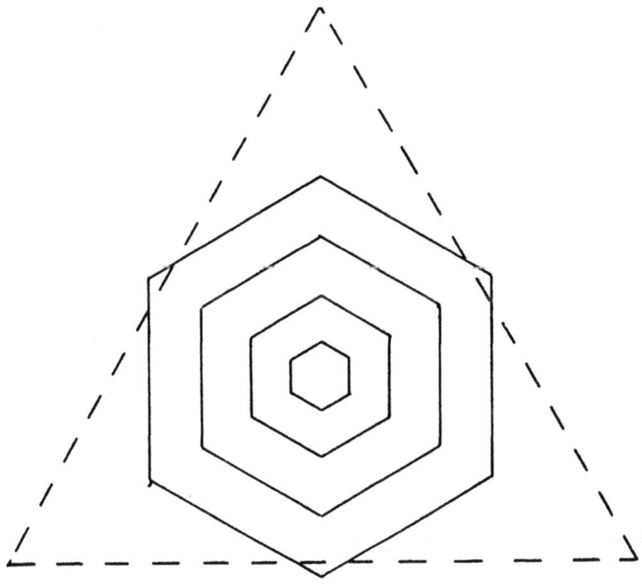

Figure 2.3(a)

[9] This issue will be taken up in more detail in Chapter 3.

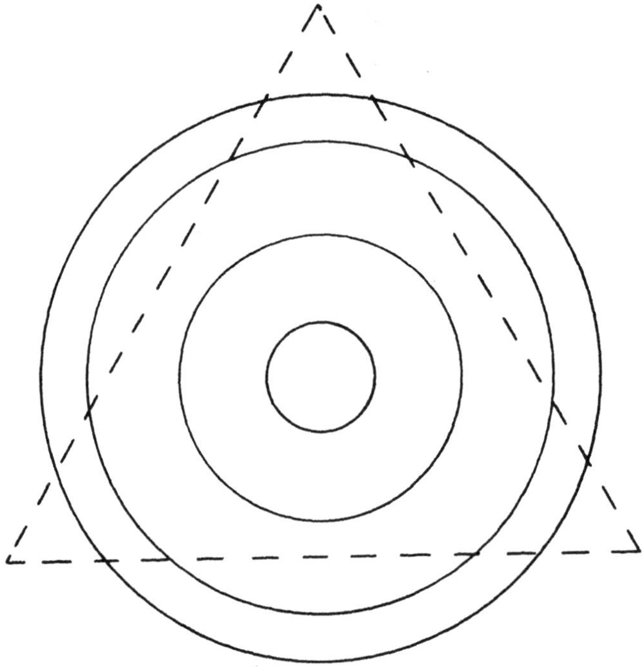

Figure 2.3(b)

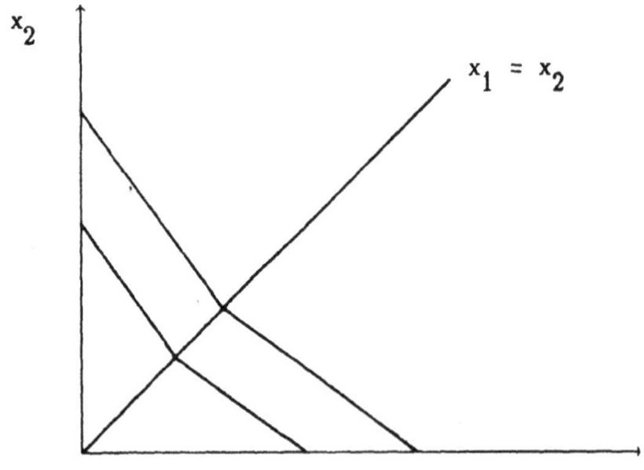

Figure 2.4(a)

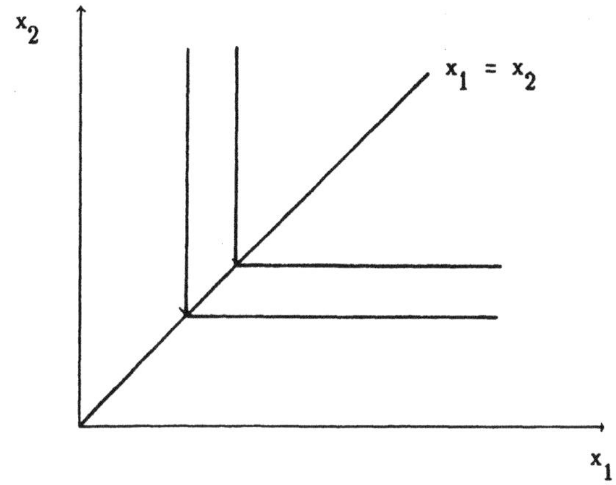

Figure 2.4(b)

From figure 2.3 we observe that the shape of the contours does not alter as we move away from the central point of equality. Blackorby and Donaldson refer to SEFs which have this property as being distributionally homothetic. If an SEF satisfies this property, then the marginal rate of substitution between two incomes in a given simplex is independent of incomes. What is more important is, the SEF allows income trades off among individuals in a way that is independent of how unequal the income profile is. On the other hand, the contours of E_T^3 (not drawn here) will become more triangular as we move outwards, indicating that the more unequal the income profile, the more we are concerned with the welfare of the poorest. This property is also shared by the symmetric mean of order r (< 1)

$$E_r^n(x) = \left(\frac{1}{n} \cdot \sum_{i=1}^{n} x_i^r\right)^{1/r}, \qquad (2.45)$$

the ordinal SEF associated with the Atkinson index I_2^n. For $r = 0$, E_r is the geometric mean. On the other hand, if r takes the value -1, E_r becomes the harmonic mean. The transfer sensitivity parameter r determines the curvature of the social indifference surfaces. To see this, we assume a 2–person society, where one individual has 3 units of in–

come and the other has 1 unit. We then draw indifference curves corresponding to the cases $r = 1$, $r = -\infty$ and an intermediate case lying somewhere between these two extreme situations.

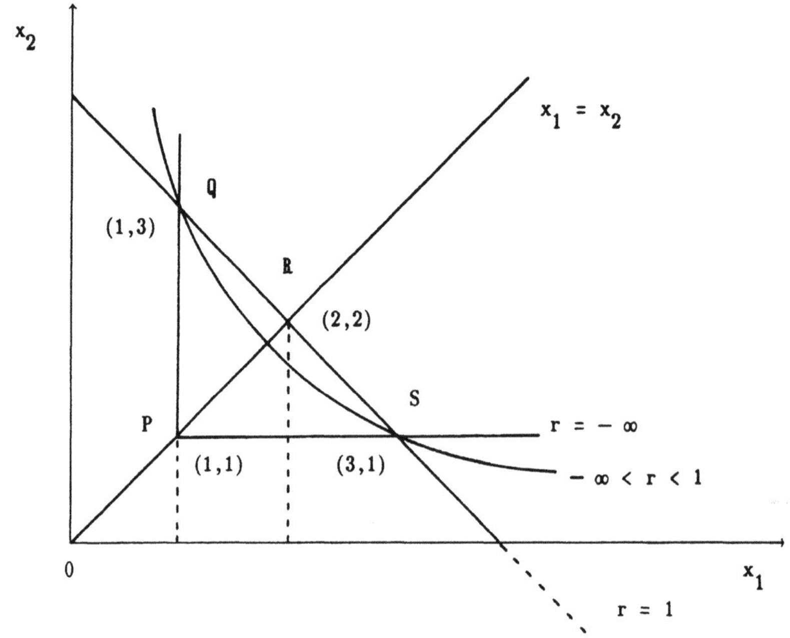

Figure 2.5

The symmetric linear SEF E_1^n has no distributional content: individuals feel indifferent between (3, 1) and (2, 2). The Rawlsian rule allows no trade–off between total income and its distribution: society feels indifferent between (1, 1) and (1, 3). The intermediate case is represented as a trade off between total income and its distribution.

2.4 Cardinally Significant Ethical Indices of Absolute and Intermediate Inequality

The concept of an absolute inequality index was introduced by Kolm(1976, 1976a). Blackorby and Donaldson(1980) made a detailed investigation on the properties of the SEFs associated with alternative absolute inequality indices. In their study, Blackorby and Donaldson(1980) proposed the use of $A_1: \mathbb{R}_+ \longrightarrow \mathbb{R}^1$ as an inequality index , where for all $n \in \mathbb{N}$, $x \in \mathbb{R}^n_+$,

$$A^n_1(x) = \lambda(x) - E^n(x) \;, \tag{2.46}$$

the shortfall of the AKS EDE income from the mean.

For a regular strictly S–concave W, A_1 is continuous, strictly S–convex and bounded by zero from below, where this bound is achieved whenever incomes are equal. A_1 is cardinally significant and satisfies the Daltonian population principle if E satisfies the same. A_1 gives the per capita income that could be saved if society distributed incomes equally without any loss of social welfare. A_1 can also be interpreted as the size of absolute welfare loss associated with the existence of inequality. Given a functional form for A^n_1, we can recover W^n using (2.46), (2.24) and (2.23).

Since in (2.46) two functions of income appear in a difference form, it is intuitively reasonable to regard A_1 as an absolute inequality index. In general, A_1 is not an absolute index. Using figure 2.2 it can be seen that for A_1 to be an absolute index we require the slope of W to be constant along lines which have constant slope equal to one. That is, any straight line which is parallel to the line of equality cuts all indifference curves at points of equal slopes. Such SEFs are called <u>homothetic to minus infinity</u> or <u>translatable</u>. Formally, $W^n\colon \mathbb{R}^n_+ \longrightarrow \mathbb{R}^1$ is translatable if for all $x \in \mathbb{R}^n_+$,

$$W^n(x) = \phi(\overset{*}{W}{}^n(x)) \tag{2.47}$$

where ϕ is increasing in its argument and

$$\overset{*}{W}{}^n(x + \alpha\cdot 1^n) = \overset{*}{W}{}^n(x) + \alpha \;, \tag{2.48}$$

α being any scalar such that $x + \alpha\cdot 1^n \in \mathbb{R}^n_+$. A function that meets the condition (2.48) is called <u>unit–translatable</u>. Thus, unit–translatable functions are those translatable functions for which ϕ is the identity mapping. An SEF $W\colon \mathbb{R}_+ \longrightarrow \mathbb{R}^1$ is translatable if for all $n \in \mathbb{N}$, W^n is translatable. Requiring a translatable function to be unit–translatable is analogous to requiring a homothetic function to be linearly homogeneous. Clearly, translatability of an SEF relates to an absolute index the way homotheticity of the SEF relates to a relative inequality index. We summarise the above observation rigorously in the following theorem:

Theorem 2.8 (Blackorby and Donaldson 1980)

The Blackorby–Donaldson–Kolm inequality index A_1 is an absolute index if and only if W is translatable.

Proof[10]

Sufficiency:

Suppose that W^n is translatable. That is, W^n can be written in the form given by (2.47). In this case the EDE income x_f associated with $x \in \mathbb{R}^n_+$ is given by

$$\overset{*}{W}{}^n(x_f \cdot 1^n) = \overset{*}{W}{}^n(x) . \tag{2.49}$$

Since $\overset{*}{W}{}^n$ is unit–translatable, we have

$$x_f = E^n(x) = \overset{*}{W}{}^n(x) - \overset{*}{W}{}^n(0 \cdot 1^n) , \tag{2.50}$$

and

$$A_1^n = \lambda(x) - \overset{*}{W}{}^n(x) + \overset{*}{W}{}^n(0 \cdot 1^n) . \tag{2.51}$$

Since $\lambda(x)$ is unit–translatable, A_1^n given by (2.51) is translation invariant. That is, A_1^n is an absolute index.

Necessity:

Suppose that A_1^n is an absolute inequality index. From (2.46),

$$\begin{aligned} E^n(x + \alpha \cdot 1^n) &= \lambda(x + \alpha \cdot 1^n) - A_1^n(x + \alpha \cdot 1^n) \\ &= \lambda(x) + \alpha - A_1^n(x) \\ &= E^n(x) + \alpha , \end{aligned} \tag{2.52}$$

---

10 Again our proof is much simpler than the Blackorby–Donaldson proof.

which shows unit–translatability of E^n. Now

$$W^n(x) = W^n(x_f \cdot 1^n) = W^n(E^n(x) \cdot 1^n) = \Psi(E^n(x)) \ , \tag{2.53}$$

where Ψ is increasing in its argument (since W^n is ordinally significant). Hence W^n is translatable. Clearly, our proof holds for all $n \in \mathbb{N}$. Thus, A_1 is an absolute index if and only if W is translatable[11]. ■

The absolute inequality index A_1^n tells us how much must be added in absolute terms to the income of every member of an n–person community to reach the same level of social welfare that would be achieved if everyone received the mean income of the original distribution. Thus, from a policy point of view the absolute inequality index A_1^n gives the total cost of per capita inequality (see Blackorby and Donaldson(1980)).

All absolute inequality indices imply and are implied by translatable SEFs. The absolute index suggested by Kolm(1976) is

$$A_2^n(x) = \begin{cases} 0 & , \alpha = 0 \\ \frac{1}{\alpha} \cdot \log \frac{1}{n} \cdot \sum_{i=1}^{n} e^{\alpha(\lambda(x) - x_i)} & , \alpha > 0 \end{cases}$$

which can be rewritten as

$$A_2^n(x) = \begin{cases} \lambda(x) - \lambda(x) & , \alpha = 0 \\ \lambda(x) - (-\frac{1}{\alpha} \cdot \log \frac{1}{n} \cdot \sum_{i=1}^{n} e^{-\alpha x_i} & , \alpha > 0 \ . \end{cases} \tag{2.54}$$

The EDE income associated with (2.54) is, therefore, given by

[11] Since the index A_1 is well–defined on $\mathbb{R}_+$, we have proved Theorem 2.8 on this extended domain. Noting that the AKS index I_3 is discontinuous at the origin in $\mathbb{R}_+$ we have defined it on D.

$$E_{\alpha}^{n}(x) = \begin{cases} \lambda(x) & , \alpha = 0 \\ -\frac{1}{\alpha} \cdot \log \frac{1}{n} \cdot \sum_{i=1}^{n} e^{-\alpha x_i} & , \alpha > 0 \ . \end{cases} \tag{2.55}$$

Pollak(1971) determined the class of additive utility functions that are homothetic to minus infinity. A very simple symmetric representation is

$$W_P^n(x) = -\sum_{i=1}^{n} e^{-\alpha x_i} , \alpha > 0 \ . \tag{2.56}$$

This function can be written as an increasing transform of E_{α}^{n}, since

$$W_P^n(x) = -n \cdot \exp(-\alpha \cdot E_{\alpha}^{n}(x)) \ . \tag{2.57}$$

Alternatively, we can start with $W_P^n(x)$ and find the associated EDE income. It is then easy to verify that the Blackorby–Donaldson–Kolm (BDK) index in this case is given by (2.54), which is the Kolm function. The class of SEFs in (2.56) and its indices has a free parameter α that determines the curvature of the social indifference surfaces. As $\alpha \longrightarrow 0$, E_{α}^{n} approaches the symmetric linear SEF $\lambda(x)$, whereas it approaches the Rawlsian maximin function when α tends to plus infinity. The latter extreme situation produces the absolute maximin index of inequality: $\lambda(x) - \min_i \{x_i\}$. For $0 < \alpha < \infty$, the indifference curve is strictly convex to the origin.

Some SEFs are both homothetic and translatable – they are <u>compromise</u> SEFs. Both the Gini and coefficient of variation SEFs have this property, consequently, it is possible to calculate the corresponding absolute indices. In view of (2.42) and (2.43), the Gini absolute index can be written as

$$G_A^n(x) = \lambda(x) - \frac{1}{n^2} \cdot \sum_{i=1}^{n} (2i-1) \cdot \mathring{x}_i \tag{2.58}$$

$$= \lambda(x) - \frac{1}{n^2} \cdot \sum_{i=1}^{n} [2 \cdot (n-i) + 1] \cdot \bar{x}_i \ . \tag{2.59}$$

The absolute index that corresponds to the SEF (2.37) is the normalised standard deviation $\sigma_n/\sqrt{n-1}$. Thus, the Gini index and the coefficient of variation are <u>compromise</u> relative indices – they can be converted into absolute inequality indices by multiplying with mean income.

Other interesting examples of compromise SEFs are the symmetric linear SEF $\lambda(x)$ and the maximin SEF $\min_i \{x_i\}$. In fact, all compromise SEFs are distributionally homothetic. That is, any such SEF can be expressed as an ordinal transform of a distributionally homogeneous function (Blackorby and Donaldson(1982)). Formally, $W^n\colon D^n \longrightarrow \mathbb{R}^1$ is distributionally homothetic if for all $x \in D^n$

$$W^n(x) = \phi(\hat{W}^n(x)) , \tag{2.60}$$

where ϕ is increasing in its argument and $\hat{W}^n$ is distributionally homogeneous. $\hat{W}^n$ is called distributionally homogeneous if

$$\hat{W}^n(cx + \alpha \cdot 1^n) = c \cdot W^n(x) + \alpha , \tag{2.61}$$

where $c > 0$ and α are scalars such that $cx + \alpha 1^n \in D^n$. An SEF $W\colon D \longrightarrow \mathbb{R}^1$ is distributionally homothetic if for all $n \in \mathbb{N}$, W^n is distributionally homothetic.

The following propositions, which are easy to prove, indicate the relationship between distributionally homothetic SEFs and compromise indices.

<u>Proposition 2.1</u>

The Atkinson–Kolm–Sen relative inequality index I_3 in (2.27) is a compromise relative index, that is, $\lambda(x) \cdot I_3$ is an absolute index if and only if W is distributionally homothetic.

<u>Proposition 2.2</u> (Blackorby and Donaldson 1980)

The Blackorby–Donaldson–Kolm absolute inequality index A_1 in (2.46) is a compromise absolute index , that is, $A_1(x)/\lambda(x)$, $\lambda(x) > 0$, is a relative index if and only if W is distributionally homothetic.

Following Blackorby and Donaldson(1980) we now argue that 'if absolute and relative indices represent moral judgements of the 'left' and 'right' respectively, as Kolm thinks they do, one must either decide where one stands, or else commit oneself to distributionally homogeneous social evaluation functions'.

In their study on intermediate inequality, Bossert and Pfingsten(1989) suggested $B_\mu: D \longrightarrow \mathbb{R}^1$, where for all $n \in \mathbb{N}$, $x \in D^n$ and $0 \leq \mu \leq 1$,

$$B_\mu^n(x) = \frac{\lambda(x) - E^n(x)}{\mu \cdot \lambda(x) + 1 - \mu} \tag{2.62}$$

as an index of inequality. B_μ seems to be natural generalisation of the AKS and BDK indices in (2.27) and (2.46) respectively. (These two indices become polar cases of B_μ corresponding to $\mu = 1$ and $\mu = 0$ respectively.) The following theorem which parallels Theorems 2.7 and 2.8 provides a necessary and sufficient condition for B_μ, $0 < \mu < 1$, to be an intermediate index.

<u>Theorem 2.9</u> (Bossert and Pfingsten 1989)

B_μ, $0 < \mu < 1$, is an intermediate inequality index if and only if E^n satisfies

$$E^n(\alpha[x + \epsilon \cdot 1^n] - \epsilon \cdot 1^n) = \alpha[E^n(x) + \epsilon] - \epsilon \tag{2.63}$$

for all $x \in D^n$, $\alpha > 0$, where $\epsilon = (1 - \mu)/\mu$ and $n \in \mathbb{N}$.

<u>Proof</u>

With $\epsilon = (1 - \mu)/\mu$, (2.3) can be written as $I^n(\alpha[x + \epsilon \cdot 1^n] - \epsilon \cdot 1^n) = I^n(x)$ and (2.62) becomes $[\lambda(x) - E^n(x)]/\mu \cdot (\lambda(x) + \epsilon)$. The theorem then can be established using arguments which are analogous to those employed in the proof of Theorem 2.7. ■

Thus, Theorem 2.9 identifies all SEFs whose associated inequality indices, as defined in (2.62), are required to satisfy intermediate inequality equivalence concept. The Gini SEF provides an example of such SEFs.

2.5 Inequality as an Ordinal Concept

The concern of this section is the connection between social welfare and the measurement of inequality, where the concept of inequality is purely ordinal. We examine the distributions of income over a given population size $n \geq 2$. As a first step let us suppose that the AKS relative inequality index I_3^n has ordinal significance. Following Blackorby and Donaldson(1978) we may consider the SEF $\lambda(x)\cdot(1 - I_3^n(x))$ as a representation of the associated welfare ordering. But it is evident that two ordinally equivalent indices of inequality, for example, the Gini index $G^n(x)$ and its square $(G^n(x))^2$, will imply two ordinally different SEFs – namely $\lambda(x)\cdot(1 - G^n(x))$ and $\lambda(x)\cdot(1 - (G^n(x))^2)$. That is, the SEF $\lambda(x)\cdot(1 - (G^n(x))^2)$ cannot be expressed as an ordinal transform of the SEF $\lambda(x)\cdot(1 - G^n(x))$. This shows that if inequality of income distribution is an ordinal concept, then the Blackorby–Donaldson procedure of recovering the SEF from an inequality index is inappropriate.

Ebert(1987) suggested a new procedure which avoids the above difficulty and this is the issue of our discussion here. The starting point is an ordering $\gtrsim_I n$ defined on D^n, that is, $\gtrsim_I n$ is a reflexive, transitive and complete relation. $\gtrsim_I n$ reflects the inequality within the vectors – $x \gtrsim_I n\ y$ means that x is more unequal than y. $\sim_I n$ stands for the symmetric component of $\gtrsim_I n$ – $x \sim_I n\ y$ means that $x \gtrsim_I n\ y$ and $y \gtrsim_I n\ x$. Additional properties of $\gtrsim_I n$ are summarised by the following assumption.

Assumption 1

(a) $\gtrsim_I n$ is continuous.

(b) $\gtrsim_I n$ is a relative ordering; $x \sim_I n\ \Theta\cdot x$ for all $x \in D^n$, $\Theta > 0$.

Assumption 1(a) implies the existence of a continuous indicator I^n: $D^n \longrightarrow \mathbb{R}^1$, where I^n is scale invariant according to assumption 1(b).

By means of $\gtrsim_I n$ it is possible to get a partition of D^n into the set of equivalence classes $X_I n$. If $x_I n$ denotes the equivalence class to which $x \in D^n$ belongs, then $X_I n = \{x_I n\text{: } x \in D^n\}$. A topology of $X_I n$ is introduced by requiring that the mapping k: $X_I n \longrightarrow \mathbb{R}^1$, which maps $x_I n$ onto $I^n(y)$ for any $y \in x_I n$, becomes a homeomorphism.

To express value judgements about the trade-off between the mean income and the inequality of an income vector, we now presume the existence of an ordering $\gtrsim_V$ defined on $D^1 \times X_I n$, which satisfies

Assumption 2

$\gtrsim_V$ is continuous.

For any two pairs $(\alpha, x_I n)$ and $(\alpha', y_I n)$ of mean incomes $\alpha, \alpha' \in D^1$ and grades of inequality $x_I n, y_I n \in X_I n$, the ordering $\gtrsim_V$ specifies whether the combination $(\alpha, x_I n)$ is better than, indifferent to or worse than $(\alpha', y_I n)$. The next assumption ensures that $\gtrsim_V$ is consistent with $\gtrsim_I n$:

Assumption 3

For all $\alpha > 0$, $(\alpha, x_I n) \lesssim_V (\alpha, y_I n) \Leftrightarrow x \gtrsim_I n\ y$, where $x, y \in D^n$ are arbitrary.

In words, assumption 3 implies that two income vectors possessing the same mean income are ranked by $\gtrsim_V$ according to their inequality. Clearly, this property is a kind of monotonicity of $\gtrsim_V$.

By means of $\gtrsim_I n$ and $\gtrsim_V$ we can define an ordering $\gtrsim_W n$ on D^n in terms of social welfare:

$$x \gtrsim_W n\ y \Leftrightarrow (\lambda(x), x_I n) \gtrsim_V (\lambda(y), y_I n) \quad , \tag{2.64}$$

where $x, y \in D^n$ are arbitrary. We now have

Theorem 2.10 (Ebert 1987)

If assumptions 1, 2 and 3 are satisfied, then the ordering $\gtrsim_W n$ possesses the following properties:

(a) It is continuous.

(b) For all $x, y \in D^n$, at least one of the following conditions hold:

(i) $(\alpha \cdot \frac{x}{\lambda(x)}) \gtrsim_W n\ (\alpha \cdot \frac{y}{\lambda(y)})$, $\alpha > 0$ is arbitrary, or

(ii) $(\alpha \cdot \frac{x}{\lambda(x)}) \lesssim_{W^n} (\alpha \cdot \frac{y}{\lambda(y)})$, $\alpha > 0$ is arbitrary.

Proof

(a) Continuity of $\gtrsim_{W^n}$ follows from continuity of $\gtrsim_{I^n}$ and $\gtrsim_V$.

(b) By completeness of $\gtrsim_{I^n}$, we have either $x \gtrsim_{I^n} y$ or $x \lesssim_{I^n} y$. This along with assumption 1(b) shows that either $\frac{x}{\lambda(x)} \gtrsim_{I^n} \frac{y}{\lambda(y)}$ or $\frac{x}{\lambda(x)} \lesssim_{I^n} \frac{y}{\lambda(y)}$. Finally, assumption 3 implies $(\alpha, (\frac{x}{\lambda(x)})_{I^n}) \gtrsim_V (\alpha, (\frac{y}{\lambda(y)})_{I^n})$ or $(\alpha, (\frac{x}{\lambda(x)})_{I^n}) \lesssim_V (\alpha, (\frac{y}{\lambda(y)})_{I^n})$, from which the desired result follows. ■

Condition (b) in theorem 2.10 means that $\gtrsim_{W^n}$ ranks two income profiles $\alpha \cdot \frac{x}{\lambda(x)}$ and $\alpha \cdot \frac{y}{\lambda(y)}$ of the same total income $n \cdot \alpha$ independently of total income. Thus, the component size does not play any role here. Clearly, this property is weaker than homotheticity.

A simple consequence of the definition of $\gtrsim_{W^n}$ is the decomposition of SEFs which represent $\gtrsim_{W^n}$. If $W^n: D^n \longrightarrow \mathbb{R}^1$ is an ordinal indicator of $\gtrsim_{W^n}$, it follows that we can choose an ordinal indicator V of $\gtrsim_V$ such that

$$W^n(x) = V(\lambda(x), x_{I^n}) \; . \tag{2.65}$$

Moreover, if I^n represents $\gtrsim_{I^n}$ we can express W^n by a function f based on I^n:

$$W^n(x) = f(\lambda(x), I^n(x)) \; , \tag{2.66}$$

where, by assumption 3, f is non–increasing in I^n.

To see that W^n is ordinally significant, choose $\hat{W}^n = g(W^n)$, $h(I^n) = \hat{I}^n$, where g and h are increasing. Then we have

$$\begin{aligned}\hat{W}^n(x) &= g(W^n(x)) \\ &= g(f(\lambda(x), h^{-1} 0\, h(I^n(x)))) \\ &= \hat{g}(\lambda(x), \hat{I}^n(x)) \ ,\end{aligned} \tag{2.67}$$

where h^{-1} is the inverse of h and '0' means the composition of functions.

Additional properties of f will depend on corresponding properties of $\gtrsim_V$ and $\gtrsim_{W^n}$ respectively. For example, the monotonicity of $\gtrsim_V$ in its first argument (that is, if $x \sim_{I^n} y$, then $\lambda(x) > \lambda(y) \rightarrow (\lambda(x), x_{I^n})) \gtrsim_V (\lambda(y), y_{I^n}))$ is necessary and sufficient for increasingness of f in $\lambda(x)$. Similarly increasingness of $\gtrsim_{W^n}$ along rays ($\Theta x \gtrsim_{W^n} x$ for all $\Theta > 1$) implies and is implied by monotonicity of $\gtrsim_V$ in mean income.

It is also easy to check that $\gtrsim_{I^n}$ is weakly normatively significant for $\gtrsim_{W^n}$ in the sense of Blackorby and Donaldson(1978). That is, suppose that assumptions 1, 2 and 3 hold. Then for arbitrary x, y with $\lambda(x) = \lambda(y)$, $x \lesssim_{I^n} y \Leftrightarrow x \gtrsim_{W^n} y$ and $x >_{W^n} y \Rightarrow x <_{I^n} y$.

We now attend to the converse problem. The following theorem shows that the procedure proposed can be reversed.

Theorem 2.11 (Ebert 1987)

(a) If the ordering $\gtrsim_{W^n}$ satisfies conditions (a) and (b) in Theorem 2.10, then one can get two orderings $\gtrsim_{I^n}$ and $\gtrsim_V$ satisfying assumptions 1, 2 and 3.

(b) If one derives an ordering $\gtrsim_{F^n}$ from $\gtrsim_{I^n}$ and $\gtrsim_V$ by the procedure described above, this ordering $\gtrsim_{F^n}$ coincides with $\gtrsim_{W^n}$.

(c) If one derives $\gtrsim_{W^n}$ from the orderings $\gtrsim_V$ and $\gtrsim_{I^n}$ which satisfy assumptions 1, 2, 3 and uses this $\gtrsim_{W^n}$ to derive the orderings $\gtrsim_{V'}$ and $\gtrsim_{I'^n}$ according to the procedure used below, then $\gtrsim_{I'^n} = \gtrsim_{I^n}$ and $\gtrsim_{V'} = \gtrsim_V$.

Proof

(a) For $x, y \in D^n$, define

$$x \gtrsim_{I^n} y \Leftrightarrow \alpha \cdot \frac{x}{\lambda(x)} \lesssim_{W^n} \alpha \cdot \frac{y}{\lambda(y)}, \ \alpha > 0 \ . \tag{2.68}$$

It is clear that the relation $\gtrsim_{I^n}$ is reflexive, transitive and complete. Again by continuity of $\gtrsim_{W^n}$, it is ordinally representable by the continuous function

$$I^n(x) = -W^n(x/\lambda(x)) \ , \tag{2.69}$$

where W^n is a continuous indicator of $\gtrsim_{W^n}$. Obviously $x \sim_{I^n} \alpha \cdot x$, $\alpha > 0$. Therefore $\gtrsim_{I^n}$ satisfies assumption 1.

Let X_{I^n} denote the set of equivalence classes x_{I^n} with respect to $\gtrsim_{I^n}$ endowed with the natural topology. Then we can define the ordering $\gtrsim_v$ on $D^1 \times X_{I^n}$ by

$$(\delta, x_{I^n}) \gtrsim_v (\Theta, y_{I^n}) \ = \ \delta \cdot \frac{x}{\lambda(x)} \gtrsim_{W^n} \Theta \cdot \frac{y}{\lambda(y)} \tag{2.70}$$

for $x \in x_{I^n}$, $y \in y_{I^n}$ and for all $\delta, \Theta \in D^1$, $x_{I^n}, y_{I^n} \in X_{I^n}$.
This definition is independent of the choice of x, y because of conditions (a), (b) in Theorem 2.10 and the definition of $\gtrsim_{I^n}$. Continuity of $\gtrsim_v$ follows from continuity of $\gtrsim_{W^n}$.
Assumption 3 can be checked easily.

(b) It is obvious that starting with $\gtrsim_{I^n}$ and $\gtrsim_v$ we arrive at $\gtrsim_{W^n}$ again.

(c) This part follows from part (a) and uniqueness of $\gtrsim_{I^n}$ and $\gtrsim_v$. ■

The following theorem, whose proof is very easy, shows why an ordering $\gtrsim_{I^n}$ derived from $\gtrsim_{W^n}$ can be interpreted in terms of inequality.

<u>Theorem 2.12</u> (Ebert 1987)

Suppose that assumptions 1, 2, 3 and conditions (a) and (b) in Theorem 2.10 hold.

(a) $\gtrsim_{W^n}$ is S–concave $\Leftrightarrow$ $\gtrsim_{I^n}$ is S–convex[12].

---

[12] An ordering $\gtrsim_{W^n}$ defined on D^n is S–concave (S–convex) if $Qx \gtrsim_{W^n} x$ ($Qx \lesssim_{W^n} x$) for all bistochastic matrices Q of order n and for all $x \in D^n$.

(b) $\gtrsim_{W^n}$ is symmetric $\Leftrightarrow$ $\gtrsim_{I^n}$ is symmetric.

Thus, the above theorem shows that $\gtrsim_{W^n}$ and $\gtrsim_{I^n}$ take into account the Pigou–Dalton condition correctly.

Finally, by assuming that $\gtrsim_{W^n}$ is increasing along rays and homothetic, we can show that the AKS inequality index becomes an ordinal indicator of $\gtrsim_{I^n}$. This is formally stated as:

Theorem 2.13 (Ebert 1987)

Suppose that the ordering $\gtrsim_{W^n}$ satisfies conditions (a) and (b) in Theorem 2.10. Furthermore, let $\gtrsim_{W^n}$ be increasing along rays ($\Theta \cdot x \gtrsim_{W^n} x$ for all $\Theta > 1$) and homothetic ($x \sim_{W^n} y \;\Rightarrow\; \Theta \cdot x \sim_{W^n} \Theta \cdot y$ for all $\Theta > 0$). Then the AKS inequality index $J^n(x) = 1 - x_f/\lambda(x)$ is an ordinal indicator of $\gtrsim_{I^n}$. That is, the ordering implied by $J^n(x)$ coincides with $\gtrsim_{I^n}$.

Proof

Let $W^n(x)$ be a homothetic indicator of $\gtrsim_{W^n}$: $W^n(\Theta \cdot x) = \Theta \cdot W^n(x)$, $\Theta > 0$, $x \in D^n$. By Theorem 2.11, we can regard $I^n(x) = - W^n(x/\lambda(x))$ as an ordinal indicator of $\gtrsim_{I^n}$. Now

$$
\begin{aligned}
J^n(x) &= 1 - \frac{x_f}{\lambda(x)} \\
&= 1 - \frac{x_f \cdot W^n(1^n)}{\lambda(x) \cdot W^n(1^n)} \\
&= 1 - \frac{W^n(x_f \cdot 1^n)}{\lambda(x) \cdot W^n(1^n)} \\
&= 1 - \frac{W^n(x/\lambda(x))}{W^n(1^n)} \\
&= f(I^n(x)) , \qquad (2.71)
\end{aligned}
$$

where $f(r) = 1 + \dfrac{1}{W^n(1^n)} \cdot r$. Since $W^n(1^n) > 0$, f is monotone and continuous. ∎

We can now illustrate the theoretical framework established above with an example. For simplicity, let n = 2. Suppose that the ordering $\gtrsim_{I^n}$ is represented by the Gini coefficient

$$G^2(x) = 1-(x_1 + 3x_2)/2(x_1 + x_2), \text{ where } x_1 \geq x_2.$$

We represent the set of equivalence classes X_{I^2} by the interval [0, 1/2], the range of $G^2(x)$, and identify classes x_{I^2} with $k = k(x_{I^2}) \in [0, 1/2]$ if and only if $G^2(y) = k$ for any $y \in x_{I^2}$.

Now $\gtrsim_V$ is defined on $D^1 \times [0, 1/2]$ by the function

$$f(\alpha, k) = \alpha \cdot (1-k), \; k \in [0, 1/2]^{13}. \tag{2.72}$$

We will now demonstrate the procedure of deriving $\gtrsim_{W^2}$. We define

$$W^2(x) = f(\lambda(x), k(x_{I^2})) \; . \tag{2.73}$$

Then we have

$$\begin{aligned} W^2(x) &= \lambda(x) \cdot (1-G^2(x)) \\ &= \frac{1}{4} \cdot (x_1 + 3x_2) \end{aligned} \tag{2.74}$$

and this determines $\gtrsim_{W^2}$.

If we start with $(G^2(x))^2$, the set X_{I^2} remains unchanged. Furthermore, we can use [0,1/2] as the representation of X_{I^2} again. But now x_{I^2} is identified by $k = k(x_{I^2}) \in [0,1/2]$: if and only if $(G^2(y))^2 = k^2$ for any $y \in x_{I^2}$. Assuming the same functional form for $\gtrsim_V$ and f we again arrive at $W^2(x) = [x_1 + 3x_2]/4$ and the same $\gtrsim_{W^2}$. This

[13] This representation of $\gtrsim_V$ is by no means unique. What is actually necessary is a specification of $\gtrsim_V$ such that assumptions 2 and 3 are satisfied.

shows that we do not face the problem embodied in the Blackorby–Donaldson approach.

We can consider a second example to illustrate the framework when the SEF is not homothetic. We define an ordering $\gtrsim_{W^n}$ by an (ordinal) SEF W^n:

$$W^n(x) = \begin{cases} \lambda(x) - \lambda(x) \cdot G^n(x) \ , \lambda(x) \leqq \lambda_0 \\ \lambda(x) - \dfrac{\lambda_0^2}{\lambda(x)} \cdot G^n(x) \ , \lambda(x) > \lambda_0 \end{cases} \tag{2.75}$$

where $\lambda_0 > 0$. Clearly, W^n is not homothetic. As long as the mean income is less than or equal to the minimum level of standard of living, inequality does play an important role. But if mean income increases, inequality is taken into account less and less. The ordering underlying W^n in (2.75) possesses property (b) in Theorem 2.10. The implied inequality ordering $\gtrsim_{I^n}$ can be represented by the Gini index and is unique.

2.6 Decomposition of Inequality Indices by Population Subgroups and by Factor Components

Many of the commonly used inequality indices have been used by different authors interested in decomposition of the overall degree of inequality. In this context, two particular applications stand out. The first concerns a partition of the population into disjoint subgroups, such as groups by age, sex, race, region etc., and the researcher is interested in examining how the overall degree of inequality can be appropriately resolved into contributions due to (i) inequality within each of the groups, and (ii) inequality between groups, that is, due to variations in average levels of income across these groups (see Mendershausen(1946), Soltow(1960), Bhattacharya and Mahalanobis (1967), Theil(1967, 1972), Mehran(1975), Paglin(1975, 1977, 1979, 1989), Love and Wolfson(1976), Pyatt(1976), Danziger et. al.(1977), Johnson(1977), Kurien(1977), Minarik(1977), Nelson(1977), Bourguignon(1979), Murray(1979), Wertz(1979), Cowell (1980, 1985, 1988), Formby and Seaks(1980), Shorrocks(1980, 1984, 1988), Cowell and Mehta (1982), Mookherjee and Shorrocks(1982), Foster(1983, 1985), Adelman and Levy (1984, 1986), Kanbur(1984), Russell(1985), Maasoumi(1986), Satchell(1987), Ebert (1988) and Formby et. al.(1989)). The other main application disaggregates total income of each individual into amounts earned from different sources (or factor components) and examines the impact of each of these sources on overall degree of inequality (see Mahalanobis(1960), Rao(1969), Mangahas and Gamboa(1976), Kakwani (1977), Fei, Ranis and Kuo(1978, 1979), Fields(1979, 1979a, 1980), Layard and Zabalza(1979), Theil (1979), Pyatt, Chen and Fei(1980), Shorrocks(1982, 1983a, 1988), Lerman and Yitzhaki (1985) and Silber(1989)).

2.6.1 Subgroup Aggregation

We first address ourselves to the problem of subgroup decomposition. Let $\{N^1, N^2, ..., N^k\}$ be a disjoint exhaustive partition of the population set $\{1, 2, ..., n\}$. Hence $j \in N^k$ means that individual j is a member of group k and x^i is a vector of incomes of group i. Accordingly the income profile $x \in D^n$ can now be written as $x = (x^1, ..., x^k)$, where $x^i \in D^{n_i}$ and n_i is the number of persons in group i. Following Shorrocks (1980) we say that an inequality index $I: D \to \mathbb{R}^1$ is additively decomposable if for all $n \in \mathbb{N}$, for all partitions $\{N^1, ..., N^k\}$ of $\{1, 2, ..., n\}$ and for all $x \in D^n$

$$I^n(x^1, x^2, ..., x^k) = \sum_{g=1}^{k} w_g^k(\underline{\lambda}(x), \underline{n}) I^{n_g}(x^g) + I^n(\lambda(x^1)\cdot 1^{n_1}, \lambda(x^2)\cdot 1^{n_2}, ..., \lambda(x^k)\cdot 1^{n_k}), \tag{2.76}$$

where w_g^k is the positive weight attached to subgroup g in a decomposition into k subgroups, shown to depend on the vector of subgroup means $\underline{\lambda}(x) = (\lambda(x^1), ..., \lambda(x^k))$ and the vector of subgroup populations $\underline{n} = (n_1, n_2, ..., n_k)$ but is independent of the level of inequality within the subgroups. The second term on the right hand side of (2.76) is the between group inequality and the first term is a weighted average of within group inequalities.

Shorrocks(1980) has shown that a relative index $I: D \to \mathbb{R}^1$ has continuous first order derivatives, and satisfies NM, IM, PD, PP, CON and additive decomposability in (2.76) if and only if it is a positive multiple of an index from the family $S_c: D \to \mathbb{R}^1$, where for all $n \in \mathbb{N}$, $x \in D^n$

$$S_c^n(x) = \frac{1}{nc(c-1)} \cdot \sum_{i=1}^{n} \left[\left(\frac{x_i}{\lambda(x)}\right)^c - 1\right] \quad , c \neq 0,1,$$

$$S_1^n(x) = \frac{1}{n} \cdot \sum_{i=1}^{n} \frac{x_i}{\lambda(x)} \cdot \log \frac{x_i}{\lambda(x)} , \qquad (2.77)$$

$$S_0^n(x) = \frac{1}{n} \cdot \sum_{i=1}^{n} \log \frac{\lambda(x)}{x_i} .$$

The decomposition coefficients for these indices are given by $w_g^k(\underline{\lambda}, \underline{n}) = \frac{n_g}{n} \cdot (\frac{\lambda(x^g)}{\lambda(x)})^c$ and sum to unity only when c = 0 or c = 1. Consequently, in general, the total within group contribution to inequality

$$\sum_{g=1}^{k} w_g^k(\underline{\lambda}, \underline{n}) \, I^{n_g}(x^g)$$

is not a weighted average of subgroup inequality values $I^{n_g}(x^g)$. Shorrocks(1980) argued that $1 - \sum_{g=1}^{k} w_g^k$ is proportional to the between group term in the appropriate decomposition formula. This means that except for two Theil indices (c = 0,1), the decomposition coefficients are not independent of the between group contribution.

The class of indices given by (2.77) is popularly referred to as the Generalised Entropy family. The parameter c in S_c reflects different perceptions of inequality. As c decreases, S_c becomes more sensitive to transfers lower down the scale. S_c includes the Theil entropy index (c = 1), the mean logarithmic deviation (c = 0) and monotonic transformation of the coefficient of variation (c = 2). Bourguignon(1979) characterised the index S_0 using the rather restricted form of (2.76) where w_g^k is given by n_g/n. Foster (1983), on the other hand, characterised S_1 using the decomposability postulate (2.76) where $w_g^k = n_g \cdot \lambda(x^g)/n\lambda(x)$.

Shorrocks(1984) replaces (2.76) with the following more modest requirement: for all $n_1, n_2 \in \mathbb{N}, x^1 \in D^{n_1}, x^2 \in D^{n_2}$,

$$I^{n_1+n_2}(x^1, x^2) = A(I^{n_1}(x^1), I^{n_2}(x^2), \lambda(x^1), \lambda(x^2), n_1, n_2), \qquad (2.78)$$

where the 'aggregation' function A is continuous in first two arguments. Following Foster(1985) we say that an inequality index $I: D \longrightarrow \mathbb{R}^1$ is aggregative if (2.78) is satisfied for some aggregation function A. Clearly, any additively decomposable index is aggregative with A having a very special form. Shorrocks(1984) demonstrated that an aggregative relative index satisfies the assumptions NM, IM, PP, PD and CON if and only if it is an increasing transformation of a member from the Generalised Entropy family (2.77). Since the distributional rankings generated by indices remain unaffected under monotone transformations, we do not gain much from replacement of (2.76) by (2.78) so far as the choice of decomposable inequality index is concerned.

We may wish to note that the Atkinson index I_2 in (2.22) corresponds to the index S_c with $r = c$ via the monotonically increasing transformation

$$I_2^n(x) = \begin{cases} 1 - [c(c-1)S_c^n(x) + 1]^{1/c}, & c < 1 \\ 1 - e^{-S_c^n(x)}, & c = 0 \, . \end{cases} \qquad (2.79)$$

That is, I_2 gives precisely the same inequality ordering as S_c when $r = c < 1$. Since I_2 is an increasing transform of S_c, it is an aggregative inequality index for all $r < 1$ (see Shorrocks(1980), Foster(1985)).

It will now be an interesting exercise to investigate whether the Gini index can be interpreted as an aggregative inequality index. Many authors (e.g., Bhattacharya and Mahalanobis(1967), Pyatt(1976), Mookherjee and Shorrocks(1982), Foster(1985) and Ebert(1988)) noted that if we allow partitions of the population to be non-overlapping, then the overall Gini index can be decomposed into between and within group components. Symbolically, if we partition the ordered vector $x \in D^n$ into ordered vectors x^1, x^2, ..., x^k such that the range of incomes in group i does not overlap with that of group i+1 and that $x = (x^1, x^2, ..., x^k)$, then the Gini coefficient may be decomposed as follows:

$$G^n(x) = \sum_{j=1}^{k} \left(\frac{n_j}{n}\right)^2 \cdot \frac{\lambda(x^j)}{\lambda(x)} \cdot G^{n_j}(x^j)$$

$$+ \frac{1}{2} \sum_{j=1}^{k} \sum_{h=1}^{k} \frac{n_j}{n} \frac{n_h}{n} \left| \frac{\lambda(x^j) - \lambda(x^h)}{\lambda(x)} \right| . \tag{2.80}$$

Thus, the Gini index satisfies a particular form of aggregativity where the vectors x^1, x^2, ..., x^k as well as the vector x are ordered. Ebert(1988) showed that if in (2.76) we restrict ourselves to non–overlapping partitions of the population, then the Generalised Entropy class and the Gini index are the only additively decomposable relative inequality indices which possess continuous first and second order partial derivatives and satisfy NM, PD, PP and CON.

Blackorby, Donaldson and Auersperg(1981) began with a rather different definition of intergroup inequality. Instead of defining intergroup inequality as the inequality that arises if each person receives his subgroup's mean income, they defined it as the inequality that results if each person enjoys his group's AKS EDE income. Their procedure can be illustrated with a simple example. We consider a population consisting of two men whose incomes are (10, 10) and two women whose incomes are (15, 5). Since the subgroup means are 10, according to the conventional procedure intergroup inequality becomes zero. But it is clear that in this economy the two sexes are not treated equally. Fifty percent of the woman population receives less income than all of the men. Thus, if we assume that it is better to have less inequality, then the women as a group are worse off than the men. The EDE income for the men is 10 and the EDE income for the women will be less than 10 for any strictly S–concave SEF.

For the income vector $x \in D^n$ and the partition $\{N^1, N^2, ..., N^k\}$ of the population set $\{1, 2, ..., n\}$, Blackorby, Donaldson and Auersperg(1981) considered the following three reference vectors:

$$\begin{aligned} &(a)\ x = (x^1, x^2, ..., x^k), \\ &(b)\ (x_f^1 \cdot 1^{n_1}, x_f^2 \cdot 1^{n_2}, ..., x_f^k \cdot 1^{n_k}), \\ &(c)\ (x_f \cdot 1^n), \end{aligned} \tag{2.81}$$

where x_f is the EDE income of the population and x_f^i is the EDE income of group i. It is assumed that all the three vectors (a), (b) and (c) have the same level of social welfare. In (b) there is no intragroup inequality and in (c) there is no inequality at all. They defined the AKS intragroup inequality index I_A^n as the fraction of income saved in moving from (a) to (b), and the AKS intergroup index I_B^n as the fraction saved in moving from (b) to (c). Thus

$$I_A^n(x) = \frac{n\lambda(x) - \sum_{i=1}^{k} n_i x_f^i}{n\lambda(x)} .$$

$$I_B^n(x) = \frac{\sum_{i=1}^{k} n_i x_f^i - n x_f}{\sum_{i=1}^{k} n_i x_f^i} . \tag{2.81a}$$

It is easy to see that the overall AKS index I_3^n can be written as

$$I_3^n(x) = I_A^n(x) + I_B^n(x) - I_A^n(x) \cdot I_B^n(x) . \tag{2.82}$$

(2.82) can also be written in the multiplicative form $[1 - I_3^n(x)] = [1 - I_A^n(x)][1 - I_B^n(x)]$. It is now necessary to determine the (symmetric) homothetic SEF for which the vectors (a), (b) and (c) in (2.81) are socially indifferent. Eichhorn(1978) and Blackorby and Donaldson(1978, 1982) showed that the only homothetic SEF that satisfies this requirement is the symmetric mean of order r (< 1). Therefore, the Atkinson index is the only relative index which satisfies the decomposability condition (2.82).

Blackorby, Donaldson and Auersperg(1981) did a similar analysis for absolute indices also. Using the three reference vectors (a), (b), (c) in (2.81) the per capita income saved in moving from (a) to (b) is the intragroup index $A_A^n(x)$, given by

$$\begin{aligned} A_A^n(x) &= \lambda(x) - \frac{1}{n} \cdot \sum_{i=1}^{k} n_i x_f^i \\ &= \sum_{i=1}^{k} \frac{n_i}{n} \cdot [\lambda(x^i) - x_f^i] \end{aligned}$$

$$= \sum_{i=1}^{k} \frac{n_i}{n} \cdot A_1^{n_i}(x^i) \ . \tag{2.83}$$

Thus, intragroup inequality is simply the weighted average of group inequalities. The per capita income saved in moving from (b) to (c) is the intergroup index A_B^n, given by

$$A_B^n(x) = \frac{1}{n} \cdot \sum_{i=1}^{n} n_i \cdot x_f^i - x_f \ . \tag{2.84}$$

It is immediate that overall per capita inequality A_1^n is the sum of the two sub–indices in (2.83) and (2.84), and we have

$$A_A^n(x) + A_B^n(x) = A_1^n(x) \tag{2.85}$$

as the aggregation rule in the per capita case. Blackorby and Donaldson(1980, 1982) showed that the only symmetric translatable SEF for which (a), (b) and (c) remain socially indifferent is the Kolm–Pollak SEF (2.55). Thus, the Kolm–Pollak index (2.54) is the only absolute inequality index which verifies the aggregation rule (2.85).

2.6.2 Component Aggregation

The problem can be formally stated if for any income vector $x \in D^n$, we denote the income of individual i from source j by x_{ij} (j = 1, 2, ..., k). The distribution of factor j incomes is represented by $(x_{1j}, ..., x_{nj}) = x_{(j)}$. Assuming that the factor income categories are mutually exclusive, and that total income is the sum of individual factor incomes we have $x = \sum_{j=1}^{k} x_{(j)}$. Thus, the assesment of inequality contribution of factor j becomes the problem of determining the impact of $x_{(j)}$ on x.

If for any inequality index I we have some way of writing $I^n(x) = \sum_{j=1}^{k} B_j$, where B_j depends on income from source j, then B_j might be regarded as the contribution of factor j to aggregate inequality. Equivalently, the fractions $b_j = \frac{B_j}{I^n(x)}$ can be interpreted as proportional factor contributions. Following Shorrocks(1982, 1983a) we say that a function is a <u>decomposition rule</u> if it produces suitable values of b_j with the property that $\sum_{j=1}^{k} b_j = 1$.

Shorrocks(1982, 1983a) noted that the decomposition rules can be ascertained very simply for inequality indices of the form

$$I^n(x) = \sum_{i=1}^{n} a_i(x) \cdot x_i \ . \tag{2.86}$$

On substituting $x_i = \sum_{j=1}^{k} x_{ij}$ in (2.86), we get

$$I^n(x) = \sum_{j=1}^{k} \sum_{i=1}^{n} a_i(x) \cdot x_{ij} = \sum_{j=1}^{k} B_j \ , \tag{2.87}$$

where $B_j = \sum_{i=1}^{n} a_i(x)\, x_{ij}$. $\qquad$ (2.88)

Shorrocks(1982) provided conditions that enable us to express I^n in the quasi–separable form (2.86). The above procedure can now be applied directly to many inequality indices that can be written in the form (2.86). To illustrate this, let us consider the formulation of the Gini index for the illfare ranked permutation of incomes. In this case the relative Gini index can be written as

$$G^n(x) = \frac{2}{n^2 \cdot \lambda(x)} \cdot \sum_{i=1}^{n} \left(i - \frac{n+1}{2}\right) \cdot \bar{x}_i \ . \tag{2.89}$$

Consequently, the contribution of factor j to overall inequality is given by

$$\begin{aligned} B_j &= \frac{2}{n^2 \cdot \lambda(x)} \cdot \sum_{i=1}^{n} \left(i - \frac{n+1}{2}\right) \cdot \bar{x}_{ij} \\ &= \frac{\lambda(x_{(j)})}{\lambda(x)} \cdot \left[\frac{2}{n^2 \cdot \lambda(x_{(j)})} \cdot \sum_{i=1}^{n} \left(i - \frac{n+1}{2}\right) \cdot \bar{x}_{ij}\right] \end{aligned}$$

$$= \frac{\lambda(x_{(j)})}{\lambda(x)} \cdot G_S^n(x_{(j)}) \,, \tag{2.90}$$

where $\lambda(x_{(j)})$ is the mean of the vector $x_{(j)}$ and $G_S^n(x_{(j)})$ is the pseudo–Gini value for the income component j (see Shorrocks(1982)). The decomposition formula (2.90) has been proposed and used by Fei, Ranis and Kuo(1978, 1979), Fields(1979), Pyatt, Chen and Fei(1980). If we express the contribution (2.90) as a proportion of the overall Gini index we get the Gini decomposition rule

$$R_G: b_j = \frac{\sum_{i=1}^{n} [i - \frac{n+1}{2}] \cdot \bar{x}_{ij}}{\sum_{i=1}^{n} [i - \frac{n+1}{2}] \cdot \bar{x}_i} \,. \tag{2.91}$$

Shorrocks(1982, 1983a) also showed that the decomposition rules for the coefficient of variation, Theil's entropy index and the mean logarithmic deviation are given respectively by

$$R_C: b_j = \frac{\text{Covariance between } x_{(j)} \text{ and } x}{\text{Variance of } x} \,, \tag{2.92}$$

$$R_T: b_j = \frac{\sum_{i=1}^{n} x_{ij} \cdot \log\left(\frac{x_i}{\lambda(x)}\right)}{\sum_{i=1}^{n} x_i \cdot \log\left(\frac{x_i}{\lambda(x)}\right)} \,, \tag{2.93}$$

$$R_m: b_j = \frac{\sum_{i=1}^{n} \frac{x_{ij}}{x_i} \cdot \log \frac{\lambda(x)}{x_i}}{\sum_{i=1}^{n} \log \frac{\lambda(x)}{x_i}} \,. \tag{2.94}$$

It is important to note that the above mentioned method of calculating factor contributions suffers from one defect: the decomposition rule is not unique. It depends on the particular formula used to represent the inequality of income distribution. For instance, we can write any inequality index $I^n(x)$ as $\sum_{i=1}^{n} \frac{x_i}{n\lambda(x)} \cdot I^n(x)$, so that the coefficients of the equation in (2.86) becomes $a_i(x) = I^n(x)/n\lambda(x)$ and the corresponding decomposition rule is $\lambda(x_{(j)})/\lambda(x)$. This shows that we can have multiple decomposition rules. Consequently, the inequality contribution of a particular income source can vary arbitrarily, depending on the choice of the decomposition rule. Shorrocks(1982) examined the problem whether every inequality index can be decomposed in only one way. He showed that CON, NM, IM, PD and quasi-separability in (2.86) along with two additional restrictions are sufficient to solve the non-uniqueness problem. The first of these additional restrictions requires that a given income source will make no contribution to total inequality if incomes in this source are equally distributed. For the second restriction suppose that total income arises from two factors only. Then it says that the components will make same contribution to total inequality if the distribution of the first factor incomes is a permutation of that for the second factor. Shorrocks(1982) calls this 'two factor symmetry'. The unique decomposition rule is then determined as

$$R_I n\colon b_j = \frac{\text{Covariance between } x_{(j)} \text{ and } x}{\text{Variance of } x} . \tag{2.95}$$

This rule does not depend on the inequality index chosen, so the contribution made by different income components will be independent of the functional form of the inequality index.

2.7 Concluding Remarks

This chapter has distinguished among three classes of inequality indices: relative, absolute and intermediate indices. In Section 2 of this chapter we have discussed the postulates that an arbitrary index of inequality should satisfy. The concern of Sections 3, 4 and 5 is the connection between measurement of inequality and social welfare. Section 6 discussed the problem of decomposition of inequality indices by population subgroups and by factor components.

It may by worthwhile now to have a discussion of inequality indices which cannot be interpreted in the frameworks of Sections 3, 4 and 5. A very simple example of an index of this type is the range $e_1\colon D \longrightarrow \mathbb{R}^1$, where in terms of the illfare ranked permutation $\bar{x}$ of $x \in D^n$

$$e_1^n(x) = \bar{x}_n - \bar{x}_1 , \qquad (2.96)$$

$n \in \mathbb{N}$. Closely related to e_1^n are the indices $e_1^n(x)/\lambda(x)$ (the relative range), $e_1^n(x)/\bar{x}_n$ (the normalised range) and $(e_1^n(x) + \bar{x}_1)/\bar{x}_1$ (the maximin ratio). By concentrating on extreme values only all these indices fail to possess many desirable properties of inequality indices.

Some authors, including Bowley(1937), Wiles(1974) and Tinbergen(1975, 1975a) suggested the use of measures based on income shares of selected ordinal groups rather than using indices that concentrate only on extreme values of the profile. Measures belonging to this category are the ratios of shares of total income held by two fractile or quantile groups, such as the upper and lower 25 percent (quartiles), 20 percent (quintiles), 10 percent (deciles) and 5 percent. Slightly different from this approach is the method of percentiles used, among others, by Lydall(1959) to look at changes in the pattern of distribution in its different ranges over years. A formalisation of this approach for purposes of comparisons can be found in Esberger and Malmquist(1972) (see Cowell (1977)). Measures of this type are advocated by those who argue that measures based on the entire profile may not reflect changes in the lower/upper brackets of the profile which are of primary interest for policy. Such measures, do not, however, meet the transfers principle.

We will now discuss some indices based on the entire income profile[14]. Eltetö and Frigyes(1968) suggested indices which may be defined in terms of three ratios:

$$e_2^n(x) = \frac{\lambda(x)}{\lambda_1(x)}, \; e_3^n(x) = \frac{\lambda_2(x)}{\lambda_1(x)}, \; e_4^n(x) = \frac{\lambda_2(x)}{\lambda(x)}, \qquad (2.97)$$

where λ_1 and λ_2 are respectively the means of observations below the mean income and incomes at or above the mean income λ. e_3 is a measure of inequality for the entire profile. It is possible to compress the essential information contained in e_2, e_3 and e_4 in the

14 Sometimes measures of skewness have been used as measures of inequality (Young(1917)). But Sen(1973) pointed out that this is a wrong identification of equality with symmetry of a profile around the mean. A symmetric profile can as well be unequal (Stark(1972)).

following index (Kondor(1971)):

$$e_5^n(x) = \frac{(e_2^n(x) - 1) \cdot (e_4^n(x) - 1)}{(e_3^n(x) - 1)}$$

$$= \frac{1}{2n\lambda(x)} \cdot \sum_{i=1}^{n} |x_i - \lambda(x)| \ . \qquad (2.98)$$

Twice of e_5 is popularly known as the relative mean deviation. Sometimes referred to as Kuznets'(1963) ratio, this index has been used extensively (vide Rosenbluth(1951), Schutz(1951), McCabe(1974), Kondor(1975a), Mehran(1976)). The UN Economic Commission for Europe(1957) called e_5^n the 'maximum equalisation percentage' since, when expressed as a percentage, it gives the percentage of income which has to be transferred from earners above the mean income level to those below it in order to achieve perfect equality of incomes. $e_5^n = 0$ for perfect equality and $e_5^n = (n - 1)/n$ if one individual receives all the income. The indices e_i, i = 2, 3, 4, 5; violate the transfers principle – they are not affected at all if income is transferred between two individuals on the same side of the mean. Clearly, e_5 is a compromise relative index.

Gastwirth(1974) proposed an inequality index using absolute differences between all possible pairs of values of the income variable. This index is defined as

$$e_6^n(x) = [\binom{n}{2}]^{-1} \sum_{i<j} \frac{|x_i - x_j|}{(x_i + x_j)} \ . \qquad (2.99)$$

The direct computation of this measure is complicated since all the $\binom{n}{2}$ pairs must be used. Gastwirth, however, suggested an approximation to the measure when the data are arranged in (k + 1) groups with n_i observations in group i and suppose that λ_i, the mean of the ith group is also given. Then e_6^n is approximated by

$$e_7^n(x) = 2 \sum_{i<j} \frac{|\lambda_i - \lambda_j|}{(\lambda_i + \lambda_j)} \cdot \frac{n_i}{n} \cdot \frac{n_j}{n} \ . \qquad (2.100)$$

van Praag(1977, 1978) suggested the use of the variance of log–marginal income utilities as a measure of welfare inequality. If U stands for the identical individual income utility function, then the van Praag index is defined as

$$e_8^n(x) = \frac{1}{n} \sum_{i=1}^{n} [\log U'(x_i) - \overline{\log U'}]^2, \tag{2.101}$$

where U' and $\overline{\log U'}$ stand respectively for the marginal utility and the mean of log–marginal utility. Depending on the functional form of U, e_8^n may be relative or an absolute index. Thus, if $U(x_i) = 1 - \exp(-x_i)$, then van Praag's formula becomes the variance. Again if U is given by (2.16), then e_8^n takes the form

$$\frac{(r-1)^2}{n} \cdot \sum_{i=1}^{n} (\log x_i - \nu)^2 , \tag{2.102}$$

where ν = mean log–income. For $r = 0$, the above index is referred to as the variance of logarithm of incomes. Unlike variance or its positive square root, the index in (2.102) is scale invariant. This index is more sensitive to transfers at lower income levels than to transfers at higher income levels. But at very high levels of income the index actually decreases instead of increasing with transfer from a relatively poor to a rich person. Creedy(1977) argues that the extent to which the variance of logarithms violate the Pigou–Dalton condition is very minor for empirical profiles. Clearly, the view of welfare based on comparison of marginal utilities is rather limited, since it is concerned with concepts of optimality rather than inequality.

Sometimes it is assumed that some continuous type distribution fits the personal income distribution. In such cases some parameter appearing in the density of the fitted distribution is considered as a measure of inequality. A notable example is Pareto's (1897) α, where α is the slope of the line showing the cumulative frequency of persons with incomes above each stated level plotted on a double–log scale against the size of income. Samuelson(1972) shows that within the Pareto–Levy family (vide Mandelbrot (1960)) the coefficient α is not a valid measure of inequality in the usual sense of the word. Chipman(1974) confines himself to the Pareto– Levy family and shows that for distributions with the same subsistence level an increase in α actually decreases social welfare. The result is due to the lowering of the mean income with increase in α which outweighs the effect of the associated reduction in inequality. Chipman proved this result assuming that the SEF is in essence a sum of individual utilities and that the common utility function for all individuals is twice continuously differentiable, non-decreasing and concave. Gibrat(1931) demonstrated that in many situations income follows three-parameter log-normal distribution (vide Aitchison and Brown(1957)) and proposed standard deviation of $\log(x - x_0)$, where x is income and x_0 is the threshold parameter, as a measure of inequality[15].

It may be mentioned that some of the indices discussed in this chapter have large sample properties (see Wold(1935), Ramasubban(1959), Iyengar(1960), Glasser(1961), Taguchi(1967, 1968), David(1968), Levine and Singer(1970), Gastwirth(1974a), Krieger (1979), McDonald and Jensen(1979), Sendler(1979) and Beach and Davidson(1983)). The estimation problems associated with many of the inequality indices have also been discussed by different authors (vide Nair(1936), Lomnicki(1952), Kamat(1953), Ramasubban(1958), Blitz and Brittain(1962), Brittain(1962), Glasser(1962), Martic (1970) Gastwirth(1971, 1972, 1975), Kakwani and Podder(1973, 1976), Kakwani(1974, 1976, 1980a), Hart(1975), Mehran(1975a), Gastwirth and Glauberman(1976), Jean and Helms (1977), Gail and Gastwirth(1978), Krieger(1979), Petersen(1979), Seiver(1979), Rasche et. al.(1980), Aghevli and Mehran(1981), Beach and Richmond(1985), Shalit (1985), Arnold(1986) and Guerrero(1987))[16,17].

Before we conclude this section we may mention, following Cowell(1977), that several studies based on attributes other than income or wealth provide interesting material for comparison. A few notable studies may be mentioned here. In Jencks(1973) income inequality has been put in the much wider sense of social inequality. Addo(1973) considered international inequality in such things as school enrolement, calorie/energy consumption and numbers of physicians; Alker(1965) made a discussion on quantification of voting power; Russett(1964) related land ownership inequality to political instability. (For additional references, see Atkinson(1983a).)

---

[15] For further discussion, see Chapter 3.

[16] For an econometric approach to the measurement of inequality in the distribution of individual welfare, see Jorgenson and Slesnick(1984). See also Jorgenson and Slesnick (1984a, 1985) and Slesnick(1986, 1986a).

[17] A discussion of inequality indices in a topological framework can be found in LeBreton(1986). See also Le Breton(1984, 1986a).

CHAPTER 3

THE GINI INDICES OF INEQUALITY

3.1 Introduction

The most frequently used index of inequality is perhaps the Gini coefficient attributed to Gini(1912) and analysed, among others, by Dalton(1920), Atkinson(1970), Newbery (1970), Kats(1972), Sheshinski(1972), Dasgupta, Sen and Starrett(1973), Rothschild and Stiglitz(1973), Sen(1973, 1974, 1976, 1976a, 1978), Chipman(1974), Pyatt(1976), Graaff (1977), Hagerbaumer(1977), Blackorby and Donaldson(1978, 1980), Michal(1978), Dorfman(1979), Schwartz and Winship(1979), Takayama(1979), Yitzhaki(1979, 1980, 1982, 1982a, 1983), Donaldson and Weymark(1980, 1983), Hey and Lambert(1980), Kakwani (1980, 1980b, 1981, 1984, 1985, 1988), Amiel(1981), Berrebi and Silber(1981, 1985, 1987, 1987a, 1987b), Weymark(1981), Nygård and Sandström(1982), Thon(1982), Zagier (1983), Chakravarty and Chakraborty(1984), Lerman and Yitzhaki(1984, 1985), Shalit and Yitzhaki(1984), Foster(1985), Lambert(1985), Trannoy(1986), Basu(1987), Chakravarty(1988), Ebert(1988, 1988a) and Bossert(1989a).

The Gini coefficient is a relative index of inequality, scaling incomes proportionally does not alter the value of the index. When multiplied by the mean income the index becomes the Gini index of absolute inequality, which depends, as do all absolute indices, on income differentials only. The two versions of the Gini formula implicitly define a common Gini social evaluation function (SEF) which represents an ethical ordering of alternative income profiles.

The Gini index has many advantages. It is easy to compute, bounded by zero and one and it satisfies the Dalton(1920) population principle. It has a natural geometric interpretation as two times the area enclosed between the Lorenz curve (LC) and the diagonal line representing perfect equality. It can be interpreted in terms of the expected value of a game in which each individual is able to compare himself with some other drawn at random from the total population (Pyatt(1976)). The absolute Gini index can be shown to be equal to two times the covariance between income and proportional rank of income. It can be interpreted as an index of aggregate relative deprivation (Yitzhaki (1979), Chakravarty and Chakraborty(1984)). It has recently been used for comparing uncertain prospects (Yitzhaki(1982), Shalit and Yitzhaki(1984)). If a population is partitioned into non–overlapping groups, then the overall Gini can be uniquely decomposed into between and within group components of inequality (Bhattacharya and Mahalanobis(1967), Pyatt(1976), Zagier(1983), Foster(1985), Ebert(1988)). The index can also be used to examine the impact of different sources of income on total income inequality (Kakwani(1977), Fei et. al.(1978, 1979), Shorrocks(1982), Lerman and Yitzhaki (1985)). It has also the characteristic of being sensitive to the Pigou–Dalton condition, a requirement which states that inequality should reduce under a transfer of income from rich to poor.

With a given rank order of incomes the Gini index is linear. That is why, we cannot find a strictly concave SEF that corresponds to the Gini index in a negative monotonic way. Thus, the index fails to attach greater weight to transfers lower down the income scale. In Section 4 of this chapter we propose an extension of the Gini index that will rank income profiles from a given simplex in an exactly opposite way as a strictly concave SEF. This extension uses the LC of an income profile as the basis.

The next section of this chapter presents a formal definition of the LC for a continuum of population. Section 3 discusses a general definition of the LC put forward by Gastwirth(1971a, 1972). This general formulation is applicable to both discrete and continuous income distributions. These two sections also present some alternative formulations of the Gini index. In Section 5 we discuss some of the existing generalisations of the Gini index. Section 6 provides a numerical illustration of the extended Gini index and some of the widely used indices of inequality. In Section 7 we summarise our conclusions and discuss the absolute version of the extended Gini index.

3.2 A Formal Definition of the Lorenz Curve for a Continuum of Population

We begin this section with the assumption that income profiles are defined on the continuum. In such a framework, the income X of an individual is a random variable defined on the interval [0,T], where $0 < T \leqq \infty$. Let F be the cumulative distribution function (F(x) is the proportion of individuals receiving income less than or equal to x) defined on [0,T]. $F(0) = 0$, $F(T) = 1$ and F is monotonically increasing. Often F is assumed to be continuously differentiable. The continuous function f, the derivative of the cumulative income distribution function F, is called the income density function. Then

$$F(t) = \int_0^t f(X)\, dX . \tag{3.1}$$

Any element of the income space $\mathbb{R}^n_+$ (or D^n) can now be assumed to constitute a random sample of size n drawn from the distribution of the random variable having distribution function F.

The mean income $\lambda = \int_0^T X\, dF(X)$, which is assumed to be positive, can be rewritten as

$$\lambda = \int_0^T (1 - F(X))\, dX . \tag{3.2}$$

Now, the proportional share of total income enjoyed by earners with income less than or equal to $t \geq 0$ is given by

$$F_1(t) = \frac{1}{\lambda} \cdot \int_0^t X\, dF(X) . \tag{3.3}$$

The derivative of F_1 with respect to t is

$$\frac{dF_1(t)}{dt} = \frac{tf(t)}{\lambda} . \tag{3.4}$$

The positivity of this derivative implies that like F, F_1 rises monotonically as t rises from 0 to T. Also, $F_1(0) = 0$ and $F_1(T) = 1$. F_1 is called the first moment distribution function of X.

The Lorenz curve (LC) associated with the continuous type random variable X is the graph of F_1 against F, as X rises from 0 to T. Often we can eliminate X between them and can express F_1 explicitly as a function of F. Obviously, the curve goes through (0,0) corresponding to X = 0 and through (1,1) corresponding to X = T. In view of (3.1) and (3.4), we have

$$\frac{dF_1(t)}{dF(t)} = \frac{t}{\lambda}, \tag{3.5}$$

which is positive for positive incomes. Again,

$$\frac{d^2F_1(t)}{d\,F^2(t)} = \frac{d}{dF(t)} \cdot \left(\frac{dF_1(t)}{dF(t)}\right) = \frac{1}{\lambda f(t)}, \tag{3.6}$$

which is also positive. (3.5) and (3.6) demonstrate rigorously that the LC is monotonically increasing and convex to the F–axis. So, except when F = 0 or F = 1, $F_1 < F$. In the case of equality where all incomes are equal, that is, when the random variable X assumes a constant value c, we have $F_1 = F$ –the LC coincides with the egalitarian line. For an unequal profile the gap $F - F_1$ takes the maximum value at $X = \lambda$. That is, half of the relative mean deviation $F(\lambda) - F_1(\lambda)$ can be regarded as the maximum distance between the egalitarian line and the LC.[1]

The area enclosed between the LC and the egalitarian line, expressed as a proportion of the area under the curve for the perfectly equal income profile, has been considered as an index of inequality. This index is popularly known as the Lorenz ratio (see Lorenz (1905)). Now, the area under the LC for an equal profile of income is 1/2. (In terms of figure 1.1 this area is nothing but the area of the triangle OAB). By a similar argument, the area enclosed between the line of equality and the LC is given by $(\frac{1}{2}$ – area under the LC). Consequently, the Lorenz ratio LR(F) associated with the distribution having distribution function F becomes

$$\begin{aligned} LR(F) &= 2 \cdot \left(\frac{1}{2} - \text{area under the LC}\right) \\ &= 1 - 2 \cdot \int_0^1 F_1 \, dF . \end{aligned} \tag{3.7}$$

[1] For a proof, see Kakwani(1980, Chapter 3).

Theorem 3.1

The Lorenz ratio equals the Gini index of relative inequality.

Proof

For income profiles on the continuum, the Gini index of relative inequality is defined as

$$G(F) = \frac{1}{2\lambda} \cdot \int_0^T \int_0^T |x_1 - x_2| \, dF(x_1) \, dF(x_2) \, , \tag{3.8}$$

where x_1 and x_2 are two independent random drawings from the distribution having distribution function F. G(F) in (3.8) can be rewritten as

$$G(F) = \frac{1}{2\lambda} \Big[\int_0^T \int_0^{x_1} (x_1 - x_2) f(x_1) f(x_2) \, dx_1 \, dx_2$$

$$+ \int_0^T \int_{x_1}^T (x_2 - x_1) f(x_1) f(x_2) \, dx_1 \, dx_2 \Big] \, . \tag{3.9}$$

The two integrals on the right hand side of (3.9) are equal because of symmetry. Hence

$$G(F) = \frac{1}{\lambda} \cdot \int_0^T \int_0^{x_1} (x_1 - x_2) f(x_1) f(x_2) \, dx_1 \, dx_2$$

$$= \frac{1}{\lambda} \int_0^T \Big[x_1 F(x_1) f(x_1) - \lambda F_1(x_1) f(x_1) \Big] dx_1 \, , \tag{3.10}$$

where in (3.10) use has been made of (3.1) and (3.3). Using integration by parts, the first integral on the right hand side of (3.10) gives

$$\frac{1}{\lambda} \int_0^T x_1 F(x_1) f(x_1) dx_1 = 1 - \int_0^T F_1(x_1) f(x_1) dx_1, \tag{3.11}$$

which, on substitution in (3.10) yields

$$G(F) = 1 - 2\int_0^T F_1(x_1) f(x_1)\, dx_1 \ . \qquad (3.12)$$

G(F) in (3.12) is nothing but the Lorenz ratio (see (3.7)). This completes the proof of the theorem. ■

Our next result is

Theorem 3.2

For an income distribution having cumulative distribution function F and mean income $\lambda > 0$, the Gini index of relative inequality G(F) is given by

$$G(F) = 1 - \frac{1}{\lambda} \cdot \int_0^T (1 - F(t))^2\, dt \ . \qquad (3.13)$$

Proof[2]

From Theorem 3.1,

$$G(F) = 1 - 2\int_0^T F_1(t)\, dF(t)\, , \qquad (3.14)$$

where F_1 is the first moment distribution function associated with F.

G(F) in (3.14) can be rewritten as

$$G(F) = 1 - \frac{2}{\lambda} \int_0^T \left[\int_0^t X\, dF(X) \right] dF(t) \ . \qquad (3.15)$$

Applying Fubini's theorem (Apostol 1975, p. 410) in (3.15) we have

$$G(F) = 1 - \frac{2}{\lambda} \int_0^T \left[\int_t^T dF(X) \right] t dF(t)$$

[2] Theorem 3.2 has been proved by Dorfman(1979). A much simpler proof is provided here. However, Dorfman's proof does not assume differentiability of F.

$$= 1 - \frac{2}{\lambda} \int_0^T \left[1 - F(t)\right] t dF(t)$$

$$= 1 + \frac{2}{\lambda} \int_0^T t \left[1 - F(t)\right] d(1 - F(t)) \ . \qquad (3.16)$$

Using integration by parts, we can write G(F) in (3.16) as

$$G(F) = 1 - \frac{1}{\lambda} \cdot \int_0^T (1 - F(t))^2 \, dt \ , \qquad (3.17)$$

which is the desired result. ■

Formula (3.13) has a clear advantage over the formula (3.12). While for (3.12) to be defined the distribution function needs to be continously differentiable, (3.13) does not require any such assumption. Formula (3.13) will apply to both continuous and discrete distributions. Moreover, it is easy to compute.

Our next result is

<u>Theorem 3.3</u> (Stuart 1954, Lerman–Yitzhaki 1984)

The relative Gini index for an income distribution X represented by the distribution function F can be written as

$$G(F) = \frac{2 \text{ (Covariance between X and F(X))}}{\lambda} \ , \qquad (3.18)$$

where $\lambda > 0$ is the mean income.

<u>Proof</u>

From Theorem 3.2 we have

$$G(F) = \frac{\lambda - \int_0^T (1 - F(X))^2 \, dX}{\lambda}$$

$$= \frac{\int_0^T \left[(1 - F(X)) - (1 - F(X))^2\right] dX}{\lambda}$$

$$= \frac{\int_0^T F(X)\ (1 - F(X))\ dX}{\lambda} . \tag{3.19}$$

Using integration by parts we write G(F) in (3.19) as

$$G(F) = \frac{2}{\lambda} \int_0^T X(F(X) - \frac{1}{2})\ dF(X) , \tag{3.20}$$

which reduces to

$$G(F) = \frac{2\left[\int_0^T XF(X)\ dF(X) - \frac{\lambda}{2}\right]}{\lambda} . \tag{3.21}$$

Note that F is uniformly distributed between [0,1], so that its mean is 1/2. This means that (3.21) can be written as

$$G(F) = \frac{2\ (\text{Covariance between } X \text{ and } F(X))}{\lambda} , \tag{3.22}$$

which is the desired result. ■

For a discrete profile $x \in D^n$, r_i/n is the representation of $F(x_i)$, where r_i is the rank of income x_i in the profile x. Thus, we can interpret formula (3.18) as follows: the Gini index is two times the covariance between income and proportional rank of income expressed as a proportion of the mean income. It is interesting to note that unlike standard approaches for calculating the Gini from empirical data, this method requires no grouping of the data to economise on computations. Thus, the method is not only easier, but also more accurate than the standard methods.

We will now compute the Gini index for two theoretical income distributions – the gamma and the lognormal. While a discussion on the Gini index for the latter can be found in many places (for example, Aitchison and Brown(1957) and Kakwani(1980)), a discussion on the same for the former has rarely been made. A continuous type random variable X has a gamma distribution with parameters (c,α), c, $\alpha > 0$, if it has a density

$$f(X) = [\Gamma(\alpha)]^{-1}\exp(-cX)\,(cX)^{\alpha-1}\cdot c\ , \qquad X \geqq 0, \tag{3.23}$$

where $\Gamma(\alpha) = \int_0^\infty e^{-t}\, t^{\alpha-1}\, dt$ is the gamma function. Salem and Mount(1974) fitted the gamma distribution to personal income data in the United States for the years 1960 to 1969. Their empirical results show that the gamma distribution fits better than the lognormal. When the distribution function F has a density given by (3.23), substituting (3.23) in (3.3) shows that F_1 corresponds to a gamma variate with parameters (c, α+1). Now, (3.12) can be rewritten as

$$G(F) = 1 - 2\,P(U \leqq V)\ , \tag{3.24}$$

where U and V are an arbitrary pair of random variables with distribution functions F_1 and F respectively, and the operator P stands for probability. Thus, when X is gamma (c,α), for computing the Gini index we set in (3.24) a pair of independent gamma variates with parameters (c, α+1) and (c, α) for U and V respectively. But in this case $\frac{U}{U+V}$ has a beta distribution with parameters $(\alpha+1,\ \alpha)$[3]. Consequently, the Gini index for the gamma distribution is

$$\begin{aligned} G_\alpha(F) &= 1 - 2\,P(U \leqq V) \\ &= 1 - 2\,P\left(\frac{U}{U+V} \leqq \frac{1}{2}\right) \\ &= 1 - \frac{2}{B(\alpha+1,\alpha)} \int_0^{1/2} t^{\alpha}(1-t)^{\alpha-1}\, dt\ , \end{aligned} \tag{3.25}$$

3 See Rao(1969, Chapter 3).

where B(m,n) is the beta function defined by

$$B(m,n) = \int_0^1 t^{m-1}(1-t)^{n-1}\,dt \;. \tag{3.26}$$

$G_\alpha(F)$ in (3.25) can also be written in terms of the incomplete beta function $\beta_z(m,n)$, which is tabulated in Pearson(1934), as follows:

$$G_\alpha(F) = 1 - 2\beta_{.5}(\alpha+1,\alpha) \;. \tag{3.27}$$

Since the Gini index is a relative index, the scale parameter c did not appear in (3.27). The index depends only on the skewness parameter α.

The lognormal distribution is one of the most frequently used distributions of income. A continuous type random variable X is said to have lognormal distribution with parameters λ and σ^2 if log X follows normal distribution with mean λ and variance σ^2. Equivalently, $(\log X - \lambda)/\sigma$ is a normal variate with mean 0 and variance 1. The density function of the lognormal variate X is given by

$$f(X) = \frac{1}{X\sqrt{2\pi}\,\sigma}\, e^{-\frac{1}{2}\left(\frac{\log X - \lambda}{\sigma}\right)^2} \;, \quad X > 0 \,. \tag{3.28}$$

When the distribution function F has a density function given by (3.28), substitution of (3.28) in (3.3) shows that F_1 corresponds to the distribution function of a lognormal variate with parameters $(\lambda + \sigma^2, \sigma^2)$. To derive the equation for the LC of the lognormal distribution, let us write ϕ for the distribution function of a normal (0,1) variate Y. Thus

$$\phi(t) = \int_{-\infty}^{t} \frac{1}{\sqrt{2\pi}}\, e^{-Y^2/2}\, dY \;. \tag{3.29}$$

We can now express F and F_1 in terms of the same function ϕ:

$$F(t) = \phi\left[\frac{\log t - \lambda}{\sigma}\right] \;, \tag{3.30}$$

$$F_1(t) = \phi\left[\frac{\log t - \lambda - \sigma^2}{\sigma}\right] . \tag{3.31}$$

Eliminating log t from (3.30) and (3.31) gives the equation of the LC

$$\phi^{-1}(F_1(t)) = \phi^{-1}(F(t)) - \sigma , \tag{3.32}$$

which depends only on the parameter σ. Of two lognormal distributions, the one with greater σ has a uniformly lower LC. As $\sigma \to 0$, the LC coincides with the line of equality. As $\sigma \to \infty$, $F_1 = 0$ whenever $F < 1$, case of perfect inequality. Since a higher σ generates a lower LC, any strictly S–convex inequality index should be a monotone increasing function of σ. Hence σ, wich is nothing but the standard deviation of log X, is also a sensible measure of inequality in this case.

In view of (3.24), the Gini index for the lognormal distribution is given by $1 - 2P(U \leq V)$, where U and V are independent lognormal variates with parameter $(\lambda + \sigma^2, \sigma^2)$ and (λ, σ^2) respectively. Using the observation that $\log U - \log V$ is a normal variate with mean σ^2 and variance $2\sigma^2$, the required Gini index can be written as $1 - 2\phi(-\frac{\sigma}{\sqrt{2}})$. Now, by symmetry of the normal distribution we have $\phi(-t) = 1 - \phi(t)$. Consequently, the Gini coefficient for the lognormal distribution becomes

$$G_\sigma(F) = 2\phi(\frac{\sigma}{\sqrt{2}}) - 1 . \tag{3.33}$$

G_σ is increasing in σ. As $\sigma \to 0$, $G_\sigma \to 0$, as $\sigma \to \infty$, $G_\sigma \to 1$. These are consistent with the observations we have made for the LC of a lognormal distribution.

3.3 A General Definition of the Lorenz Curve

The definition of the LC discussed in Section 3.2 assumes absolute continuity (that is, differentiability) of the income distribution function. This is a very strong requirement. Gastwirth(1971a, 1972) proposed an alternative definition of the LC, which applies to discrete as well as to continuous random variables. This definition of the LC is expressed in terms of the generalised inverse $F^{-1}: [0,1] \to [0,T]$ of the income distribution function

F: [0,T] $\longrightarrow$ [0,1]. This generalised inverse is defined as

$$F^{-1}(t) = \inf_{U} \{ U: F(U) \geq t \} . \tag{3.34}$$

If F is continuously differentiable, that is, the income density function f is continuous, then for a given value of F(z) we can always find a value of z. But in the case of a discrete profile for a given value of F(z), z may not exist[4]. (3.34) ensures the existence of a value of z for a discrete profile also. For any t in the range of F, $F^{-1}(t)$ is defined as the minimum income U in the domain of F such that F(U) $\geq$ t. Since F is monotone, F^{-1} is also a monotone non–decreasing function. Hence it has, at most, a countable number of points of discontinuity. This is compatible with Lebesgue or Stieltjes integration.

We can calculate the mean income λ using the inverse distribution function F^{-1} as follows:

$$\lambda = \int_0^1 F^{-1}(t)\, dt . \tag{3.35}$$

Let F_x^{-1} stand for the inverse distribution function for $x \in D^n$. Then the following are some of the interesting properties of F_x^{-1} (Ebert(1984)).

(i) F_x^{-1} is independent of the ordering of the components of the vector x. In particular $F_x^{-1} = F_{\bar{x}}^{-1}$, where $\bar{x}$ is the illfare ranked permutation of x.

(ii) F_x^{-1} does not depend on the size of the population. That is, $F_x^{-1} = F_{x^{(k)}}^{-1}$, where $x^{(k)}$ is the k–fold replication of x, k $\geq$ 1.

(iii) If the inverse distribution functions F_x^{-1} and F_y^{-1} coincide, then $x \in D^n$ and $y \in D^m$ can differ only in size or order.

---

[4] We have already noted that in the discrete case the distribution function F_x associated with $x \in D^n$ (or $\mathbb{R}_+^n$) is defined as $F_x(t) = \# \{i | x_i \leq t\}/n$, where $x_1 \leq x_2 \leq \ldots \leq x_n$.

The LC associated with the distribution having distribution function F is now defined as

$$L(F,p) = \frac{1}{\lambda} \int_0^p F^{-1}(t)\, dt \ , \qquad (3.36)$$

where $0 \leq p \leq 1$. The function F^{-1} is a monotone function and the interval $[0,p]$ is finite for all $p \in [0,1]$. Consequently, the integral in (3.36) exists for all $p \in [0,1]$[5]. The monotonicity of F^{-1} ensures convexity of $L(F,p)$. $p - L(F,p)$, the divergence between the line of equality and the LC, is called the Lorenz divergence function.

The Gini index of relative inequality is then given by

$$\begin{aligned} G(F) &= 1 - 2 \int_0^1 L(F,p)\, dp \\ &= 2 \int_0^1 [p - L(F,p)]\, dp \ . \end{aligned} \qquad (3.37)$$

We will now illustrate the formulae (3.36) and (3.37) using two examples. As a first example[6], let $x = (6,1,8) \in D^3$. The distribution function F is defined by

$$F(t) = \begin{cases} 0 & , \ t < 1 \\ 1/3 & , \ 1 \leq t < 6 \\ 2/3 & , \ 6 \leq t < 8 \\ 1 & , \ 8 \leq t \end{cases} \ , \qquad (3.38)$$

so that F^{-1} is defined by

$$F^{-1}(t) = \begin{cases} 0 & , \ t = 0 \\ 1 & , \ 0 < t \leq 1/3 \\ 6 & , \ 1/3 < t \leq 2/3 \\ 8 & , \ 2/3 < t \leq 1 \end{cases} \ . \qquad (3.39)$$

---

5 See Apostol(1975, Chapter 7).

6 This example is due to Foster(1985).

Hence

$$L(F,p) = \begin{cases} \frac{1}{5}p & , 0 \leq p < \frac{1}{3} \\ \frac{1}{15} + \frac{6}{5}(p - \frac{1}{3}) & , \frac{1}{3} \leq p < \frac{2}{3} \\ \frac{1}{15} + \frac{2}{5} + \frac{8}{5}(p - \frac{2}{3}) & , \frac{2}{3} \leq p \leq 1 \,. \end{cases} \tag{3.40}$$

The Gini index for this distribution is 14/45.

The second example assumes that income X follows the log–logistic distribution function:

$$F(x) = 1 - \frac{1}{1 + \left[\frac{x}{x_0}\right]^a} \,, \; x \geq 0 \,, \tag{3.41}$$

where $a > 1$ is a parameter and x_0 is the median income. F in (3.41) is also known as the Sech square distribution (Fisk(1961)). This distribution function coincides with a special case of a family of distribution functions considered by Champernowne(1952). The inverse log–logistic distribution function is given by

$$F^{-1}(t) = x_0 \, t^{\frac{1}{a}} (1-t)^{-\frac{1}{a}} \,. \tag{3.42}$$

In terms of the beta function the mean of the log–logistic distribution is $x_0 \, B(1 + \frac{1}{a}, 1 - \frac{1}{a})$. Consequently, the LC for this distribution is given by

$$L(F,p) = \frac{1}{B(1 + \frac{1}{a}, \, 1 - \frac{1}{a})} \int_0^p t^{\frac{1}{a}} (1-t)^{-\frac{1}{a}} \, dt$$

$$= \beta_p(1 + \frac{1}{a}, 1 - \frac{1}{a}) \,, \tag{3.43}$$

where $0 \leq p \leq 1$ and β_p is the incomplete beta function. The corresponding Gini index is

$$G_a(F) = 1 - \frac{2}{B(1+\frac{1}{a}, 1-\frac{1}{a})} \int_0^1 [\int_0^p t^{\frac{1}{a}} (1-t)^{-\frac{1}{a}} dt]\, dp$$

$$= 1 - \frac{2}{B(1+\frac{1}{a}, 1-\frac{1}{a})} \int_0^1 [\int_t^1 dp]\, t^{\frac{1}{a}} (1-t)^{-\frac{1}{a}} dt$$

$$= 1 - \frac{2}{B(1+\frac{1}{a}, 1-\frac{1}{a})} \int_0^1 t^{\frac{1}{a}} (1-t)^{1-\frac{1}{a}} dt$$

$$= 1 - \frac{2B(1+\frac{1}{a}, 2-\frac{1}{a})}{B(1+\frac{1}{a}, 1-\frac{1}{a})} = \frac{1}{a}, \tag{3.44}$$

where use has been made of Fubini's theorem (Apostol 1975, p. 410) for changing the order of integration. Now, the parameter a can be shown to be inversely proportional to the standard deviation of the logarithm of income. Thus, the Gini index for the log –logstic distribution is directly proportional to a measure of variation, as we might expect.

The examples discussed in this section show that the Gastwirth formulation for the Lorenz curve given by (3.36) is applicable to discrete as well as to continuous income distributions.

Before we conclude this section let us define the generalised Lorenz curve GL(F,p) in terms of the inverse distribution function:

$$GL(F,p) = \lambda L(F,p) = \int_0^p F^{-1}(t)\, dt . \tag{3.45}$$

Then the absolute Gini index $G_A(F)$ is given by

$$G_A(F) = \lambda G(F)$$

$$= \int_0^1 (\lambda p - GL(F,p))\, dp . \tag{3.46}$$

Clearly, we can have formulations for the absolute Gini which are analogous to the relative Gini formulations given by (3.13) and (3.18).

3.4 An Extension of the Gini Index of Relative Inequality

We have noted in Chapter 2 that the Gini index fails to rank income profiles in an exactly opposite way as a strictly quasi–concave SEF. The purpose of this section is to suggest an extension of the Gini index that will avoid this shortcoming. (This extension was advanced by Chakravarty(1988).) The extension is based on the Gastwirth formulation for the LC L(F,p) given by (3.36) for any arbitrary income distribution function F.

We begin our discussion by considering the following divergence function between the line of equality p and the LC L(F,p):

$$\Psi(p) = [p - L(F,p)]^b , \tag{3.47}$$

where $\Psi:[0,1] \longrightarrow \mathbb{R}^1_+$ and $b > 1$ is a constant. The reason why the Gini index does not rank income profiles according to some strictly quasi–concave SEF is that the transformation function Ψ in the Lorenz divergence function $p - L(F,p)$ is linear, that is $b = 1$.

We now define the representative divergence d_e for F as that level of divergence which is independent of p and for which the following equality holds:

$$\int_0^1 [d_e]^b \, dp = \int_0^1 \Psi(p) \, dp . \tag{3.48}$$

This gives

$$d_e = [\int_0^1 [p - L(F,p)]^b \, dp]^{1/b} . \tag{3.49}$$

As an index of inequality we suggest the use of

$$I_b^R = 2d_e = 2\,[\int_0^1 [p - L(F,p)]^b\,dp]^{1/b} \;. \tag{3.50}$$

For a finite population of size n, I_b^R in (3.50) is equivalent to

$$I_b^R = 2\cdot(\frac{1}{n}\sum_{i=1}^{n}[\frac{i}{n} - \frac{\sum_{j=1}^{i} x_j}{\sum_{j=1}^{n} x_j}]^b)^{1/b} \;, \tag{3.51}$$

where $x \in D^n$ and $x_1 \leqq x_2 \leqq \ldots \leqq x_n$.

Clearly, I_b^R is a relative index. I_b^R will be called the extended Gini (E–Gini for short) index of relative inequality.

Theorem 3.4

Assume that the Lorenz curve L(F,p) is continuous at p = 0,1. Then the extended Gini index of relative inequality I_b^R is continuous, bounded by zero and two, satisfies Dalton's population principle, symmetric and on income profiles in a given simplex it is strictly convex.

Proof

The LC L(F,p) is convex. Since any convex function defined on a closed set is continuous on the interior of its domain (Rudin 1976, p. 101), L(F,p) is continuous on (0,1). This along with the assumption that L(F,p) is continuous at p = 0,1 makes L(F,p) continuous on its domain [0,1]. This shows the continuity of the Lorenz divergence function p – L(F,p). Now, the function h: $[0,1] \longrightarrow \mathbb{R}_+^1$ defined by $h(z) = z^b$, where b > 1, is continuous and increasing on [0,1]. Consequently, the composite mapping Ψ defined by (3.47) is continuous (Apostol 1975, p. 79). Now, d_e in (3.49) can be written as $\Psi^{-1}[\int_0^1 \Psi(p - L(F,p))\,dp]$. For a real valued strictly increasing, continuous function f defined on a compact interval [c,d], the inverse function f^{-1} is continuous and strictly increasing on [f(c),f(d)] (Apostol

1975, p.95).This, therefore, demonstrates continuity of I_b^R. By construction, $0 \leq I_b^R < 2$, where the lower bound is achieved whenever incomes are equal.

Now, exact replication of a population, income by income, leaves L(F,p) and hence I_b^R unchanged. Thus, I_b^R satisfies the Dalton population principle. I_b^R is obviously symmetric.

To prove strict convexity of I_b^R on income profiles in a given simplex, let us consider two arbitrary income profiles with the same mean λ and having distribution functions F_1 and F_2 respectively. Then we consider another income profile with distribution function F_3 such that

$$F_3^{-1}(t) = \mu F_1^{-1}(t) + (1-\mu)F_2^{-1}(t) \ , \tag{3.52}$$

where $0 < \mu < 1$ and $0 \leq t \leq 1$[7]. The mean of the profile having distribution function F_3 is obviously λ.

Using (3.52) it can be easily seen that

$$L(F_3,p) = \mu L(F_1,p) + (1-\mu)L(F_2,p) \tag{3.53}$$

for all $p \in [0,1]$. Let $I_b^R(i)$ represent the E–Gini index of relative inequality corresponding to the distribution function F_i, i = 1,2,3. Then

$$I_b^R(3) = 2\left[\int_0^1 [p - L(F_3,p)]^b \, dp\right]^{1/b}$$

---

[7] In the discrete case consider two income vectors $u = (u_1, u_2, \ldots, u_n)$ and $v = (v_1, v_2, \ldots, v_n)$, where $u_1 \leq u_2 \leq \ldots \leq u_n$, $v_1 \leq v_2 \leq \ldots \leq v_n$ and $\sum_{i=1}^{n} u_i = \sum_{i=1}^{n} v_i$. Consider a third profile $z = (z_1, z_2, \ldots, z_n)$ where $z_i = \mu u_i + (1-\mu)v_i$, $i = 1,2,\ldots,n$. If F_1 and F_2 are distribution functions for u and v respectively, then F_3 is the distribution function for z.

$$= \quad 2\left[\int_0^1 [\mu(p-L(F_1,p)) + (1-\mu)(p-L(F_2,p))]^b \, dp\right]^{1/b} \quad \text{(by (3.53))}$$

$$< \quad 2\left[\int_0^1 [\mu(p-L(F_1,p))]^b \, dp\right]^{1/b} + 2\left[\int_0^1 [(1-\mu)(p-L(F_2,p))]^b \, dp\right]^{1/b}$$

(by Minkowski's inequality)[8]

$$= \quad 2\mu\left[\int_0^1 [p-L(F_1,p)]^b \, dp\right]^{1/b} + 2(1-\mu)\left[\int_0^1 [p-L(F_2,p)]^b \, dp\right]^{1/b}$$

$$= \quad \mu\, I_b^R(1) + (1-\mu)\, I_b^R(2) \; . \tag{3.54}$$

Since the inequality $I_b^R(3) < \mu I_b^R(1) + (1-\mu)I_b^R(2)$ holds for all $\mu \in (0,1)$, we can now conclude that I_b^R is strictly convex on income profiles in a given simplex. This completes the proof of the theorem. ■

The following are some of the additional properties of I_b^R:

(i) I_b^R is increasing in b. For $b = 1$, I_b^R coincides with the Gini index. In this case I_b^R is convex but not strictly so. On the other hand, as $b \to \infty$, $I_b^R \to 2 \sup_{p\in[0,1]} (p - L(F,p))$, two times the Pietra index of inequality or the relative mean deviation.

(ii) For $b > 1$, a transfer of income from person i to person j will increase I_b^R by a larger amount the richer is person j. As b increases, I_b^R becomes more sensitive to income transfers at the lower end than at the upper and middle ends of the profile. Hence I_b^R possesses desired types of sensitivity to income transfers affecting earners at different income levels and is thus superior to the Gini index.

As a <u>dual</u> of the E–Gini index I_b^R we can consider the SEF

$$W_b^R = \lambda(2 - I_b^R) \; . \tag{3.55}$$

---

[8] See Hardy, Littlewood and Polya(1934, p. 146).

Since I_b^R is strictly convex on incomes, W_b^R is strictly concave on income profiles in a given simplex. Also W_b^R is continuous, symmetric, population replication invariant and linearly homogeneous. When efficiency considerations are absent, that is, λ is fixed, an increase in I_b^R is equivalent to a reduction in W_b^R. We, therefore, have

Theorem 3.5

For income profiles in a given simplex there exists a strictly concave SEF that ranks income profiles in exactly the same way as the negative of the E–Gini index of relative inequality.

Let e_λ and e_b represent the elasticities of the SEF W_b^R in (3.55) with respect to λ and I_b^R respectively. Then $e_\lambda = 1$ and $e_b = -I_b^R/(2 - I_b^R)$. Hence if $I_b^R < 1$, we have $|e_b| < e_\lambda$. Thus, the SEF W_b^R in (3.55) is more (less) sensitive to the mean income than to income inequality if the E–Gini index I_b^R is less (more) than one.

In order to illustrate the formula in (3.50), we assume that income X follows the Pareto distribution. Then

$$F(t) = \begin{cases} 0 & \text{if } t < m, \ m > 0 \\ 1 - (\frac{m}{t})^\alpha & \text{if } t \geq m \end{cases}, \tag{3.56}$$

where $\alpha > 1$ is a parameter. The mean income λ is given by $m\alpha/(\alpha - 1)$. The inverse Pareto distribution becomes

$$F^{-1}(p) = m(1-p)^{-1/\alpha}, \tag{3.57}$$

where $0 \leq p \leq 1$. Then applying the Gastwirth formula (3.36) yields the following equation of the LC:

$$L(F,p) = 1 - (1-p)^{\frac{\alpha-1}{\alpha}}. \tag{3.58}$$

(3.58) shows that the position of the LC depends on the parameter α only. An LC corresponding to a higher α is uniformly interior to the LC with a lower α. Using (3.58) we can determine the E–Gini index I_b^R for the Pareto distribution in terms of the beta function as $I_b^R = 2[\alpha B(b + 1, b\alpha + \alpha - b)]^{1/b}$. For b = 1 this expression reduces to $1/(2\alpha - 1)$, the Gini index for the Pareto distribution. The Gini SEF $\lambda(1 - G(F))$ for this distribution then becomes $2m\alpha/(2\alpha - 1)$. Thus, for distributions with a given subsistence income level m an increase in the value of α reduces social welfare. Hence α, which we refer to as the Pareto inequality parameter, is a valid index of inequality. This confirms Chipman's(1974) interpretation of α as an inequality measure. (See Chapter 2, Section 2.7, for a discussion on Chipman's result.)

3.5 Alternative Generalisations of the Gini Index

Many authors have suggested alternative generalisations of the Gini index from different perspectives. The purpose of this section is to make a brief discussion on some of these generalisations.

From (2.42) we observe that when incomes are ranked in descending order, the Gini SEF can be written as a weighted average of incomes with the weights being the odd natural numbers in increasing order. But there does not appear to be any strong argument in favour of this particular weight sequence in the Gini SEF. Replacing the weight sequence $\{2i - 1\}$ in (2.42) by an arbitrary positive increasing weight sequence $\{a_i^n\}$, Weymark(1981) suggested a generalisation of the Gini index. This generalised index is given by I_W: $D \longrightarrow \mathbb{R}^1$, where for all $n \in \mathbb{N}$, $x \in D^n$,

$$I_W^n(x) = 1 - \frac{1}{\lambda(x) \sum_{i=1}^{n} a_i^n} \cdot \sum_{i=1}^{n} a_i^n \overset{\circ}{x}_i , \tag{3.59}$$

and without loss of generality we can assume that $a_1^n = 1$ for all $n \in \mathbb{N}$. While unlike the Gini weight sequence $\{2i - 1\}$, the general sequence $\{a_i^n\}$ may depend on the population size n, they have one common property – the weight attached to the ith ranked income is independent of the income profile.

I_W is a compromise index – it can be converted into an absolute index by multiplying with mean income $\lambda(x)$. But the E–Gini index I_b^R in (3.50) is not a compromise index for

$b > 1$. I_W is strictly S–convex – but not strictly quasi–convex. With respect to the Pigou–Dalton transfers principle its behaviour is similar to the Gini index. Weymark(1981) proposed a characterisation of the absolute version of (3.59) using normalisation, impartiality, Pigou–Dalton principle and a mild separability condition[9]. According to this separability condition if in two income profiles the incomes from all but one type of income are the same in both the profiles, then the overall judgement that one profile is more unequal than a second profile is completely determined by the comparison of the distributions of income from the variable source.

The inequality index I_W, in general, does not satisfy the principle of population. Donaldson and Weymark(1980) assumed that a_i^n's are independent of n, that is $a_i^n = a_i$, $i, n \in \mathbb{N}$, and that a_i's are related to the function f: $\{0,N\} \to \mathbb{R}^1$ as follows:

$$f(m) = \begin{cases} 0 \quad , & m = 0 \\ \sum_{i=1}^{m} a_i \quad , & m \in \mathbb{N} \; . \end{cases} \tag{3.60}$$

Thus,

$$a_i = f(i) - f(i-1), \; f(0) = 0, \; f(1) = 1. \tag{3.61}$$

They showed that under these assumptions about a_i^n's the strictly S–convex inequality index I_W satisfies the population principle if and only if $f(m) = m^\delta$, where $\delta > 1$ is a parameter. The requirement $\delta > 1$ is necessary to maintain increasingness of the sequence $\{a_i\}$ in (3.61). (Increasingness of the sequence $\{a_i^n\}$ is necessary and sufficient for strict S–convexity of I_W in (3.59).) Thus, the selection of the single parameter $\delta > 1$ is sufficient to determine a_i for all i in (3.61). This defines a family of single–parameter Gini (S–Gini) inequality indices. This family is, therefore, defined by J_δ: $D \to \mathbb{R}^1$, where for all $n \in \mathbb{N}$, $x \in D^n$

---

9 Related and independently obtained results can be found in Yaari(1987, 1988). See also Chew(1983), Chew and Epstein(1987) and Chew, Epstein and Seigel(1987).

$$J^n_\delta(x) = 1 - \frac{1}{\lambda(x) \cdot n^\delta} \sum_{i=1}^{n} [i^\delta - (i-1)^\delta] \, \mathring{x}_i \; . \tag{3.62}$$

The index J_δ becomes more sensitive distributionally as δ increases from one to plus infinity. For $\delta = 1$, the S–Gini SEF $E^n_\delta(x) = \lambda(x) \cdot (1 - J^n_\delta(x))$ becomes the symmetric linear SEF $\lambda(x)$. In this case $J^n_\delta(x) = 0$ for all $x \in D^n$. Consequently, in this case the ranking of income profiles will be completely determined by the strong Pareto condition. If $\delta = 2$, J_δ in (3.62) becomes the relative Gini index. As $\delta \longrightarrow \infty$, $E^n_\delta(x) \longrightarrow \min_i \{x_i\}$, the maximin criterion. The corresponding S–Gini inequality index is the relative maximin index. Thus, as δ increases the underlying norm becomes closer to the Rawlsian maximin criterion.

Many of the useful properties of the Gini are possessed by J_δ: non–positive incomes can be easily accommodated, boundedness between zero and one for non–negative incomes and inequality can be decomposed by income source if the rank order of incomes remain constant over income sources. The <u>absolute S–Gini</u> inequality index $K_\delta = \lambda(x)J_\delta$ also possesses similar interesting properties. K_δ is the absolute Gini for $\delta = 2$ and as $\delta \longrightarrow \infty$, K_δ becomes the absolute maximin index[10].

Donaldson and Weymark(1983) studied the continuous analogue to J_δ, which is given by

$$J_\delta(F) = 1 - \frac{1}{\lambda} \int_0^T (1 - F(t))^\delta \, dt \; , \tag{3.63}$$

where F: $[0,T] \longrightarrow [0,1]$ is the income distribution function, and $\lambda > 0$ is the mean income. The particular case $\delta = 2$ in (3.63) is the Dorfman(1979) formula for the Gini index. Using alternative assumptions, Yitzhaki(1983) also suggested $J_\delta(F)$ as a generalisation of the Gini index. Yitzhaki developed conditions in terms of the SEF $E_\delta(F) = \lambda(1 - J_\delta(F))$ for a distribution function F to be preferred to another distribution func-

[10] Ebert(1988a) provides a joint characterisation of the Atkinson family, the Kolm – Pollak family and J_δ.

tion G according the stochastic dominance criteria. To explain these results, we need to discuss first the stochastic dominance conditions. The necessary and sufficient conditions for F to stochastically dominate G are:

$$F(t) \leqq G(t) \text{ for all } t \in [0,T] \tag{3.64}$$

for first degree stochastic dominance, and

$$\int_0^t F(z)dz \leqq \int_0^t G(z)\,dz \text{ for all } t \in [0,T] \tag{3.65}$$

for second degree stochastic dominance, where at least one strict inequality must hold[11]. (3.64) is equivalent to the condition that F is preferred to G by the utilitarian rule for any increasing utility function U, that is, $\int_0^T U(x)\,dF(x) > \int_0^T U(x)\,dG(x)$, where U is increasing. Thus, efficiency preference, or the preference for higher incomes, <u>ceteris paribus</u>, is the main distinguishing characteristic for first order stochastic dominance. (3.65), on the other hand, holds if and only if F is preferred to G by the utilitarian rule for all increasing, strictly concave utility functions. Thus, under second degree stochastic dominance F is preferred to G by all utilitarians who approve of both efficiency and equity[12]. Yitzhaki showed that a necessary condition for (3.64) to hold is that $E_\delta(F) \geqq E_\delta(G)$ for all $\delta \geqq 0$ (> for at least one δ). The analogous condition for (3.65) to hold is $E_\delta(F) \geqq E_\delta(G)$ for all $\delta \geqq 1$ (> for at least one δ).

The above discussion enables us to present a method for comparing uncertain prospects. This method is based on using the mean λ and the absolute Gini index G_A as the summary statistics to describe the distribution (the MG approach). Precisely speaking, for any two prospects F and G, $\lambda(F) \geqq \lambda(G)$ and $G_A(F) \leqq G_A(G)$ are necessary conditions for F to dominate G according to (3.64) and (3.65). Thus, the use of mean and the absolute Gini as summary statistics of a risky investment allows the derivation of

[11] For detailed discussions see Hader and Russell(1969, 1974), Hanoch and Levy(1969), Rothschild and Stiglitz(1970), Bawa(1975), Testfatsion(1976), Yitzhaki(1982) and Foster and Shorrocks(1988).

[12] Atkinson(1970) used this result (under the assumption of equality of means) to prove Theorem 1.1.

necessary conditions for stochastic dominance, enabling us to discard from the efficient set prospects that are stochastically dominated by others. It is well–known that the mean–variance analysis, which is one of the most frequently used methods for comparing uncertain alternatives, may lead to unwarranted conclusions. For example, assuming that efficiency considerations are absent, with non–quadratic concave utility function the ranking of prospects by variance and the ranking by expected utility can be different. (See Hanoch and Levy(1969) and Rothschild and Stiglitz(1970).) Thus, the MG approach is superior to the mean–variance approach (see Yitzhaki(1982a) and Shalit and Yitzhaki(1984)).

The stochastic dominance conditions defined in (3.64) and (3.65) can be easily extended to the nth degree stochastic dominance rule. Of two distribution functions F and G, the former is said to dominate the latter by the nth degree stochastic dominance criterion if and only if

$$F_n(x) \leqq G_n(x) \tag{3.66}$$

for all $x \in [0,T]$, with $<$ for at least one x, where

$$F_n(x) = \int_0^x F_{n-1}(t)\, dt \tag{3.67}$$

and $F_1(x) = F(x)$. (3.66) is equivalent to the condition that the expected utility under F is greater than the expected utility under G, where all odd order derivatives of the utility function U through n are positive, and all of its even order derivatives are negative (see Fishburn(1980, 1982) and Fishburn and Willing(1984)). For $n = 3$, this condition means that F is preferred to G by all utilitarians who argue in favour of efficiency, equity and the diminishing transfers principle that put more emphasis to income transfers taking place at the lower end of the distribution.

Kakwani(1980b) suggested an alternative generalisation of the Gini index which, when written in terms of the LC L(F,p), is given by

$$C_q(F) = 1 - q(q+1) \int_0^1 (1-p)^{q-1}\, L(F,p)\, dp \ , \tag{3.68}$$

where $q > 0$ is a parameter. $C_q(F)$ is the Gini index when q takes on the value 1. Equation (3.68) shows that changing q affects only the weight $q(q + 1)(1 - p)^{q-1}$ attached to the each point of the LC L(F,p). This weight is independent of the income profile – a property which is also possessed by J_δ. In fact, when the Donaldson –Weymark formula $J_\delta(F)$ in (3.63) is written in terms of the LC L(F,p), it coincides with $C_q(F)$ in (3.68), where $q = \delta - 1 > 0$ (see Yitzhaki(1983)). The compromise index $C_q(F)$, whose discrete analogue is given by

$$C_q^n(x) = \sum_{i=1}^{n} (\lambda(x) - x_i)(n + 1 - i)^q / (\lambda(x) \sum_{i=1}^{n} i^q), \text{ where } x_1 \leq x_2 \leq \ldots \leq x_n,$$

was introduced to make it more sensitive to income transfers at the lower end of the profile. It can be seen that there does not exist a value of q with which this objective can be fulfilled for all income profiles. (Though for a given profile one can find a value of $q > 1$ that will enable $C_q(F)$ to meet this objective.) An alternative compromise formula that will avoid this shortcoming of $C_q(F)$ is given by

$$V_t^n(x) = [\frac{1}{n^2} \sum_{i=1}^{n} \sum_{j=1}^{n} |x_i - x_j|^t]^{1/t} , \tag{3.69}$$

where $t \geq 1$ and $x \in D^n$. V_1^n is twice of the absolute Gini index, V_2^n is a positive scalar multiple of the standard deviation, and as $t \to \infty$, $V_t^n \to \max_{i,j} |x_i - x_j|$, the income range. For any $t > 2$, V_t^n evaluates a rank preserving transfer from a person with income $x_i + h$ to a poorer person with income x_i as more progressive as x_i decreases.

Donaldson and Weymark(1980) also considered another single–parameter family of compromise indices, which was constructed by employing the illfare ranked permutation $\bar{x}$ of the vector $x \in D^n$. Formula for these indices is given by

$$J_\beta^n(x) = 1 - \frac{1}{n^\beta \lambda(x)} \sum_{i=1}^{n} [i^\beta - (i-1)^\beta] \bar{x}_i , \tag{3.70}$$

where $0 < \beta < 1$. Letting $\beta = 1$ corresponds to the degenerate index, while $\beta = 0$ gives the relative maximin index. The illfare ranked S–Gini SEF $E^n_\beta(x) = \lambda(x)(1 - J^n_\beta(x))$ has an important property – it is completely strictly recursive, that is, the ordering over any set of poor is strictly separable from (the incomes of) anyone who is richer. Bossert (1989a) attempted to single out the class of SEFs that simultanously satisfies strict S–concavity, homotheticity, translatability and complete strict recursivity. The class turns out to be the illfare ranked single series Gini SEF $\sum_{i=1}^{n} b_i \bar{x}_i / \sum_{i=1}^{n} b_i$, where $\{b_i\}$ is positive, decreasing, independent of the population size n and $b_1 = 1$[13]. Berrebi and Silber (1981) combined the Donaldson–Weymark welfare and illfare ranked indices in (3.62) and (3.70) to propose the following multi–parameter generalisation of the Gini:

$$B^n_\nu(x) = 1 - \frac{\sum_{i=1}^{n} c_i \mathring{x}_i}{\lambda(x) \sum_{i=1}^{n} c_i}, \tag{3.71}$$

where $c_i = [(i^\delta - (i-1)^\delta)/n^\delta]^\nu [((n+1-i)^\beta - (n-i)^\beta)/n^\beta]^{1-\nu}$

and $0 \leq \nu \leq 1$. When $\nu = 1$, $B^n_\nu = J^n_\delta$ and when $\nu = 0$, $B^n_\nu = J^n_\beta$. Thus, in B^n_ν the weight attached to the ith ranked income depends on the number of individuals having higher, as well as, lower incomes than it. This formula, however, is not population replication invariant.

Nygård and Sandström(1982) have considered indices of the form

$$I_N(F) = \int_0^1 v(p)\,[p - L(F,p)]\,dp \;, \tag{3.72}$$

where $v(p) > 0$ is a weighting function. The idea of attaching a weight to the Lorenz divergence function $p - L(F,p)$ is essentially the same as one used in the case of the Gini index or the S–Gini index, where a sequence of increasing weights is attached to welfare ranked incomes. For $I_N(F)$ to be sensitive to the Pigou–Dalton principle we require non–increasingness of $v(p)$. If $v(p) = 6(1-p)$, then $I_N(F)$ is the Mehran(1976) family of

[13] For further discussion on such SEFs, see Chapter 6

linear inequality measures. Obviously, $I_N(F)$ is the Gini if $v(p) = 2$.

Michal(1978) proposed a generalisation of the Gini index which is given by

$$I_M^n(x) = \frac{1}{2n^2\,\lambda(x^c)} \sum_{i=1}^{n} \sum_{j=1}^{n} |x_i^c - x_j^c| \,, \tag{3.73}$$

where $x \in D^n$, $c > 1$ is a parameter and $\lambda(x^c)$ is the mean of $(x_1^c, x_2^c, \ldots, x_n^c)$. I_M was introduced to enable it to satisfy the diminishing transfers principle. For any $c > 1$, a rank preserving regressive transfer gives rise to changes both in the denominator and numerator of (3.73). It is very difficult to give a clear verdict about the direction of net change in inequality in such a situation.

Before we conclude this section let us discuss briefly an inequality index proposed by Kakwani(1980) which is closely related to the LC. This index is given by

$$K_l(F) = \frac{l - \sqrt{2}}{2 - \sqrt{2}} \,, \tag{3.74}$$

where $l \in [\sqrt{2}, 2]$ is the length of the LC $L(F,p)$. This length can be written in terms of mean income λ as

$$l = \frac{1}{\lambda} \int_0^T \sqrt{\lambda^2 + t^2}\, dF(t) \,. \tag{3.75}$$

Taguchi(1968) proposed l as a dispersion indicator of the LC $L(F,p)$. Kakwani showed that K_l is more sensitive to transfers at lower income levels. It is, however, quite difficult to interpret K_l as an ethical index.

3.6 Empirical Estimation of Inequality Indices from Grouped Data

The purpose of this section is to estimate the Atkinson(1970) index I_2, the Donaldson – Weymark(1980) – Kakwani(1980b) – Yitzhaki(1983) index $C_q(F)$, the Generalised

Entropy inequality index S_c introduced by Shorrocks(1980) and the E–Gini inequality index I_b^R from the per capita expenditure (PCE) data for rural India thrown up by the Indian National Sample Survey (NSS) Organisation for three different accounting periods.

The NSS PCE data are available in grouped form, i. e., distributed over expenditure classes giving PCE and percentage of population for different classes. We assume that the price changes between any two accounting periods are the same for all expenditure classes. For estimating I_b^R and $C_q(F)$ we adopt the procedure suggested by Kakwani (1980b). From the basic data, for each accounting period, we derive the data on p's (the cumulative relative frequencies of earners) and L(F,p)'s (the proportions of total income enjoyed by bottom p percents of earners) for each expenditure class, which in turn can be used to compute I_b^R and C_q from (3.50) and (3.68) respectively. For this purpose, we fit the following equation of the LC by ordinary least–squares method after applying a logarithmic transformation:

$$L(F,p) = p - ap^{c_1}(1-p)^{c_2}, \tag{3.76}$$

where a, c_1, $c_2 > 0$ are parameters. For convexity of L(F,p) in (3.76) we need $0 < c_1, c_2 \leq 1$. Values of squared multiple correlation coefficient (the coefficient of determination) which were not less than 0.99 for all accounting periods and parameter estimates are not reported here. For each accounting period, the estimated L(F,p)'s were very close to the corresponding actual L(F,p)'s for all the expenditure classes showing a very good fit of the LC in (3.76). Now, on substituting the functional form of L(F,p) given by (3.76) in (3.50) and (3.68) we determine I_b^R and C_q in terms of the complete beta function as $2a[B(c_1b+1, c_2b+1)]^{1/b}$ and $1 - q(q+1)[B(2,q) - aB(c_1+1, c_2+q)]$ respectively. Using the estimates of a, c_1 and c_2 for different accounting periods we can now estimate I_b^R and C_q for these periods assuming different values of the respective parameters b and q. These estimates are reported in Table 3.1. The same table also reports estimates of the Atkinson index and the Generalised Entropy index for different accounting periods. The estimation procedure of these indices from grouped data is straightforward and hence has not been discussed.

From Table 3.1 we observe that all the four indices are sensitive to respective para–

Table 3.1

NUMERICAL ESTIMATES OF INEQUALITY INDICES

Accounting Period	I_b^R values of b				C_q values of q				I_2 values of r				S_c' values of c			
	1	2	3	4	1	2	3	4	.5	-.5	-1.5	-2.5	-1	0	1	2
October 1973 - June 1974 (28th Round)	.284	.307	.320	.330	.284	.387	.443	.481	.065	.174	.264	.342	.142	.131	.139	.175
July 1977 - June 1978 (32nd Round)	.342	.368	.384	.396	.342	.436	.486	.519	.102	.237	.346	.481	.205	.195	.245	.430
January - December 1983 (38th Round)	.301	.323	.337	.347	.301	.393	.445	.482	.073	.190	.282	.361	.156	.145	.158	.202

meters. While I_b^R, C_q, and I_2 are monotonic in b, q and r respectively, S_c is not monotonic in c. The reason for S_c not being monotonic is as follows: for large negative values of c, while the terms $\frac{1}{c(c-1)}\left[\frac{x_i}{\lambda(x)}\right]^c$ with $\frac{x_i}{\lambda(x)} > 1$ decrease arbitrarily to zero, for $\frac{x_i}{\lambda(x)} < 1$ the same terms increase as c decreases (since the rate of increase is exponential in the numerator and polynomial in the denominator). As a result S_c increases as c decreases for large negative values of c. By a similar argument S_c increases as c increases for large positive values of c. Thus, on the left side of an interval S_c is monotonically decreasing in c and on the right side of the interval S_c is monotonically increasing. The behaviour of S_c in that interval will depend on the income profile under consideration.

Table 3.1 also shows that the ranking of the different accounting periods produced by any one of the four indices is the same for all values of the corresponding parameter. A comparison across inequality indices shows that the ranking of the accounting periods produced by all of the four indices are the same for all values of the respective parameters. However, we do not have any a priori reason to believe that the rankings will always be the same.

3.7 Concluding Remarks

This chapter began with alternative formulations of the Lorenz curve (LC) and the Gini indices. Next, an extension of the relative Gini index based on the LC is presented. While the Gini index does not correspond to any strictly concave SEF this extension is able to meet this criterion. We have also discussed some other generalisations of the Gini index and estimated many of the commonly used indices of inequality.

The absolute version of the extended Gini (E–Gini) index is based on the generalised Lorenz curve (GLC) GL(F,p). Proceeding in a fashion similar to that employed in Section 3.4 we introduce

$$I_b^A(F) = 2\left[\int_0^1 [\lambda p - GL(F,p)]^b \, dp\right]^{1/b} , \tag{3.77}$$

where b > 1, as an inequality index. I_b^A is an absolute index and will be called the E–Gini index of absolute inequality. We now have the following theorem whose proof is analogous to that of Theorem 3.4.

Theorem 3.6

Assume that GL(F,p) is continuous at p = 0,1. Then I_b^A is continuous, bounded by zero from below (but not by two from above), symmetric and on income profiles in a given simplex it is strictly convex.

We define the SEF which corresponds to I_b^A in a negative monotonic way by

$$W_b^A = 2\lambda - I_b^A \, . \tag{3.78}$$

W_b^A is strictly concave on a given simplex, continuous, symmetric and translatable of degree two. We, therefore, have

Theorem 3.7

For income profiles in a given simplex there exists a strictly concave SEF that ranks income profiles in exactly the same way as the negative of the E–Gini index of absolute inequality.

CHAPTER 4

ETHICAL INDICES OF DISTANCE BETWEEN INCOME PROFILES

4.1 Introduction

In the growing literature on the welfare comparisons of income profiles, a concept which has recently received some attention is that of economic distance between income profiles. The economic distance (or distance for short) between two income profiles is supposed to reflect the degree of affluence or well–being of one population relative to another. Hence this rules out a simple comparison of the inequality of incomes (according to some inequality index) within the respective populations, since this approach neglects differences in mean incomes and so ignores an important factor which influences the relative well–being of two populations.

Dagum (1980) proposed two indices which he called economic distance ratios. However, Shorrocks (1982a) showed that Dagum's indices have a number of shortcomings – they are ambiguous in some comparisons and do not possess the properties normally associated with a distance function. Using a social evaluation function (SEF), Shorrocks argued that the absolute value of the difference between the Atkinson (1970) – Kolm (1969) – Sen (1973) equally distributed equivalent (EDE) incomes of the two income profiles under consideration can be regarded as the distance between them. Ebert (1984), in an interesting paper, presented a class of statistical indices of distance between two income profiles. Ebert's indices are based on income distribution functions and the class is derived by an axiomatic approach.

Chakravarty and Dutta (1987) demonstrated that Ebert's indices cannot serve as economic distance functions since the distance between pairs of income profiles do not reflect, in any meaningful way, the differences in average welfares of the different populations. They then axiomatically characterised an ethical distance function that meets the above requirement. Interestingly enough, this distance index becomes a positive scalar multiple of the Shorrocks distance index. Some properties of this distance index have also been discussed by them.

In Section 2 we begin by presenting a result on SEFs that satisfy Dalton's (1920) principle of population (PP). We then formalise the notion of an ethical distance function and finally show that Ebert's indices cannot serve as economic distance functions. Section 3 contains the characterisation of the ethical distance index and also discusses its properties. Section 4 makes some concluding remarks and a brief discussion on the Dagum indices.

4.2 Ethically Coherent Distance Functions

Throughout this chapter we will assume that the set of income profiles over a given population size n is given by the $\mathbb{R}^n_+$. Consequently, the set of all possible income profiles is $\mathbb{R}_+ = \bigcup_{n \in \mathbb{N}} \mathbb{R}^n_+$. Before formalising the notion of a distance function between income profiles, let us discuss a property of the SEFs that are population replication invariant. As a first step we have

Definition 4.1

Let $W : \mathbb{R}_+ \longrightarrow \mathbb{R}^1$ be any regular SEF and E be its EDE income function. Then W satisfies scaling consistency if and only if for all m, n $\in \mathbb{N}$, for all $x \in \mathbb{R}^m_+$, $y \in \mathbb{R}^n_+$,

$$W^m(x) = W^n(y) \Leftrightarrow E^m(x) = E^n(y) \ . \tag{4.1}$$

Scaling consistency of an SEF W requires that if two income profiles x and y over two arbitrary population sizes are judged equally well off by W, then they should be judged equally well off by the associated EDE income function E also. The following result establishes relationship between scale consistent SEFs and the SEFs that are population replication invariant.

Theorem 4.1

Suppose that the SEF $W : \mathbb{R}_+ \longrightarrow \mathbb{R}^1$ is regular. Then W satisfies scaling consistency if and only if W satisfies PP.

Proof:

Suppose that PP holds. Since W is regular, the EDE income function E exists. Remembering that W and E are ordinally equivalent and that W satisfies PP, we have for all $m \in \mathbb{N}$, $x \in \mathbb{R}^m_+$,

$$W^m(x) = W^{mn}(x^{(n)}) \Leftrightarrow E^m(x) = E^{mn}(x^{(n)}) \ , \tag{4.2}$$

where $x^{(n)}$ is the n–fold replication of x, $n \in \mathbb{N}$. Again, since the SEF W is regular and PP holds, we can construct an income profile $y \in \mathbb{R}^n_+$ such that $W^n(y) = W^{mn}(x^{(n)})$. Hence we have for all $n \in \mathbb{N}$, $y \in \mathbb{R}^n_+$

$$W^n(y) = W^{mn}(x^{(n)}) \Leftrightarrow E^n(y) = E^{mn}(x^{(n)}) \ . \tag{4.3}$$

From (4.2) and (4.3) we have for all $m,n \in \mathbb{N}$, $x \in \mathbb{R}^m_+$, $y \in \mathbb{R}^n_+$,

$$W^m(x) = W^n(y) \Leftrightarrow E^m(x) = E^n(y) \ , \tag{4.4}$$

which is nothing but scaling consistency of W. Similarly it can be shown that a regular, scale consistent W is population replication invariant. ∎

Let us now consider any non–negative scalar function d defined on $\mathbb{R}_+ \times \mathbb{R}_+$, that is, $d\colon \mathbb{R}_+ \times \mathbb{R}_+ \longrightarrow \mathbb{R}^1_+$. Define for all m, $n \in \mathbb{N}$,

$$d_{m,n} : \mathbb{R}^m_+ \times \mathbb{R}^n_+ \longrightarrow \mathbb{R}^1_+ \tag{4.5}$$

by

$$d_{m,n} = d \Big|_{\mathbb{R}^m_+ \times \mathbb{R}^n_+} \ . \tag{4.6}$$

Thus, the function $d_{m,n}$ is the restriction of d on the domain $\mathbb{R}^m_+ \times \mathbb{R}^n_+$. We then have

Definition 4.2

The function $d: \mathbb{R}_+ \times \mathbb{R}_+ \longrightarrow \mathbb{R}^1_+$ is an ethical distance function if and only if for all $m,n \in \mathbb{N}$ and for all $x \in \mathbb{R}^m_+$, $y \in \mathbb{R}^n_+$, the following properties are satisfied:

$d_{m,n}$ is continuous, (4.7)

$d_{m,n}(x,y) = 0$ if and only if the EDE incomes of x and y are equal for any regular SEF, (4.8)

$$d_{m,n}(x,y) = d_{n,m}(y,x), \tag{4.9}$$

$$d_{m,n}(x,y) \leq d_{m,k}(x,z) + d_{k,n}(z,y) \tag{4.10}$$

for all $z \in \mathbb{R}^k_+$, $k \in \mathbb{N}$,

$$d_{mk,nl}(x^{(k)},y^{(l)}) = d_{m,n}(x,y) \tag{4.11}$$

for all $k, l \in \mathbb{N}$, where $x^{(k)}$, $y^{(l)}$ denote respectively the k and l–fold replications of x and y.

Properties (4.9) and (4.10), which are popularly known respectively as symmetry and triangle inequality, are the same as in Ebert(1984). Symmetry means that the distance from x to y is the same as the distance from y to x. Triangle inequality requires that the length of one side of a triangle be no longer than the sum of the lengths of the other two sides. Ebert uses a stronger reflexivity property than (4.8). Under Ebert's definition the distance function takes the value zero if and only if the inverse distribution functions[1] coincide. However, the EDE incomes of two profiles may be equal even if the inverse distribution functions do not coincide. But if one is interested in measuring the distance between average well–being of two populations, then (4.8) seems to be a quite reasonable condition. In fact, in view of assumption (4.8) we can say that $d_{m,n}$, as defined by us, is not a metric on the space of all income profiles, but on the space of all equivalence classes of income profiles, where $x \in \mathbb{R}^m_+$ and $y \in \mathbb{R}^n_+$ belong to the same equivalence class if and only if the EDE income of x equals that of y. Property (4.11), which is parallel to

[1] See Chapter 3, for a discussion.

Dalton's population principle, means that the distance function is independent of population sizes. Property (4.7) requires the distance function to vary continuously with its arguments.

Since an economic distance function between two income profiles is supposed to reflect the difference in average well-being (or welfare) of the two populations, the distance function will have ethical significance only if it is related in some way to the SEF used to rank alternative income profiles. The following is a mild restriction on when a distance function can be said to be ethically significant.

Definition 4.3

Let the SEF W: $\mathbb{R}_+ \longrightarrow \mathbb{R}^1$ be regular and scale consistent and let E be the EDE income function of W. A distance function d: $\mathbb{R}_+ \times \mathbb{R}_+ \longrightarrow \mathbb{R}^1_+$ is ethically coherent with W if and only if for all n_1, n_2 n_3, $n_4 \in \mathbb{N}$ and for all $x^1 \in \mathbb{R}^{n_1}_+$, $x^2 \in \mathbb{R}^{n_2}_+$, $x^3 \in \mathbb{R}^{n_3}_+$, $x^4 \in \mathbb{R}^{n_4}_+$,

$$\left[|E^{n_1}(x^1) - E^{n_2}(x^2)| \geqq |E^{n_3}(x^3) - E^{n_4}(x^4)|\right]$$

$$\longrightarrow \left[d_{n_1,n_2}(x^1,x^2) \geqq d_{n_3,n_4}(x^3,x^4)\right] . \tag{4.12}$$

Condition (4.12) is a very reasonable restriction because all it requires is that the distance between any pair of profiles $x^1 \in \mathbb{R}^{n_1}_+$ and $x^2 \in \mathbb{R}^{n_2}_+$ be related in a monotonic way to the absolute value of the difference between $E^{n_1}(x^1)$ and $E^{n_2}(x^2)$[2]. Of course, apart from monotonicity no other restriction is imposed on the functional form of the dependence between $d_{n_1,n_2}(x^1,x^2)$ and $E^{n_1}(x^1) - E^{n_2}(x^2)$.

In order to introduce the class of indices proposed by Ebert, let us consider the illfare

---

2 It is implicitly assumed here that the EDE income function E has cardinal significance, so that differences of the form $(E^{n_1}(x^1) - E^{n_2}(x^2))$ can be compared in a meaningful way.

ranked permutation $\bar{x}$ of any $x \in \mathbb{R}^m_+$. Then Ebert's class of statistical distance function is $d^E: \mathbb{R}_+ \times \mathbb{R}_+ \longrightarrow \mathbb{R}^1_+$, where for all $m \in \mathbb{N}$, $x,y \in \mathbb{R}^m_+$,

$$d^E_{m,m}(x,y) = \left[\frac{1}{m} \sum_{i=1}^{m} |\bar{x}_i - \bar{y}_i|^{\rho}\right]^{1/\rho} \tag{4.13}$$

and ρ is a parameter. For the triangle inequality to hold we require $\rho \geq 1$. Because the distance function d^E satisfies the population principle (4.11), no loss of generality happens for restricting attention to the same population size in (4.13). d^E is increasing in ρ. For $\rho = 1$, d^E in (4.13) is simply the mean of the absolute income gaps. On the other hand, if $\rho \longrightarrow \infty$, $d^E_{m,m} \longrightarrow \max_i |\bar{x}_i - \bar{y}_i|$, the maximum absolute income gap. If y in (4.13) is replaced by $\lambda(x)\cdot 1^m$, the equal income profile associated with x, then $d^E_{m,m}$ becomes the absolute mean deviation for $\rho = 1$. If ρ takes on the value 2, then in this particular case $d^E_{m,m}$ becomes the standard deviation.

Now suppose that the income profiles x and y constitute random samples from distributions of non–negative random variables whose distribution functions are given respectively by F_x and F_y. Denote the corresponding inverse distribution functions by F_x^{-1} and F_y^{-1} respectively. Then the continuous analogue to the distance function d^E proposed by Ebert takes the form

$$d^E(F_x,F_y) = \left[\int_0^1 |F_x^{-1}(t) - F_y^{-1}(t)|^{\rho}\, dt\right]^{1/\rho} . \tag{4.13a}$$

We are now ready for the main result of this section.

Theorem 4.2

Suppose that the SEF $W: \mathbb{R}_+ \longrightarrow \mathbb{R}^1$ is regular, strictly S–concave and scale consistent. Then a distance function of the form given by (4.13) is not ethically coherent with W.

Proof

The proof consists of an example. Let $m = 2$ and consider $x^1 = (1/2, 1/2)$, $x^2 = (1/2, 3/2)$, $x^3 = (1, 0)$, $x^4 = (1, 1)$ (see the figure below).

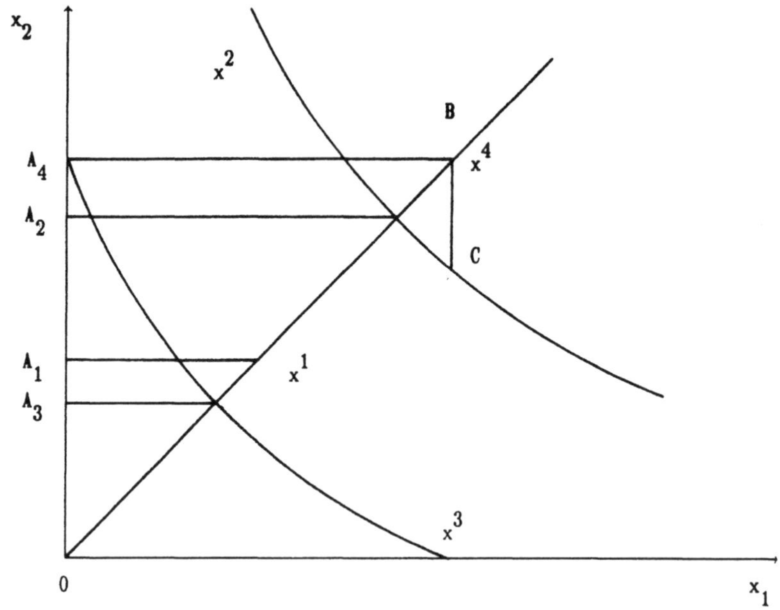

Figure 4.1

For the distance function (4.13), we have

$$d^{E}_{2,2}(x^1,x^2) = d^{E}_{2,2}(x^3,x^4) = \left[\frac{1}{2}\right]^{\rho} . \tag{4.14}$$

Given that W is regular, the EDE income function E exists and possess all the properties of W. Since contours of E are numbered, we have

$$E^2(x^1) = \frac{1}{2} , \tag{4.15}$$

$$E^2(x^4) = 1 . \tag{4.16}$$

Again from strict S–concavity and regularity of E, we have

$$\frac{1}{2} < E^2(x^2) < 1 , \tag{4.17}$$

$$E^2(x^3) < \frac{1}{2} . \tag{4.18}$$

$$\text{Hence } E^2(x^2) - E^2(x^1) < \frac{1}{2} < E^2(x^4) - E^2(x^3) . \tag{4.19}$$

For all $p \in (0,1)$, define $x(p) = (1, 1-p)$.

Clearly, $d^E_{2,2}(x^3,x(p)) < d^E_{2,2}(x^3,x^4)$. Hence from (4.14), we have

$$d^E_{2,2}(x^3,x(p)) < d^E_{2,2}(x^1,x^2) . \tag{4.20}$$

Since $E^2(x^4) > E^2(x^2)$, and since E is continuous, one can choose p small enough (say p^*) such that $E^2(x(p^*)) > E^2(x^2)$. Remembering that $E^2(x^3) < E^2(x^1)$, it follows that

$$E^2(x(p^*)) - E^2(x^3) > E^2(x^2) - E^2(x^1) . \tag{4.21}$$

(4.20) and (4.21) show that d^E is not ethically coherent with W.

In our proof so far we have not made use of scaling consistency of W. Clearly, scaling consistency of W will be necessary for proving the theorem whenever we compare income profiles over differing population sizes. ■

4.3 A Characterisation Theorem

Theorem 4.2 suggests that ad hoc distance indices may fail to have any ethical relevance. Since these distance indices are supposed to reflect differences in the average well–being of two populations, and since the EDE income of any profile is a numerical representation of the average welfare, it makes sense to express the distance between two profiles in terms of the two EDE incomes. This provides the motivation for the following definition.

Definition 4.4

An ethical index of distance d is a function d: $\mathbb{R}_+ \times \mathbb{R}_+ \longrightarrow \mathbb{R}^1_+$ satisfying conditions (4.7) – (4.11), and for all m,n $\in \mathbb{N}$, for all $x \in \mathbb{R}^m_+$, $y \in \mathbb{R}^n_+$, $d_{m,n}$ can be written as

$$d_{m,n}(x,y) = f(E^m(x),E^n(y)) , \tag{4.22}$$

where f: $\mathbb{R}^2_+ \longrightarrow \mathbb{R}^1_+$ and E is the EDE income function associated with an arbitrary SEF W: $\mathbb{R}_+ \longrightarrow \mathbb{R}^1$, which is assumed to be regular.

Clearly, the conditions (4.7) – (4.11) impose corresponding restrictions on E and f in (4.22). For instance, the principle of population (4.11) will require scaling consistency of the SEF. Similarly, continuity of d will imply continuity of f, and so on.

We now impose three additional axioms on an ethical distance index d: $\mathbb{R}_+ \times \mathbb{R}_+ \longrightarrow \mathbb{R}^1_+$.

Linear Homogeneity (LH)

For all m,n $\in \mathbb{N}$, for all $x \in \mathbb{R}^m_+$, $y \in \mathbb{R}^n_+$, and for all scalars $c > 0$,

$$d_{m,n}(cx,cy) = c\, d_{m,n}(x,y) . \tag{4.23}$$

Translation Invariance (TI)

For all m,n $\in \mathbb{N}$, for all $x \in \mathbb{R}^m_+$, $y \in \mathbb{R}^n_+$,

$$d_{m,n}(x + \alpha 1^m, y + \alpha 1^n) = d_{m,n}(x,y) \tag{4.24}$$

where α is any scalar such that $x + \alpha 1^m \in \mathbb{R}^m_+$ and $y + \alpha 1^n \in \mathbb{R}^n_+$.

Normalisation (NORM)

For m $\in \mathbb{N}$, for all $x \in \mathbb{R}^m_+$,

$$d_{m,m}(x, \lambda(x)\cdot 1^m) = A^m_1(x) = \lambda(x) - E^m(x) , \tag{4.25}$$

where $\lambda(x)$ is the mean of the profile x and non–negativity of the distance index d requires strict S–concavity of the SEF W: $\mathbb{R}_+ \longrightarrow \mathbb{R}^1$ associated with the EDE income function E.

By axiom LH, the ethical distance index depends on the scale of the profiles in the sense that an equiproportional variation in all incomes in both the profiles will lead to the same type of variation in the distance index. According to axiom TI, the distance index should remain unchanged when all the incomes in both the profiles are augmented (diminished) by the same absolute amount. The axiom of normalisation states that the distance between a particular profile and the egalitarian profile that corresponds to it is given by the Blackorby–Donaldson–Kolm (BDK) index of inequality. This seems quite reasonable, because an index of inequality treats perfect equality of incomes as the benchmark and measures the distance separating the income profile under study from the state of perfect equality.

Theorem 4.3

(a) An ethical index of distance $d: \mathbb{R}_+ \times \mathbb{R}_+ \longrightarrow \mathbb{R}^1_+$ satisfies axioms LH and TI if and only if its restriction $d_{m,n}$ on $\mathbb{R}^m_+ \times \mathbb{R}^n_+$ can be written as

$$d_{m,n}(x,y) = k\,|E^m(x) - E^n(y)| \ , \tag{4.26}$$

where $m,n \in \mathbb{N}$, $x \in \mathbb{R}^m_+$, $y \in \mathbb{R}^n_+$ are arbitrary, the EDE income function E is distributionally homogeneous and k is a positive constant.

(b) d also satisfies axiom NORM if and only if $d_{m,n}$ can be written as

$$d_{m,n}(x,y) = |E^m(x) - E^n(y)| \ , \tag{4.27}$$

where $m,n \in \mathbb{N}$, $x \in \mathbb{R}^m_+$, $y \in \mathbb{R}^n_+$ are arbitrary.

Proof

By definition, $d_{m,n}(x,y) = f(E^m(x),E^n(y))$. Let (p,q) be an element in the domain of f. Consequently, there must exist income profiles $x \in \mathbb{R}^m_+$, $y \in \mathbb{R}^n_+$ such that $E^m(x) = p$ and $E^n(y) = q$. Since contours of E are numbered, we can choose $x = p \cdot 1^m$ and $y = q \cdot 1^n$. Hence

$$d_{m,n}(p \cdot 1^m, q \cdot 1^n) = f(p,q) \ . \tag{4.28}$$

Now consider any scalar c such that (p + c, q + c) is in the domain of f. Then

$$f(p+c, q+c) = d_{m,n}((p+c)1^m, (q+c)1^n)$$

$$= d_{m,n}(p \cdot 1^m, q \cdot 1^n) \quad \text{(by axiom TI)}$$

$$= f(p,q) \ . \tag{4.29}$$

Again consider $\alpha > 0$. Then

$$f(\alpha p, \alpha q) = d_{m,n}(\alpha p 1^m, \alpha q 1^n)$$

$$= \alpha\, d_{m,n}(p 1^m, q 1^n) \quad \text{(by axiom LH)}$$

$$= \alpha f(p,q) \ . \tag{4.30}$$

Now suppose $p > q$. Then

$$f(p,q) = f(p-q,0) \quad \text{(from (4.29))}$$

$$= (p-q)f(1,0) \quad \text{(from(4.30))}$$

$$= k\,(p-q) \tag{4.31}$$

where $k = f(1,0)$. Positivity of k follows from the reflexivity condition (4.8). Using analogous arguments, if $q > p$, since $f(1,0) = f(0,1)$ by symmetry of d,

$$f(p,q) = k(q-p) \ . \tag{4.32}$$

From (4.31) and (4.32) we have,

$$f(p,q) = k \cdot |p-q| \ . \tag{4.33}$$

This shows that $d_{m,n}$ must be written in the form

$$d_{m,n}(x,y) = k\cdot|E^m(x) - E^n(y)| \ . \tag{4.34}$$

Clearly, this result is true for all $m,n \in \mathbb{N}$ and for all $x \in \mathbb{R}^m_+$, $y \in \mathbb{R}^n_+$.

Now for α, $c > 0$, $x \in \mathbb{R}^m_+$, we have

$$d_{m,m}(cx, c\alpha 1^m) = k|E^m(cx) - c\alpha| \ . \tag{4.35}$$

By axiom LH we have

$$\begin{aligned} d_{m,m}(cx, c\alpha 1^m) &= c\cdot d_{m,m}(x, \alpha 1^m) \\ &= ck\cdot|E^m(x) - \alpha| \ . \end{aligned} \tag{4.36}$$

Evaluate the expressions in (4.35) and (4.36) as $\alpha \longrightarrow 0$. Since by continuity of d the two limiting expressions are also identical, we must have $E^m(cx) = cE^m(x)$, where $x \in \mathbb{R}^m_+$ and $c > 0$ are arbitrary. This shows that E^m is linearly homogeneous.

Again for $x \in \mathbb{R}^m_+$ and $\alpha > 0$,

$$d_{m,m}(x, \alpha 1^m) = k|E^m(x) - \alpha| \ . \tag{4.37}$$

For any real β such that $(x + \beta 1^m, (\alpha+\beta)1^m) \in \mathbb{R}^m_+ \times \mathbb{R}^m_+$, we have

$$d_{m,m}(x + \beta 1^m, (\alpha+\beta)1^m) = k|E^m(x+\beta 1^m) - (\alpha+\beta)| \ . \tag{4.38}$$

By translation invariance of d, (4.37) and (4.38) imply

$$k|E^m(x) - \alpha| = k|E^m(x + \beta 1^m) - (\alpha + \beta)| \ . \tag{4.39}$$

Evaluating both sides of (4.39) as $\alpha \longrightarrow 0$, by continuity of d we have

$$E^m(x + \beta 1^m) = E^m(x) + \beta \ . \tag{4.40}$$

Since $x \in \mathbb{R}^m_+$ is arbitrary and (4.40) holds for any β such that $x + \beta 1^m \in \mathbb{R}^m_+$, (4.40) proves unit–translatability of E^m. Since E^m has been shown to be linearly homogeneous as well, E^m is distributionally homogeneous. Clearly, this result is true for all $m \in \mathbb{N}$. Hence E is distributionally homogeneous. This completes the necessity part of the proof of Theorem 4.3(a). The sufficiency can be verified easily.

(b) In orer to prove part (b) of the theorem, consider any $x \in \mathbb{R}^m_+$, where $m \in \mathbb{N}$ is arbitrary. Then

$$d_{m,m}(x,\lambda(x)\cdot 1^m) = k\cdot |E^m(x) - \lambda(x)|$$

$$= k(\lambda(x) - E^m(x)) \ . \qquad (4.41)$$

Axiom NORM along with (4.41) shows that $k = 1$. Hence $d_{m,n}$ in (4.34) can now be written as

$$d_{m,n}(x,y) = |E^m(x) - E^n(y)| \ . \qquad (4.42)$$

The converse can be proved very easily. This completes the proof of Theorem 4.3(b). ∎

It is interesting to note that the proof of Theorem 4.3 does not use the condition of triangle inequality. Of course d defined by (4.26) or (4.27) satisfies this condition.

Shorrocks(1982a) has proposed $|E^m(x) - E^n(y)|$, where $x \in D^m$, $y \in D^n$, as an index of economic distance. Theorem 4.3 shows that this index satisfies the seemingly mild axioms LH and TI only if E is distributionally homogeneous.

Since E is unit–translatable, we can express d in (4.27) in terms of the BDK absolute inequality index A_1:

$$d_{m,n}(x,y) = |(\lambda(x) - A_1^m(x)) - (\lambda(y) - A_1^n(y))| \ . \qquad (4.43)$$

But E is also linearly homogeneous. Consequently, the inequality index A_1 in (4.43) is a compromise index. Hence it is also possible to express d in terms of the Atkinson–Kolm–Sen relative inequality index I_3:

$$d_{m,n}(x,y) = |\lambda(x)(1 - I_3^m(x)) - \lambda(x)(1 - I_3^n(y))| \ , \tag{4.44}$$

where it is assumed that the means $\lambda(x)$, $\lambda(y)$ are positive. Obviously, the index I_3 in (4.44) is a compromise relative index. (4.43) and (4.44) establish the intuitive notion that an ethical index of distance between income profiles should depend both on the size (efficiency) and inequality of the profiles.

Theorem 4.3 shows that for every distributionally homothetic SEF, there is a different index of distance. We give below an example for the case k = 1, i. e., when the distance function also satisfies axiom NORM.

<u>Example 1</u>

Consider the Donaldson–Weymark(1980) single parameter Gini SEF E_δ, where $\delta > 1$. Its associated distance index is given by

$$d_{m,m}(x,y) = |\frac{1}{m^\delta} \sum_{i=1}^{m} [i^\delta - (i-1)^\delta](x_i - y_i)| \ , \tag{4.45}$$

where $x_1 \geq x_2 \geq \dots \geq x_n$ and $y_1 \geq y_2 \geq \dots \geq y_n$. For $\delta = 1$ (E_δ is not strictly S–concave in this case), d in (4.45) becomes the absolute value of the difference between the means of the profiles x and y. For $\delta = 2$, E_δ is the Gini SEF and in this case d in (4.45) can be called the <u>Gini index of distance</u>[3]. On the other hand if $\delta \longrightarrow \infty$, $E_\delta^m \longrightarrow \min_i \{x_i\}$.

Hence we have the <u>maximin distance</u> index:

$$d_{m,m}(x,y) = | \min_i x_i - \min_i y_i| \ . \tag{4.46}$$

We now have

[3] A numerical illustration of the Gini distance index and the Ebert index for $\rho = 2$ can be found in Silber and Berrebi(1988).

Theorem 4.4

The distance index given by (4.27) satisfies the following properties:

(i) for all $m \in \mathbb{N}$, $x \in \mathbb{R}^m_+$, $d_{m,m}(x + \alpha 1^m, x) = \alpha$, where $\alpha > 0$ is a constant.

(ii) for all $m \in \mathbb{N}$, $d_{m,m}(\alpha \cdot 1^m, \beta \cdot 1^m) = |\alpha - \beta|$, where $\alpha, \beta > 0$ are scalars.

(iii) for all $m \in \mathbb{N}$, $x \in \mathbb{R}^m_+$, $d_{m,m}(x, 0 \cdot 1^m) = E^m(x)$.

Proof

The proof follows easily from the properties of the EDE income function E and hence omitted. ■

Condition (i) in Theorem 4.4 says that if all the incomes in a given profile are augmented by the same absolute amount α, then the distance between the original profile and the augmented profile is simply the common absolute amount α by which the incomes increase. This property seems reasonable, because a distance index should reflect the difference between the average well–being of the populations. Condition (ii) expresses the intuitive notion that when incomes are equally distributed, then only differences in size matter[4]. According to condition (iii) the distance between the origin in $\mathbb{R}^m_+$ and any other profile x in $\mathbb{R}^m_+$ is simply the EDE income of the profile x.

The following examples show the importance of axioms LH and TI.

Example 2

For $m,n \in \mathbb{N}$, for all $x \in \mathbb{R}^m_+$, $y \in \mathbb{R}^n_+$,

$$d_{m,n}(x,y) = |(E^m(x))^\alpha - (E^n(y))^\alpha|^{1/\alpha}, \tag{4.47}$$

where $\alpha > 1$.

Example 3

For $m,n \in \mathbb{N}$, for all $x \in \mathbb{R}^m_+$, $y \in \mathbb{R}^n_+$,

$$d_{m,n}(x,y) = \sqrt{|(E^m(x))^q - (E^n(y))^q|^{2/q} + |(E^m(x))^\Theta - (E^n(y))^\Theta|^{2/\Theta}}, \tag{4.48}$$

where $q, \Theta > 1$.

---

[4] Properties (i) and (ii) are shared by d^E also.

If E is linearly homogeneous, then the above measures satisfy LH. However, even if E is distributionally homogeneous, these measures violate axiom TI.

Example 4

For m,n $\in \mathbb{N}$, for all $x \in \mathbb{R}^m_+$, $y \in \mathbb{R}^n_+$,

$$d_{m,n}(x,y) = \sqrt{|E^m(x) - E^n(y)|}\ . \tag{4.49}$$

Example 5

For m,n $\in \mathbb{N}$, for all $x \in \mathbb{R}^m_+$, $y \in \mathbb{R}^n_+$,

$$d_{m,n}(x,y) = \frac{|E^m(x) - E^n(y)|}{1 + |E^m(x) - E^n(y)|}\ . \tag{4.50}$$

In these examples the distance functions satisfy axiom TI if E is unit–translatable. However, axiom LH is violated even if E is linearly homogeneous.

4.4 Concluding Remarks

This chapter has argued that distance measures between income profiles should be related in some way to the social evaluation functions (SEFs) used to rank alternative income profiles. It is then shown that the class of indices proposed by Ebert(1984) fail to satisfy the mild restriction of ethical coherence with respect to any regular, scale consistent and strictly S–concave SEF. Finally, a characterisation of the distance function proposed by Shorrocks(1982a) is provided. The axioms used place restrictions not only on the functional form of the distance function, but also on the SEF.

For completeness we may now briefly discuss the Dagum(1980) indices of distance. Dagum's first index d^0 is defined as follows: of the two income profiles $x \in \mathbb{R}^m_+$, $y \in \mathbb{R}^n_+$, suppose that x has a higher mean. Dagum selected x as a kind of reference profile and examined the incomes in the other profile. If x and y contain no common values, then d^0 is defined as

$$d^0_{m,n}(x,y) = \frac{1}{mn} \sum_{i=1}^{m} \sum_{j=1}^{n} c(x_i - y_j)\ , \tag{4.51}$$

where $c(z) = 1$ or 0 according as $z > 0$ or $z \leq 0$. d^0 will have discontinuity corresponding to any pair of profiles which either have common mean or contain at least one common value. To demonstrate that d^0 does not meet the triangle inequality, Shorrocks(1982a) considered the profiles $x^2 = (1, 1, 8)$, $x^1 = (2, 2)$ and $x^3 = (3, 3)$. Then $d^0_{2,3}(x^1,x^2) = 1/3$, $d^0_{3,2}(x^2,x^3) = 1/3$ and $d^0_{2,2}(x^1,x^3) = 1$, showing that d^0 violates the triangle inequality. d^0 also violates reflexivity.

As an alternative to d^0, Dagum(1980) proposed a second index, which in terms of our earlier notation is given by

$$d^1_{m,n}(x,y) = \frac{1}{mn} \sum_{i=1}^{m} \sum_{j=1}^{n} (x_i - y_j)c(x_i - y_j) \,. \tag{4.52}$$

Shorrocks noted that d^1 is closely related to the interaction term that would arise in the Gini index decomposition if x and y are regarded as subgroup profiles in the partitioning of the aggregate profile (x,y).
d^1 meets the triangle inequality. But d^1 violates the reflexivity condition: $d^1_{m,m}(x,x)$ = Absolute Gini index of the profile x. Thus, both d^0 and d^1 have a number of shortcomings.

Dagum, in a subsequent contribution (Dagum(1985)) considered a normalised form of d^1 as a distance index. Yitzhaki(1989) showed that in the normalised form this index is given by

$$d^2_{m,n}(x,y) = \frac{d^1_{m,n}(x,y) - \min\,(G^m_A(x),\ G^n_A(y))}{2d^1_{m,n}(x,y) + \lambda(x) - \lambda(y) - \min\,(G^m_A(x),\ G^n_A(y))}\,, \tag{4.53}$$

where G_A denotes the absolute Gini index. Although for $x = y$, d^2 takes the value zero, the converse need not be true. To see this, let $x = (3, 5, 6)$ and $y = (1, 3, 4)$. Then $d^2_{3,3}(x,y) = 0$ but $x \neq y$. It is reasonable to argue that the economic distance between x and y here should be 2. Since d^1 appears both in the numerator and denominator of d^2, a clear verdict about the triangle inequality is difficult to draw in the case of d^2.

CHAPTER 5

THE MEASUREMENT OF RELATIVE DEPRIVATION

5.1 Introduction

Deprivation can roughly be defined as the utility foregone because of not possessing the economic variable under consideration, here income. Deprivation is relative because people feel deprived by comparing themselves with persons who have higher incomes. In this chapter we are mainly concerned with interpretations and quantifications of alternative definitions of relative deprivation put forward by Runciman(1966).

Runciman(1966) uses the example of promotion and writes: 'The more people a man sees promoted when he is not promoted himself, the more people he may compare himself within a situation where the comparison will make him relatively deprived' (op. cit., p.19). Thus, the extent of deprivation felt by an individual because of not possessing something is an increasing function of the number of individuals who have it. By quantifying a particular case of this statement, Yitzhaki(1979, 1982a) showed that a plausible index of aggregate deprivation in a society can be represented by the absolute Gini index for the society. This is discussed in Section 2 of this chapter. In this chapter we also discuss general relationships between unambigous relative deprivation comparisons and unambigous social welfare comparisons, where means of the income profiles under consideration are not necessarily the same. These results provide interesting new perspectives on the question of relative deprivation measurement and its relation to inequality and welfare.

In Section 3 we propose a family of indices of aggregate relative deprivation. Each index implies and is implied by at least one social evaluation function (SEF). The construction of these indices is quite general in the sense that each index is defined for a finite population of any size and for income profiles in the continuum. The absolute Gini index is shown to be related to a special case of one of these indices. Finally, Section 4 makes some concluding remarks and a discussion of related works.

5.2 A Simple Index of Relative Deprivation and the Implied Welfare Ordering[1]

Runciman pointed out that the notion of 'reference group' is important in explaining the feeling of deprivation. Loosely speaking, a reference group means a group within which an individual confines his aspirations. Sometimes the society to which the particular individual belongs may be the reference group, and indeed this is the case when we compute inequality for the entire society. We assume here that the reference groups are closed by which we mean that if individual i is in individual j's reference group, then j is in i's reference group. For the time being let us suppose that any two individuals in the society are comparable. Consequently, the entire society constitutes the reference group[2].

Runciman(1966) defined relative deprivation as follows: 'We can roughly say that a person is relatively deprived of (income) z when (i) he does not have z, (ii) he sees some other person or persons, which may include himself at some previous or expected time, as having z (whether or not this is or will be in fact the case), (iii) he wants z and (iv) he sees it as feasible that he should have z' (op. cit., p.10).

The feeling of deprivation is described by (i) and (iii), and the relativity of deprivation is due to (ii) and (iv). Condition (iii) implicitly assumes the existence of a reference group. The income z can be regarded as the reference point for the individual. Now suppose that the possible income range for each individual in the society is $[0,T]$, where $0 < T \leq \infty$. The income level T can be treated as the reference point for the entire society. For each person i, his own income x_i partitions the income range $[0,T]$ into two segments: $[0,x_i]$, the range of income for which he is satisfied, and $(x_i,T]$, the range of income for which he is deprived. Thus, loosely speaking, satisfaction of having and deprivation of not having are complements of each other.

For simplicity of exposition let us now assume that income follows a continuous type distribution represented by the distribution function $F: [0,T] \rightarrow [0,1]$. Then $1 - F(t)$ is the proportion of persons whose income is higher than t. Now, a person with income z is deprived of all incomes which are greater than z. Therefore, in view of discussions made

---

[1] This section is mainly based on Yitzhaki(1979, 1982a), Hey and Lambert(1980) and Stark and Yitzhaki(1988).

[2] For discussions on closely related issues, see Duesenberry(1949) and Buchanan(1965).

in the opening section of this chapter the extent of deprivation $d_z(F)$ felt by an individual with income z is found by integrating the function $h(1 - F(t))$ over the interval $[z,T]$, where the real–valued function h defined on $[0,1]$ is assumed to be continuous, increasing and $h(0) = 0$. For simplicity we suppose that h is the identity function: $h(p) = p$ for all $p \in [0,1]$. Then $d_z(F)$ is given by

$$d_z(F) = \int_z^T (1 - F(t))\, dt \; . \tag{5.1}$$

In an analogous manner the satisfaction function $s_z(F)$ of an individual possessing income z is

$$s_z(F) = \int_0^z (1 - F(t))\, dt \; . \tag{5.2}$$

Since $\int_0^T (1 - F(t))\, dt = \lambda$, where λ is the mean of the distribution with distribution function F, we say that the deprivation and satisfaction functions complement each other in the following way:

For any income z,

$$d_z(F) + s_z(F) = \lambda \; . \tag{5.3}$$

(5.3) shows that in evaluating a change in satisfaction of an individual in a given reference group, it does not matter which function is used.

Using integrations by parts we can rewrite $s_z(F)$ in (5.2) as

$$\begin{aligned} s_z(F) &= z[1 - F(z)] + \int_0^z t\, dF(t) \\ &= z[1 - F(z)] + \lambda F_1(z) \; , \end{aligned} \tag{5.4}$$

where F_1 is the first moment distribution function of income (see equation (3.3)). From (5.4), we have $s_0(F) = 0$ and $s_T(F) = \lambda$. That is, the satisfaction of the poorest person is zero and that of the richest person is λ. Using (5.4) we can also deduce that the marginal satisfaction function $ds_z(F)/dz$ is given by $(1 - F(z))$, from which it follows that $-d^2s_z(F)/dz^2 = f(z)$, the income density function. Thus, the satisfaction function increases at non–increasing rate.

(5.3) and (5.4) enable us to write $d_z(F)$ as

$$d_z(F) = \lambda[1 - F_1(z)] - z[1 - F(z)] \ . \tag{5.5}$$

$d_z(F)$ in (5.5) is simply the gap between the total income of those with income more than z and their total income if they all had income z. From (5.5) we also note that $d(d_z(F))/dz = -(1 - F(z))$ and $d^2(d_z(F))/dz^2 = f(z)$. Hence individual deprivation is a decreasing, convex function of income. That is, as income increases, deprivation decreases at an increasing rate. If $z = \lambda$, $d_z(F) = \lambda(F(\lambda) - F_1(\lambda))$, half of the absolute mean deviation. Thus, if the population is divided into two groups so that in the first (second) group all the persons have income less (greater) than the population mean, the aggregate amount of income (as a fraction of the population size n) that should be transferred from the richer group to the poorer group to bring perfect equality of incomes is given by the extent of relative deprivation felt by the average citizen.

The functions $s_z(F)$ and $d_z(F)$ can be presented graphically using the generalised Lorenz curve (GLC) λF_1. OAB is the GLC of F. The line AC is tangent to the GLC at F(z). Now $CE = z[1 - F(z)]$ and $CD = z[1 - F(z)] + \lambda F_1(z)$. BC is the deprivation of an individual with income z whereas CD is the satisfaction enjoyed by him. (This figure has been taken from Stark and Yitzhaki(1988)).

We now define the degree of relative deprivation [satisfaction] in the society d(F)[s(F)] as the average (or aggregate) deprivation [satisfaction]. Formally,

$$\begin{aligned} d(F) &= \int_0^T d_z(F)\, dF(z) \ , \\ s(F) &= \int_0^T s_z(F)\, dF(z) \ . \end{aligned} \tag{5.6}$$

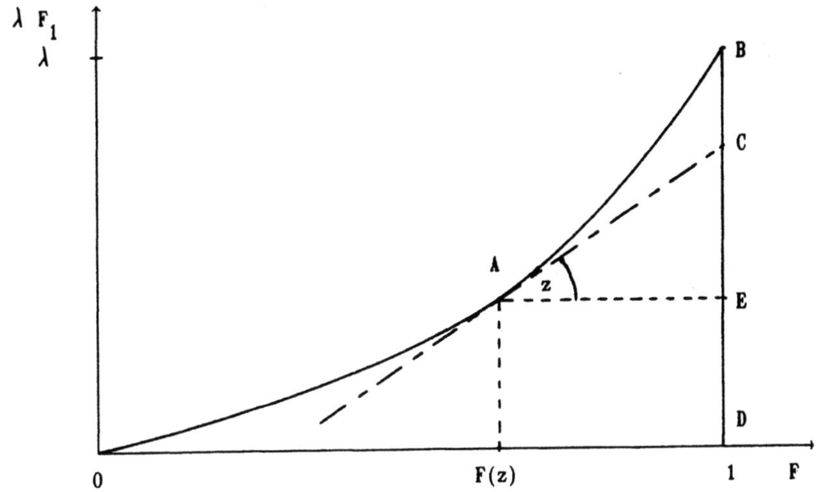

Figure 5.1

Theorem 5.1 (Yitzhaki 1979, 1982a)

The aggregate relative deprivation d(F) and the aggregate relative satisfaction s(F) are given respectively by the absolute Gini index for the society G_A and the Gini social evaluation $\lambda - G_A$, λ being the mean income.

Proof

(i) Since the absolute Gini index G_A is obtained by scaling up the relative Gini by the mean income λ, from (3.10) we have

$$G_A = \int_0^T [zF(z) - \lambda F_1(z)]\, dF(z) \tag{5.7}$$

$$= \int_0^T [zF(z) - \lambda F_1(z) + \lambda - z]\, dF(z)$$

$$= \int_0^T [\lambda(1 - F_1(z)) - z(1 - F(z))] \, dF(z)$$

$$= \int_0^T d_z(F) \, dF(z) = d(F) , \qquad (5.8)$$

where in (5.8) use has been made of (5.5).

(ii) Given that for all $z \in [0,T]$, $s_z(F) = \lambda - d_z(F)$,

we have

$$\begin{aligned} s(F) &= \int_0^T s_z(F) \, dF(z) \\ &= \lambda - \int_0^T d_z(F) \, dF(z) \\ &= \lambda - G_A . \quad \blacksquare \qquad (5.9) \end{aligned}$$

The above theorem enables us to rank income profiles in terms of relative desirability – at least as far as the relative deprivation of the entire society is concerned. Thus, when we try to choose between two income profiles the above theorem implies that we need to choose the profile with the lower absolute Gini coefficient if we want to minimise the aggregate relative deprivation.

As pointed out by Hey and Lambert(1980), the Yitzhaki theorem says nothing about ranking of profiles using individual levels of relative deprivation (or satisfaction). However, results along this direction can be derived exploiting Yitzhaki's insight. For this we consider two income distribution functions F and H, where relative satisfaction under F is not less than that under H at each income level and more at some income level(s). That is,

$$\int_0^z (1 - F(t)) \, dt \geqq \int_0^z (1 - H(t)) \, dt \qquad (5.10)$$

for all $z \in [0,T]$ and > for some z. We rewrite (5.10) as

$$\int_0^z (F(t) - H(t)) \, dt \leqq 0 \qquad (5.11)$$

for all $z \in [0,T]$ and < for some z. Condition (5.11) corresponds to the statement that F dominates H by the second order stochastic dominance criterion (see Chapter 3, Section 3.5). But condition (5.11) is equivalent to the statement that

$$\int_0^p (F^{-1}(t) - H^{-1}(t))\, dt \geqq 0 \tag{5.12}$$

for all $p \in [0,1]$ and > for some p (Foster and Shorrocks(1988)). (5.12) simply means that the GLC of F strictly dominates the GLC of H. Therefore, we can now state

Proposition 5.1 (Hey and Lambert 1980)

For any two income distribution functions F and H, the following statements are equivalent:

(i) Relative satisfaction under F is not less than that under H at all income levels and more at some income level(s).

(ii) Generalised Lorenz curve of F strictly dominates that of H.

(iii) For all increasing, strictly concave utility functions U defined on [0,T], the expected utility value under F is greater than that under H.

The above proposition thus says that the relative satisfaction ordering (5.10) holds if and only if F is unambigously preferred to H by all utilitarians who value both efficiency and equity in ranking income profiles.

Now suppose that the distribution functions F and H in Proposition 5.1 have a common mean. Then the generalised Lorenz ranking coincides with the Lorenz ranking. In such a case F is regarded as more equal than H by any inequality index that satisfies the Pigou–Dalton condition and impartiality (see Theorem 2.3)[3]. Thus, we have the following corollary to Proposition 5.1.

Corollary 5.1

For any two income distribution functions F and H with a common mean, the following statements are equivalent:

(i) Relative deprivation (satisfaction) under F is not more (less) than that under H at each income level and less (more) at some income level(s).

[3] It is important to note that the Daltonian population principle is a property of all indices defined on income profiles in the continuum.

(ii) F is regarded as more equal than H by any inequality index that satisfies the Pigou–Dalton condition and impartiality.

Corollary 5.1, therefore, provides a relationship between the question of relative deprivation measurement and the measurement of inequality.

However, in many cases we have to assume that the society contains many reference groups. For instance, the poorest person may not consider T, the maximum income existing in the society as feasible. Consequently, T cannot be a reference point for this person. In such a case the poorest and the richest persons belong to two different reference groups. We will now show that dividing a society with a given income distribution into reference groups reduces the deprivation in the society. Let us assume a society with k non–overlapping reference groups. For simplicity we assume that the society is comprised of n persons. Then the aggregate relative deprivation G_A^n is related to the group relative deprivations $G_A^{n_j}$ in the following way

$$G_A^n = \sum_{j=1}^{k} w_j G_A^{n_j} + A \tag{5.12a}$$

where n_j is the population size in reference group j, $w_j > 0$ is the weight attached to jth group's deprivation, and $A > 0$ is the intergroup inequality which is ignored by reference groups (see equation (2.80) in Chapter 2). Since $A > 0$, the aggregate deprivation, $\sum_{j=1}^{k} w_j G_A^{n_j}$, felt in a society decomposed into reference groups is smaller than that felt in the society with one reference group only. If we assume that a particular group, say i, is further subdivided into two groups, then the intergroup inequality term will increase while $\sum_{j=1}^{k} w_j G_A^{n_j}$ falls. Thus, increasing the number of reference groups reduces the deprivation in the society. The result, therefore, says that one way of reducing the magnitude of deprivation in a society is to subdivide the latter into some reference groups. We have already discussed in Chapter 2 (Section 2.6) that such subdivisions can be done in many ways.

5.3 Ethical Indices of Relative Deprivation[4]

While discussing the magnitude of relative deprivation, Runciman(1966) defines it as 'the extent of the difference between the desired situation and that of the person desiring it' (op. cit., p.10). This motivates us to define the deprivation felt by an individual with income z relative to income t as

$$d'_z(t) = \begin{cases} (t-z) , & t \geq z , \\ 0 , & t < z . \end{cases} \tag{5.13}$$

Now, the larger the number of individuals with income more than z, the more is the feeling of deprivation for the person possessing income z. Thus, to arrive at an overall measure of relative deprivation for this person we weigh $d'_z(t)$ by dF(t), the proportion of persons with income t, and integrate the weighted function over the range [z,T]:

$$d'_z(F) = \int_z^T (t-z)\, dF(t) . \tag{5.14}$$

Consequently, the average or aggregate deprivation for the society is given by

$$d'(F) = \int_0^T \int_z^T [(t-z)\, dF(t)]\, dF(z) . \tag{5.15}$$

In view of relations (3.9) and (3.10), d'(F) in (5.15) is identical to the absolute Gini index for the society. Thus, (5.15) lends support to Yitzhaki's characterisation of aggregate relative deprivation.

Having established that the two definitions of aggregate deprivations given by (5.6) and (5.15) are identical, we will exploit the formulation (5.14) to construct a general index of relative deprivation. We begin our discussion by assuming that the society is comprised of a finite population of size n. Now, for any income profile x over the population size n, the amount by which the total income of those with income more than x_i exceeds their total income if they all had income x_i, when expressed as an average of the

[4] This section is based on Hey and Lambert(1980) and Chakravarty and Chakraborty (1984).

population size n, is $\sum_{j=i+1}^{n} [x_j - x_i]/n$, where $x_1 \leq x_2 \leq \ldots \leq x_n$. This is compatible with the formulation (5.14). As a general deprivation function of individual i we may, therefore, consider the use of

$$d^{\varphi}(x_i) = \varphi\left(\sum_{j=i+1}^{n} [x_j - x_i]/n\right) \tag{5.16}$$

where the function φ: $[0,T] \longrightarrow \mathbb{R}^1$ is continuous, increasing, convex and $\varphi(0) = 0$, $T < \infty$ being the maximum income existing in the society. Increasingness of the function φ reflects the view that deprivation increases as the gap $(x_j - x_i)$ increases. Convexity of φ means that the rate of change deprivation is increasing. Let C stand for the class of real–valued functions defined on [0,T] satisfying the aforesaid restrictions on φ.

The following are some of the interesting properties possessed by the general deprivation function d^{φ} for an arbitrary $\varphi \in C$:

(i) $d^{\varphi}(x_i) \geq d^{\varphi}(x_j)$ whenever $x_j \geq x_i$. (5.13) ensures that d^{φ} takes on the value zero for the richest person.

(ii) $d^{\varphi}(x_i)$ is independent of incomes of the persons poorer than individual i.

(iii) $d^{\varphi}(x_i)$ remains unaffected when income transfers takes among persons, who are all richer than individual i, assuming that the donor's income does not fall below x_i as a result of the transfer.

(iv) $d^{\varphi}(x_i)$ decreases when rank preserving income transfers take place from a person richer than i to someone poorer than i.

(v) An increase in the income of a person richer than i increases $d^{\varphi}(x_i)$.

(vi) An increase in the income of all persons by a constant absolute amount keeps $d^{\varphi}(x_i)$ unchanged – it is a translation invariant function.

(vii) When all the incomes are increased proportionally $d^{\varphi}(x_i)$ increases. For while scaling up the income profile leaves the relative positions of the individuals unchanged, absolute differences between incomes are widened. Consequently, $d^{\varphi}(x_i)$ increases.

(viii) If the population is replicated, income by income, $d^{\varphi}(x_i)$ remains unaltered.

(ix) d^{φ} is continuous in its argument.

We now define the representative relative deprivation d_e for the income profile x as that level of deprivation which if felt by each individual makes the total deprivation indifferent to the actual aggregate deprivation in x (as determined from (5.16)). Formally,

$$\sum_{i=1}^{n} \varphi(d_e) = \sum_{i=1}^{n} \varphi\left(\sum_{j=i+1}^{n} [x_j - x_i]/n\right) , \tag{5.17}$$

where $\varphi \in C$.

As an index of relative deprivation in the society we suggest the use of

$$I_{\varphi}^{n}(x) = d_e = \varphi^{-1}\left[\frac{1}{n} \sum_{i=1}^{n} \varphi\left(\sum_{j=i+1}^{n} \frac{(x_j - x_i)}{n}\right)\right] . \tag{5.18}$$

I_{φ}^{n} is a particular cardinalisation of the aggregate deprivation $a(x) = \sum_{i=1}^{n} \varphi\left(\sum_{j=i+1}^{n} \frac{(x_j - x_i)}{n}\right)$. That is, for two income profiles x and y over a given population size n,

$$I_{\varphi}^{n}(x) \gtreqless I_{\varphi}^{n}(y) \Leftrightarrow a(x) \gtreqless a(y) . \tag{5.19}$$

We then have

<u>Theorem 5.2</u>

If $\varphi \in C$, then the relative deprivation index I_{φ}^{n} is continuous, bounded between zero and T, translation invariant, symmetric, quasi–convex and satisfies the Daltonian population principle.

Proof

By construction $0 \leq I_{\varphi}^{n}(x) < T$. Proof of continuity of I_{φ}^{n} is analogous to that of the E–Gini index (see Theorem 3.4). Since the identical individual deprivation functions in (5.16) are defined on the ordered profile x, I_{φ}^{n} is symmetric for any $\varphi \in C$. Translation invariance of I_{φ}^{n} follows from the fact that the individual deprivation functions are invariant to equal absolute changes in all incomes. Monotonicity φ implies that the inverse function φ^{-1} is also monotonic. By convexity of φ, $\sum_{i=1}^{n} \varphi(\sum_{j=i+1}^{n} \frac{(x_j - x_i)}{n})$ is convex. Consequently, the deprivation index I_{φ}^{n} is quasi–convex (Madden(1986), pp. 204 – 206). A replication of the population, income by income, leaves the individual deprivation functions of the form (5.16) unchanged for any $\varphi \in C$. Hence I_{φ}^{n} remains invariant to replications of populations.

■

Theorem 5.2 shows that for any $\varphi \in C$ there exists a particular continuous, symmetric, translation invariant, quasi–convex aggregate relative deprivation index. The index achieves its lower bound when all the incomes are equal. The maximum, on the other hand, is obtained when the richest person enjoys income T and all the other persons have zero income. These indices will differ only in the manner in which we decide to aggregate the individual deprivations into an overall indicator by employing a particular $\varphi \in C$.

I_{φ}^{n} has some additional interesting properties:

(i) It is increasing in individual deprivation levels showing that each $d^{\varphi}(x_i)$ $(i = 1,2,...,n)$ really affects the average level of deprivation.

(ii) Adding an individual earning zero income to the society increases the average deprivation level.

(iii) Average deprivation increases whenever a person with income greater than the existing highest income migrates to the society.

To interpret I_{φ}^{n} as an ethical index we need to relate it to some well–defined SEF. We define the SEF associated with I_{φ}^{n} by

$$W^{n}(x) = T - I_{\varphi}^{n}(x) \tag{5.20}$$

where $\varphi \in C$. W^n corresponds to I_φ^n in a negative monotonic way in the sense that for a given population size n and a given $\varphi \in C$, an increase in I_φ^n is equivalent to a reduction in W^n. Thus, increases or reductions in I_φ^n are normatively significant. The following theorem which follows from Theorem 5.2 shows the properties of W^n.

Theorem 5.3

For any $\varphi \in C$, the SEF W^n in (5.20) is continuous, symmetric, bounded between zero and T, where the upper bound is achieved whenever incomes are equal, and quasi–concave and unit–translatable.

When income profiles are represented by a distribution function F, I_φ^n in (5.18) is equivalent to

$$I_\varphi(F) = \varphi^{-1}[\int_0^T (\int_z^T \varphi(t-z)\, dF(t))\, dF(z)], \tag{5.21}$$

where $\varphi \in C$.

We may now illustrate the general formula I_φ^n by two examples. As a first example let us suppose that $\varphi(z) = z^\alpha$, where $\alpha \geq 1$. The resulting index is given by

$$I_\alpha^n(x) = \left[\frac{1}{n}\sum_{i=1}^{n}\left(\sum_{j=i+1}^{n}\frac{x_j - x_i}{n}\right)^\alpha\right]^{1/\alpha}. \tag{5.22}$$

If $\alpha = 1$, I_α^n becomes the Yitzhaki index of deprivation. As α increases, I_α^n becomes more sensitive to deprivation of poorer persons. As $\alpha \longrightarrow \infty$, $I_\alpha^n \longrightarrow \max_i \sum_{j=i+1}^{n} (x_j - x_i)/n = \sum_{j=2}^{n} (x_j - x_1)/n$, the relative deprivation of the poorest person. This limiting case can be referred to as the maximin index of relative deprivation – the deprivation of the worst–off person is the only criterion for ranking income profiles.

An alternative of interest arises if $\varphi(z) = e^{\Theta z} - 1$, where $\Theta > 0$. The resulting index becomes

$$I_\Theta^n(x) = \frac{1}{\Theta} \log[\frac{1}{n} \sum_{i=1}^{n} \exp(\Theta \sum_{j=i+1}^{n} (\frac{x_j - x_i}{n}))] . \qquad (5.23)$$

As Θ increases the deprivations of poorer persons get more importance. When $\Theta \to \infty$, I_Θ^n becomes the maximin index of relative deprivation.

5.4 Concluding Remarks

This chapter began with a discussion of a simple index of relative deprivation suggested by Yitzhaki(1979, 1982a). It has been obtained by quantifying the definition of relative deprivation put forward by Runciman(1966). We then studied the social welfare ordering implied by this index. Next, a general ethical index of relative deprivation has been proposed and its properties are studied in detail.

Sen(1973) provided an interesting interpretation of the Gini index which can be incorporated in the relative deprivation framework. According to Sen, in any pairwise comparison the individual with lower income may suffer from depression upon discovering that his income is lower. If it is assumed that this depression is proportional to the difference in incomes, the average of all such depressions in all pairwise comparisons leads to the Gini index. Kakwani(1980) assumes that an individual's depression is proportional to the square of the income difference and shows that the average of all such depressions leads to the coefficient of variation. On multiplication with the mean income this index becomes a positive scalar multiple of I_α^n in (5.22) when α takes on the value 2.

Berrebi and Silber(1985a) claim that many of the commonly used indices of inequality or some monotonic transformations of them can be written as indices of aggregate deprivation. For example, if individual deprivation functions d_i are given respectively by $\left[\frac{s_i}{n}\right]^r$ and $\log(\frac{1}{n}) - \log s_i$, where s_i is the income share of person i and $r < 1$, then the corresponding aggregate deprivation indices $\sum_{i=1}^{n} d_i s_i$ become functions of the Atkinson (1970) and Theil(1967) indices of inequality. Again, if d_i is of the form $(1 - ns_i)$, then the aggregate deprivation index $\sum_{i=1}^{n} d_i s_i$ is the coefficient of variation. But it is clear that this method of interpreting the inequality indices as indices of relative deprivation is quite ad hoc. One has to look at the functional form of the inequality index to select the corresponding individual deprivation function. Moreover, the individual deprivation functions considered by Berrebi–Silber do not satisfy most of the properties outlined in Section 5.3.

CHAPTER 6

ETHICALLY FLEXIBLE INDICES OF POVERTY

6.1 Introduction

In the decades since the World War II, lot of attention has been paid by economists to the problem of development of the Third World countries and the associated problems of poverty. Even in the developed countries poverty remains one of the major issues of current economic and social policy. To understand the threat that the problem of poverty poses, it is necessary to know its dimensions and the process through which it seems to be aggravated. In this chapter and in the next chapter of this book we are interested in the quantification of poverty.

In his pioneering article on the measurement of poverty, Sen(1976a) noted that the evaluation of poverty requires the solution of two distinct but not unrelated exercises: (i) The problem of identification of the set of the poor people in the total population, and (ii) the problem of aggregation of the information available on the poor persons into a device that will quantify the extent of poverty. The identification problem requires the specification of a poverty line – a demarcation line separating the poor individuals from the set of non–poor individuals in the total population. We assume that the poverty line representing the level of income necessary to maintain the subsistence standard of living, is given exogenously[1].

Once the poor persons are identified, the next step is to aggregate the characteristics of the poor into an indicator of poverty, that is, the construction of poverty index. This particular problem, the problem of aggregation, is the main issue of our discussion. Until very recently, the aggregation problem was handled using crude indices such as the proportion of persons below the poverty line (the head–count ratio) and the ratio of the

---

[1] The problems regarding the determination of an appropriate poverty line are discussed in Rowntree(1901), Orshansky(1965), Rein(1968), Atkinson(1969, 1983a), Kilpatrick (1973), Rainwater(1974), Rudra(1974), Goedhart et. al. (1977), Riffault and Rabier (1977), Srinivasan(1977), Sen(1979, 1981, 1983, 1986a), van Praag et. al. (1980), Osmany(1982), Hagenaars(1986) and Seidl(1988).

total shortfall from the poverty line of all poor persons' income to the product of the poverty line and the total number of poor individuals (the income gap ratio).

Sen(1976a, 1981) argued that an index of poverty should obey some generally agreed upon principles, which he called axioms for an index of poverty. He proposed three axioms for an index of poverty – the focus axiom, the monotonicity axiom and the transfer axiom. The focus axiom requires the poverty index to be sensitive to the income and the number of the poor only. The monotonicity axiom requires sensitivity of a poverty index to the gap between the poverty line and the income of a poor person. The transfer axiom, on the other hand, requires a poverty index to be sensitive to the redistribution of income involving the poor, a postulate which is verified by neither the head–count ratio nor the income gap ratio.

Sen(1976a) also suggested a sophisticated index of poverty. His index is the normalized weighted aggregate income gap of the poor from the poverty line, the weight on the ith poor person's gap being the rank order of individual i in the inter–personal income ordering of the poor. Kakwani(1980b) suggested a generalisation of the Sen index, where the weight on the ith individual's income gap is the Θth power ($\Theta \geq 1$) of the income rank used in Sen's formula. The motivation for introducing the new index is to make it more sensitive to income transfers in the lower end of the income profile.

Blackorby and Donaldson(1980a) offered an alternative interpretation and a generalisation of the Sen index as an ethical index. Essential to the construction of this generalised index is the notion of representative income of the poor. This representative income is that level of income which, if given to each poor person, would prove ethically equivalent to the existing income profile of the poor according to a social evaluation function (SEF) satisfying certain regularity conditions. They noted that the Sen index can be written as the product of the head–count ratio and the proportionate gap between the poverty line and the Gini representative income of the poor. The generalised index retains the shape of the Sen index but allows the use of an arbitrary representative income of the poor. However, the Sen–Blackorby–Donaldson–Kakwani indices violate some version of the transfer axiom.

With a view to accommodating deprivation relative to individuals above the poverty line, Takayama(1979) defined the censored income profile as one where all incomes above the poverty line are set equal to the poverty line, and he then used the Gini index of the censored income profile as an index of poverty. Other indices of inequality have been applied to the censored income profile to derive corresponding indices of poverty by Hamada and Takayama(1977). But all such indices violate the monotonicity axiom.

In an interesting paper Clark, Hemming and Ulph(1981) defined the SEF on the censored income profile and used a Blackorby–Donaldson type approach to construct their poverty index. However, they did so only for the symmetric mean of order r ($\leq$ 1) SEF. Chakravarty(1983) recognised that the Clark–Hemming–Ulph approach does not depend upon the use of such a restricted SEF and presented the general approach implicit in the Clark–Hemming–Ulph example. The general index also contains the Thon(1979) index as a special case. All these indices are 'relative' indices of poverty. Chakravarty(1983) also presented a general 'absolute' index of poverty. The relative indices are related to the Atkinson(1970) – Kolm(1969) – Sen(1973) (AKS) relative inequality indices and absolute indices to the Blackorby–Donaldson(1980) – Kolm(1976, 1976a) (BDK) absolute inequality indices, if applied to the censored income profiles. These indices are continuous and avoid many of the shortcomings of other indices. In the first four subsections of Section 3 of this chapter we present the crude indices, the Sen index, the Blackorby –Donaldson–Kakwani indices, and the Takayama and the Hamada–Takayama indices respectively. In the fifth subsection we present the Clark–Hemming–Ulpph–Chakravarty (CHUC) relative indices and discuss their properties. In Section 4 an analysis of absolute indices is presented.

Section 2 sets out the properties for an index of poverty and discuss their implications. Section 5 makes some concluding remarks and deals with some alternative classes of poverty indices proposed by Anand(1977), Kakwani(1977a, 1980) Hagenaars (1987), Vaughan(1987) and CHUC. It is interesting to note that if the poverty line is taken as the reference point, then this alternative class of indices proposed by CHUC determines the average relative deprivation of the poor persons in the sense of Runciman (1966). The Sen and the Kakwani(1980b) indices are revisited in this general set–up.

Lewis and Ulph(1988), in a rigorous framework, considered some of the factors advanced by Townsend(1979), Sen(1983, 1986a) and Desai and Shah(1985) as decisive factors of poverty and analysed the implications of these for individual utility. Assuming that the SEF is of the utilitarian type, they have demonstrated how the overall welfare measure can be decomposed into measures of poverty and inequality. Section 5 also contains a discussion on the Lewis–Ulph model.

6.2 Properties for an Index of Poverty

Throughout this chapter and the next chapter we assume that the set of individuals $\{1, 2, ..., n\}$, the poverty line $\pi > 0$ are fixed, and that the income space is given by $\mathbb{R}^n_+$. The poverty line π seperates income levels at which a person is considered poor from those income levels at which he is considered rich. Two alternative definitions of the set of poor persons are possible, depending on how individuals on the poverty line are treated. Following Donaldson and Weymark(1986) we refer to these as the weak and the strong definitions of the poor.

Weak Definition of the Poor(WP)

For all $x \in \mathbb{R}^n_+$, the set of poor people is $\pi^W(x) = \{i \in \{1, 2, ..., n\} | x_i < \pi\}$.

Strong Definition of the Poor(SP)

For all $x \in \mathbb{R}^n_+$, the set of poor people is $\pi^S(x) = \{i \in \{1, 2, ..., n\} | x_i \leqq \pi\}$.

$\pi(x)$ denotes the set of poor persons without specifying which definition is employed. In the literature dealing with the construction of poverty indices strong definition is more common.

An index of poverty is a real valued function P which, given a poverty line π, associates to each income profile $x \in \mathbb{R}^n_+$, a value $P(x,\pi)$ indicating its associated level of poverty. Thus, this may be denoted by $P: \mathbb{R}^{n+1}_+ \longrightarrow \mathbb{R}^1$. A poverty index is a relative index or an absolute index according as it is invariant to equiproportional or equal absolute changes in all incomes and the poverty line itself.

We now set out some properties which are common for an absolute and for a relative poverty index. Discussions along this line have been made by Sen(1976a, 1977, 1979a, 1981), Thon(1979, 1981, 1983, 1983a), Kakwani(1980, 1980b, 1981a), Chakravarty (1983,1983a), Kundu and Smith(1983), Foster(1984), Donaldson and Weymark(1986), Hagenaars(1987), Pyatt(1987), Vaughan(1987), Foster and Shorrocks(1988c) and Lewis and Ulph(1988). The suggested postulates are listed below.

Independence of the Incomes of the Rich(IIR)

For all $x,y \in \mathbb{R}^n_+$, if $\pi(x) = \pi(y)$ and $x_i = y_i$ for all $i \in \pi(x)$, then $P(x,\pi) = P(y,\pi)$.

IIR specifies that once the poverty line is set we disregard information relating to the incomes of the non–poor individuals in constructing a poverty index. That is, for two income profiles x and y with the same population size n, if x is obtained from y by changing some non–poor incomes then according to IIR poverty levels associated with the profiles x and y must be the same. This axiom, which is quite appropriate for a poverty index, has been called Focus axiom by Sen(1981). Henceforth a poverty index satisfying IIR will be called a focussed poverty index.

Monotonicity axioms are concerned with effects on poverty of changing a poor person's income, other incomes remaining unchanged. Two monotonicity axioms are considered.

Weak Monotonicity Axiom (WM)

For all $x,y \in \mathbb{R}^n_+$, if $x_j = y_j$ for all $j \neq i$, $i \in \pi(x)$ and $x_i > y_i$, then $P(x,\pi) < P(y,\pi)$.

WM, which says that a reduction in a poor person's income, holding other incomes constant, must increse poverty, was suggested by Sen(1976a). The following stronger version of the monotonicity axiom was proposed by Donaldson and Weymark(1986).

Strong Monotonicity Axiom (SM)

For all $x,y \in \mathbb{R}^n_+$, if $x_j = y_j$ for all $j \neq i$, $i \in \pi(x)$ and $y_i > x_i$, then $P(\pi,y) < P(\pi,x)$.

SM requires poverty to decrease if a poor person's income increases, given that other incomes are fixed. Thus, SM includes the possibility that the beneficiary of the income increase may become rich. Consequently, for any definition of the poor SM implies WM, but the converse is not true. A direct implication of SM is that for a given n and a given $\pi^S(x)$, a poverty index achieves the lower bound when all the poor persons have the largest income consistent with their being poor.

While monotonicity axioms are concerned with situations where a single person's income is changed, given that other incomes remain unchanged, transfer axioms deal with situations in which redistributions of a fixed amount of income occur between two individuals. Following Donaldson and Weymark(1986) we distinguish among four transfer axioms.

Minimal Transfer Axiom(MT)

For all $x,y \in \mathbb{R}^n_+$, if $x_i = y_i$ for all $i \neq j,k$ and $x_j > y_j \geq y_k > x_k$, $x_j - y_j = y_k - x_k$ for $j,k \in \pi(x) \cap \pi(y)$, then $P(x,\pi) > P(y,\pi)$.

MT says that for two income profiles x and y with a fixed population size and a fixed number of poor persons, if x is obtained from y by an upward transfer of Θ ($= x_j - y_j$) amount of income from the poorer poor k to richer poor j, then given other things, x should display more poverty than y. Income transfers involved in MT cannot change the number of poor persons. Symmetrically, a downward transfer between two poor persons should reduce poverty.

Weak Transfer Axiom(WT)

For all $x,y \in \mathbb{R}^n_+$, if $x_i = y_i$ for all $i \neq j,k$ and $x_j > y_j \geq y_k > x_k$, $x_j - y_j = y_k - x_k$, $k \in \pi(x)$ and $\pi(x) = \pi(y)$, then $P(x,\pi) > P(y,\pi)$.

WT demands an increase in poverty only if the poorer of the two individuals involved in the upward transfer is poor and if the set of poor people does not change.

Strong Upward Transfer Axiom (SUP)

For all $x,y \in \mathbb{R}^n_+$, if $x_i = y_i$ for all $i \neq j,k$ and $x_j > y_j \geq y_k > x_k$, $x_j - y_j = y_k - x_k$ for $k \in \pi(x) \cap \pi(y)$, then $P(x,\pi) > P(y,\pi)$.

In SUT the poorer of the two persons concerned in the upward transfer is initially poor and remains poor after the transfer. The richer of the poor persons involved may be made rich as a result of the transfer.

Strong Downward Transfer Axiom (SDT)

For all $x,y \in \mathbb{R}^n_+$, if $x_i = y_i$ for all $i \neq j,k$ and $x_j > y_j \geq y_k > x_k$, $x_j - y_j = y_k - x_k$, for $k \in \pi(x)$, then $P(x,\pi) > P(y,\pi)$.

SDT requires poverty to decrease whenever a person originally poor receives an income transfer from someone remaining richer than the recipient after the transfer, even if the recipient crosses the poverty line as a result of the transfer.

It is clear that for either definition of the poor, the following chain of implication is true: SDT $\Rightarrow$ SUT $\Rightarrow$ WT $\Rightarrow$ MT. Sen(1976a) had chosen SUT as his transfer axiom, but in later works (Sen(1977, 1979a, 1981)) he questioned the merit of using a transfer axiom that allows the possibility of a change in the number of poor persons occuring as a result of transfers considered in the axiom and opted for WT. WT does not allow the number of poor persons to change and demands an unambiguous increase of poverty whenever there is a disequalising transfer from a poor person to a richer person. But with strong axioms the arguments are less clearcut, since while a disequalising transfer worsens the position of the donor, the recipient of the transfer may cross the poverty line because of the transfer. These effects work in opposite directions, the first increasing poverty and the second decreasing it. Hence the strong transfer principles became a source of controversy.

Before we discuss the implications of the transfer axioms, for the sake of completeness, we formulate some other general axioms for a poverty index.

Weak Diminishing Transfer Axiom (WDT)

If an upward transfer takes place from the ith poor with income x_i to a person with income $x_i + h$, then for a given $h > 0$, the magnitude of increase in $P(x,\pi)$ decreases as x_i increases, given that the number of poor persons remains unchanged as a result of the transfer.

This axiom gives more weight to transfers considered in WT at the lower end of the profile than at upper ends. This axiom, in a sense, is a stronger version of WT. The corresponding versions for the remaining forms of the transfer principle can be stated analogously.

Impartiality (IMP)

For all $x,y \in \mathbb{R}^n_+$, if x is obtained from y by a permutation of incomes, then $P(y,\pi) = P(x,\pi)$.

Clearly, an implication of this axiom is that poverty may be defined over ordered income profiles without loss of generality.

If the poverty line varies, then the poverty index should be sensitive to such variations. The following axiom reflects this for a given income profile.

Increasingness in Subsistence Income (ISI)

For a given $x \in \mathbb{R}^n_+$, $P(x,\pi)$ is increasing in π.

We assume that a poverty index varies continuously with incomes.

Continuity (CONT)

For all $(x,\pi) \in \mathbb{R}^{n+1}_+$, $P(x,\pi)$ is jointly continuous in (x,π).

However, for a fixed poverty line we require continuity of P in x only.

In addition to the above properties a poverty index may be required to satisfy the following axiom:

Population Invariance Axiom (PI)

For all $x \in \mathbb{R}^n_+$, $P(x,\pi) = P(x^{(k)},\pi)$ where $x^{(k)}$ denotes the k–fold replication of x.

This axiom is parallel to Dalton's(1920) population principle for inequality indices.

Donaldson and Weymark(1986) studied implications of different combinations of the above axioms. Below we shall discuss some of these implications which will enable us to eliminate/modify some troublesome postulates. We first look at the implication of CONT and SM when the strong definition of the poor is adopted. It is impossible to decrease the value of a focussed poverty index, as required by SM, and keep it constant at the same time, as required by CONT, when a person right at the poverty line has income increase. Thus, using the strong definition of the poor, no focussed poverty index can satisfy both SM and CONT (Donaldson and Weymark(1986)). However, if the weak definition of the poor is adopted, then for a focussed poverty index satisfying CONT, SM and WM are equivalent. It should also be clear that WM is not consistent with CONT for a focussed poverty index when the strong definition of the poor is adopted.

When the weak definition of the poor is adopted, IMP, IIR, WM and WT are equivalent to requiring that for a fixed number of poor persons, the poverty index should be a decreasing, strictly S–convex function of incomes of the poor. In other words, the poverty index corresponds to an increasing, strictly S–concave SEF in a negative monotonic way. That is, the poverty index agrees with the generalised Lorenz quasi–ordering.

This enables us to state the following:

Theorem 6.1

Let $x,y \in \mathbb{R}^n_+$ be arbitrary, where $\pi(x) = \pi(y)$. Then the following statements are equivalent:

(i) Using the weak definition of the poor, $P(x,\pi) > P(y,\pi)$ for all focussed poverty indices $P: \mathbb{R}^{n+1}_+ \to \mathbb{R}^1$ that satisfy IMP, WM and WT.

(ii) y^p strictly dominates x^p in the generalised Lorenz sense, where y^p (x^p) is the income profile of the poor in y (x).

We noted that SUT implies WT, but the converse is not true. The following theorem shows under what conditions the converse will be true:

Theorem 6.2 (Donaldson and Weymark 1986)

For either definition of the poor, if a focussed poverty index satisfies CONT and WT, then it satisfies SUT.

Proof

Since WT is satisfied we consider only a transfer from a poor person to a richer poor person that will enable the recipient to become rich.

Case 1 Strong definition of the poor: The transfer is broken into a sequence of steps. (i) If necessary, transfer just enough income to put the richer person at the poverty line. By WT, poverty increases. (ii) Increase rich person's income by $\Theta > 0$. There is no change in poverty by CONT and IIR. (iii) Transfer $\delta > 0$ amount of income not used in step (i). By WT poverty increases. (iv) Take back Θ amount of income from the richer person. There is no change in poverty by IIR.

Case 2 Weak definition of the poor: (i) Transfer some amount of income so that the income of the richer person is $(\pi - \delta)$, where $\delta > 0$ is sufficiently small. By WT poverty increases. (ii) Continuity ensures that if δ amount of income is given to the richer person, change in poverty from the initial profile will be positive. (iii) Transfering the rest of income (which is not used in step (i)) increases poverty by WT. (iv) Taking back δ amount of income from the richer person does not change poverty by IIR. ■

If we adopt the weak definition of poor, a similar theorem is obtained when SUT is combined with CONT.

Theorem 6.3 (Donaldson and Weymark 1986)

Using the weak definition of the poor, if a focussed poverty index satisfies CONT and SUT, then it satisfies SDT.

Proof

Since SUT is satisfied, we only consider a simple downward transfer of $\delta > 0$ amount of income from a rich person to a poor person such that both become rich. (i) Transfer just enough income to put the poor person at $\pi - t$, where $t > 0$. By SUT, poverty decreases. (ii) By choosing t in the previous step sufficiently small, CONT ensures that increasing the poor person up to π keeps the change in poverty from the initial profile negative. (iii) Reduce the rich person's income by t. By IIR, there is no change in poverty. (iv) If necessary, complete the rest of the transfer. Again, by IIR, there is no change in poverty. ■

But in Theorem 6.3 if the weak definition of poor is replaced by the strong definition, then an impossibility arises.

Theorem 6.4 (Donaldson and Weymark 1986)

Let $n \geq 3$. Using the strong definition of the poor, no focussed poverty index can satisfy SDT.

Proof

Suppose that the incomes of all but two individuals i and j are fixed: $x_k = \hat{x}_k$ for all $k \neq i,j$, where for at least one k, $\hat{x}_k > \pi$. (Clearly, at this point we need the assumption $n \geq 3$). The following figure gives the projection of $\mathbb{R}^n_+$ obtained by setting $x_k = \hat{x}_k$ for $k \neq i,j$.

Suppose SDT is satisfied. Since there is at least one rich person, an increase in x_j will obviously reduce poverty. Thus, poverty decreases monotonically as x_j increases along the interval [A,B). In other words, the poverty index P is a monotonically decreasing function along [A,B). Hence P has at most a countable number of points of discontinuity in [A,B)[2]. Let $\tilde{x} = (\hat{x}_1, \hat{x}_2, ..., \hat{x}_{i-1}, \pi, \hat{x}_{i+1}, ..., \hat{x}_{j-1}, \tilde{x}_j, \hat{x}_{j+1}, ..., \hat{x}_n)$ be a point of continuity in x_j of P in [A,B).

[2] See Rudin(1976, p. 96)

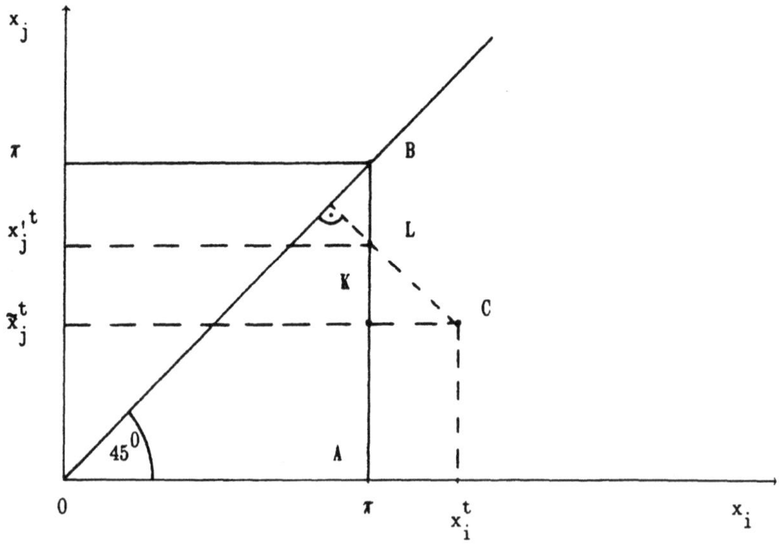

Figure 6.1

Construct a pair of sequences of profiles x^t, x'^t for t = 1, 2, ... in the following way:

(a) $x^t = (\tilde{x}_1, ..., \tilde{x}_i + \delta_t, ..., \tilde{x}_j, ..., \tilde{x}_n)$,

(b) $x'^t = (\tilde{x}_1, ..., \tilde{x}_i, ..., \tilde{x}_j + \delta_t, ..., \tilde{x}_n)$,

(c) $0 < \delta_t < (\pi - \tilde{x}_j)$, (6.1)

(d) $\lim_{t \to \infty} \delta_t = 0$.

The construction is illustrated in figure 6.1. K corresponds to $\tilde{x}$, C to x^t and L to x'^t. Now by SDT,

$$P(\tilde{x},\pi) > P(x^t,\pi) . \tag{6.2}$$

The profile x^t is obtained from x'^t by an upward transfer from j to i. Thus, by

SDT, $P(x^t,\pi) > P(x'^t,\pi)$. Hence for all t,

$$P(\tilde{x},\pi) > P(x^t,\pi) > P(x'^t,\pi) \ . \tag{6.3}$$

Since $\tilde{x}$ was chosen to be a point of continuity in x_j for P, $\lim_{t\to\infty} P(x'^t,\pi) = P(\tilde{x},\pi)$. Thus, from (6.3) we have

$$\lim_{t\to\infty} P(x^t,\pi) = P(\tilde{x},\pi) \ . \tag{6.4}$$

Because of IIR, $P(x^t,\pi)$ is independent of t. Hence by (6.4), $P(\tilde{x},\pi) = P(x^t,\pi)$ for all t, which contradicts (6.2). ■

In the proof of Theorem 6.4, appeal has been made to monotonicity arguments. The necessary monotonicity properties can be obtained by the use of SM instead of using SDT. However, to establish the inequality $P(x^t,\pi) > P(x'^t,\pi)$ use of a transfer principle is necessary. It should be clear that this inequality can as well be established using SUT instead of SDT. Consequently, Theorem 6.4 can be restated as:'Using the strong definition of the poor, no focussed poverty index can satisfy SM and SUT'. However, a possibility result arises if in this theorem the strong definition of the poor is replaced by the weak definition. To see this, suppose SUT is satisfied. We need only to consider a simple transfer of $\Theta > 0$ from a rich person to a poor person such that the poor person becomes rich. If we first take Θ units of income away from the rich person, there will be no change in poverty because of IIR. Now giving Θ to the poor person decreases poverty by SM. Thus, using the weak definition of the poor, if a focussed poverty index satisfies SM and SUT, it also satisfies SDT. By an analogous argument it can be shown that for either definition of the poor, if a focussed poverty index satisfies WM and MT, it also satisfies WT (Donaldson and Weymark(1986)).

The above discussion shows that the identification of individuals having subsistence income has significant implications for poverty indices. Clearly, one way out of the above impossibilities is to adopt the weak definition of the poor. Thon(1979) and Donaldson and Weymark(1986) suggested that a second alternative will be to adopt the strong definition of poor but adjust the axioms SM and SDT for a person right at the poverty line (that is, an increase in income of this person does not change poverty and changing the strict inequality to a weak inequality in SDT for this person).

Up till now we have assumed a fixed set of individuals. Kundu and Smith(1983) proposed two axioms for variable populations, one for poverty growth and one for non–poverty growth. These two axioms can be combined into the following axiom:

Population Growth (PG)

For all $x \in \mathbb{R}^n_+$, denote $\hat{x}$ by $(x_1, x_2, ..., x_n, x_{n+1})$, where $x_{n+1} \geq 0$. Then

(a): $P(\hat{x},\pi) > P(x,\pi)$ if $x_{n+1} < \pi$

(b): $P(\hat{x},\pi) < P(x,\pi)$ if $x_{n+1} > \pi$

PG states that when a poor (non–poor) person is added to the population, poverty should increase (decrease). In defence of their axiom Kundu and Smith contend that 'it may be argued that growth of non–poor in no way helps the poor, and in fact deteriorates their situation relative to the average citizen. However, if one compares poverty between large countries and small countries having the same absolute number of the poor (with respect to some relevant poverty line) then it seems hard to argue that the degree of poverty in the small country is not greater'. The main theorem of Kundu and Smith is that even if the weak definition of the poor is employed any poverty index that satisfies PG must violate SUT. According to Sen this result arises because of a conflict in the way the axioms regard the poverty line: The growth axiom 'treats the line as the great divider', whereas the transfer axiom 'takes no note whatever of the poverty line' (Sen(1981)). The Kundu–Smith result might be taken as a criticism of SUT. (WT does not conflict with PG. WT does take into account the poverty line.)

Kundu and Smith illustrated their result by presenting a table of indices. It is shown that the aggregate shortfall of the incomes of the poor from the poverty line and the head–count ratio are the only indices in their table which satisfy respectively (a), and (a) and (b) of PG. Foster(1984) noted that in the Kundu–Smith table every index that satisfies (a) and violates (b) of PG can be transformed by a suitable normalisation into another index which will satisfy (b) and violate (a). This remains true if positions of (a) and (b) are reversed. Further it can be seen that while (a) and (b) appear to be concerned with different aspects of poverty measurement, the transfer axiom is quite consistent with either of the two approaches (Foster(1984)). At this stage it seems worthwhile to mention the suggestion made by Sen(1981) on the purpose for selecting a poverty index: If we are interested in knowing how poor the poor are, the inequality of their income profile and the proportion of total population they represent, then we should not expect the poverty index to be sensitive to their absolute number. On the other hand, if we want to know how poor the poor are, the inequality of their income profile and their absolute number, then we should not be too concerned if the index does not increase when a non–poor person is added to the population.

6.3 Relative Indices of Poverty

6.3.1 The Crude Indices

We will now formally define the crude indices and discuss their properties. For a given $x \in \mathbb{R}^n_+$ and given $\pi > 0$, let $q(x,\pi)$ or simply q stand for the number of persons in $\pi(x)$. Then the head–count ratio (the proportion of poor persons in a given population) is defined as

$$P_1(x,\pi) = \frac{q}{n} . \tag{6.5}$$

P_1 has been used for most poverty studies since the works of Booth(1889) and Rowntree(1901)[3]. P_1 satifies IIR. But on income profiles with a given q, P_1 is a constant function and hence insentive to the incomes of the poor. That is, P_1 violates monotonicity and transfer axioms.

The second crude index is based on the aggregate poverty gap. For a given $x \in \mathbb{R}^n_+$ and given $\pi > 0$, the poverty gap of individual i in $\pi(x)$ is defined as $g_i = \pi - x_i$. The aggregate poverty gap is then defined as $\sum_{i \in \pi(x)} g_i$. Assuming the strong definition of the poor, this gap gives the amount of money necessary to put all the poor persons at the poverty line. The aggregate poverty gap, which has been developed by the Social Security Administration of the United States (see Batchelder(1971)), is normalised to ob–

3 The measure has been used extensively to study the trends in the incidence of poverty in India. See, for example, Ojha(1970), Bardhan(1970, 1971, 1973), Minhas(1970, 1971), Dandekar and Rath(1971), Mukherjee, Bhattacharya and Chatterjee(1972), Vaidyanathan(1974), Lal(1976), Pal, Chakravarty and Bhattacharya(1986).

tain the income gap ratio:

$$P_2(x,\pi) = \frac{\sum_{i\in\pi(x)} g_i}{\pi q} . \qquad (6.6)$$

P_2 can also be referred to as the normalised poverty gap. P_2 is obviously decreasing in incomes of the poor. But it is clear that P_2 is constant on income profiles with a given q and a given mean income of the poor. Thus, P_2 goes against the transfer axioms.

6.3.2 The Sen Index

Sen(1976a) begins by assuming that the poverty index P_3 is a weighted average of the income shortfalls of all people who are judged to be poor:

$$P_3(x,\pi) = A(x,\pi) \sum_{i\in\pi(x)} g_i v_i(x,\pi) , \qquad (6.7)$$

where $x \in \mathbb{R}^n_+$ and $A(x,\pi) > 0$ is a normalisation coefficient. It is presumed that $A(x,\pi) = A(y,\pi)$ whenever $q(x,\pi) = q(y,\pi)$ and the positive weights $v_i(x,\pi)$ may depend on the entire income profile.

In the next step Sen chooses a weighting scheme based on a person's relative rank.

Ranked Relative Deprivation

The weight $v_i(x,\pi)$ on individual i's poverty gap equals i's rank $r_i(x,\pi)$ in the income profile of the poor:

$$v_i(x,\pi) = r_i(x,\pi) \text{ [4]}. \qquad (6.8)$$

---

[4] This weighting rule is taken in Sen(1976a) as an axiom. But it is easy to derive it from more primitive axioms (Sen(1974)). The rank order weighting scheme has been used extensively in voting theory (see Black(1958), Fishburn(1973), Hansson(1973), Fine and Fine(1974) and Gardenfors(1974)).

This weighting scheme can be justified in two ways. First, as Sen himself stated, (6.8) has been borrowed from Borda's rank order method for social choice. 'This makes the weights equi-distanced, ...choosing equal distances in the absence of a convincing case for any alternative assumption' (Sen 1981). Secondly, Sen argued that if we assume that $\pi(x)$ represents a poor person's reference group, then $r_i(x,\pi)$ might be regarded as a measure of i's sense of relative deprivation[5] (also see Runciman(1966), Sen(1970) and Pattanaik(1971)).

The third step is to specify the normalisation factor A. It has already been noted that independently P_1 and P_2 are subject to many shortcomings. Sen argued that in the special case when all the poor persons have the same income a combination of the two might produce an adequate picture of poverty. Hence we might require the poverty index to depend only on P_1 and P_2 in this special case. The following simple formulation takes care of this.

Normalised Absolute Deprivation

If for all $i \in \pi(x)$, $x_i = c$, then

$$P_3(x,\pi) = P_1(x,\pi)\cdot P_2(x,\pi)^6 . \tag{6.9}$$

The Sen theorem can then be stated: If we assume the conditions of normalised absolute deprivation and ranked relative deprivation in the context of general form (6.7), then the poverty index turns out to be

$$P_3(x,\pi) = \frac{2}{(q+1)n\pi} \sum_{i\in\pi(x)} g_i r_i(x,\pi)$$

which, when rewritten in terms of the illfare ranked permutation $\bar{x}$ of x, becomes

$$P_3(x,\pi) = \frac{2}{(q+1)n\pi} \sum_{i=1}^{q} (\pi - \bar{x}_i)(q+1-i) . \tag{6.10}$$

[5] This approach of attaching higher weight to the income shortfall of a poorer person is closely related to the social assessment of 'named good vectors'. See Sen(1976b).

[6] Basu(1985) has constructed an axiomatic framework that implies (6.9).

For large q, $P_3(x,\pi)$ in (6.10) can be written as

$$P_3(x,\pi) = P_1[P_2 + (1 - P_2)G_p^q], \tag{6.11}$$

where G_p^q is the relative Gini index of the income profile of the poor[7].

Clearly, the above discussion enables us to interpret P_3 as an index of aggregate relative deprivation of the poor. In addition P_3 is related to G_p^q in a positive monotonic way. For income profiles with the same number of poor and the same mean income of the poor, the ranking of profiles produced by G_p^q is the same as that produced by P_3. Also if n replaces q, the mean income $\lambda(x)$ of x replaces π, P_3 becomes a multiple of the Gini coefficient of x.

Sen's work has led to a large body of literature dealing with the aggregation aspects of the measurement of poverty. This literature has been surveyed by Sen(1979a, 1981), Chakravarty(1983a), Foster(1984), Kanbur(1984), Donaldson and Weymark(1986), Atkinson(1987) and Seidl(1988). It is clear that alternatives and variations of the Sen index can be obtained in many ways, e.g., by varying the weights $v_i(x,\pi)$ on g_i, changing the normalisation rule, choosing a form which is different from the general form in (6.7), replacing the Gini index of inequality in (6.11) by some other index of inequality and so on. In the remaining part of this section we discuss alternatives and variations of the Sen index.

6.3.3 The Blackorby–Donaldson Approach

Before we discuss the Blackorby–Donaldson(1980a) generalised index, we need to define the representative income of the poor. For $x \in \mathbb{R}_+^n$, let x^p be the income profile of the poor, and let W_p^q be their SEF. Then the representative income of the poor x_f^p is defined by

---

[7] The Sen measure has been used extensively to study the incidence of poverty in different countries (see, for example, Bhatty(1974), Anand(1977, 1983), Kakwani(1977a, 1980, 1980b), Ahluwalia(1978), Dutta(1978), Osmany(1982) and Pal, Chakravarty and Bhattacharya(1986)).

$$W^q_p(x^p_f \cdot 1^q) = W^q_p(x^p) . \tag{6.12}$$

W^q_p is assumed to be <u>smooth</u> (continuous, increasing, strictly S–concave) and homothetic. We can write x^p_f as $E^q(x^p)$, where E^q is the normalised form of W^q_p (see Chapter 2, Subsection 2.3.3).

Blackorby and Donaldson(1980a) noted that the Sen index in (6.11) can be written using $\mathring{x}$, the welfare ranked permutation of x, as follows:

$$P_3(x,\pi) = \frac{q}{n}[1 - \frac{1}{q^2\pi} \sum_{i \in \pi(x)} (2i-1)\mathring{x}_i] . \tag{6.13}$$

In accordance with the formula for the Gini SEF in (2.42), $\sum_{i \in \pi(x)} (2i-1)\mathring{x}_i/q^2$ can be called the Gini representative income of the poor. Now, if the Gini representative income in (6.13) is replaced by some other representative income of the poor (for example, the one produced by the symmetric mean of order $r(<1)$ SEF of the poor), then we get a different index. This is the line along which Blackorby and Donaldson(1980a) generalised the Sen index. Accordingly, the Blackorby–Donaldson relative poverty index is defined as the product of the proportion of population in poverty and the relative gap between π and x^p_f:

$$P_4(x,\pi) = \frac{q}{n} \cdot [\frac{\pi - x^p_f}{\pi}] . \tag{6.14}$$

Given homotheticity of the SEF of the poor, we have $W^q_p(x^p) = \phi(\bar{W}_p(x^p))$, where $\bar{W}_p$ is linearly homogeneous and ϕ is increasing in its argument. Suppose that in terms of the illfare ranked permutation of the incomes of the poor, $\bar{W}_p(x^p)$ is given by $\sum_{i=1}^{q} \bar{x}_i(q+1-i)^\Theta$, where $\Theta > 0$. Then P_4 becomes the Kakwani(1980b) index of poverty:

$$\frac{q}{n\,\pi \sum_{i=1}^{q} i^{\Theta}} \cdot \sum_{i=1}^{q} (\pi - \bar{x}_i)(q + 1 - i)^{\Theta} \ . \tag{6.15}$$

When $\Theta = 0$, the index is simply $P_1 \cdot P_2$. The Sen index corresponds to the case $\Theta = 1$, 'making it equally sensitive to a transfer of income at all income positions' (Kakwani (1980b)). The motivation for introducing the index in (6.15) is to enable it to satisfy WDT. Kakwani has shown that for a given profile there exist a $\Theta > 1$, such that $P_4(x,\pi)$ in (6.15) meets WDT. But different values of Θ would be needed for different profiles to meet WDT. This is clearly a disadvantage associated with the formula in (6.15).

Thus, given (6.14), to every homothetic SEF, there exists a different focussed relative poverty index. Assuming the weak definition of the poor, P_4 satisfies WM and WT (since W_p^q is increaing and strictly S–concave). The general index retains all the properties of the Sen index: (i) it is sensitive to the head–count ratio, (ii) it is sensitve to how poor the poor are and (iii) it is sensitive to the inequality among the poor themselves ($x_f^p = (1 - I_3^q)\lambda(x^p)$, where I_3^q is the AKS relative inequality index corresponding to W_p^q and $\lambda(x^p)$ is the mean of income of the poor, which is assumed to be positive). P_4 can be easily converted into the AKS relative inequality index I_3 in (2.27) by replacing π by $\lambda(x)$, q by n and x^p by the entire profile x. (A characterisation of the general formula (6.14) by the population invariance axiom can be found in Bossert(1989b).)

Blackorby and Donaldson pointed out that if the SEF underlying P_4 is required to be ethically significant then it must reflect a set of ethical judgements for the whole society. To explain this let us write $\mathring{x}$ as $(\mathring{x}^R, \mathring{x}^p)$, where $\mathring{x}^R(\mathring{x}^p)$ is the welfare–ranked permutation of the income profile $x^R(x^p)$ of the non–poor (poor). By fixing $\mathring{x}^R$ at $\hat{\mathring{x}}^R$, an SEF for the poor W_p^q is generated from W^n and is written as

$$\hat{W}_p^q = W^n(\hat{\mathring{x}}^R, \mathring{x}^p) \ . \tag{6.16}$$

But in this case $\hat{W}_p^q$ depends on the non–poor incomes also. If W^n is continuous and increasing, then the minimal condition needed for $\hat{W}_p^q$ not to depend upon non–poor incomes is that income profile of the poor is separable from that of the non–poor. Then the SEF W^n can be written as

$$W^n(\overset{\circ}{x}) = \overset{*}{W}^n(\overset{\circ}{x}^R, W_p^q(\overset{\circ}{x}^p)) . \tag{6.17}$$

But this does not guarantee that W^n is increasing in W_p^q. To ensure that the general SEF W^n is increasing in $W_p^q(x^p)$, we need strict separability of the poor from the non–poor. Now, both $\overset{*}{W}^n$ and W_p^q depend upon π. To avoid this we assume that every group of people is separable from anyone with higher income. This implies that the SEF is completely strictly recursive (Blackorby, Primont and Russell 1978, Chapter 6). That is

$$W^n(\overset{\circ}{x}) = W^n(\overset{\circ}{x}_1, w_2) \tag{6.18}$$

where, $w_j = W^{n-j+1}(\overset{\circ}{x}_j, w_{j+1})$, $j = 2, 3, ..., n-1$,

$$w_n = W^1(\overset{\circ}{x}_n) ,$$

and W^{n-j+1} is increasing in w_{j+1}.

Thus, we have two classes of functions from which to choose –completely separable class and non–separable class. The symmetric mean of order $r < 1$ is a member of the former class and the Gini is a member of the latter class.

For the remainder of this section we assume that the SEF W^n is smooth and homothetic. In the context of the Blackorby–Donaldson index we will assume additionally that W^n is completely strictly recursive. We now have

<u>Theorem 6.5</u>

Using the strong definition of the poor, the Blackorby–Donaldson relative poverty index violates CONT and SUT.

<u>Proof</u>

For $z \in \mathbb{R}_+^n$, let us consider its welfare ranked permutation $\overset{\circ}{z}$. Then by complete strict recursivity of W^n the representative income of the poor z_f^p is given by

$$W^n(\overset{\circ}{z}) = W^n(\overset{\circ}{z}_1, ..., \overset{\circ}{z}_{n-q}, z_f^p, ..., z_f^p) .$$

To show that P_4 is discontinuous, choose $x \in \mathbb{R}_+^n$ such that $\overset{\circ}{x}_{n-q+1} = \pi$ and $\overset{\circ}{x}_{n-q+2} < \pi$. Now define $\overset{\circ}{y} = (\overset{\circ}{y}_1, \overset{\circ}{y}_2, ..., \overset{\circ}{y}_n)$ as follows: $\overset{\circ}{y}_i = \overset{\circ}{x}_i$ for all $i \neq n-q+1$, $\overset{\circ}{y}_{n-q+1} = \overset{\circ}{x}_{n-q+1} + \otimes$, where $\otimes > 0$. Thus, we have increased the income of the richest poor person lowering the number of poor to (q–1).

Since W^n is completely strictly recursive, we have

$$W^n(\overset{\circ}{y}) = W^n(\overset{\circ}{y}_1, ..., \overset{\circ}{y}_{n-q}, \pi + \otimes, y_f^p, ..., y_f^p), \tag{6.19}$$

and

$$W^n(\overset{\circ}{x}) = W^n(\overset{\circ}{x}_1, ..., \overset{\circ}{x}_{n-q}, \pi, y_f^p, ..., y_f^p)$$

$$= W^n(\overset{\circ}{x}_1, ..., \overset{\circ}{x}_{n-q}, x_f^p, ..., x_f^p) . \tag{6.20}$$

By strict S–concavity of W^n, $y_f^p < \pi$ (since $\overset{\circ}{x}_{n-q+2} < \pi$) and

$$x_f^p < [(q-1)y_f^p + \pi]/q. \tag{6.21}$$

Now,

$$P_4(\overset{\circ}{x},\pi) = \frac{q}{n} \cdot \left[\frac{\pi - x_f^p}{\pi}\right]$$

$$> \frac{q}{n} \cdot \left[\frac{q\pi - (q-1)y_f^p - \pi}{q\pi}\right]$$

$$= \frac{q}{n} \cdot \left[\frac{(q - 1)\cdot(\pi - y_f^p)}{q\pi}\right]$$

$$= \frac{(q - 1)}{n} \cdot \left[\frac{\pi - y_f^p}{\pi}\right]$$

$$= P_4(\overset{\circ}{y},\pi)\,. \tag{6.22}$$

(6.22) must hold for all $\Theta > 0$. But $P_4(\overset{\circ}{x},\pi)$ is independent of $\Theta > 0$, and because of IIR (guaranteed by strict recursivity) so is $P_4(\overset{\circ}{y},\pi)$. Therefore, continuity of P_4 requires, $P_4(\overset{\circ}{x},\pi) > P_4(\overset{\circ}{x},\pi)$, a contradiction!

To show that P_4 violates the strong upward transfer axiom, consider the income profile $(y_1, \ldots, y_{n-q}, \pi - \frac{\Theta}{q}, \pi - \frac{2\Theta}{q}, \ldots, \pi - \frac{(q-1)\Theta}{q}, \pi - \Theta)$, where $\Theta > 0$ is small, and $y_1 \geqq y_2 \geqq \ldots \geqq y_{n-q} > \pi$. Transfer Θ amount of income from the poorest person to the richest poor person. The new income profile is $x = (x_1, \ldots, x_{n-q}, x_{n-q+1}, \ldots, x_n)$ where $x_i = y_i$ for all $i \neq n-q+1,n$ and $x_{n-q+1} = \pi + \Theta(1 - \frac{1}{q}) > \pi$, $x_n = \pi - 2\Theta$. Since the SEF is continuous and $\Theta > 0$ is arbitrary, we can make $(\pi - y_f^p)$ very close to $(\pi - x_f^p)$ such that the inequality

$$\frac{q}{n}\left[\frac{\pi - y_f^p}{\pi}\right] < \frac{(q-1)}{n}\left[\frac{\pi - x_f^p}{\pi}\right] \tag{6.23}$$

does not hold. This shows that P_4 violates the strong upward transfer axiom. This completes the proof of the theorem. ■

We conclude this subsection with the remark that the failure of the Sen–Blackorby–Donaldson–Kakwani indices to meet a strong transfer axiom remains to be rather disturbing.

6.3.4 The Takayama and the Hamada–Takayama Approach

Takayama(1979) pointed out that the Sen index is insensitive to relative deprivation of the poor with respect to non–poor incomes, that is, relative deprivation stops at the poverty line. According to Takayama(1979) in measuring poverty ' we cannot neglect the existence of the people above the poverty line', because 'someone in poverty compares his income with that of others in the community as a whole, not only with that of individuals below the poverty line'.

Keeping the above in mind Takayama defined the censored income profile x^* corresponding to the income profile x as

$$x_i^* = \min\{x_i, \pi\}, i = 1, 2, ..., n, \tag{6.24}$$

that is, all incomes above the poverty line are replaced by the poverty line itself. The Takayama poverty index $P_5(x,\pi)$ for the income profile x is then defined as the Gini index of the profile x^*:

$$P_5(x,\pi) = \frac{1}{2n^2\lambda(x^*)} \sum_{i=1}^{n} \sum_{j=1}^{n} |x_i^* - x_j^*|, \tag{6.25}$$

where $\lambda(x^*) > 0$ is the mean of the censored income profile x^*. Other indices of relative inequality have been applied to derive corresponding indices of poverty in Hamada and Takayama(1977).

The approach has a clear merit – it ignores information on actual incomes of the non–poor, but counts them in with the poverty line income. The main drawback of the Takayama and the Hamada–Takayama indices lie in their robust violation of WM. To see this, consider a society in which all the n–persons are poor (using either definition of the poor)[8]. Now, multiply all the incomes by a positive scalar $c < 1$. Then by WM, a poverty index should increase. But the Takayama and the Hamada–Takayama indices remain invariant under such circumstances. To strengthen our criticism, let us prove the following result also.

Theorem 6.6

Let $x \in D^n$ be such that $x_i < \pi$ for all i = 1, 2, .., n. Suppose that $I_R^n: D^n \to \mathbb{R}^1$ is a relative inequality index that satisfies the Pigou–Dalton transfers principle (PD). Increase the richest person's income by $\Theta > 0$ such that he still remains poor. Then

---

[8] In such a case, if all the incomes assume a common value, then the Takayama and the Hamada–Takayama indices take the value zero, irrespective of the common income. Clearly, this is undesirable. Moreover, these indices are not even defined when all the incomes take the value zero.

$$I_R^n(x_1 + \Theta, x_2, ..., x_n) > I_R^n(x_1, x_2, ..., x_n)$$

where $x_1 \geq x_2 \geq ... \geq x_n$.

Proof

Given that I_R^n verifies PD, a transfer of income from a rich person to a poor person will decrease I_R^n. Consequently,

$$I_R^n(x_1 + \Theta, x_2, \dots, x_n)$$

$$> \quad I_R^n\left(x_1 + \frac{\Theta x_1}{n\lambda(x)}, x_2 + \frac{\Theta x_2}{n\lambda(x)}, ..., x_n + \frac{\Theta x_n}{n\lambda(x)}\right)$$

$$= \quad I_R^n(cx_1, cx_2, \dots, cx_n)\ , \tag{6.26}$$

where $c = 1 + \dfrac{\Theta}{n\lambda(x)}$. Since I_R^n is a relative index, we have

$$I_R^n(cx_1, cx_2, \dots, cx_n) = I_R^n(x_1, x_2, \dots, x_n).$$

The desired result now follows from this equality and the inequality in (6.26). ■

Theorem 6.6 tells us that an increase in the richest person's income will increase inequality. But SM demands an unambiguous reduction of poverty in this case (since the richest person is assumed to be poor). We therefore have

Theorem 6.7

If a relative inequality index defined on the censored income profile is used as a relative poverty index (the Takayama and the Hamada–Takayama approach), then

(a) using either definition of the poor, the poverty index will violate WM.

(b) using the weak definition of the poor, the poverty index will violate SM. ■

The broad question that now arises is whether we can propose indices based on censored income profiles that would meet WM, SUT and CONT. The next subsection answers this question.

6.3.5 The Clark – Hemming – Ulph – Chakravarty Approach

This approach is a combination of the Blackorby–Donaldson and the Takayama approaches. To make the notion explicit, let us denote the AKS equally distributed equivalent (EDE) income associated with the censored income profile x^* corresponding to $x \in \mathbb{R}^n_+$ by x^*_f. That is, x^*_f is defined implicitly by, $W^n(x^*_f \cdot 1^n) = W^n(x^*)$. Then the Clark–Hemming–Ulph–Chakravarty (CHUC) relative poverty index $P_6(x,\pi)$ is defined as the proportionate gap between the poverty line π and x^*_f:

$$P_6(x,\pi) = \frac{\pi - x^*_f}{\pi} . \tag{6.27}$$

P_6 lies in the interval [0,1], the lower and upper limits being attained, respectively, when $x_i \geq \pi$ for all $i = 1,2,...,n$ and when $x_i = 0$ for all $i = 1,...,n$.
We now have

Theorem 6.8

Using the strong definition of the poor, the CHUC relative poverty index $P_6(x,\pi)$ satisfies IIR, WM, SUT, IMP, ISI and CONT.

Proof

By construction, P_6 is a focussed poverty index. Since W^n is a smooth SEF, x^*_f can be written as $E^n(x^*_1, x^*_2, \ldots, x^*_n)$, where E^n is also smooth (see Chapter 2, Subsection 2.3.3). Homotheticity of W^n implies that E^n is linearly homogeneous. Therefore, we can rewrite P_6 in (6.27) as

$$\begin{aligned} P_6(x,\pi) &= \frac{\pi - E^n(x^*_1, \ldots, x^*_n)}{\pi} \\ &= 1 - E^n\left[\frac{x^*_1}{\pi}, \frac{x^*_2}{\pi}, \ldots, \frac{x^*_n}{\pi}\right] . \end{aligned} \tag{6.28}$$

By increasingness of E^n, P_6 is increasing in π. Continuity of P_6 follows from continuity of E^n. Since E^n is increasing, a decrease in the income of a poor person will obviously increase the value of P_6. Hence WM is satisfied. Impartiality of P_6 is implied by symmetry of E^n.

Because of strict S–concavity of E^n, a rank preserving transfer of income from a poor person to any one who is richer such that the set of the poor remains unchanged, will decrease E^n. This shows that P_6 satisfies WT. Now P_6 is a continuous, focussed poverty index. Hence by Theorem 6.2 we can conclude that P_6 will meet SUT. This completes the proof of the theorem. ■

The specific functional form of W^n will determine whether the index satisfies the population invariance axiom or not.

Our next result is

Theorem 6.9

If the social evaluation function is completely strictly recursive, then P_4 and P_6 are related by

$$P_4(x,\pi) < P_6(x,\pi) < (\pi - x_f^p)/\pi \tag{6.29}$$

as long as $x_f^p < \pi$ and $q < n$.

Proof

Using complete strict recursivity of W^n we have

$$\begin{aligned} x_f^* &= E^n(\pi, \pi, \ldots, \pi, x_{n-q+1}, \ldots, x_n) \\ &= E^n(\pi, \pi, \ldots, \pi, x_f^p, \ldots, x_f^p), \end{aligned} \tag{6.30}$$

where E^n is the normalised form of W^n (see Chapter 2, Subsection 2.3.3) and it has been assumed that $x_1 \geq x_2 \geq \ldots \geq x_{n-q} > \pi \geq x_{n-q+1} \geq \ldots \geq x_n$.

Now, by strict S–concavity of E_n we have

$$x_f^* < [qx_f^p + (n-q)\pi]/n \ . \tag{6.31}$$

$$P_6(x,\pi) = \frac{\pi - x_f^*}{\pi} > \frac{n\pi - qx_f^p - (n-q)\pi}{n\pi}$$

$$= \frac{q}{n} \cdot [\frac{\pi - x_f^p}{\pi}] . \tag{6.32}$$

In (6.30), since $x_f^p < \pi$ and E^n is strictly S–concave, $x_f^* > x_f^p$. Hence

$$P_6(x,\pi) = (\pi - x_f^*)/\pi < (\pi - x_f^p)/\pi \ . \tag{6.33}$$

The desired result now follows from (6.32) and (6.33). ■

Note that the bounds in (6.29) are actually attained with $W^n(x) = \min_i \{x_i\}$ (the maximin rule) and $W^n(x) = \sum_{i=1}^{n} x_i$ (the income sum criterion). Both these SEFs are S–concave but not strictly so.

We can rewrite $P_6(x,\pi)$ in (6.27) in terms of the AKS relative inequality index I_3^n as

$$P_6(x,\pi) = 1 - \lambda(x^*)(1 - I_3^n(x^*))/\pi \ , \tag{6.34}$$

where $\lambda(x^*) > 0$. Therefore, for two censored income profiles x^* and y^* with the same mean $\lambda(x^*) = \lambda(y^*) > 0$, we have

$$P_6(x,\pi) \geqq P_6(y,\pi) \Leftrightarrow I_3^n(x^*) \geqq I_3^n(y^*) \ . \tag{6.35}$$

It is now clear that given (6.27), to every homothetic SEF there corresponds a different relative poverty index. These indices will differ only in the manner in which the amount of relative inequality in the censored income profile is taken into account. Therefore, the index P_6 is a fairly natural translation of a relative inequality index of a censored income profile into a relative poverty index.

Example 1

Assume that the SEF is the symmetric mean of order r (< 1). Then P_6 in (6.27) becomes

$$P_6(x,\pi,r) = \begin{cases} 1-[\frac{1}{n}\sum_{i=1}^{n}(x_i^*)^r]^{1/r}/\pi & , r<1, r\neq 0 \\ 1-[\prod_{i=1}^{n}x_i^*]^{1/n}/\pi & , r=0 . \end{cases} \quad (6.36)$$

This index satisfies WDT for all r < 1. We can rewrite $P_6(x,\pi,r)$ as

$$P_6(x,\pi,r) = 1 - [P_1((1 - I_2^q(x^P))(1 - P_2))^r + (1 - P_1)]^{1/r} . \quad (6.37)$$

P_6 in (6.37) is increasing in P_1, P_2, the Atkinson(1970) inequality index for the poor $I_2^q(x^P)$ and π. It is decreasing in r reaching finally $P_6(x,\pi,1) = P_1P_2$. On the other hand, as $r \to -\infty$, $P_6(x,\pi,r) \to 1 - \min_i \{x_i^*\}/\pi$, the relative maximin index of poverty. For any $r < 0$, $P_6(x,\pi,r) \to 1$ as any one income tends to zero.

Example 2

If x_f^* is given by

$$x_f^* = \frac{2}{n(n+1)}\sum_{i=1}^{n} x_i^*(n+1-i) , \quad (6.38)$$

where $x_1 \leq x_2 \leq ... \leq x_q \leq \pi < x_{q+1} \leq ... \leq x_n$, then P_6 in (6.27) becomes the Thon(1979) index[9]. The motivation for introducing the new index was to enable it to satisfy SUT. Clearly, this index does not meet WDT.

---

[9] Thon, however, did not suggest this index using the CHUC approach. Instead, he defined the poverty index as a normalised weighted sum of income gaps of the poor, the weight on ith poor's gap being his rank in the entire income profile.

Corresponding to an income profile $x \in \mathbb{R}^n_+$, Pyatt(1987) defined, what he called 'the affluence' of individual j, by $b_j = x_j - x^*_j$; $j = 1,2,...,n$. b_j is positive or zero according as individual j rich or poor. Then employing the generalised Gini SEF, the EDE income corresponding to x can be written as $x_f = \pi + b_f - \pi P_6(x,\pi)$, where b_f is the EDE income for b. Thus, an average measure of social welfare has been decomposed into the poverty line π, the gain in social welfare due to affluence, b_f, and the loss in social welfare due to poverty, πP_6. If the poverty line is set equal to the mean income, the generalised Gini inequality index is simply the net difference between the poverty index P_6 and a normalised measure of affluence b_f/π.

In view of the discussion carried out in this section it is clear that the CHUC index is one of the most satisfactory indices of poverty with respect to its compliance with the important general axioms considered.

6.4 Absolute Indices of Poverty

Throughout this section we will assume that the SEF W^n is smooth and translatable. In the case of the Blackorby–Donaldson poverty index we will further assume that it is completely strictly recursive.

One might consider an absolute inequality index, when applied to the censored income profile, as an absolute poverty index. However, the approach is not fruitful one in view of Theorem 6.10, which is easy to demonstrate.

Theorem 6.10

> If an absolute inequality index defined on the censored income profile is used as an absolute poverty index, then
> (a) for either definition of the poor, the poverty index will violate WM,
> (b) for the weak definition of the poor, the poverty index will violate SM.

Blackorby and Donaldson(1980a) suggested the use of the following as a general absolute poverty index.

$$Q_1(x,\pi) = nP_1[\pi - x_f^p]$$

$$= q[\pi - x_f^p] \ , \tag{6.39}$$

where $x \in \mathbb{R}_+^n$ and x_f^p is the representative income of the poor. The following theorem, whose proof is completely analogous to that of Theorem 6.5, shows that as an absolute poverty index Q_1 is not a suitable candidate.

<u>Theorem 6.11</u>

Using the strong definition of the poor, the Blackorby–Donaldson absolute poverty index violates SUT and CONT.

In contrast, as a general absolute poverty index we introduce the measure

$$Q_2(x,\pi) = \pi - x_f^*$$

$$= \pi - E^n(x_1^*, x_2^*, ..., x_n^*) \ . \tag{6.40}$$

where the AKS EDE income function E^n is smooth and unit–translatable. Q_2 lies between zero and π, where the bounds are attained, respectively, when $x_i \geq \pi$ for all i = 1, 2, ..., n and when $x_i = 0$ for all i = 1, 2, ..., n. It measures the <u>per capita</u> poverty. In a censored income profile if each person were given $(\pi - x_f^*)$ amount of money, then the index would be zero (since E^n is unit–translatable) at an aggregate cost of n $Q_2(x,\pi)$. Hence $nQ_2(x,\pi)$ gives the total money unit cost of poverty. Therefore, we can also use the index

$$Q_3(x,\pi) = n(\pi - x_f^*) \ , \tag{6.41}$$

as an absolute poverty index. This index measures <u>total</u> absolute poverty rather than per capita poverty. Clearly, the index Q_1 can also be given similar interpretation. The specific functional form of W^n determines whether the per capita index meets the population invariance axiom or not. If the per capita index meets this axiom, then repli cating the population would raise Q_3 in proportion to n.

The following theorems can be proved easily

Theorem 6.12

Using the strong definition of the poor, the absolute poverty index Q_2 satisfies IIR, WM, SUT, IMP, ISI and CONT.

Theorem 6.13

If the social evaluation function is completely strictly recursive, then Q_1 and Q_2 are related by

$$Q_1(x,\pi) < n \cdot Q_2(x,\pi) < n(\pi - x_f^p) \ , \tag{6.42}$$

as long as $x_f^p < \pi$ and $q < n$.

We can rewrite Q_2 in (6.40) in terms of the BDK absolute inequality index $A_1^n(x^*)$ and $\lambda(x^*)$, the mean of the censored income profile x^* as follows:

$$Q_2(x,\pi) = \pi - \lambda(x^*) + A_1^n(x^*) \ . \tag{6.43}$$

Therefore for two censored income profiles x^* and y^* with the same mean $\lambda(x^*) = \lambda(y^*)$, we have

$$Q_2(x,\pi) \gtreqless Q_2(y,\pi) \iff A_1^n(x^*) \gtreqless A_1^n(y^*) \ . \tag{6.44}$$

Example 1

An interesting example of Q_2 arises from the Kolm–Pollak SEF. Its implicit poverty index is

$$Q_2(x,\pi,\alpha) = \frac{1}{\alpha} \log[\frac{1}{n} \sum_{i=1}^{n} e^{\alpha(\pi - x_i^*)}] \tag{6.45}$$

where $\alpha > 0$. The index in (6.45) is an increasing function of α. For $\alpha = 0$, $Q_2(x,\pi,0) = \pi - \lambda(x^*)$, the average gap of the individuals in the distribution x^* from the poverty line. On the other hand, as $\alpha \longrightarrow \infty$, $Q_2(x,\pi,\alpha) \longrightarrow \pi - \min_i \{x_i^*\}$, the absolute maximin index of poverty. Q_2 satisfies WDT for all $\alpha > 0$ and PI for all $\alpha \geq 0$.

Example 2

Another interesting example of Q_2 in (6.40) can be constructed from the single–parameter Gini SEF. In this case the poverty index is

$$Q_2(x,\pi,\delta) = \frac{1}{n^\delta} \sum_{i=1}^{n} [\pi - x_i^*] (i^\delta - (i-1)^\delta) , \tag{6.46}$$

where $x_1^* \geq x_2^* \geq \ldots \geq x_n^*$ and $\delta > 1$. The properties of Q_2 in (6.46) will follow from the properties of the associated SEF. For $\delta = 2$, Q_2 can be called the absolute Gini index of poverty. By dividing this with π we get the relative Gini poverty index.

The general measure introduced in this section incorporates an absolute measure of inequality and exists for every translatable SEF. Alternative examples of the general measure will differ among themselves only in the way they take account of the absolute inequality in the censored income profile.

6.5 Concluding Remarks

While the Takayama and the Hamada–Takayama indices violate the weak monotonicity axiom and the Sen–Blackorby–Donaldson–Kakwani indices violate the strong upward transfer axiom, the general ethical indices introduced by Clark–Hemming–Ulph –Chakravarty satisfy these axioms. These indices are based on the equally distributed equivalent income corresponding to a censored income profile.

Anand(1977) suggested two simple variations of the Sen index. Anand's first index is

$$P_7(x,\pi) = \frac{a}{b} P_3(x,\pi) , \tag{6.47}$$

where $a = n\pi$ is the amount of income necessary to put all persons at the poverty line and $b = \sum_{i=1}^{n} x_i$ is the aggregate income in x. The second Anand index is given by

$$P_8(x,\pi) \;=\; \frac{a}{b_1} \cdot P_3(x,\pi) \;, \tag{6.48}$$

where $b_1 = \sum_{i \notin \pi(x)} x_i$ is the aggregate income of the non–poor. When all the poor persons have the same income, P_7 reduces to the aggregate poverty gap as a proportion of the total income and P_8 reduces to the aggregate poverty gap as a proportion of the total non–poor income. P_7 and P_8 violate IIR. However, Anand is careful to note that P_7 and P_8, unlike P_3, determine the degree of ease with which poverty can be alleviated rather than the extent of poverty. Sen(1981) also pointed out that if the purpose of measurement is to check the country's potential ability to meet the challenge of poverty, then the first Anand index has some clear advantage.

Vaughan(1987) derived poverty indices 'from an explicit view of the loss of welfare which results from the existence of poverty' in comparison with a society in which poverty has been eliminated by raising all the persons below the poverty line to the poverty line itself. In terms of the notation used in the context of the Blackorby –Donaldson formulae, the gross relative and absolute indices are defined respectively by $[W^n(\mathring{x}^R,\pi \cdot 1^q) - W^n(\mathring{x}^R,\mathring{x}^p)]/W^n(\mathring{x}^R,\pi \cdot 1^q)$ and $W^n(\mathring{x}^R,\pi \cdot 1^q) - W^n(\mathring{x}^R,\mathring{x}^p)$. These indices determine respectively the proportional and absolute loss in society's welfare generated by the existence of poverty. If we assume that the welfare gains arise solely from the elimination of poverty within a society of fixed initial resources, then it is necessary to impose some taxes on rich incomes to raise the poor to the poverty line. Denoting the welfare ranked permutation of the tax vector of the rich by $\mathring{T}^R$, the net Vaughan indices are defined by $[W^n(\mathring{x}^R-\mathring{T}^R,\pi \cdot 1^q) - W^n(\mathring{x}^R,\mathring{x}^p)]/W^n(\mathring{x}^R-\mathring{T}^R,\pi \cdot 1^q)$ and $W^n(\mathring{x}^R-\mathring{T}^R,\pi \cdot 1^q) - W^n(\mathring{x}^R,\mathring{x}^p)$. These indices ensure that welfare gains arise from the elimination of poverty when resources are fixed. These latter indices are, obviously, based on two assumptions: (i) No rich person falls below the poverty line as a result of taxation, (ii) the society is potential enough for eliminating poverty – the aggregate income gap of the poor must not be greater than the total tax proceeds.

Kakwani(1980) derived several poverty indices, investigated the effect of negative in come tax schemes with the help of these indices and gave a numerical illustration based on Malaysian data (some of these indices were presented earlier in Kakwani(1977a)). He assumed a more general dependence between the poverty index and G_p^q than that exists in the Sen formula (6.11) and presented the following class of indices:

$$P_9(x,\pi) = \frac{q}{n\lambda(x)}[\pi - \lambda(x^p)f(G_p^q)], \tag{6.49}$$

where $\lambda(x^p)$, the mean income of the poor, is positive and f is monotone decreasing in its arguments such that $0 \leq f(G_p^q) \leq 1$, $f(G_p^q) = 1$ if $G_p^q = 0$. Two particular cases of P_9 using the transformations $f(G_p^q) = 1 - G_p^q$ and $f(G_p^q) = 1 / (1+G_p^q)$ were given and used in the empirical illustration. Clearly, P_9 is <u>not</u> a focussed index. It also violates WM.

Hagenaars(1987) employed a Dalton(1920) type averaging rule to propose an alternative poverty index. Letting U stand for the identical, individual utility function, this index can be written as $\sum_{i\in\pi(x)} [U(\pi) - U(x_i)]/nU(\pi)$. Hagenaars proposed some alternative forms of U and derived corresponding indices of poverty. Obviously, the index suffers from the same shortcoming as the Dalton formula in (2.14).

To present the second CHUC index, let us consider, without loss of generality, the illfare ranked permutation $\bar{x}$ of $x \in \mathbb{R}_+^n$, so that $\pi(x) = \{1, 2, \ldots, q\}$. Suppose that the aggregate illfare function of the poor is denoted by F^q, ,where the arguments of F^q are the individual poverty gaps g_i, $i = 1, 2, \ldots, q$. This may be represented by $F^q: \mathbb{R}_+^q \to \mathbb{R}^1$. It is assumed that F^q is continuous, decreasing in x_i's and strictly S-convex.

Now if the poverty line is taken as a reference point, then the magnitude of relative deprivation of the ith individual is g_i[10]. Clearly, with this interpretation the function F^q determines the extent of deprivation for the poor persons as a whole in Runciman's

[10] Townsend(1979) noted that a sizeable proportion of the poor in the United Kingdom regard the poverty line as a reference point.

(1966) sense[11].

What is needed now is a translation of F^q into a poverty index. For this, we define the representative income gap (g_e) of the poor as the gap which, if shared by all the poor would make the existing distribution of income gaps socially indifferent. g_e is implicitly defined by

$$F^q(g_e \cdot 1^q) = F^q(g) \tag{6.50}$$

where $g = (g_1, g_2, \dots, g_q)$.

As a general poverty index we introduce

$$P_{10}(x,\pi) = \frac{q}{n} \cdot \frac{g_e}{\pi} . \tag{6.51}$$

If the weak definition of the poor is adopted, then for a homothetic illfare function F^q, P_{10} is a focussed relative poverty index that satisfies CONT, WM, WT and IMP. P_{10} is the aggregate income gap of the poor which, if equally shared, would yield the same level of deprivation as the actual distribution of gaps generates, expressed as a proportion of the aggregate gap when each member of the population has zero income.

If F^q is given by any increasing transform of $\sum_{i=1}^{q} g_i(q + 1 - i)^{\Theta}$, where $\Theta \geq 0$, then P_{10} in (6.51) becomes the Kakwani(1980b) index. The case $\Theta = 1$ generates the Sen formula. P_{10} becomes the second Clark–Hemming–Ulph index C_α if F^q is of the form $(\sum_{i=1}^{q} g_i^{\alpha-1})$, where $\alpha \geq 2$. (Chakravarty(1983b) presented the general formula (6.51) underlying the Clark–Hemming–Ulph example C_α.)

We can also define an absolute poverty index corresponding to F^q by

11 See Chapter 5 for further discussions.

$$Q_4(x,\pi) = q \cdot g_e \, . \tag{6.52}$$

Q_4 is the aggregate income gap of the poor, which if equally shared, would yield the same level of deprivation as the actual distribution of gaps. When $x_i = 0$, for all $i = 1, \ldots, n$, Q_4 determines the amount of money necessary to put all persons at the poverty line. Given continuity, decresingness and strict S–convexity of F^q, Q_4 is an absolute focussed poverty index that verifies WM and WT (if the weak definition of the poor is assumed).

Lewis and Ulph(1988) made an attempt to measure inequality and poverty by comparing the actual welfare with that which would exist when poverty and inequality have been eliminated. They viewed poverty as the problem of incapability of individuals to participate in some forms of social interaction. In doing so they followed arguments advanced by Townsend(1979), Sen(1983, 1986a) and Desai and Shah(1985). In the framework considered the identical, individual utility function U is assumed to depend on three arguments (α,Z,Θ). α is a perfectly divisible, normal consumption good, giving only private consumption benefits. In their model basic physical survival is not a question, consequently, α 'should be interpreted as consumption beyond physical subsistence requirements'.

The consumption of the second commodity Z not only gives rise to direct satisfaction, but it is also necessary for individual's participation in certain activities that generates extra benefits. It is supposed that for such participation Z has to reach $\underline{Z} > 0$.'.... The benefits arising from participation at $\underline{Z}$ are so great that a deprived individual would be willing to sacrifice all other discretionary consumption to acquire them. As soon as a consumer's income is large enough to make $\underline{Z}$ a feasible choice, it is chosen. In other words what makes Z a poverty good is that not having it is such a severe deprivation for the consumer that they never choose not to purchase it'. Θ is a dummy variable which takes the value 1 or 0 according as the individual participates in the extra activities or not.

$U(\alpha,Z,\Theta)$ is assumed to be increasing and strictly concave in α and Z for $\Theta = 0,1$. In accordance with the arguments put in favor of Z's purchase, $U(0,\underline{Z},1) > U(\alpha,Z,0)$ for all $\alpha \geq 0$, $Z < \underline{Z}$. Also $U(\alpha,Z,1) > U(\alpha,Z,0)$.

The indirect utility function V is then defined as

$$V(p,q,x) = \max_{\substack{\alpha \geq 0,\ Z \geq 0 \\ \Theta \in \{0,1\}}} U(\alpha,Z,\Theta) \tag{6.53}$$

subject to $p\alpha + qZ \leq x$ and $\Theta = 1 \Rightarrow Z \geq \underline{Z}$, where p, q are the (positive) prices of the two goods and x is individual's income. It is also necessary to define the conditional indirect utility functions:

$$V_0(p,q,x) = \max_{\alpha \geq 0,\ Z \geq 0} U(\alpha,Z,0) \text{ subject to } p\alpha + qZ \leq x \ .$$

$$V_1(p,q,x) = \max_{\alpha \geq 0,\ Z \geq \underline{Z}} U(\alpha,Z,1) \text{ subject to } p\alpha + qZ \leq x \ . \tag{6.54}$$

Interestingly enough, $V_1(p,q,q\underline{Z}) = U(0,\underline{Z},1)$. The unconditional indirect utility function V can now be characterised by

$$V(p,q,x) = \begin{cases} V_0(p,q,x) & 0 \leq x \leq q\underline{Z} \\ V_1(p,q,x) & x \geq q\underline{Z} \end{cases} \ . \tag{6.55}$$

Clearly, $q\underline{Z}$ represents the poverty line in this framework.

Since the gap $d(p,q,\underline{Z}) = V_1(p,q,q\underline{Z}) - V_0(p,q,q\underline{Z})$ determines the increment in individual's utility from participation in additional activities, it can be regarded as an index of the extent of deprivation due to being poor. d can be used to define the function

$$\omega(p,q,x) = \begin{cases} V_0(p,q,x) + d(p,q,\underline{Z}) & 0 \leq x \leq q\underline{Z} \\ V_1(p,q,x) & x \geq q\underline{Z} \end{cases} \ . \tag{6.56}$$

Thus, ω measures utility in the absence of any poverty. Clearly, (6.56) enables us to express V in terms of ω and d.

Then assuming that income x is represented by a continuous type distribution function $F:[a,b] \longrightarrow [0,1]$, the actual (average) welfare is given by

$$U^* = \int_a^b V(x)\, dF(x) , \tag{6.57}$$

which, using (6.55) and (6.56), can be written as

$$U^* = \int_a^b \omega(x)\, dF(x) - p^* , \tag{6.58}$$

where p^* is an index of poverty given by the product of the measure of the degree of deprivation, $d(\underline{Z})$, and the proportion of population in poverty – the head–count ratio, P_1. Using the mean income λ, we can rewrite U^* in (6.58) as

$$U^* = \omega(\lambda) - \left[\omega(\lambda) - \int_a^b \omega(x)\, dF(x)\right] - p^* . \tag{6.59}$$

Clearly, $\omega(\lambda)$ measures average welfare in a hypothetical society with the same mean income, but in which poverty and inequality have been eliminated. The term in square brackets on the right hand side of (6.59) is positive whenever the income profile is unequal. Thus, this term, which we denote by I^*, can be regarded as an index of inequality.

We now rewrite (6.59) as

$$U^* = \omega(\lambda) - I^* - p^* . \tag{6.60}$$

Thus, (6.60) reveals how the actual (average) welfare falls short of its ideal level (which could be attained by redistributing incomes equally) because of existence of poverty and inequality.

It is now necessary to distinguish between the following cases: (a) $\lambda \geq q\underline{Z}$, and (b) $\lambda < q\underline{Z}$. With $\lambda \geq q\underline{Z}$, $V(\lambda) = \omega(\lambda)$, and so (6.60) becomes

$$\omega(\lambda) = U^* + I^* + p^* \tag{6.61}$$

(6.61) means that equalisation of incomes will increase aggregate well–being and the equalisation plan will eliminate both poverty and inequality. If $\lambda < q\underline{Z}$, then $V(\lambda) = \omega(\lambda) - d(\underline{Z})$. Consequently,

$$V(\lambda) = \omega(\lambda) + I^* - \left[1 - P_1\right] d(\underline{Z}) . \tag{6.62}$$

Thus, in this case also we can improve social well–being by redistributing incomes equally. But the equalisation plan will make the non–poor persons poor, though inequality is eliminated.

The Lewis–Ulph decomposition of welfare is quite helpful for calculating the percentage contributions made by different components of welfare. But we should note that the development of this model rests on three crucial assumptions: (i) a consumer possesses the basic income necessary for survival, (ii) poverty arises only from non–participation in certain extra activities, (iii) the participation in extra activities is possible only if the consumption of the second commodity does not fall below an a priori level. Clearly, the alternative approaches to the aggregation problem discussed in the chapter have a somewhat different purpose than the Lewis–Ulph model.

CHAPTER 7

ADDITIVELY DECOMPOSABLE INDICES OF POVERTY

7.1 Introduction

Ranking income profiles by summary indices is just a first step in the analysis of poverty. For deeper analysis we should inquire into the factors contributing to poverty using time series or cross–section income data. For carrying out such analysis we need a poverty index that exhibits additive decomposability: for any partitioning of the population, defined along ethnic or geographical or other lines, the total poverty is a weighted average of the subgroup poverty levels. Clearly, this will enable us to calculate a particular subgroup's contribution to total poverty. Hence this type of poverty breakdown becomes suitable for identifying causal factors of poverty and in choosing and implementing poverty alleviation policies.

In Section 3 of this chapter we present a class of additively decomposable poverty indices derived from a normalised aggregate utility gap of the poor assuming an identical, increasing and strictly concave utility function of income. This index is continuous, attaches more weight to income transfers lower down the scale and satisfies other postulates of a poverty index. Furthermore, the index can be easily converted into an index of inequality. This inequality index, when normalised on the closed set [0,1], coincides with the normalised Theil(1967) entropy index in a limiting case. Another class of additively decomposable indices which was suggested by Foster, Greer and Thorbecke (1964) is also discussed in this section. The class satisfies the basic properties of a poverty index and can be justified by a relative deprivation concept of poverty. The inequality index associated with a member of this class is the squared coefficient of variation.

The next section discusses the decomposability axiom. Section 4 makes a numerical illustration of the additively decomposable indices and the Sen(1976a) index using Indian data. Section 5 makes some concluding remarks and a brief discussion on the works of Foster and Shorrocks(1988, 1989a) who considered the problem of ranking income profiles with respect to poverty indices when the poverty line is not fixed.

7.2 Decomposability

Suppose that the population, which is assumed to be of fixed size n, is partitioned into k groups with respect to some characteristic. The income profile $x \in \mathbb{R}^n_+$ can now be written as $x = (x^1, x^2, \ldots, x^k)$, where x^j is the distribution of incomes in subgroup j over the population size n_j ($j = 1, 2, \ldots, k$; $\sum_{j=1}^{k} n_j = n$). Foster–Greer– Thorbecke (FGT) suggested that 'in analysing poverty by population subgroups, the following axiom can be taken as a basic consistency requirement'.

Subgroup Monotonicity Axiom (SUM)

> Let $\hat{x}$ be the vector of incomes obtained from x by changing the incomes in subgroup j from x^j to $\hat{x}^j$, where n_j is unchanged. If $\hat{x}^j$ has more poverty than x^j, then $\hat{x}$ must also have a higher level of poverty than x.

The axiom says that the total poverty should be a strictly increasing function of individual subgroup poverty levels. That is, if incomes of a particular subgroup change (the rest remaining fixed), then subgroup poverty and total poverty should move along the same direction. Thus, SUM is an analogue of the monotonicity axioms discussed in Chapter 6. This property can be regarded as a minor requirement if regional and national policies aiming at poverty alleviation are to be coherent. A poverty index satisfying SUM will be called subgroup consistent. Clearly, the indices of poverty which are based on the ordinal rank weights (e. g., the Sen(1976a) index and its variants proposed by Takayama(1979), Thon(1979) and Kakwani(1980b)) will violate this axiom. Violators of SUM also include the income gap ratio and the general Blackorby – Donaldson(1980a) formula. The head–count ratio and the CHUC particular formula given by (6.36) are two examples that satisfy SUM.

Although SUM can be regarded as a minor logical requirement for poverty indices, it is not of much help in formulating any effective antipoverty policy. This is performed by the additive decomposability postulate, which implies SUM. According to the additive decomposability condition, overall poverty is a weighted average of subgroup poverty levels, where the weights are given by the subgroup population shares[1]. Formally,

Additive Decomposability Axiom (AD)

Let $x \in \mathbb{R}^n_+$ be an income profile broken down into k subgroup income profiles x^1, $x^2, \ldots, x^k$. Then a poverty index $P(x,\pi)$ is additively decomposable with population share weights $\frac{n_i}{n}$; i = 1, 2, ..., k, if

$$P(x,\pi) = \sum_{i=1}^{k} \frac{n_i}{n} P(x^i,\pi), \tag{7.1}$$

where π is the given poverty line.

$\frac{n_s}{n} P(x^s,\pi)$ is the contribution of subgroup s to total poverty, the amount by which national poverty will decrease if poverty in the subgroup is eliminated. $[n_s P(x^s,\pi)/nP(x,\pi)]\cdot 100$ is the percentage contribution of subgroup s to total poverty. Each of these statistics is useful to planners and analysts.

Foster and Shorrocks(1988c) showed the class of subgroup consistent poverty indices, which is continuous, contains only monotonic continuous transformations of continuous additively decomposable indices. Thus, corresponding to each continuous subgroup consistent index there is a continuous additively decomposable poverty index that will rank income profiles in precisely the same way. Hence subgroup consistency provides a means of justifying the use of additively decomposable poverty indices.

7.3 Additively Decomposable Indices of Poverty

7.3.1 An Ethical Approach[2]

Let U stand for the identical, continuous, increasing and strictly concave income

[1] The additive decomposability axiom was proposed independently by Anand(1977), Kakwani(1980), Chakravarty(1983a) and Foster, Greer and Thorbecke(1984).

[2] This approach was developed in Chakravarty(1983a).

utility function. Denote the 'utility gap' $U(\pi) - U(x_i)$ of individual i by h_i. Using the strong definition of the poor, h_i's are non–negative for the poor and negative for others.

For a given income configuration $x \in \mathbb{R}^n_+$, the index of poverty $H(x,\pi)$ is defined as the normalised aggregate utility gap of the poor. That is,

$$H(x,\pi) = A(n,\pi) \sum_{i\in\pi(x)} [U(\pi) - U(x_i)] , \tag{7.2}$$

where $\pi(x)$ is the set of poor in x and $A(n,\pi) > 0$ is the coefficient of normalisation, shown to depend on the population size and the poverty line. Given π, $H(x,\pi)$ can be regarded as a (cardinal) measure of distance separating the income profile of the poor from the social state $\pi \cdot 1^q$, where q is the number of persons in $\pi(x)$.

For deriving the explicit form $H(x,\pi)$, we will impose the following axiom:

Normalisation (NOM)

If all the n–persons in the society have zero income, then the poverty index takes the value unity[3].

Theorem 7.1

For either definition of the poor, the only relative poverty index of the form (7.2) that satisfies NOM is given by

$$H(x,\pi) = \frac{1}{n} \sum_{i\in\pi(x)} [1 - (\frac{x_i}{\pi})^e] , \tag{7.3}$$

where $0 < e < 1$.

Proof

(a) Weak definition of the poor:

Let us assume that $x_1 \leq x_2 \leq ... \leq x_q < \pi \leq x_{q+1} \leq ... \leq x_n$. Now $H(x,\pi)$ in (7.2) satisfying the normalisation axiom gives

[3] This axiom rules out any utility function which is undefined for zero incomes, e. g., a logarithmic utility function.

$$A(n,\pi) = \frac{1}{n[U(\pi) - U(0)]}, \tag{7.4}$$

which on substitution in (7.2) yields

$$H(x,\pi) = \frac{\sum_{i=1}^{q} [U(\pi) - U(x_i)]}{n \cdot [U(\pi) - U(0)]} \tag{7.5}$$

$$= \frac{1}{n} \sum_{i=1}^{q} [1 - \frac{f(x_i)}{f(\pi)}], \tag{7.6}$$

where $f(v) = U(v) - U(0)$.

For $n = 1$ and $0 < x_1 < \pi$, the index in (7.6) is $1 - f(x_1)/f(\pi)$. But $H(x,\pi)$ being a relative index should depend only on x_1/π in such a case. Therefore, $f(v)/f(t)$ is of the form $g(v/t)$ for some continuous function g. This shows that $f(t) = \beta t^e$, where β and e are constants (see Aczél, 1966, p. 144). Increasingness and strict concavity of f require that $\beta > 0$ and $0 < e < 1$. Substituting $U(t) = \alpha + \beta t^e$, where $\alpha = U(0)$, in (7.5) we get the desired form of $H(x,\pi)$. This establishes the necessity part of the theorem. The sufficiency can be verified by checking that $H(x,\pi)$ in (7.3) is a relative index that satisfies NOM.

(b) Strong definition of the poor:
From (7.2) it follows that if all the poor persons are at the poverty line, then the index value is zero. We, therefore, assume in this case that there is at least one poor person whose income is less than the poverty line. The proof then parallels that of part (a) of the theorem. ∎

We will discuss the properties of the index in (7.3) using the strong definition of the poor. The discussion for the weak case can be done in an analogous manner.

<u>Theorem 7.2</u>

Assuming the strong definition of the poor, the poverty index $H(x,\pi)$ in (7.3) satisfies the following postulates: Independence of the Incomes of the Rich (IIR), Continuity (CONT), Impartiality (IMP), Increasingness in Subsistence Income

(ISI), Weak Monotonicity (WM), Strong Upward Transfer (SUT), Weak Diminishing Transfer (WDT) and Additive Decomposability (AD).

Proof

Continuity of H follows from continuity of U. It is obvious that H satisfies IIR, ISI, WM, IMP and AD. When $0 < e < 1$, H embodies an SEF which is strictly concave in the incomes of the poor, and WT is satisfied. This along with continuity of H shows that it satisfies SUT (see Theorem 6.2). The change in H due to a transfer of income between two individuals depends on the difference in the marginal utilities of the individuals concerned. Therefore, H satisfies WDT. ∎

The poverty index H possesses some additional properties:
(i) It lies in the interval [0,1], the lower limit is attained in the case when there is no person below the poverty line and the upper limit in the extreme case described in NOM.

(ii) H remains invariant under affine transformations of U.

(iii) For a given x and π, H increases as e increases. As $e \longrightarrow 0$, $H \longrightarrow 0$ and for $e \longrightarrow 1$, H approaches P_1P_2, the product of head-count ratio and the income gap ratio. As e decreases over the interval (0,1), H becomes more sensitive to income transfers lower down the scale. $(e - 1)$, it may be noted, is the constant elasticity of marginal utility with respect to income. Thus, the Arrow(1971)–Pratt(1964) measure of relative risk aversion takes a constant value for the utility function underlying the poverty index in (7.3)[4].

(iv) When H is applied to the entire income profile in the sense that n replaces q, the population mean $\lambda(x) > 0$ replaces π, we obtain the following relative inequality index:

$$H^n(x) = \frac{1}{n} \sum_{i=1}^{n} [1 - (\frac{x_i}{\lambda(x)})^e] \ . \tag{7.7}$$

For $0 < e < 1$, $0 \leq H^n(x) < 1$, where the lower bound is achieved in the case of perfect equality. Clearly, H^n satisfies the diminishing transfers principle of inequality. We can normalise H^n on the closed interval [0,1] assuming that it takes the value unity when the

4 The Arrow–Pratt measure of relative risk aversion is minus one time the elasticity of marginal utility of income. This meaasure determines how averse the individual is to a risky outcome. The Arrow–Pratt absolute risk aversion measure is obtained by dividing the relative measure with income.

richest individual monopolises the entire income. The normalised index is given by

$$\frac{1}{1 - n^{e-1}} \sum_{i=1}^{n} [1 - (\frac{x_i}{\lambda(x)})^{e}] \; . \qquad (7.8)$$

As $e \longrightarrow 1$, the inequality index in (7.8) approaches $\frac{1}{n\log n} \sum_{i=1}^{n} \frac{x_i}{\lambda(x)} \cdot \log \frac{x_i}{\lambda(x)}$, the normalised Theil(1967) entropy index. Thus, we have a normative characterisation of the Theil inequality formula.

7.3.2 The Foster – Greer – Thorbecke Index

FGT presented the following parametric family of poverty indices:

$$G_\alpha(x,\pi) = \frac{1}{n} \sum_{i \in \pi(x)} (\frac{g_i}{\pi})^{\alpha-1} \, , \qquad (7.9)$$

where $x \in \mathbb{R}^n_+$, $g_i = \pi - x_i$ and $\alpha \geqq 1$. Clearly, using the either definition of the poor, G_α is a focussed relative poverty index which is increasing in π, symmetric in incomes and jointly continuous in (x,π) for all $\alpha > 1$. When α takes on the value 1, the head–count ratio P_1 is obtained. When $\alpha = 2$, G_α becomes P_1P_2. Using the strong definition of the poor, G_α satisfies WM for $\alpha > 1$, SUT for $\alpha > 2$ and WDT for $\alpha > 3$. G_α satisfies AD for all permissible values of α. When the poverty line is taken as a reference point, the poverty index G_α can be regarded as an index of average deprivation for the poor persons in the sense of Runciman(1966). (For arguments leading to such interpretations of G_α, see Chapters 5 and 6.)

For $\alpha \geqq 2$, $G_\alpha(x,\pi)$ is related the second Clark – Hemming – Ulph poverty index $C_\alpha(x,\pi)$ in the following way[5]:

$$G_\alpha(x,\pi) = (P_1)^{2-\alpha} (C_\alpha(x,\pi))^{\alpha-1} \; . \qquad (7.10)$$

[5] For a discussion on C_α, see Chapter 6, Section 6.5.

This shows that for income profiles on which the head–count ratio P_1 is constant, the ranking of profiles generated by G_α will be the same as that generated by C_α. Moreover, G_α coincides with C_α when α takes on the value 2.

For $\alpha = 3$, G_α is closely related to a well–known inequality index in the same way as the Sen index is related to the Gini coefficient:

$$G_3(x,\pi) = P_1[(P_2)^2 + (1 - P_2)^2(C_p^q)^2] , \tag{7.11}$$

where C_p^q is the coefficient of variation among the poor. This implies that over the income profiles with the same number of poor and the same mean income of the poor, the ranking of profiles generated by G_3 is the same as that generated by $(C_p^q)^2$.

It may be noted that the following inequality index can be derived from G_α by replacing q, the number of poor persons, by n and the poverty line π by $\lambda(x) > 0$, the mean of the income profile x:

$$F_\alpha^n(x) = \frac{1}{n}\sum_{i=1}^{n}\left|\frac{\lambda(x) - x_i}{\lambda(x)}\right|^{\alpha-1} . \tag{7.12}$$

For $\alpha = 1$, F_α^n takes a constant value of 1. When $\alpha = 2$, F_α^n becomes the relative mean deviation. If α takes on the value 3, the squared coefficient of variation is obtained. Obviously, F_α^n satisfies the Pigou–Dalton transfers principle for all $\alpha > 2$ and the diminishing transfers principle whenever $\alpha \in (3,\infty)$. As α increases more weight is attached to transfers lower down the scale. For $\alpha > 1$, the monotonic transformation $\bar{F}_\alpha^n$ defined by $\bar{F}_\alpha^n(x) = (F_\alpha^n(x))^{1/(\alpha-1)}$, generates the following relative inequality index:

$$\bar{F}_\alpha^n(x) = \left[\frac{1}{n}\sum_{i=1}^{n}\left|\frac{\lambda(x) - x_i}{\lambda(x)}\right|^{\alpha-1}\right]^{\frac{1}{\alpha - 1}} . \tag{7.13}$$

$\bar{F}^n$ preserves all the properties of F^n and has the additional advantage of being a compromise relative index[6]. Consequently, $\bar{F}^n$ can be converted into a family of absolute inequality indices by multiplying it by the mean income $\lambda(x)$. As $\alpha \to \infty$, $\bar{F}^n_\alpha(x) \to \max_i \left| \frac{\lambda(x) - x_i}{\lambda(x)} \right|$, the relative maximin index. As $\alpha \to 1$, $\bar{F}^n \to \left[\prod_{i=1}^{n} | x_i - \lambda | \right]^{1/n} / \lambda(x)$, the relative geometric mean deviation. On multiplication with the mean $\lambda(x)$, this becomes the absolute geometric mean deviation.

7.4 Empirical Estimation of Poverty Indices from Grouped Data

The numerical illustration provided in this section is based on a special tabulation of NSS 28th round (October 1973 – June 1974) household budget data for rural India carried out by Pal, Chakravarty and Bhattacharya(1986) using a copy of the updated Honeywell tape supplied by the authorities of the NSS organisation, Government of India. The data were collected by the interview method through a 'consumer expenditure inquiry' schedule. A probability sample of households was drawn from practically the whole of India and each household was interviewed for collecting data on expenditure on all items of consumption during the last '30 days' preceding the data of inquiry. Consumption consisted of consumption of goods and services out of (a) purchases in cash and credit, (b) receipts in exchange of goods and services, (c) home–grown stock and (d) transfer receipts like gifts, loans, free collections etc..

The rural population of the country has been divided into groups by states, and groupwise and overall poverty indices were computed to create a profile of poverty, revealing those groups which are most afflicted by poverty. As the relevant sample sizes were small, poverty estimation had to be given up for the Union Territories of Delhi, Chandigarh, Pandichery and Goa, Daman and Diu. However, all these regions were included in the assessment of poverty for the entire rural population of the country.

The population has also been divided into subgroups using the following socio–economic characteristics (i) social groups, (ii) occupations, (iii) size classes of land possessed for poverty analysis. Information on these characteristics was collected in the inquiry on consumer expenditure. The partitioning of the population with respect to the 'social groups' category has been done as follows: (a) Scheduled Castes (SC), (b) Scheduled

---

6 An axiomatic characterisation of $\bar{F}^n$ can be found in Ebert(1988b).

Tribes (ST), (c) 'Other' Hindus, (d) 'Other' Muslims and (e) 'Others' comprising the remaining sections of the population. At the stage of tabulation, it was found that some non–Hindu households had reported themselves as SC. Actually, according to the instructions issued to the field workers, only Hindu and Sikh households could be put in the SC category. In the present study, for the sake of simplicity, only Hindu SC households have been considered as forming the SC social group; the remaining SC households have been included in group (d) or (e) depending on their religion. The Other Hindus category was formed by excluding from all Hindu households those households which belonged to either SC or ST; and the other Muslims, by considering Muslim households which did not belong to ST. It should be mentioned that the social groups SC and ST are recognised in the Indian constitution as economically and socially depressed classes, and the Government of India follows a policy of reservation of educational facilities, employment prospects etc. for them.

The codes given for household principal occupation as per National Classification of Occupations (Government of India, Central Statistical Organisation, 1968) for India have been employed to divide all households into eight occupation groups: (i) professional, technical, administrative, executive, managerial, clerical and related workers, (ii) sales workers, (iii) service workers, (iv) cultivators (owners), (v) cultivators (tenants), (vi) agricultural labourers, (vii) other agricultural workers, and (viii) production, transport and related workers. Approximately half of the rural population turned out to belong to owner cultivator households, with agricultural labourers making up the next largest number.

Finally, the rural population was partitioned by size classes of 'land possessed by household' defined as the total land owned by the household plus land leased in (homestead land is included) minus land leased out. Seven size classes of land possessed were chosen after some experiments.

There has been some debate over the issues relating to the selection of an appropriate poverty line for India. In 1962, a distinguished study group of the Government of India recommended per capita monthly consumption expenditure (PCE) of Rs. 20.00 at 1960–61 all India prices as representing a 'minimum level of living'[7]. It has been a common practice in Indian studies on poverty to adopt this value of PCE as the all India

[7] The study group, while recommending the minimum PCE of Rs. 20.00 excluded health and education, both of which were expected to be provided by the state.

poverty line. Unfortunately, the basis of this magic figure of Rs. 20.00 is obscure (see Rudra(1974), for a critical examination).

Bardhan(1971) adopted PCE = Rs. 15.00 at 1960–61 rural prices as the poverty line for rural India, considering that rural prices tend to be lower than urban prices and derived separate poverty lines for rural areas of different states at 1960–61 prices utilising the interstate price differential indices estimated by Chatterjee and Bhattacharya (1974).[8] More precisely, he averaged the Fisher price indices for the two bottom quintile groups of the rural population of each state with prices faced by the corresponding quintile groups of rural India as bases estimated by Chatterjee and Bhattacharya. He then used such averages to adjust the all India rural poverty line of Rs. 15.00 at 1960–61 prices to get the poverty lines for rural areas of different states.

The present study being based on NSS 28th round household budget data relating to the period October 1973 – June 1974, the statewise rural poverty lines at 1960–61 prices used by Bardhan were expressed at NSS 28th round prices using the average monthly value of the statewise Consumer Price Index (CPI) numbers for Agricultural Labourers (published by the Government of India Labour Bureau) during the 28th round period. This is the most appropriate series of CPI numbers for the rural poor in India and has been frequently used for similar studies (vide Bardhan(1971), Ahluwalia(1978))[9].

Numerical estimates of poverty for different partitionings of the rural India population are now presented in Tables 7.1 – 7.4, the formats of which are identical. The first column gives the partitioning of the population with respect to a characteristic. The second column presents the proportion of total population in different subgroups, whereas the third column reports the mean income of the poor within each subgroup. The fourth column gives the numerical values of the head–count ratio P_1, which is equal to the proportion of all households living in poverty. The figures in parantheses in this column are the number of sample households in different groups. In columns 5 and 6 we present respectively the Gini index and the squared coefficient of variation of the poor.

[8] The Chatterjee–Bhattacharya indices were based on NSS 18th round household budget data relating to the year 1963–64; Bardhan assumed this pattern of interstate consumer price differentials to hold for the year 1960–61 also.

[9] The CPI for Agricultural Labourers for Assam covers Manipur, Tripura and Meghalaya in addition to Assam. Similarly, there is one index for the Punjab, Haryana, Himachal Pradesh and Delhi. In each case, therefore, the same poverty line is used for all the states/union territories covered in a composite CPI number.

The computed values of the Sen index, the FGT index G_α (for $\alpha = 2$) and the ethical index H given by (7.2) (for e = 0.5) are reported in columns 7, 8 and 9 respectively. The subgroup poverty levels (as determined by P_1, G_α and H) are now weighted by the corresponding population shares to determine the contributions of different subgroups to total poverty, which are given as percentages of total poverty in columns 10 – 12. Complete elimination of poverty within a subgroup would lower aggregate poverty precisely by the percentage by which it contributes to total poverty.

It may be mentioned that different poverty lines were used for different states for the table using state as a classification on the ground that in doing so we are really correcting the PCEs for price variation across states. Clearly, the additive decomposability relation remains valid in this case also because the ratios x_i/π and g_i/π remain unaltered when x_i's and π are deflated by the same price index number measuring the price level of the state relative to the all India price level. For Tables 7.2 – 7.4 only the all India (rural) poverty line was used and all PCEs have been expressed at all India rural prices of the poor using the Chatterjee – Bhattacharya Fisher price indices for the two bottom quintile groups of the rural population.

Table 7.1 presents the different indices of poverty for the rural areas of the states. Three of the poorest states (West Bengal, Bihar and Orissa) are in the eastern region. West Bengal is the worst off among these with nearly 70% of the rural population below the poverty line. The picture is also dismal for several other states like Kerala, Madhya Pradesh and Uttar Pradesh, where about half of the population existed under the subsistence level. As is well–known some of the relatively prosperous states e. g., Haryana and the Punjab are found to be in the north–western region of the country.

The ranking of states by H agree very well with that based on G_α or P_1. The same can be said about the ranking by P_3. Spearman's rank correlation coefficient is about 0.98 between the head–count ratio and P_3 or G_α, while that between P_3 and H is about 0.99.

The last column of Table 7.1 shows that the three poorest states, namely, West Bengal, Orissa and Bihar, all of which are in the eastern region, constitute 24% of total population and report 31.2% of the poor in rural India judged by P_1. Their contribution

Table 7.1: Measures of poverty for the rural population in India, by states (October 1973 – June 1874).

State (Poverty line)	Percentage of all India rural population	Head-count ratio P_1 (Number of sample households)	Mean PCE of the poor	Gini index of the poor	Squared coefficient of variation of the poor	Alternative indices of poverty: Sen's index P_3	FGT index G_α ($\alpha = 2$)	The ethical index H (e = .5)	Percentage contributions to total poverty based on: P_1	G_α	H
(1)	(2)	(3)	(4)	(5)	(6)	(7)	(8)	(9)	(10)	(11)	(12)
Andhra Pradesh (Rs.37.82)	7.9	.395 (1236)	28.60	.126	.055	.134	.036	.054	6.3	5.3	5.5
Assam (Rs.43.83)	2.9	.386 (600)	34.55	.101	.042	.113	.028	.045	2.3	1.5	1.7
Bihar (Rs.55.28)	11.1	.603 (1288)	38.09	.147	.076	.248	.080	.108	13.7	16.7	15.5
Gujrat (Rs.42.11)	4.4	.351 (530)	33.38	.096	.036	.100	.023	.040	3.1	1.9	2.3
Haryana (Rs.44.52)	1.9	.275 (603)	35.52	.085	.033	.074	.017	.031	1.1	0.6	0.7
Himachal Pradesh (Rs.44.52)	0.8	.183 (394)	36.44	.080	.038	.045	.011	.018	0.3	0.2	0.2
Jammu and Kashmir (Rs.40.68)	0.4	.336 (657)	33.00	.091	.032	.088	.019	.035	0.3	0.1	0.2

Table 7.1 (Contd.)

(1)	(2)	(3)	(4)	(5)	(6)	(7)	(8)	(9)	(10)	(11)	(12)
Karnataka (Rs.43.56)	5.1	.488 (621)	31.88	.114	.047	.172	.048	.074	5.1	4.6	4.8
Kerala (Rs.45.79)	4.3	.503 (645)	31.81	.142	.071	.204	.064	.088	4.4	5.2	4.9
Madhya Pradesh (Rs.45.14)	8.2	.561 (1320)	32.11	.126	.057	.212	.063	.092	9.4	9.7	9.8
Maharashtra (Rs.44.39)	7.9	.466 (1135)	32.56	.115	.048	.163	.045	.070	7.5	6.7	7.1
Manipur (Rs.43.83)	0.2	.369 (222)	35.55	.085	.030	.095	.021	.038	0.2	0.1	0.1
Meghalaya (Rs.43.83)	0.2	.219 (225)	35.01	.108	.066	.064	.018	.026	0.1	0.1	0.1
Orissa (Rs.41.57)	4.7	.611 (671)	29.17	.137	.062	.241	.073	.104	5.9	6.5	6.4
Punjab (Rs.44.52)	2.5	.179 (670)	36.89	.059	.023	.040	.008	.017	0.9	0.4	0.5
Rajasthan (Rs.42.68)	4.9	.289 (613)	32.91	.101	.039	.089	.022	.037	2.9	2.0	2.3
Tamil Nadu (Rs.41.27)	6.4	.495 (910)	29.89	.125	.052	.131	.051	.077	6.4	6.2	6.3

Table 7.1 (Contd.)

(1)	(2)	(3)	(4)	(5)	(6)	(7)	(8)	(9)	(10)	(11)	(12)
Tripura (Rs.43.83)	0.3	.435 (187)	33.97	.103	.042	.133	.033	.054	0.3	0.2	0.2
Uttar Pradesh (Rs.45.61)	17.7	.506 (1784)	34.46	.098	.039	.161	.042	.069	18.2	13.8	15.7
West Bengal (Rs.52.01)	8.2	.695	33.07	.170	.095	.328	.119	.148	11.6	18.2	15.8
All-India rural (Rs.43.57)	100.0	.491 .461* (15341) (15452)*	32.00*	.127*	.165*	.054*	.051 .046*	.077 .069*	100.0	100.0	100.0

Note: The starred figures for all India rural in Table 7.1 indicate the values of the indices when one poverty line (that is, Rs. 43.57) is used for the entire country. These estimates take into account the Union Territories of Chandigarh, Delhi, Pondichery and Goa, Daman and Diu. For all other figures statewise poverty lines were used.

to overall poverty rises to 37.7% (41.4%) if one uses H (G_α). The higher contribution of these three states according to H or G_α is partly due to higher than average Gini index or squared coefficient of variation of PCE among the poor for these three states. Madhya Pradesh and Uttar Pradesh come next in the ranking by percentage contributions by P_1. The five states taken together account for about half of the rural population and for about 59% of the total poverty according to P_1 and for about 62 – 63% of total poverty by H.

In Table 7.2 the entire population in rural India is disaggregated according to social groups. The SC and ST are by far the poorest among the groups, followed by other Muslims who are somewhat poorer than the general (all–groups) level. Other Hindus are somewhat better off than the average while others are the most prosperous of the five social groups. If one pools SC and other Hindus one gets a head–count ratio of about 0.446. Some Hindus are still left out, being in the ST group. Clearly, all Hindus taken together would have poverty measures close to the general level. The ranking of social groups by H agrees completely with that generated by G_α or P_3. This ranking is very close to that produced by P_1.

From column 10 of Table 7.2 we see that of the poor in rural India 23.1% belonged to ST who made up of 17.3% of the population. According to G_α (H) the SC and ST taken together contributed nearly 43% (41%) to total poverty. In contrast other Hindus who constituted 58% of the population contributed about 50% to total poverty according to P_1 and about 45% according to H.

The breakdown of the rural India population according to size classes of land possessed is presented in Table 7.3. It is obserbed that the landed households possessing less than one acre (and more than 0.005 acre) of land appear to be the poorest with about 58% of the population in them lying below the poverty line. Interestingly, landless households are somewhat better off with the head–count ratio about 53%. There is a clear trend in poverty over the size classes. For landed households, as one moves to higher size classes of land possessed, the incidence of poverty decreases. Thus, P_1 falls to about 25% for households possessing 15 acres or more of land.

When we come to the question of ranking of alternative size classes by poverty

Table 7.2: Measures of poverty for the rural population in India, by social groups (October 1973 – June 1974).

Social group	Percentage of all India rural population	Head-count ratio P_1 (Number of sample households)	Mean PCE of the poor	Gini index of the poor	Squared coefficient of variation of the poor	Alternative indices of poverty			Percentage contributions to total poverty based on		
						Sen's index P_3	FGT index G_α ($\alpha = 2$)	The ethical index H (e = .5)	P_1	G_α	H
(1)	(2)	(3)	(4)	(5)	(6)	(7)	(8)	(9)	(10)	(11)	(12)
Scheduled Caste	17.3	.656 (2669)	30.01	.147	.071	.271	.086	.117	23.1	28.1	26.3
Scheduled Tribe	9.4	.649 (1614)	30.11	.140	.064	.264	.082	.114	12.7	14.7	14.1
Other Hindus	58.2	.422 (8311)	32.77	.120	.049	.143	.038	.059	49.4	41.7	44.5
Other Muslims	9.5	.532 (1670)	31.22	.142	.066	.205	.061	.086	10.7	11.1	10.7
Others	5.6	.387 (1077)	31.70	.137	.061	.144	.041	.060	4.1	4.4	4.4
All groups	100.0	.492 (15341)	31.59	.134	.059	.183	.053	.077	100.0	100.0	100.0

Table 7.3: Measures of poverty for the rural population in India, by size classes of land possessed (October 1973 – June 1974).

Land possessed (in acres)	Percentage of all India rural population	Head-count ratio P_1 (Number of sample households)	Mean PCE of the poor	Gini index of the poor	Squared coefficient of variation of the poor	Alternative indices of poverty			Percentage contributions to total poverty based on		
						Sen's index P_3	FGT index G_α ($\alpha = 2$)	The ethical index H (e = .5)	P_1	G_α	H
(1)	(2)	(3)	(4)	(5)	(6)	(7)	(8)	(9)	(10)	(11)	(12)
Landless (< .005)	3.7	.652 (681)	30.13	.152	.075	.232	.074	.099	4.1	5.1	4.8
.005 - 1.00	31.8	.623 (5477)	29.80	.152	.075	.262	.084	.113	40.0	50.8	46.9
1.00 - 2.50	16.6	.544 (2705)	32.24	.126	.053	.192	.053	.080	18.6	16.6	17.2
2.50 - 5.00	17.5	.455 (2727)	33.34	.108	.040	.145	.036	.059	16.4	12.0	13.6
5.00 - 7.50	10.8	.387 (1467)	33.13	.114	.043	.126	.032	.052	8.8	6.6	7.3
7.50 - 15.00	11.2	.356 (1399)	33.47	.103	.037	.111	.027	.046	8.0	5.8	6.7
15.00 -	8.4	.257 (885)	33.88	.111	.043	.079	.019	.032	4.1	3.1	3.5
All classes	100.0	.492 (15341)	31.59	.134	.059	.183	.053	.077	100.0	100.0	100.0

Table 7.4: Measures of poverty for the rural population in India, by occupational groups (October 1973 – June 1974).

Household occupation	Percentage of all India rural population	Head-count ratio P_1 (Number of sample households)	Mean PCE of the poor	Gini index of the poor	Squared coefficient of variation of the poor	Alternative indices of poverty			Percentage contributions to total poverty based on		
						Sen's index P_3	FGT index G_α ($\alpha = 2$)	The ethical index H (e = .5)	P_1	G_α	H
(1)	(2)	(3)	(4)	(5)	(6)	(7)	(8)	(9)	(10)	(11)	(12)
Professional, technical and related administrative, executive and managerial workers, clerical and related workers	3.1	.292 (555)	33.03	.119	.047	.097	.025	.039	1.8	1.5	1.6
Sales workers	2.8	.431 (455)	32.60	.129	.057	.150	.041	.061	2.4	2.2	2.2
Service workers	1.7	.558 (296)	31.61	.133	.063	.207	.061	.087	1.9	1.9	1.9
Cultivators (owners)	52.9	.387 (7580)	33.49	.109	.041	.122	.030	.050	42.6	30.4	34.4
Cultivators (tenants)	1.7	.564 (255)	31.77	.134	.058	.208	.059	.086	1.9	1.9	1.9
Agricultural labourers	25.9	.707 (4025)	29.43	.151	.074	.302	.098	.132	36.7	48.4	44.6

Tabelle 7.4 (Contd.)

(1)	(2)	(3)	(4)	(5)	(6)	(7)	(8)	(9)	(10)	(11)	(12)
Other agriculture, fishermen, hunters, loggers and related workers	2.2	.604 (383)	29.97	.142	.066	.248	.078	.108	2.6	3.3	3.1
Production and related workers, transport, equipment operators and labourers	7.9	.526 (1319)	31.91	.133	.059	.192	.054	.080	8.4	8.2	8.3
Non-response	1.8	.495 (473)	30.47	.157	.081	.203	.064	.086	1.7	2.2	2.0
All occupations		.492 (15341)	31.59	.134	.059	.183	.053	.077	100.0	100.0	100.0

indices, we observe that P_3, G_α and H depict a similar picture. Households with small landholdings (0.005 – 1.00 acre) having about 32% of the total population contributed 46% to total poverty according to H. In fact, the three poorest size classes, namely, the landless households and households possessing upto 2.5 acres of land account for 68% (73%) of total poverty according to H (G_α) and 63% of the same according to P_1, as against 52% of the total population in rural India. The contribution of 'landless households' taken separately is, however, quite small, mainly because such households covered only 3.7% of the rural population.

Next, the decomposition of poverty according to household occupation is considered. Table 7.4 shows that agricultural labourers were the poorest (P_1 = 0.67) among the occupational classes covered in the table, followed by 'other agricultural households', 'tenant cultivators' and 'service workers'. The poorest group is also seen to possess the minimum mean PCE among all groups. The ranking of groups by H is very close to that generated by G_α. The rankings generated by G_α and H deviate from that produced by P_3.

From Table 7.4 we see that households of agricultural labourers showing the highest head–count ratio formed about 26% of the rural population and included nearly 37% of the poor. Their contribution to rural poverty by H is 44%. But the cultivators (owners) who made up 53% of the total population accounted for 35% of total poverty by H.

7.5 Concluding Remarks

In this chapter we have discussed indices of poverty that are additively decomposable in the sense that for any partitioning of the population the overall poverty index is a weighted average of subgroup poverty indices. Thus, we can identify the subgroups that are most susceptible to poverty and implement policies for the reduction of poverty. A numerical illustration of such indices using Indian data has also been presented.

The axiomatic poverty indices are certainly a major advance on ad hoc poverty indices. But the alternative approaches discussed in Chapters 6 and 7 pre–suppose that the poverty line is given. It is not quite unreasonable to claim that the choice of the poverty line is done arbitrarily. Therefore, it will be interesting to look at the rankings of income profiles generated by different poverty indices when the poverty line is not fixed.

Two pioneering articles by Foster and Shorrocks(1988, 1988a) can be regarded as the first step in this direction. Rather than the complete ordering generated by a poverty index with a fixed poverty line, they consider the partial ordering generated by allowing the poverty line to vary. Symbolically, given any poverty index P and two income profiles $x,y \in \mathbb{R}^n_+$, we say that x has unambigously less poverty than y, written x P y, if $P(x,\pi) \leqq P(y,\pi)$ for all $\pi > 0$, with strict inequality for some π.

Foster and Shorrocks(1988) studied the partial orderings generated by the members of the FGT class G_α. They showed that the poverty ordering generated by G_α is equivalent to the αth degree stochastic dominanee condition, where $\alpha > 0$ can take any integral value. Thus, when income profiles are represented by distribution functions, for $\alpha = 1$ an unambiguous poverty rankings by a pair of distributions occurs if and only if one of the distribution functions point–wise dominates the other. For $\alpha = 2$ the induced poverty ordering corresponds to the generalised Lorenz ranking. Clearly, the close relationship between stochastic dominance and utilitarian welfare orderings will lead to very interesting welfare interpretations of the poverty orderings generated by the members of the FGT class[10].

Foster and Shorrocks(1988a) provided an extensive examination of the orderings generated by G_α in the context of discrete profiles for α taking on the value 1, 2 and 3. In this case connections between poverty orderings and general types of SEFs which are <u>not</u> necessarily additively separable can be established. For example, x G_1 y holds if and only if x is preferred to y by all symmetric, increasing SEFs. Again, x G_2 y is equivalent to the condition that x is regarded as better than y by all increasing, strictly S–concave SEFs. Finally, the ordering generated by G_3 coincides with that generated by all SEFs which are increasing, strictly S–concave, and transfer sensitive in the sense that they emphasize transfers at lower income levels. By assuming that the SEFs are population replication invariant these results can be used for comparing income profiles over differing population sizes also. In view of the above discussion we can conclude that the selection of a particular member from the FGT family automatically specifies how one

[10] A detailed discussion on these relationships can be found in Chapter 3 (Section 3.5).

has decided to evaluate alternative income profiles of the poor using an SEF[11].

[11] Anand and Kanbur(1975) used the FGT index to study the poverty implications of the development models put forward by Kuznets(1955) and Todaro(1969). Taking explicit account of the budget constraint and technology, Besley and Kanbur(1988) used this index for reallocating food subsidy in a manner that would reduce poverty. Also see Kanbur(1986) and Kanbur and Keen(1988) for application of the FGT formula to related problems. Greer and Thorbecke(1986) provided a numerical illustration of the formula using Kenyan data.

CHAPTER 8

MEASUREMENT OF TAX PROGRESSIVITY AND HORIZONTAL INEQUITY

8.1 Introduction

Various economic decisions taken by the government affect us in several ways. The taxation principle adopted by the government is an appropriate example of this. An important job is, therefore, to look at the degree of progression of the tax structure. Traditionally, a fiscal system is qualified as progressive if the average rate of taxation increases with income before tax. Equivalently, we say that the elasticity of income after tax with respect to income before tax is less than unity at all income levels. But these indices are local indices of progression. Such indices measure the deviation from proportionality of the tax function at a particular income level. On the other hand, '... effective progression measures the extent to which a given tax structure results in a shift in the distribution of income toward equality' (Musgrave and Thin(1948)). In Section 3 of this chapter we propose an ethical index of global tax progressivity that measures shifts in the income profile toward equality caused by the tax system taken as a whole. This index is constructed by comparing the welfare value (as measured by the sum of identical individual utility functions) of the actual post–tax income profile with the welfare value of the hypothetical income profile that would arise if the same aggregate amount of tax were realised through a proportional tax rule. Consequently, a tax system will be regarded as progressive by this index if the actual post–tax income profile strictly Lorenz dominates the hypothetical post–tax income profile. In a limiting situation the index equals the proportionate gap between the Theil(1967) entropy index of inequality of the pre–tax income profile and that of the post–tax income profile. For completeness and also for preparing the background for constructing the ethical index in Section 3, we discuss the Musgrave – Thin(1948) indices of local tax progressivity and their consistency in terms of the Lorenz quasi–ordering in Section 2.

A tax rule may alter the ranking of individuals within the income profile. This particular effect of a tax system corresponds to horizontal inequity. We should be aware of the extent of this negative effect. Thus, we need useful indicators of the magnitude of h-orizontal inequity. Section 4 of this chapter discusses ethical indices for the measurement of 'relative' and 'absolute' horizontal inequity. These indices determine respectively the fraction of total ex–post income and the per capita ex–post income that could be saved without any welfare loss if society eliminated all changes in ranking. The relative indices proposed are a generalisation of King's(1983) index of horizontal inequity. In Section 5 we discuss alternative indices of tax progressivity and horizontal inequity. Section 7 discusses the impact of strict convexity of a tax schedule on disaggregation of income into different components, the revenue responsiveness effect of a fiscal scheme and the Blackorby–Donaldson(1984b) ethical indices of benefit and net tax/benefit progressivity.

8.2 Indices of Local Progression

The purpose of this section is to discuss alternative point measures of tax progression and their consistency with the Lorenz quasi–ordering.

We write $x_i \in D^1$ for the 'taxable income' of individual i in a community of n persons. We do not wish to make here any discussion of what constitutes the proper basis of taxation. The topic has been discussed extensively in the public finance literature. The vector $x = (x_1, x_2, \dots, x_n) \in D^n$ will stand for the vector of taxable incomes in the community under consideration[1]. Let $t_i = f(x_i)$ be the tax owed on x_i, where $f: D^1 \to \mathbb{R}^1$ is the tax schedule. f will be called feasible or income positive if net incomes are positive under f. More precisely, a tax method $f: D^1 \to \mathbb{R}^1$ is said to be feasible if for all $z \in D^1$, $f(z) < z$. Throughout this chapter we will assume that f is feasible. We do not restrict ourselves to positive taxes and f(z) may be considered as either a tax or an allowance/ subsidy. The post tax income vector associated with $x \in D^n$ is denoted by $y \in D^n$. Obviously, $y = x - t$, where t stands for the vector of taxes $(t_1, t_2, \dots, t_n)$. In this section we will assume that the tax function t is incentive preserving – after–tax income is an increasing function of before–tax income. Clearly, this condition preserves incentive for the individuals to earn a higher income (see Fei(1981)).

A tax schedule f is progressive if f(z)/z is increasing in z, it is flat or proportional if

[1] Since we assume positivity of x_i for all $i = 1, 2, \dots, n$, strictly speaking we restrict our attention to the positive part of D^n.

f(z)/z is constant, and it is <u>regressive</u> if f(z)/z is decreasing in z. The fraction f(z)/z is popularly known as the <u>average tax rate</u>.

Let us now assume that the tax function f is twice continuously differentiable. The four local measures of tax progression suggested by Musgrave and Thin(1948) are then defined as:

(i) Average rate progression (the derivative of the average tax rate with respect to income before tax):

$$AP(z|f) = \frac{d}{dz}\left(\frac{f(z)}{z}\right).$$

(ii) Marginal rate progression (the derivative of the marginal tax rate with respect to income before tax):

$$MP(z|f) = \frac{d}{dz}\left(\frac{df(z)}{dz}\right).$$

(iii) Liability progression (elasticity of tax liability with respect to income before tax):

$$LP(z|f) = \frac{df(z)}{dz} \cdot \frac{z}{f(z)}.$$

(iv) Residual income progression (elasticity of income after tax with respect to income before tax):

$$RP(z|f) = \frac{d[z - f(z)]}{dz} \cdot \frac{z}{z - f(z)}.$$

AP and MP, record the rates of increase of the average tax rate and the marginal tax rate respectively. On the other hand, LP (RP) measures the percentage increase in tax liability (after–tax income) when before–tax income increases by one percent.

It is now necessary to verify whether each of the above measures is compatible with the basic definition of a progressive tax system –'any progressive tax is by each measure considered 'more progressive' than a proportional tax' (Jakobsson(1976)). In our notation the tax function f is progressive in the traditional sense if the index

$$AP(z|f) = \frac{1}{z}[f'(z) - \frac{f(z)}{z}] \qquad (8.1)$$

is positive for all $z > 0$, where f' is the derivative of f. The term in square brackets on the right hand side of (8.1) gives the excess of the marginal tax rate $f'(z)$ over the average tax rate $f(z)/z$. Positivity of (8.1) implies that $zf'(z)/f(z) > 1$ for $f(z) > 0$. Thus, liability progression is compatible with the basic definition of progressivity for positive taxes. Using positivity of (8.1) we also get $[z - zf'(z)]/[z - f(z)] < 1$, under feasibility of f. Thus, a tax rule is progressive with respect to residual progression whenever it is progressive with respect to average rate progression[2]. Increasingness of $f(z)/z$ only implies that $f'(z) > f(z)/z$. This, however, does not guarantee that $MP(z|f)$ is compatible with the basic notion of progression[3].

As expected, the different indices may rank alternative tax schedules in different manners (see Pfähler(1984) and Pfingsten(1986a)). One way of seeking a resolution to this conflict, at least partially, is to relate these indices to the concept of redistribution that arises through the Lorenz quasi–ordering. Now, with non–intersecting Lorenz curves (LCs) of two income profiles the first is said to be more redistributive than the second if and only if the former strictly Lorenz dominates the latter. Thus, for a fixed population size the former is regarded as more equal than the latter by any relative inequality index that decreases under a rank preserving progressive transfer (see Theorem 2.2). If the pre–tax income profile is given, the Lorenz criterion can, therefore, be used to decide whether one tax system is more redistributive than another. If two tax schedules give rise to post–tax income profiles with non–intersecting LCs, then the tax schedule related to the undominated LC can be taken as unambigously more redistributive than another. It is, therefore, logical to look for a relation between the concepts of tax progression and income redistribution. The following result due to Jakobsson(1976) can be regarded as a step in this direction.

---

2 It should be noted that the residual progression exhibits decreasing numerical values when progression is on the increase, whereas the values of the other three measures increase.

3 To see this let $f(z) = az - b - c/z$, where $0 < a < 1$, $b > 0$, $c > 0$. This function has an increasing average for all $z > 0$. But it has a decreasing marginal for $z > 0$. This example is due to Pfingsten(1986a). However, strict convexity of a tax function f along with $f(0) = 0$ guarantees that the average tax rate $f(z)/z$ is increasing in $z > 0$.

Theorem 8.1 (Jakobsson 1976)

A continuous tax function f_1 has, for all pre–tax income z, a smaller residual progression RP than a continuous tax function f_2 if and only if for every unequal pre–tax income profile the post–tax income profile associated with f_1 strictly Lorenz dominates that associated with f_2.

The proof of this theorem relies on the following lemma due to Jakobsson.

Lemma 8.1 (Jakobsson 1976)

Consider two vectors $a = (a_1, a_2, ..., a_n)$ and $b = (b_1, b_2, ..., b_n)$, where $0 < a_1 \leqq ... \leqq a_n$ and $0 < b_1 \leqq b_2 \leqq ... \leqq b_n$. If for $1 < i \leqq n$, $(b_i/b_{i-1}) < (a_i/a_{i-1})$, then b strictly Lorenz dominates a.

Proof

See appendix.

The intuitive reasoning behind this lemma is quite clear: If consecutive relative income differentials under b are term by term, smaller than the corresponding differentials under a, then b is Lorenz superior to a.

Proof of Theorem 8.1

Necessity:

Let y^1 and y^2 be the post tax income profiles resulting from the pre–tax profile $x \in D^n$ on applying the continuous tax methods f_1 and f_2 respectively. It follows by the definition of elasticity of income after tax that if $RP^1 < RP^2$, for all z, then

$$\frac{y_i^1}{y_{i-1}^1} < \frac{y_i^2}{y_{i-1}^2} ,$$

where $y_1^1 \leqq y_2^1 \leqq ... \leqq y_n^1$ and $y_1^2 \leqq y_2^2 \leqq ... \leqq y_n^2$. Hence by Lemma 8.1, y^1 strictly Lorenz dominates y^2.

Sufficiency:

Suppose $RP^1 < RP^2$ except for one interval where $RP^1 > RP^2$. Then continuity of f_i, $i = 1,2$, enables us to choose an income profile before tax that lies completely within the latter interval. Therefore, by necessity part of the theorem, for such a profile y^2 strictly Lorenz dominates y^1. This in turn implies that y^1 does not strictly Lorenz dominates y^2. Hence the inequality $RP^1 < RP^2$ must hold everywhere. ■

Since the proportional tax function is relative inequality preserving and the residual progression for such a tax function is unity at all income levels, we have the following corollary:

Corollary 8.1

A tax system is progressive everywhere if and only if the income profile before tax is strictly Lorenz dominated by the resulting income profile after tax.

Theorem 8.1 shows that residual income progression is the only function that meets the following logical requirement for a local tax progression index: 'if one tax system is everywhere, according to the measure, more progressive than the other, then it should also be unambiguously more redistributive than the other' (Jakobsson(1976)). Suppose that for a tax function the residual progression is less than unity at all income levels. Then the vertical distance evaluated at i/n between the LC of the post–tax profile and that of the post–tax profile that would result if taxes were raised proportionally gives the fraction of total ex–post income transferred from high income group (top 100(1 – i/n) percent) to low income group (bottom 100i/n percent) due to the existence of progression in the tax method. In view of these discussions we can, therefore, say that the residual progression corresponds to the redistributive effect of progressive taxation. The index of residual progression can be written as a function of the average tax rate f(z)/z and marginal tax rate f' (z) in the following way:

$$RP(z|f) = \frac{1 - f'(z)}{1 - \frac{f(z)}{z}} . \qquad (8.2)$$

The denominator of RP in (8.2) gives the shortfall of the ratio of tax payment to the ex–ante income from unity. The numerator, on the other hand, indicates how much is left to the taxpayer on the margin if before tax income increases by one unit.

It is interesting to note that there is the same relation between liability progression and the distribution of tax burden as there is between residual progression and post–tax income profile. This is formally stated as:

Theorem 8.2 (Jakobsson 1976)

A continuous tax function f_1 has, for all pre–tax income z, a greater liability progression LP than a continuous tax function f_2 if and only if for every unequal pre–tax income profile the tax burden resulting from f_2 strictly Lorenz dominates the tax burden resulting from f_1.

Proof

Similar to the proof of Theorem 8.1. ∎

The following corollary to Theorem 8.2 establishes a relation between tax progressivity (as measured by LP) and the profiles of tax–payments and pre–tax incomes.

Corollary 8.2

A tax system is progressive everywhere if and only if the pre–tax income profile strictly Lorenz dominates the profile of tax payments.

From Theorems 8.1 and 8.2 we observe that the two indices RP and LP recognise two effects of progressive taxation. Lambert(1988) calls the effect corresponding to the latter as the departure from proportionality effect of progressive income taxation. To be able to understand this let us consider the hypothetical profile of tax liabilities that would result when the same aggregate amount of tax is raised proportionally. Now look at the vertical distance evaluated at i/n between the LC of the proportional tax burden and that of the actual tax burden. If the liability progression is greater than unity at all income levels, then this vertical distance gives the fraction of total tax liability transferred to high income group (top 100(1 – i/n) percent) from low income group (bottom 100i/n percent) due to the existence of progression in the tax schedule. It should be noted that the quasi–orderings of tax functions induced by the criteria LP and RP do not coincide (see Pfähler(1984), Pfingsten(1986a, 1986b)). For a given average tax rate, the two indices vary inversely[4].

[4] This follows from the fact that RP = (1 – rLP)/(1 – r), where r is the given average tax rate.

8.3 An Ethical Index of Global Tax Progressivity

The indices of tax progression that have been discussed in Section 8.2 are local indices – they relate to progression at a given point in the income scale. Using local indices we cannot calculate global or overall progressivity caused by the tax method taken as a whole. The purpose of this section is to construct an ethical index of overall tax progressivity[5].

In constructing our index we view the proportional tax rule as the benchmark. More precisely, the index compares the actual after–tax income profile with the hypothetical after–tax profile that would result if the same aggregate amount of tax were collected proportionally. Now, a proportional tax function is relative inequality preserving – the relative inequalities of the pre– and post–tax income profiles are identical. Assuming that the tax schedule is incentive preserving, in view of Corollary 8.1 we can say that if the after–tax profile is Lorenz superior to proportionality, the tax system should be progressive. The global progressivity index to be introduced here will achieve this objective.

Let us now assume that the welfare value of a profile $x \in D^n$ is given by $\sum_{i=1}^{n} U(x_i)$, where the utility function U is continuous, increasing and strictly concave. We then define our progressivity index as the normalised value of the difference between the welfare of the actual after–tax profile and that of the after–tax profile that would be achieved by an equal yield proportional tax. In terms of the notation introduced in Section 8.2, the tax progressivity index is given by

$$B^{2n}(y,t) = h\left[\sum_{i=1}^{n} [U(y_i) - U((1-\Theta)x_i)]\right], \tag{8.3}$$

where $h > 0$ is the coefficient of normalisation and $\Theta = \left(\sum_{i=1}^{n} t_i \Big/ \sum_{i=1}^{n} x_i\right)$ is the proportionality factor. B^{2n} in (8.3) can be written in terms of $\lambda(x)$ and $\lambda(y)$, the means of the profiles x and y respectively, as follows

[5] This section is based on Chakravarty(1981).

$$B^{2n}(y,t) = h[\sum_{i=1}^{n} [U(y_i) - U(\frac{\lambda(y)}{\lambda(x)} \cdot x_i)]]. \tag{8.4}$$

B^{2n} is positive for progressivity, zero for proportionality and negative for regressivity.

We shall call a tax method most progressive if the after–tax welfare is maximised. Given pre–tax incomes, for a fixed total of tax proceeds, the SEF $\sum_{i=1}^{n} U(y_i)$ will generate its maximum value if the tax structure makes the ex–post profile equal. Equivalently, we say that the tax system should be so arranged, as to make $\sum_{i=1}^{n} [U(x_i) - U(y_i)]$, the welfare which the population gives up in paying taxes, as small as possible. This is referred to as the principle of minimum sacrifice. Since the total sacrifice in welfare is minimised only when the marginal utility of after–tax income is identical for everyone, this principle is also called the equimarginal sacrifice principle (see Dalton(1922) and Atkinson and Stiglitz(1980)). Clearly, in this extreme case the tax function is weakly incentive preserving – y_i is non–decreasing in x_i[6].

Axiom of Normalisation

For a most progressive tax system the value of the progressivity index is unity.

This axiom determines the coefficient of normalisation h. The progressivity index is then given by

$$B^{2n}(y,t) = \frac{\sum_{i=1}^{n} [U(y_i) - U(\frac{\lambda(y)}{\lambda(x)} \cdot x_i)]}{\sum_{i=1}^{n} [U(\lambda(y)) - U(\frac{\lambda(y)}{\lambda(x)} \cdot x_i)]} . \tag{8.5}$$

[6] Two other interpretations of equal sacrifice are equal absolute sacrifice and equal proportional sacrifice. While the former means that everyone gives up the same amount of utility in paying taxes, the latter demands a sacrifice of the same percentage of utility from all taxpayers. The identical individual utility function is assumed to be increasing and strictly concave. All these three rules of taxation correspond to the ability to pay taxation principle. See Dalton(1922), Samuelson(1947) and Young(1987, 1988, 1988a). This contrasts with the benefit principle of taxation which says that 'different people should be taxed in proportion to the 'benefit' they receive from public activity' (Samuelson(1980)).

Clearly, B^{2n} remains invariant under affine transformations of U. Continuity of U shows that B^{2n} is a continuous function.

The progressivity index in (8.5) is desired to be a relative index – it should remain invariant to equiproportional variations in all before – and after – tax incomes. A form of utility function that enables B^{2n} in (8.5) to fulfil this objective is the utility function given by (2.16)[7]. Substitutimg U given by (2.16) in (8.5) we get

$$B^{2n}(y,t) = \begin{cases} \dfrac{\frac{1}{n}\sum_{i=1}^{n}\left[\left(\frac{y_i}{\lambda(y)}\right)^r - \left(\frac{x_i}{\lambda(x)}\right)^r\right]}{1 - \frac{1}{n}\cdot\sum_{i=1}^{n}\left(\frac{x_i}{\lambda(x)}\right)^r}, & r < 1,\ r \neq 0 \\[2ex] \dfrac{\sum_{i=1}^{n}\left[\log\left(\frac{\lambda(x)}{x_i}\right) - \log\left(\frac{\lambda(y)}{y_i}\right)\right]}{\sum_{i=1}^{n}\log\left(\frac{\lambda(x)}{x_i}\right)}, & r = 0 \end{cases} \quad (8.6)$$

For r = 0, B^{2n} in (8.6) is simply the percentage change in Theil's(1967) mean logarithmic deviation index of inequality due to the tax system taken as a whole. This change is positive or negative according as the tax method is progressive or regressive.

In the limit as $r \to 1$,

$$B^{2n}(y,t) \to 1 - \frac{\frac{1}{n}\sum_{i=1}^{n}\left(\frac{y_i}{\lambda(y)}\right)\log\left(\frac{y_i}{\lambda(y)}\right)}{\frac{1}{n}\sum_{i=1}^{n}\left(\frac{x_i}{\lambda(x)}\right)\log\left(\frac{x_i}{\lambda(x)}\right)}, \quad (8.7)$$

which is nothing but the proportionate gap between Theil's(1967) entropy inequality index for pre– and post–tax profiles of income.

Thus, given any set of data on before– and after–tax incomes, we can employ any member of the family of progressivity indices B^{2n} in (8.6) to verify whether the latter, as a whole, has been generated from the former in a progressive manner.

---

7 But it is not clear whether U given by (2.16) is the only form that keeps B^{2n} invariant to scale transformations of pre – and post – tax incomes.

8.4 Ethical Indices for the Measurement of Horizontal Inequity

The principle of horizontal equity is usually stated as 'equal treatment of equals' (see Musgrave(1976), for a recent statement). Individuals with the same level of well–being should be liable for identical transfers or taxes. But this definition of horizontal equity is conceptually incomplete. According to King(1983) 'In practice, of course, no two individuals are ever identical, and the principle of equal treatment of equals has little empirical significance unless it can be usefully extended to include "and unequals treated accordingly". To do this we are led naturally to a comparison of the ordering of utility levels before and after tax change'. In accordance with this logic, a horizontally equitable redistribution is one that keeps unaltered the pre–tax rankings of the individuals (also see Feldstein(1976), Atkinson(1980a), Atkinson and Stiglitz(1980) and Plotnick(1982, 1985)). Equivalently, a horizontally equitable tax function is an incentive preserving method of taxation. This definition is more general than the classical definition.

There are valid reasons to believe that a tax/transfer system can give rise to changes in the ex–ante rankings of the individuals. For example, some persons with lower ex–ante incomes may be enjoying higher disposable incomes than some persons with higher ex–ante incomes by receiving some public benefit or by avoiding their just tax shares.

Now, horizontal inequity, ceteris paribus, diminishes social welfare[8]. That is, a horizontable inequitable income profile generates a lower level of social welfare than what it would have been for a horizontally equitable profile. An alteration in the ex–ante rankings of individuals causes an individual's actual income level in the ex–post profile to diverge from his rank preserving income level. These divergences in incomes, which reduce social welfare, give rise to the problem of horizontal inequity. Therefore, an ideal index of horizontal inequity should take care of such divergences. Before we go into the details of construction of indices of horizontal inequity, we clearly bring out the distinguishing features of vertical and horizontal inequity and set out the postulates for a horizontal inequity index. This discussion is based on Plotnick(1982, 1985).

[8] The belief that horizontal inequity reduces social welfare rests on an intuitive appeal to notions of fairness and redistribution of economic resources. This cannot be derived from the principle of social welfare maximisation or the Pareto preference conditions (see Atkinson(1980a) and Stiglitz(1982)).

8.4.1 Horizontal versus Vertical Inequity

Nozick(1974) has interpreted vertical inequity as an 'end–state principle'. In constructing a vertical inequity index we compare the observed income profile with an optimal or a benchmark. If they differ vertical inequity exists. The 'closer' the actual profile to the benchmark, the less is vertical inequity.

The above concept of vertical inequity satisfies impartiality and hence ignores the core of the notion of horizontal inequity. The following effects of a redistributive policy correspond respectively to vertical equity and horizontal equity: (i) altering the level of inequality, (ii) re–ranking of individuals. The concept of horizontal inequity is prior to that of vertical inequity in the sense that initially we are concerned with the fairness of the process of redistribution which can be regarded as the problem of horizontal inequity. Then we address the problem of vertical inequity, that is, how far the actual profile differs from the benchmark. In what follows, as has been done in earlier chapters, for constructing vertical inequity indices we will consider the perfectly equal income profile as the benchmark.

8.4.2 Postulates for an Index of Horizontal Inequity

A horizontal inequity index – whether relative or absolute – should satisfy the following postulates:

(a) Anonymity:

Suppose two pairs of ex–ante and ex–post profiles (x^1,y^1) and (x^2,y^2) differ only because of identity of the individuals in the ex–ante profile, but the re–ordering of ranks of individuals and hence of their incomes is identical. Then the fiscal systems should generate the same degree of horizontal inequity.

(b) Principle of Inequity Comparisons:

If one redistribution differs from a second redistribution simply because some persons' ex–post incomes are closer to what their rank–preserving (that is, horizontally equitable) ex–post incomes are, then the horizontal inequity index should make the first distribution less unequal than the second.

The anonymity condition is analogous to the symmetry or impartiality principle for inequality indices. We know that the Pigou–Dalton transfers principle for inequality indices states that of two income profiles with the same mean, over a given population size, the one which is closer to the egalitarian profile gives rise to a lower level of inequality than the other. Clearly, the principle of inequity comparisons gives us an analogous condition for horizontal inequity indices, showing that we have a constant index value for horizontally equitable income profiles.

Finally, for comparing income profiles over differing population sizes we will require a population principle which will make the horizontal inequity index invariant to replications of the population. Clearly, the Dalton(1920) population principle should be sufficient for this.

8.4.3 The Ethical Indices

We begin this subsection[9] with a discussion of the relative indices – indices that remain invariant to equiproportional changes in all ex–ante and ex–post incomes. For any ex–post income profile $y \in D^n$, we write y_{ai} for the ex–post income level corresponding to the rank of individual i in the ex–ante profile. King(1983) defined what he called 'the scaled order statistic for individual i', by $e_i = |y_i - y_{ai}|/\lambda(y)$, where $\lambda(y)$ is the mean of y. This statistic is non–negative and takes the value zero only when the individual's ranking is unchanged.

King(1983) suggested the use of the SEF

$$F^{2n}(y_1, y_2, \ldots, y_n; e_1, e_2, \ldots, e_n) \tag{8.8}$$

for summarising ethical judgements on alternative redistributions of income. It is assumed to be increasing in y_i's and decreasing in e_i's. He then suggested a particular index of relative horizontal inequality assuming that the SEF in (8.8) is additively separable. To make the King approach more flexible let us scale up y_i by $f(e_i)$ where the function $f: \mathbb{R}^1_+ \to D^1$ is continuous, positive, decreasing and $f(0) = 1$. Decreasingness of the function f relects the view that horizontal inequity is undesirable. The normalisation

9 This subsection is based on King(1983), Chakravarty(1985).

$f(0) = 1$ is necessary to attach a value of zero to the inequity index for a horizontally equitable profile. We write $yf(e)$ for $(y_1f(e_1), y_2f(e_2), \dots, y_nf(e_n))$, and assume that the SEF $W^n: D^n \longrightarrow \mathbb{R}^1$ is continuous, increasing, strictly S–concave and homothetic.

We now define the unchanged ordering equivalent proportion of income 'a' associated with $y \in D^n$ by

$$W^n(ay) = W^n(yf(e)) . \tag{8.9}$$

Increasingness of W^n implies that $0 < a \leqq 1$. The case $a = 1$ is attained when there is no change in ranks of individuals from the ex–ante profile to the ex–post profile.

The fraction of ex–post income that could be saved without any loss in welfare for eliminating all changes in ranking is $(1 - a)$, and, therefore, a natural index of horizontal inequity is

$$\begin{aligned} I_h^n(y) &= 1 - a \\ &= 1 - \frac{\bar{W}^n(yf(e))}{\bar{W}^n(y)} , \end{aligned} \tag{8.10}$$

where $\bar{W}^n$ is linearly homogeneous and is related to W^n by $\phi(\bar{W}^n(y)) = W^n(y)$, ϕ being increasing. I_h^n also gives the proportional welfare loss resulting from changes in the before–tax rankings of the taxpayers. Clearly, I_h^n is a relative index and lies between zero and unity. The lower bound corresponds to the case $a = 1$.

Next, we construct the Atkinson–Kolm–Sen (AKS) relative index of vertical inequality I_v^n by employing the equally distributed equivalent (EDE) income of y: $I_v^n(y) = 1 - \bar{W}^n(y)/\bar{W}^n(1^n)\lambda(y)$.

Finally, to construct a relative index of overall inequity, we define the equally distributed originally ranked equivalent level of income as that income Θ, for which we have

$$W^n(\Theta \cdot 1^n) = W^n(yf(e)) . \tag{8.11}$$

The relative index of overall inequity is then defined by

$$I_0^n(y) = 1 - \Theta/\lambda(y)$$
$$= 1 - \frac{\bar{W}^n(yf(e))}{\bar{W}^n(1^n)\lambda(y)} . \qquad (8.12)$$

I_0^n is continuous and bounded between zero and one, with a value of zero when there is no change from original ranking and when the ex–post profile is perfectly equal. I_0^n determines the proportion of total income which the society could sacrifice without any welfare loss to eliminate vertical and horizontal inequity.

It is now evident that

$$(1 - I_0^n) = (1 - I_h^n) \cdot (1 - I_v^n). \qquad (8.13)$$

Thus, (8.13) gives us the multiplicative decomposition rule of the overall relative inequity index into the horizontal and vertical components of inequity[10].

Therefore, given (8.10), to every homothetic SEF there is a different index of horizontal inequity. These indices explicitly take account of the distances moved from the ex–ante rankings. If W^n is the symmetric mean of order r and $f(e_i) = e^{-\alpha e_i}$, $\alpha > 0$, then I_h^n in (8.10) is the King index. An increase in the value of α decreases horizontal inequity – α measures the degree of aversion to horizontal inequity.

Next, to construct an absolute index of horizontal inequity, which remains invariant to equal translations of ex–ante and ex–post incomes, we assume that W^n defined on $\mathbb{R}_+^n$ is continuous, increasing, strictly S–concave and translatable. To incorporate the condition that the index should take account of the distance moved from pre–tax ranking, for each i, we diminish y_i by $d_i = e_i\lambda(y)$. Let us then determine ν, an equivalent income level, implicitly defined by

[10] King(1983) proved this result under the general formulation (8.8).

$$W^n(y - \nu \cdot 1^n) = W^n(y - d) , \tag{8.14}$$

where $d = (d_1, d_2, \dots , d_n)$. $\nu \geq 0$ is the per–capita income that could be saved without any welfare loss in order to eliminate all changes in ranking. ν is the unchanged ordering equivalent absolute income level. The case $\nu = 0$ indicates non–existence of horizontal inequity. As an absolute index of horizontal inequity, we can, therefore, use

$$\begin{aligned} A_h^n(y) &= \nu \\ &= \overset{*}{W}{}^n(y) - \overset{*}{W}{}^n(y - d) , \end{aligned} \tag{8.15}$$

where $\overset{*}{W}{}^n$ is unit–translatable and $\phi(\overset{*}{W}{}^n(y)) = W^n(y)$, ϕ being increasing. A_h^n is continuous. A_h^n also determines the size of absolute welfare loss resulting from the existence of horizontal inequity. Clearly, to every translatable SEF we get a particular index of horizontal inequity.

By translatability of $\overset{*}{W}{}^n$, we can write Θ, the equally distributed originally ranked equivalent income, as $\overset{*}{W}{}^n(y - d) - \overset{*}{W}(0 \cdot 1^n)$. The absolute index of overall inequity is then given by

$$\begin{aligned} A_0^n(y) &= \lambda(y) - \Theta \\ &= \lambda(y) - \overset{*}{W}{}^n(y-d) + \overset{*}{W}{}^n(0 \cdot 1^n) . \end{aligned} \tag{8.16}$$

A_0^n is the per person saving with no welfare loss for eliminating horizontal and vertical inequity. It attains a minimum value of zero when there is no change in the ex–ante ranking of individuals and the ex–post distribution is perfectly equal.

We then have the following additive decomposition rule

$$A_0^n(y) = A_h^n(y) + A_v^n(y) , \tag{8.17}$$

where A_v^n is the Blackorby–Donaldson–Kolm (BDK) absolute index of vertical inequity. Thus, (8.17) determines the percentage contributions made by individual inequity components to the overall inequity.

8.5 Alternative Indices of Tax Progressivity and Horizontal Inequity

8.5.1 Indices of Tax Progressivity

Essential to the construction of the tax progressivity index introduced in Section 8.3 is the intrinsic relation between progressivity and inequality – a tax system is progressive if post–tax incomes are less unequally distributed than pre–tax incomes. This tradition goes back at least to Musgrave and Thin(1948), who suggested the use of the following formula as a relative tax progressivity index

$$B_M^{2n}(y,t) = \frac{1 - G^n(y)}{1 - G^n(x)}, \tag{8.18}$$

where G is the Gini index of relative inequality. The Musgrave and Thin approach or some variant of it has been used through the works of Pechman and Okner(1974), Khetan and Podder(1976), Kakwani(1977b, 1979, 1984a), Reynolds and Smolensky(1977), Suits(1977, 1980), Bracewell(1979), Hutton and Lambert(1979), Davies(1980), Kienzle (1980, 1981, 1982), Fei(1981), Formby, Seaks and Smith(1981, 1984) Eichhorn(1983, 1984), Hemming and Keen(1983), Blackorby and Donaldson(1984b), Bridges(1984), Eichhorn, Funke and Richter(1984), Formby and Skyes(1984), Lambert(1984, 1985a, 1985b, 1988), Liu(1984, 1985, 1987), Kiefer(1985), Pfähler(1985, 1987, 1988), Lambert and Pfähler(1986), Pfingsten(1986, 1986a, 1987, 1988, 1988a), Thon(1987), Moyes(1988, 1988a) and many others.

Blackorby and Donaldson(1984b) defined their relative tax progressivity index B_D^{2n} as the percentage increase in the AKS EDE income of the actual after–tax profile over what it would be if taxes were raised on a proportional basis assuming that the SEF is regular, homothetic and strictly S–concave. B_D^{2n} can be written in terms of the AKS relative inequality index I_3^n as follows:

$$B_D^{2n}(y,t) = \frac{I_3^n(x) - I_3^n(y)}{1 - I_3^n(x)}. \tag{8.19}$$

B_D^{2n} is positive for progressivity, zero for proportionality and negative for regressivity. If we use the Gini index of inequality in (8.19), then $B_M^{2n}(y,t) = B_D^{2n}(y,t) + 1$. Hence in this particular case the Blackorby–Donaldson formula and the Musgrave–Thin formula are cardinally equivalent. One common feature between the progressivity indices B^{2n} in (8.6) and B_D^{2n} in (8.19) is that they use the same benchmark structure. However, they need not rank two fiscal systems in the same way.

Liu(1985) proposed $G^n(x) - G^n(y)$ as an index of tax progressivity. The same formula has also been considered by Reynolds and Smolensky(1977) and Lambert(1985a, 1988). A somewhat ad hoc variant of this is the Pechman–Okner formula $[G^n(x) - G^n(y)]/G^n(x)$. Clearly, these functions are variants of the Musgrave–Thin index of progressivity. Kiefer(1985) proposed the gap between the Atkinson(1970) index of pre– and post–tax inequalities as a progressivity index. If the tax function is incentive preserving, then all of these indices satisfy an interesting property, which Lambert(1988) refers to as the minimal requirement for a global progressivity index of redistributive effect. Suppose two tax schedules f_1 and f_2 are working on a given pre–tax income profile. Suppose also that f_1 is considered to be at least as progressive as f_2 by residual progression at each income level. Then f_1 should be at least as progressive as f_2 by any global progressivity index aiming at measuring the redistributive effect. This property is also shared by the indices B^{2n} and B_D^{2n}.

Khetan and Podder(1976) and Kakwani(1977b) proposed respectively the following indices of tax progressivity:

$$B_P^{2n}(y,t) = \frac{1 - G^n(x)}{1 - G^n(t)} , \tag{8.20}$$

$$B_K^{2n}(y,t) = G^n(t) - G^n(x) . \tag{8.21}$$

These indices are closely related: $B_P^{2n}(y,t) - 1 = B_K^{2n}(y,t)/[1 - G^n(t)]$. Blackorby and Donaldson(1984b) pointed out several shortcomings of B_P^{2n} and B_D^{2n}. If the tax structure does not modify the total income so that $\sum_{i=1}^{n} t_i = 0$, then the use of B_P^{2n} and B_K^{2n} is inappropriate. These indices are not defined when $\sum_{i=1}^{n} t_i = 0$. Moreover, multiplication of the tax vector by a positive scalar, however large or small it may be, does not affect the values of the progressivity indices B_P^{2n} and B_K^{2n}. A multiplicative change in tax levels can introduce horizontal inequity into the fiscal system. Thus, the indices may measure two fiscal systems, one of which is horizontally equitable and the other is not, as equally progressive. It is easy to see using this homogeneity property that the indices B_P^{2n} and B_K^{2n} may regard a perfectly equitable fiscal system and a non–equitable fiscal system as equally progressive. We also note that these indices are symmetric in the tax–vector – all permutations of a given tax vector are equally progressive or regressive. Finally, it is difficult to interpret these indices as ethical indices of progressivity. If the tax function is incentive preserving, then the Kakwani index is twice the area enclosed between the LC of the pre–tax incomes and that of the tax liabilities. B_K^{2n} is a suitable candidate if we want to measure the departure from proportionality effect of taxation. Suits(1977) proposed an index of progressivity which is similar to the Kakwani index. He made use of an LC which plots the cumulative proportion of tax liability against the cumulative proportion of pre–tax income. Suits' index is one minus twice the area under this LC (see also Hainsworth(1964)). This formula also can be considered as a global measure of departure from proportionality effect. The Kakwani and Suits formulae satisfy the minimal requirement for departure from proportionality effect measures using liability progression as the local progression index (Lambert(1988)).

Pfähler(1987) defined his family of progressivity indices as the weighted sum of all local relative deviations of actual taxes from 'revenue equivalent' proportional taxes. To write down the Pfähler function explicitly, let us suppose that pre–tax income z follows a continuous type distribution having distribution function F: $[0,T] \longrightarrow [0,1]$. We write t(z) for tax owed on z. The total tax ratio, or overall average tax rate, is denoted by g and defined as the ratio of arithmetic means of taxes and pre–tax incomes:

$$g = \frac{\lambda(t)}{\lambda(z)} . \tag{8.22}$$

Then the Pfähler index B_W is obtained by aggregating all the gaps of the form $[t(z) - gz]$ between the actual taxes and revenue equivalent proportional taxes as a fraction of the average tax $\lambda(t)$:

$$B_W(F) = \frac{1}{\lambda(t)} \cdot \int_0^T [t(z) - gz] \cdot w(z)\, dF(z) , \tag{8.23}$$

where w is a monotonic nonlinear weighting function. B_w is very similar to the Nygård – Sandström(1982) generalisation of the Gini index or the Mehran(1976) family of linear inequality measures. The most interesting feature of B_w is its use of a hypothetical tax structure yielding the same average revenue as the actual one. Pfähler studies some particular cases of B_w by making alternative assumptions about the functional form of w(z). For example, if $w(z) = 2F(z)$, we get the Kakwani index. On the other hand, if w(z) is twice the cumulative proportion of total taxes with income less than or equal to z, we get the Suits–Hainsworth index. B_w becomes the difference between the S–Gini inequality indices for taxes and pre–tax incomes if $w(z) = -\delta(1 - F(z))^{\delta-1}$, $\delta > 1$. If w(z) is given by $-(\lambda(z)/z)$ the resulting formula becomes the covariance between taxes and pre–tax incomes as a proportion of the average tax.

Clearly, it is impossible to interpret B_w as an ethical index. Moreover, detailed investigation of B_w will require explicit specification of the properties of the weighting function w(z). It is very difficult to draw any conclusion about general properties of a weighting function from the above specifications of w(z) – some of them possess non – overlapping properties. For B_w to increase whenever share in total tax liability of a person with income z is increased and that of a person with income $(z - c) < z$ is decreased, we require increasingness of w(z). B_w was independently proposed and discussed by Kakwani(1986). (See Kakwani(1987), Liu(1987) and Pfähler(1987) for further discussions on B_w.)

So far we have discussed indices of relative progression. Blackorby and Donaldson (1984b) also proposed an ethical index of absolute tax progressivity that remains invariant to equal translations of all pre– and post–tax incomes. They proposed to measure absolute progressivity by the difference between the AKS EDE income of the actual post–tax profile and that of the profile that would result if equal yield taxes were the same for all people, assuming that the SEF is regular, strictly S–concave and translatable. Their measure B_A^{2n} can be written using the BDK absolute inequality index A_1^n as follows:

$$B_A^{2n}(y,t) = A_1^n(x) - A_1^n(y) \quad . \qquad (8.24)$$

B_A^{2n} is positive or negative according as the tax structure is progressive or regressive[11].

In addition to Jakobsson's paper, a number of recent papers (see Eichhorn(1983, 1984), Thon(1987)) have shown that progressive taxation in the traditional sense generates a reduction of inequality on indisputable grounds – the post–tax profile is Lorenz superior to the pre–tax profile. Eichhorn, Funke and Richter(1984) gave a rigorous proof of this result under minimal assumptions. They showed that increasingness of the average tax rate along with weak incentive preservation is necessary and sufficient for this. Alternative concepts of local progressivity have also been explored. Fei(1981) introduced the concept of minimal progressivity according to which tax liability must increase with income. He showed that in the case of taxation programs that do not modify aggregate income minimally progressive taxation along with weak incentive preservation leads to a reduction of inequality in the Lorenz sense. Moyes(1988) showed that the absolute inequality of incomes is unambiguously reduced by taxation if and only if the tax function meets these two principles. This is a counterpart to the result of Eichhorn, Funke and Richter(1984).

Pfingsten(1988a) considered the parametric class of inequality concepts analysed by Bossert and Pfingsten(1989) and derived the following general equivalence result: for any (feasible), weakly incentive preserving tax function f, a necessary and sufficient condition for post–tax inequality to be less than pre–tax inequality is that the individual tax rate $f(z)/[\mu z + 1 - \mu]$ is increasing in taxable income z, where $0 \leqq \mu \leqq 1$. The result of Eichhorn, Funke and Richter(1984) is obtained for $\mu = 1$ and the corresponding result derived by Moyes(1988) drops out if $\mu = 0$. Assuming that the tax function f has a continuous derivative f' , increasingness of the tax rate implies that

$$\mu z[f'(z) - \frac{f(z)}{z}] + (1-\mu)f'(z) > 0 . \tag{8.25}$$

For $\mu = 1$, (8.25) reduces to $\frac{f(z)}{z} < f'(z)$. But if $\mu \neq 1$, a tax may be progressive in this parametric set–up even if average tax rate exceeds the marginal tax. Thus, some tax functions which are not progressive in the conventional sense may be progressive

[11] It should be noted that the benchmark structure used here may not be feasible in the sense that some of the after–tax incomes generated through the structure may be negative. Consequently, B_A^{2n} is not defined in all such cases.

according to the Pfingsten definition: $f(z)/(\mu z + 1 - \mu)$ is increasing in z. This is in particular true for the case $\mu = 0$ where (given weak incentive preservation) $f'(z) > 0$ is necessary and sufficient for progressivity (Moyes(1988)). It is immediate from (8.25) that a local tax progressivity index which will be consistent with the basic notion of progressivity introduced by Pfingsten(1988a) is

$$B_\mu(z|f) = \frac{\mu(zf'(z) - f(z)) + (1 - \mu)f'(z)}{\mu(z - f(z)) + (1 - \mu)} . \tag{8.26}$$

This index was proposed by Pfingsten(1986a, 1988). A higher value of B_μ means that the tax function is more progressive. B_μ has the convenient property of lying between zero and one, where the lower bound is achieved in the extreme case when the tax function is inequality preserving with respect to μ, that is, $f(z) = c \cdot \mu z - c(1 - \mu)$, c being the tax–yield parameter, which satisfies the condition: $c \geq 0$ or $-1 < c < 0$ and $\mu = 1$. The upper bound is obtained when the tax function is perfectly equalising, that is, for all pre–tax incomes the post–tax incomes are equal. For $\mu = 0$, B_μ becomes the marginal tax. If $\mu = 1$, B_μ becomes $1 - RP(z|f)$. Pfingsten(1988) also proposed an axiomatic characterisation of the formula (8.26).

Pfingsten(1986a) suggested to measure global progressivity using the arithmetic average of local progressivity values given by (8.26). Ebert(1987a) axiomatically characterised the geometric mean of the individual residual progressivity values as a global progressivity measure. The following are some of the interesting properties of the Ebert function: (i) It is increasing in its arguments showing that each elasticity really affects global progression. (ii) A tax system t is globally progressive for all $x \in D^n$ if and only if t is progressive by residual progression at all income levels. (iii) If there is only one person, global and local progressivity are the same. (We may note here that measures based on inequality indices are not defined in such a situation.) (iv) Of two tax functions f_1 and f_2, f_1 is globally more progressive than f_2 for all $x \in D^n$ if and only if f_1 is more progressive than f_2 by residual progression at all income levels. Pfingsten's index also satisfies similar properties.

Pfingsten(1986) developed a relation between two tax functions which are 'inequality equivalent' in the parametric sense of Bossert–Pfingsten(1989) but have different tax yields. Two feasible tax functions f_1 and f_2 are called inequality equivalent in the parametric sense if and only if for all $x \in D^n$ there exists a scalar $c(x)$ such that the corresponding post–tax income vectors y^1 and y^2 are related by

$$y^2 = y^1 + c(x)[\mu y^1 + (1-\mu)\cdot 1^n] . \tag{8.27}$$

Pfingsten(1986) showed that for (8.27) to hold it is necessary and sufficient that for all $z \in D^1$,

$$f_2(z) = (1 + \bar{c}\mu)\cdot f_1(z) - \bar{c}\mu z - \bar{c}(1-\mu) , \tag{8.28}$$

where $\bar{c}$ is a scalar and given feasibility of f_1, f_2 defined according to (8.28) is feasible if and only if

$$\bar{c} > -[z - f_1(z)]/[\mu(z - f_1(z)) + (1-\mu)] . \tag{8.29}$$

Identity (8.28) is important when a tax reform is discussed. It allows to change government's tax yield without changing inequality. If it is desired to generate a new tax function f_2 whose post–tax profile should be equally unequal to the post–tax profile resulting from the current tax function f_1, then (8.28) shows how these tax functions must be related. For $\mu = 1$, (8.28) says that a tax cut by a constant fraction of initial post–tax incomes leaves the LC of net incomes unchanged. (This result was also proved by Pfähler (1984).) The observation for the absolute view $\mu = 0$ is obvious: equal absolute changes in all tax liabilities leave inequality unchanged.

(8.28) is the case in which everybody gains or loses by the reform. That is, in this case there is a tax cut or a tax increase for all the taxpayers. Sometimes we may be interested in a reform that will increase the tax burden of the rich and decrease that of the poor. A reform may be designed to increase the tax burden of the middle income group benefiting the earners at the extremes of the range and so on. An interesting result due to Hemming and Keen(1983) shows that a reform involving transfers of net income between taxpayers occurs when the old and the new tax structures cross once. They established that of two incentive preserving tax schedules f_1 and f_2 raising the same revenue, if the former crosses the latter once, from below, then the LC of the post–tax profile generated by f_1 must lie above the LC of that generated by f_2 for all pre–tax profiles. Furthermore, the converse is also true. The intuitive appeal of this result is quite clear: relative to f_2, f_1 increases in the net–incomes of all persons having pre–tax incomes below a certain level and correspondingly reduces the net incomes of the persons with pre–tax incomes above that level, benefiting a 'poor' group at the expense of a 'rich' group (Hemming and Keen(1983)). The result can be extended to non–equal yield comparisons.

Dardanoni and Lambert(1988) showed that if f_1 and f_2 are incentive preserving tax schedules and f_1 crosses f_2 once, from below, then for any pre–tax income profile such that the overall average tax rate of f_1 does not exceed that of f_2, the post–tax profile generated by the former must dominate that generated by the latter in the strict generalised Lorenz sense. This means that a yield–neutral or yield–reducing tax change which cuts the liabilities of the low income group and increases all other liabilities must be favored by all increasing, strictly S–concave SEFs. The yield neutral case is precisely the Hemming–Keen result for the equal revenue case. Dardanoni and Lambert(1988) also showed that if f_1 crosses f_2 twice, first from below, then for any pre–tax profile such that the total yield under f_1 does not exceed the same under f_2, the GLC of net incomes corresponding to f_1 crosses the same GLC corresponding to f_2 once, from above. An application of results on crossing of GLCs yields welfare implications of this theorem. With this we conclude our discussion on tax progressivity indices and ranking of profiles using tax functions.

<u>8.5.2 Indices of Horizontal Inequity</u>

Economists have proposed a large variety of indices for the measurement of horizontal inequity. We now evaluate some of them on the basis of arguments developed in Section 4 of this chapter. (Much of this discussion is based on Plotnick(1982, 1985) and Chakravarty(1985).) Johnson and Mayer(1962) proposed two indices of horizontal inequity. Their indices are calculated as follows. Of n persons suppose that n_1 are receiving treatment t_1 and n_2 are receiving a <u>differing</u> treatment t_2, where $n_1 + n_2 = n$. Since for an arbitrary individual belonging to a particular group an inequity arises with regard to every member of the other group, total number of inequities, which is $n_1 \cdot n_2$, is the first Johnson–Mayer formula. Inequity is maximised if $n_1 = n_2$ and minimised when all but one person are placed in the same group. The second index, which has been referred to as 'the dollar value of tax discrimination', sums the money value of the inequities. Clearly, the Johnson–Mayer analysis can be extended to an arbitrary number of treatments. As an alternative, Brennan(1971) suggested the use of the ratio of the standard deviation of tax payments among equals to the average tax payment as a horizontal inequity index. The Brennan formula was also considered by White and White(1965). But all these indices ignore possible re–rankings across different groups of individuals.

Strauss and Berliant(1979) suggested an index which is based on 'the extent to which effective [tax] rates are different among all paired of comparisons of taxpayers within each income class'. A similar index was considered by Habib(1979). The implementation of this approach needs precise definitions of income classes and tax–rate intervals. This approach is very close to the Johnson–Mayer count procedure and does not address the problem of re–ranking across classes.

Rosen(1978) proposed two indices for measuring horizontal inequity. The first Rosen measure H_1^n is half of one minus the Spearman rank correlation coefficient:

$$H_1^n(y) = 3 \cdot \sum_{i=1}^{n} c_i^2/(n^3 - n) , \tag{8.30}$$

where c_i is the difference between individual i's ex–ante and ex–post ranks. H_1^n is a relative index and satisfies the principles of anonymity and inequity comparisons. But it is not clear how H_1^n can be interpreted as an ethical index. Since it does not include individual incomes as arguments, it is impossible to generate a well–defined SEF (e. g., a regular one) from (8.30). The second Rosen index is the correlation coefficient between the vectors d_x and d_y, where d_x and d_y are formed in the following way. For any randomisation of the components of x, let us arrange the components of y in the same manner. Then the ith coordinates of d_x and d_y are given respectively by $d_{x_i} = |x_i - x_{i-1}|$ and $d_{y_i} = |y_i - y_{i-1}|$. Thus, the vector d_x (d_y) gives absolute differences between consecutive pairs of incomes in x (y). A value of one for this index implies no horizontal inequity. That there should be relation between cardinal income differences in moving from initial to final distribution is a question of vertical equity. The extent of linearity between ex–ante and ex–post income differences, which is measured by the second Rosen index, is certainly not the subject matter of horizontal inequity (see Plotnick(1980) for further discussions).

The index suggested by Hettich(1979) is H_2^n, where

$$H_2^n(y) = \frac{1}{n} \cdot \sum_{i=1}^{n} (t_i - g_i)^2 , \tag{8.31}$$

where g_i is the tax payment of individual i if the preferred tax base of 'broadly defined income' is adopted. $H_2^n = 0$ is taken to signify no horizontal inequity. The novelty of (8.31) is that it measures deviation of actual tax vector from a benchmark tax vector. But the index is completely silent on re–ranking issue – the central point of horizontal inequity, its calculation does not require comparison of initial and final ranks. H_2^n takes on the value zero only when $t_i = g_i$ for all i = 1, 2, ..., n, but it may happen that the fiscal system has introduced horizontal inequity by making some alterations in the ex–ante rankings.

Atkinson(1980a) constructed a pseudo LC by ordering individuals by their ex–ante ranks, but plotting cumulative shares of ex–post incomes. This pseudo LC lies on or above the conventional LC for the ex–post profile according as we have horizontal equity or inequity. The curve may also lie above the diagonal line. This 'may be seen from the example where the first person and the last person are interchanged' (Atkinson(1980a). This pseudo LC is also referred to as the concentration curve of the ex–post profile. The curve will lie uniformly below (above) the diagonal line if residual progression is greater (less) than zero for all income levels[12]. The area enclosed between the LC of the ex–post profile and the concentration curve, suitably normalised, has been taken as a horizontal inequity index. Suppose out of n individuals m are re–ranked. Arrange these m indi-

---

[12] In general the concentration curve of a variable z with respect to another variable x is a plot of the cumulative shares of the variable z, ranked in increasing order of x. This curve coincides with the LC of z if z is increasing in x. The curve lies below (above) the diagonal line if $e_{z,x}$, the elasticity of z with respect to x, is positive (negative) everywhere. This curve will lie below, on or above the LC of x if $e_{z,x}$ is greater than, equal to or less than unity at all values of z. The shortfall of two times the area enclosed under the concentration curve from unity is called the concentration coefficient. The concentration coefficient of z is bounded between $-G_z$ and G_z, where G_z is the Gini index of z. See Kakwani(1980).

viduals in ascending order of their initial ranks. Plotnick(1982) showed that Atkinson's index can then be written as

$$H_3^n(y) = \frac{1}{n^2\lambda(y)} \sum_{i=1}^{m} (y_{ai} - y_i)r_i \ , \tag{8.32}$$

where r_i is the ex–ante rank of individual i. From the construction it is clear that H_3^n is related to impact of rank reversals on the Gini index.

Plotnick(1982, 1985) considered the index

$$H_4^n(y) = \left[\frac{\sum_{i=1}^{n} |y_{ai} - y_i|^{\alpha}}{M} \right]^{1/\alpha} , \tag{8.33}$$

where $\alpha \geq 1$ and M is the maximum attainable value of H_4^n. Maximum is associated with the redistribution giving person with initial rank i a final rank (n + 1 – i). For α = 1 and 2, H_4^n is closely related the impact of rank reversals on the Gini index and the coefficient of variation respectively. H_4^n is increasing in α. As $\alpha \longrightarrow \infty$, H_4^n becomes a function of the maximum of the gaps $|y_{ai} - y_i|$. Both H_3^n and H_4^n are relative indices and satisfy the principles of anonymity and inequity comparisons. We should be able to derive these indices from some appropriate SEFs.

Cowell(1980a, 1985a) suggested a family of one–parameter indices for measuring distributional change. These indices are readily adopted as satisfactory indices of horizontal inequity. To do so, we interpret his distributions of 'old' x_i and 'new' y_i as the distributions of y_{ai} and y_i respectively. Then the Cowell index is written as

$$H_5^n(y) = \frac{1}{\lambda(y)nc(c+1)} \sum_{i=1}^{n} y_i[(\frac{y_i}{y_{ai}})^c - 1] \ , \tag{8.34}$$

where c may assume any real value. When c $\longrightarrow$ 0, H_5^n reduces to

$\sum_{i=1}^{n} [y_i \log(y_i/y_{ai})]/n\lambda(y)$. On the other hand, as $c \rightarrow -1$, we find the specification $-\sum_{i=1}^{n} [y_{ai} \log(y_i/y_{ai})]/n\lambda(y)$. Of the infinite set of possible members of (8.34), only these two limiting cases yield useful decompositions of total horizontal inequity into between and within group components. The general formula in (8.34) can probably be interpreted as a weighted average of percentage changes in individual ex-post incomes over the corresponding rank-preserving levels, where the weights are simply the final levels of well-being. If $y_i/y_{ai} = 1$ for all i, $H_5^n = 0$, showing that for a horizontal equitable profile the index value is zero. Cowell(1985a) also developed an axiomatic framework for the family in (8.34). A natural extension of Cowell's work is to use a weighted average of the absolute gaps between actual final well-beings and the corresponding rank preserving levels as a per capita index of horizontal inequity. Berrebi and Silber(1983) used a Kolm-Pollak type averaging procedure to aggregate such gaps into a single indicator of absolute horizontal inequity.

8.6 Concluding Remarks

We started this chapter with a discussion of the Musgrave-Thin(1948) local indices of tax progressivity that relate to progression at a given point in the income scale. We then proposed an overall progressivity formula that measures shifts in the income profile caused by the fiscal system taken as a whole. Next we discussed indices of horizontal inequity that measure loss of welfare arising due to alteration in the rankings of individuals caused by the tax structure. The chapter also presents a survey of the related literature.

The Musgrave-Thin marginal rate progression index is concerned with convexity of the tax schedule. This index takes a positive value only when the tax function is strictly convex, that is, when the marginal tax rate is increasing. However, this index is not scale invariant. An alternative local progressivity index which is also concerned with convexity of the tax schedule (equivalently, concavity of after-tax income) has been proposed by Richter and Hampe(1984). In terms of the notation introduced in Section 8.2, this index is defined as

$$H(z|f) = \frac{-\,d(1 - f'(z))}{dz} \cdot \frac{z}{(1 - f'(z))} \, . \qquad (8.35)$$

This index is scale transformation invariant and takes a positive value for an incentive preserving, strictly convex tax function.

Richter and Hampe(1984) also analysed the effect of convexity of the tax schedule on splitting of income among different components. To explain this, let $z^1, z^2, \ldots, z^k$ be income components in a given tax year. It is assumed that these are liable to separate taxation under the general provisions of tax law. $(z^1, z^2, \ldots, z^k)$ can be regarded as the income profile of a family or of married couple. It can also be interpreted as the distribution of incomes received by an individual in different time periods. If the tax function f is strictly convex then by Jensen's inequality (Marshall and Olkin(1979), p. 454), we have

$$f(z) = f\left(\sum_{i=1}^{k} z^i/k\right) \leq \sum_{i=1}^{k} f(z^i)/k = f(z^0) \text{ (say)}, \tag{8.36}$$

where the equality $f(\sum_{i=1}^{k} z^i/k) = \sum_{i=1}^{k} f(z^i)/k$ holds only when z^i is the same for all $i = 1, 2, \ldots, k$. (8.36) shows that if breakdown of income into components is allowed, then the government gives up the amount $[f(z^0) - f(z)]$ on an average. Therefore, in terms of revenue the average loss from splitting is

$$AL = \left[f(z^0) - f(z)\right] . \tag{8.37}$$

Equivalently, a taxpayer will gain from splitting in terms of after–tax income. If the after–tax income function $a(z) = z - f(z)$ is strictly concave, then applying Jensen's inequality again, we have

$$\begin{aligned} a(z) &= a\left(\sum_{i=1}^{k} z^i/k\right) \\ &\geq \sum_{i=1}^{k} a(z^i)/k = a(z^*) \text{ (say)} . \end{aligned} \tag{8.38}$$

Therefore, the average gain from splitting from the view point of the taxpayer is given by

$$AG = \left[a(z) - a(z^*) \right] . \tag{8.39}$$

Clearly, AG = AL. That is, whatever the government loses, on an average, from splitting is an average taxpayer's gain. If splitting is not allowed, then this amount can be cosidered as the excess burden of progressive taxation.

Hutton and Lambert(1977) examined the effect of progression on tax yield when incomes are growing. To illustrate their results let t(z) be the tax payable on income z ($0 \leq z \leq \infty$) and f(z) be the density function of that income for a given society of k individuals. Then total income is $Z = k\cdot \int_0^\infty t(z)f(z)\,dz$ and total revenue is $T(Z) = k\cdot \int_0^\infty t(z)f(z)\,dz$. Corresponding to the Musgrave and Thin(1948) average rate progression, Hutton and Lambert(1979) and Lambert(1984) defined average rate responsiveness by

$$A(Z) = \left[T'(Z) - \frac{T(Z)}{Z} \right] , \tag{8.40}$$

where T' stands for the derivative of T. A(Z) measures the excess of the marginal rate responsiveness or the effective marginal rate T'(Z) over the economy's average tax rate T(Z)/Z. T'(Z) measures the amount taken as revenue from one unit increase in total income. T'(Z) is an indicator of built–in flexibility. ['...Built–in flexibility is the automatic sensitivity of tax yield to national income variations' (Slitor(1948)).]

The average rate responsiveness can be rewritten in terms of the revenue elasticity e(Z) = (dT(Z)/dZ)(Z/T(Z)) as follows:

$$A(Z) = \frac{T(Z)}{Z} \left[e(Z) - 1 \right] . \tag{8.41}$$

e(Z) determines the percentage by which revenue will increase whenever aggregate income increases by one percent. (8.41) shows that given positivity of T(Z) and Z, A(Z) will be positive if and only if revenue T(Z) is elastic. The following result of Lambert (1984) (see also Hutton and Lambert(1979)) establishes the relationship between revenue responsiveness and average rate progression.

Theorem 8.3

Assume equiproportionate pre–tax income growth. Then a tax function f_1 has, for all pre–tax income z, a greater average rate progression than another tax function f_2 if and only if for every unequal pre–tax income profile the average rate responsiveness of f_1 is greater than that of f_2.

The above theorem says that using average rate progression as a local index the average rate responsiveness satisfies the minimal requirement for a revenue responsiveness index when pre–tax incomes grow equiproportionately. Some authors (e. g., Snowberger and Kirk(1973)) used revenue elasticity, which has also been referred to as liability responsiveness by Lambert(1984), as a revenue responsiveness index. But this does not meet the minimal requirement with respect to any local index (Hutton and Lambert(1979)). However, the Kay–Morris(1989) gross earnings deflator (GED) fulfils the minimal requirement when residual progression is used as a local index. GED is the elasticity of before–tax aggregate income with respect to after–tax aggregate income. The reciprocal of this is residual responsiveness, the gross analogue of residual progression (Lambert(1984)). Assuming equiproportionate after–tax income growth, as Kay and Morris do, GED gives the percentage increase of total ex–ante income required to achieve an increase in all ex–post incomes by one percent.

In view of the discussions carried out in Sections 8.2 and 8.6 we can now conclude that average rate progression, residual progression, liability progression and strict convexity of a tax function correspond respectively to the following effects of taxation:

(a) Revenue responsiveness (Hutton and Lambert(1979), Lambert(1984)),
(b) Redistributive (Jakobsson(1976)),
(c) Departure from proportionality (Jakobsson(1976)) and
(d) Average gain from splitting (Richter and Hampe(1984)).

We conclude this chapter with a brief discussion on ethical indices of benefit progressivity and net/tax benefit progressivity suggested by Blackorby and Donaldson (1984b). Let $b = (b_1, b_2, ..., b_n)$ stand for the benefit vector in an n–person community. 'The assignement of benefits measured in dollars to individuals, is, of course, somewhat artificial; however this sort of exercise has been implemented, for example, by Gillespie (1976)' (Blackorby and Donaldson(1984b)). Then the net tax vector is $a = t - b$, where t is the tax vector. The actual distribution vector corresponding to the ex–ante vector $x \in$

D^n is $y^a = x - t + b = y + b$.

Analogous to B_D^{2n} in (8.19), Blackorby and Donaldson(1986) constructed their relative benefit progressivity index by comparing the AKS EDE income of the actual post–tax/benefit vector with that of the vector that would arise if benefits were proportional to the post–tax incomes. For homothetic SEFs, this index can be written in terms of the AKS relative inequality index I_3 as follows:

$$C_D^{2n}(y,b) = \frac{I_3^n(y) - I_3^n(y^a)}{1 - I_3^n(y)} . \tag{8.42}$$

Simlarly, the relative net tax/benefit progressivity index is defined as the percentage increase in the AKS EDE income of the actual vector over what it would be if net taxes were proportional to pre–tax incomes. For homothetic SEFs this index is

$$F_D^{2n}(x,a) = \frac{I_3^n(x) - I_3^n(y^a)}{1 - I_3^n(x)} . \tag{8.43}$$

Using (8.19), (8.42) and (8.43), we derive the following multiplicative decomposition rule:

$$[1 + F_D^{2n}(x,a)] = [1 + C_D^{2n}(y,b)][1 + B_D^{2n}(y,t)] . \tag{8.44}$$

This decomposition shows how two indices of tax benefit progressivity have been combined to derive a single indicator of overall progressivity. Net progressivity in (8.44) is completely determined by the benefit progressivity index if taxes are raised proportionally. Similarly when benefits are proportional to ex–post incomes only tax progressivity matters. Blackorby and Donaldson(1984b) showed that for a given pre–tax profile, F_D^{2n} can be used to rank alternative tax–benefit schemes. Lambert(1988) provides further discussion on such indices.

Blackorby and Donaldson(1984b) also suggested absolute indices analogous to (8.42) and (8.43). They used steps similar to that employed in the construction of the absolute tax progressivity index B_A^{2n} in (8.24). For translatable SEFs the benefit and net indices

C_A^{2n} and F_A^{2n} can be written using the BDK index A_1 as follows:

$$C_A^{2n}(y,b) = A_1^n(y) - A_1^n(y^a) , \tag{8.45}$$

$$F_A^{2n}(x,a) = A_1^n(x) - A_1^n(y^a) . \tag{8.46}$$

Consequently, we have the following additive decomposition rule in the absolute case:

$$F_A^{2n}(x,a) = C_A^{2n}(y,b) + B_A^{2n}(y,t) . \tag{8.47}$$

Appendix

Proof of Lemma 8.1

From the given inequality we have

$$\sum_{i=1}^{n} (b_i/b_1) < \sum_{i=1}^{n} (a_i/a_1) \tag{A.1}$$

and

$$\sum_{i=1}^{n} (b_i/b_n) > \sum_{i=1}^{n} (a_i/a_n) . \tag{A.2}$$

Since both vectors are positive, from (A.1) and (A.2), we deduce that

$$(b_1/\sum_{i=1}^{n} b_i) > (a_1/\sum_{i=1}^{n} a_i) \tag{A.3}$$

and $$(b_n/\sum_{i=1}^{n} b_i) < (a_n/\sum_{i=1}^{n} a_i) . \tag{A.4}$$

Both a and b are arranged in increasing order so there exists an integer k such that

$$(b_i/\sum_{i=1}^{n} b_i) > (a_i/\sum_{i=1}^{n} a_i) \tag{A.5}$$

where $i \leq k$, and

$$(b_i / \sum_{i=1}^{n} b_i) \leq (a_i / \sum_{i=1}^{n} a_i) \tag{A.6}$$

where $i > k$. From the identity $(\sum_{i=1}^{n} b_i / \sum_{i=1}^{n} b_i) = (\sum_{i=1}^{n} a_i / \sum_{i=1}^{n} a_i)$ and (A.6), we have

$$(\sum_{i=1}^{k'} b_i / \sum_{i=1}^{n} b_i) \geq (\sum_{i=1}^{k'} a_i / \sum_{i=1}^{n} a_i) \tag{A.7}$$

where $k' > k$. (A.7) along with (A.5) shows that b strictly Lorenz dominates a.

■

CHAPTER 9

ETHICAL INDICES OF INCOME MOBILITY

9.1 Introduction

Indices of inequality are typically summary statistics of the dispersion of incomes at a particular point of time. Even if such indices are computed for a number of successive periods, by their very nature they will ignore many features of time path of incomes which are of interest. As time progresses we observe changes in relative incomes as well as changes in the absolute income differences found in any given time period. Indices of income mobility are meant to measure the magnitude of these changes. Indices of relative mobility measure changes in relative incomes while indices of absolute mobility measure changes in income differences.

In this chapter we are concerned with ethical indices of relative income mobility. These indices are derived from explicit social evaluation functions (SEFs) and are measures of the change in welfare resulting from mobility. The concept of mobility explored consists of a comparison between the time path of incomes received over a number of periods with a hypothetical time path of incomes obtained by supposing that starting from the actual first–period profile, the remaining income receipts exhibit complete immobility. We refer to these indices as indices of relative income mobility if this benchmark maintains relative incomes through time.

By using an SEF to perform this comparison, the ethical mobility indices will allow one to determine whether the observed changes are socially desirable or not. The idea that mobility can be either socially desirable or undesirable can be illustrated by considering an example. In this example, there are two people and two time periods. In the first period incomes are (10,10), while in the second period they are (19,1). In this example, the mobility in the income profile introduces inequality into the initial egalitarian situation and is therefore judged to be socially undesirable, the ethical mobility indices assign this change a negative value. In contrast, reverse change from (19,1) to (10,10) is socially desirable and the ethical indices will indicate this fact by assigning such a change a positive index value. For many descriptive purposes only the magnitude of mobility, and not its direction, is important. For such indices, the mobility associated with the move from (10,10) to (19,1) is regarded to be equal to the mobility associated with the move in the reverse direction.

The comparison of the actual time path of the income profile with a hypothetical immobile benchmark is central to the current approach. A natural way to perform this comparison is to introduce an intertemporal SEF (defined on time paths of income profiles) and to use this function to directly compare the actual time path of incomes with the benchmark. For this approach to yield interesting conclusions, it is necessary to put some structure on the form of this intertemporal evaluation function. We assume that the evaluation function is only sensitive to the total income received by each individual over all of the time periods under consideration. This assumption has been introduced to provide a concrete illustration of how to operationalise the concept of mobility explored. Problems with this particular approach and alternative ways of measuring mobility consistent with the general ethical perspective considered are discussed in the concluding section of this chapter.

Recently a substantial number of articles has appeared which concern themselves with various aspects of mobility. Most of these articles assume that the changes over time in the variables of interest are generated by transition matrices, that is, matrices with entries which show the fraction of the population which move from one category to another in one time period. In the context of income profiles, these categories could be ranks in the income profiles or the actual incomes received. In the latter case it is typically assumed that only a finite set of income levels are attainable and that this set is fixed over time. Shorrocks(1978), in an abstract setting meant to apply to changes in such diverse phenomena as social class or place of residence, studies mobility indices directly on transition matrices. Atkinson(1980) makes an interesting discussion on such indices. Kanbur and Stiglitz(1982) and Markandya(1982a, 1984), among others, evaluate mobility in terms of the time stream of income profiles that would result from the operation of the transition matrix, rather than directly in terms of the transition matrix itself. In Atkinson(1981) the results from Atkinson and Bourguignon(1982) on ranking bivariate distributions were used to rank mobility mechanisms, with a two period SEF which emphasized non–separability of welfare over time. Kanbur and Stiglitz(1986) restricted attention on dynastic prospects and provided a necessary and sufficient characterisation of social welfare ranking on the space of mobility matrices, where it is assumed that the SEF is symmetric and quasi–concave in dynastic expected welfares and lifetime utility is the present discounted sum of expected utility over an infinite horizon. Kanbur and Stromberg(1988) analysed dominance relations between sequences of income profiles generated by transition mechanisms. Necessary and sufficient conditions on these mechanisms are derived for a dominance relation to continue once established.

In this chapter we do not assume that the time path of incomes is generated by a transition matrix. Of more relevance to the inquiry made in the present chapter are the contributions of Shorrocks(1978a), Markandya(1982), King(1983) and Chakravarty (1984). While these authors are concerned with different concepts of mobility from the one considered here, an analysis of their mobility indices will lead to a deeper understanding of the approach adopted. Accordingly these alternative mobility indices are discussed in Section 3. In Section 2 we discuss the ethical indices in detail.

9.2 Ethical Indices of Relative Mobility[1]

In the previous chapters only one time period was considered. To study income mobility, income profiles from a sequence of time periods are required. The time interval $[t_0,t_m)$ is partitioned into m equal subperiods $[t_{k-1},t_k)$, $k = 1, 2, ..., m$ where m is a fixed exogenous integer. We refer to $[t_{k-1},t_k)$ as the k–th period. For period k, let x_i^k be person i's income. Assuming that in all subperiods incomes are distributed over a fixed population of size n, the income profile in period k is the vector $x^k = (x_1^k, x_2^k, ..., x_n^k)$. Sequences of income profiles, denoted by $X = (x^1, x^2, ..., x^m)$, are called income structures. Income structures are elements of D^{nm}. Person i's income stream is $x_i = (x_i^1, ..., x_i^m)$. Over the whole time interval $[t_0,t_m)$ person i receives $x_i^a = \sum_{k=1}^{m} x_i^k$. The corresponding income profile $x^a = (x_1^a, ..., x_n^a)$ is called aggregate profile.

The mobility concept to be explored here is the one embodied in a welfare comparison of the actual income structure X with a hypothetical benchmark structure X^b. The benchmark X^b is chosen to be completely immobile and to have the same first–period profile as the actual structure X. A comparison of X and X^b yields a mobility index precisely because the benchmark is a sequence of incomes which could have resulted in the

[1] This section is mainly based on Chakravarty, Dutta and Weymark(1985).

absence of mobility given the first–period period profile x^1. The use of an SEF to perform the comparison provides an ethical interpretation of the indices. The construction of the reference income structure depends, of course, on how complete immobility is defined. Here we consider a benchmark exhibiting complete relative immobility and thus obtain indices of relative mobility.

9.2.1 A Class of Ethical Indices of Relative Mobility

Definition 9.1

X exhibits complete relative immobility if and only if for all i, $x_i^k/\lambda(x^k)$ is the same for each period k, where $\lambda(x^k)$ is the mean income in period k.

With complete relative immobility, income shares are maintained through time. For an index of relative mobility the benchmark structure X^b corresponding to X is chosen to be completely relatively immobile[2]. It is denoted by X_R^b and is equal to the completely relative immobile structure with first–period profile equal to the actual first–period profile and the mean income in each period equal to actual mean income. Formally,

$$X_R^b = [x^1, x^1 \cdot \frac{\lambda(x^2)}{\lambda(x^1)}, \ldots, x^1 \cdot \frac{\lambda(x^m)}{\lambda(x^1)}] \,. \tag{9.1}$$

Consequently, the aggregate profile for this benchmark structure, denoted by x_R^b, gives each individual the same share of actual total income as they receive in period 1.

A mobility index assigns a numerical value to each income structure X in D^{nm}, i. e., it is a function M: $D^{nm} \rightarrow \mathbb{R}^1$. The ethical approach adopted in this chapter utilises an intertemporal SEF $\mathcal{W}^{nm}$: $D^{nm} \rightarrow \mathbb{R}^1$; $\mathcal{W}^{nm}$ is the social welfare level associated with the income structure X. The mobility indices are obtained by comparing this level of social welfare $\mathcal{W}^{nm}(X)$ with the level of social welfare $\mathcal{W}^{nm}(X_R^b)$ obtained with the benchmark structure X_R^b.

---

[2] For an index of absolute mobility, the benchmark is chosen to be completely absolutely immobile, i. e., income differences are maintained through time.

To provide a concrete illustration of this approach, it is assumed that the only features of the income structures X and X_R^b relevant for the welfare comparison are their aggregate profiles x^a and x_R^b. This assumption, while important for the specific results developed here, is not an essential feature of the concept of mobility explored. Formally, we assume that there exists a regular aggregate SEF $W^n\colon D^n \longrightarrow \mathbb{R}^1$ such that

$$W^n(x^a) = \mathscr{W}^{nm}(X) \; . \qquad (9.2)$$

for all $X \in D^{nm}$. Since W^n is regular, it can be expressed in its normalised form E^n, as described in Chapter 2 (Subsection 2.3.3).

Given E^n, we propose the use of an index of relative mobility in the class $\mathscr{M}_R$ where $M \in \mathscr{M}_R$ if and only if M can be written in the form

$$M(X) = \phi\left(\frac{E^n(x^a)}{E^n(x_R^b)}\right) , \qquad (9.3)$$

where $\phi\colon D^1 \longrightarrow \mathbb{R}^1$ is a continuous, increasing function with $\phi(1) = 0$. Indices in this class are ordinally equivalent to each other and to the ratio of the Atkinson – Kolm – Sen (AKS) equally distributed equivalent (EDE) income of the actual aggregate profile to that of the aggregate profile in the hypothetical immobile benchmark structure X_R^b[3]. The normalisation employed ensures that an immobile income structure is assigned a mobility value of zero.

Among the members of the class $\mathscr{M}_R$ one index stands out because of its simple interpretation. This index is obtained by setting $\phi(t) = t - 1$ in (9.3). Formally, this is the index

---

[3] Analogously, the AKS inequality index I_3 can be thought of as a member of a general class of inequality indices obtained by taking continuous, monotonic increasing transforms of I_3 in (2.27). The appeal of the AKS index in this class lies in its simple interpretation.

$$M_R(X) = \frac{E^n(x^a)}{E^n(x_R^b)} - 1 . \tag{9.4}$$

This index measures mobility as the percentage change in the EDE income of the actual aggregate profile compared with what it would be with the immobile benchmark structure X_R^b. M_R in (9.4) can be rewritten in terms of the AKS inequality index I_3 as follows:

$$M_R(X) = \frac{I_3^n(x_R^b) - I_3^n(x^a)}{1 - I_3^n(x_R^b)} , \tag{9.5}$$

where use has been made of the fact that X and X_R^b have the same mean.

Figure 9.1 illustrates the construction of M_R. In this diagram there are two individuals and two subperiods. Since $E^n(x^a) < E^n(x_R^b)$, the situation illustrated is one where $M_R(X)$ is negative; this mobility is socially undesirable.

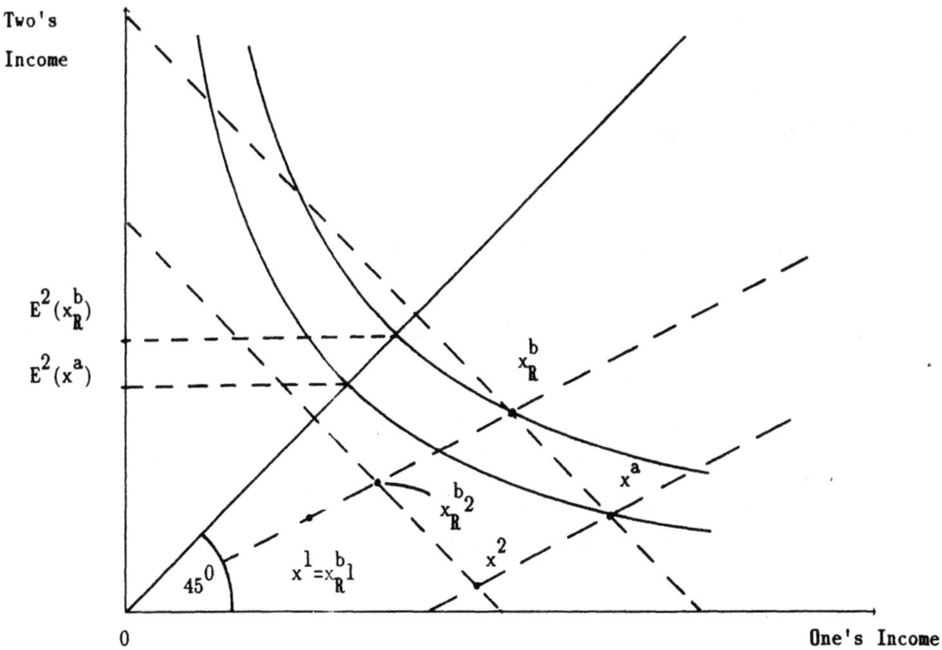

Figure 9.1

In constructing the index M_R, or any of the other indices in $\mathcal{M}_R$, the welfare (or inequality) comparisons only involve the income profiles x^a and x^b_R, profiles defined on a common time interval. Indeed, the SEF W^n in (9.2) is only constructed for income profiles on the complete interval $[t_0,t_m)$. If one assumes that we have an SEF defined on one–period incomes as well and that this function is the <u>same</u> as the m–period evaluation function W^n, then for homothetic evaluation functions we obtain

$$M_R(X) = \frac{\lambda(x^1)}{\lambda(x^a)} \cdot \frac{E^n(x^a)}{E^n(x^1)} - 1$$

$$= \frac{1 - I^n_3(x^a)}{1 - I^n_3(x^1)} - 1 \, , \tag{9.6}$$

in place of (9.4). $M_R(x)$ in (9.6) has a natural interpretation; it is the percentage change in equality of the aggregate profile compared with that of the first period profile. Thus, with <u>these additional assumptions</u> the mobility index M_R can be viewed as a measure of the change in inequality over the complete time interval compared to the inequality in the first period. As there does not appear to be convincing ethical justification for employing the same SEF (or, equivalently inequality index) over both the whole interval and over each of the subperiods, the mobility index defined in (9.3) is not, in general, an index of the change in inequality[4].

9.2.2 Properties for an Ethical Index of Relative Mobility

We now investigate the properties indices in the class $\mathcal{M}_R$ inherit from an aggregate SEF W^n. To facilitate comparisons with other indices of mobility, the formal statements of the properties are in terms of an arbitrary mobility index M: $D^{nm} \longrightarrow \mathbb{R}^1$ and an arbitrary immobile structure X^b. By an arbitrary immobile structure X^b we mean any income structure which embodies some notion of complete immobility and which has the same mean and the first period profile as the actual income structure X. To simplify the

[4] Shorrocks(1978a) presents an intriguing justification for using a common functional form.

exposition, we only verify that M_R satisfies the properties introduced in this section; it is an easy exercise to check that all members of $\mathcal{M}_R$ satisfy them as well.

The index M_R satisfies the first three properties we consider provided that the SEF W^n is regular[5].

The idea that an ethical index of mobility is obtained from a welfare comparison of the actual income structure with a reference immobile structure is formalised as Property 1.

<u>Property 1</u>

For all $X \in D^{nm}$, $M(X) = f(\mathcal{W}^{nm}(X), \mathcal{W}^{nm}(X^b))$, for some function f, with f being increasing in its first argument and decreasing in its second argument.

If the intertemporal SEF $\mathcal{W}^{nm}$ satisfies (9.2) for some regular aggregate SEF W^n, Property 1 can be equivalently expressed as Property 1'.

<u>Property 1'</u>

For all $X \in D^{nm}$, $M(X) = g(E^n(x^a), E^n(x^b))$ for some function g, with g increasing in its first argument and decreasing in its second argument.

The index M_R with the benchmark X_R^b clearly satisfies Property 1'.

The monotonicity properties of g have natural ethical interpretations. Assuming that $\mathcal{W}^{nm}$ satisfies (9.2) and that the benchmark is X_R^b, any mobility index satisfying Property 1' has the following properties as well. First in a comparison of the income structures X and Y, if $x^1 = y^1$ and $\lambda(x^a) = \lambda(y^a)$, then $M(X) \geq M(Y)$ if and only if $E^n(x^a) \geq E^n(y^a)$. This conclusion follows from the fact that $x_R^b = y_R^b$ when $x^1 = y^1$ and $\lambda(x^a) = \lambda(y^a)$[6]. Thus, we have an equivalence between increases in mobility and increases in social welfare whenever two income streams have the same total income (no incentive effects) and the same first-period profiles. Second for two income structures X and Y

---

5 Note that regularity of W^n ensures that M_R, and hence any member of $\mathcal{M}_R$, is well-defined for all $X \in D^{nm}$.

6 The benchmark structures X_R^b and Y_R^b could differ.

with $x^a = y^a$, $M(X) \gtreqless M(Y)$ if and only if $E^n(x_R^b) \lesseqgtr E^n(y_R^b)$. When two income structures have identical aggregate profiles, mobility is inversely related to the social desirability of the reference aggregate profile.

Because data are often measured imperfectly, it is desirable to have an index which is a continuous function of its arguments.

Property 2

M is continuous in X.

M_R satisfies this property since E^n is continuous and x^a and x_R^b both vary continuously with X.

If the actual income structure equals the benchmark structure, there is no mobility. As a normalisation rule, we assign immobile income structures an index value of zero.

Property 3

For all $X \in D^{nm}$, $M(X) = 0$ if $X = X^b$.

If $X = X_R^b$, then $x^a = x_R^b$ as well, so M_R satisfies this normalisation rule.

As noted in the introduction, in the current approach mobility can be socially desirable or socially undesirable. For a mobility index satisfying Properties 1, 2 and 3, socially desirable mobility is associated with income structures having positive index values while socially undesirable mobility is associated with income structures having negative index values.

If in addition to being regular, the SEF W^n is also strictly S–concave, then M_R satisfies two additional properties.

The first of these properties requires a mobility index to be symmetric. In other words, permutations of individuals in the income structure X leave the mobility index unchanged.

Property 4

M is symmetric in the income streams $(x_1, x_2, ..., x_n)$.

Permutations of income streams yield permutations of x^a and x_R^b. As strict S–concavity of W^n implies that E^n is symmetric, M_R satisfies Property 4.

We now consider the effects on mobility of a transfer of income in a single sub–period from one individual to another. The transfer is assumed to be from an individual who has at least as much income every period as the recipient, with the transfer assumed to be sufficiently small that these rankings do not change as a result of the transfer. If such a transfer occurs in the first period, both the benchmark and the actual income structures are affected, and, in general, the effect on mobility is ambiguous. However, if the transfer occurs in any other period but the first, there is no change in the benchmark profile. Using the Lorenz criterion, there is a clearcut reduction in inequality during the period in which the transfer occurs and no change in inequality in any other period. Consequently, it seems reasonable to describe the post–transfer income structure as exhibiting more mobility than the pre–transfer income structure. This poperty is stated formally as Property 5.

<u>Property 5</u>

For all X, Y $\in D^{nm}$, if $x^k = y^k$ for all $k \neq t$ with $t > 1$, $x_i^t = y_i^t$ for $i \neq j,l$, $x_j^k \geq x_l^k$ for all $k \neq t$, $x_j^t > x_l^t$, $y_j^t > y_l^t$, $y_j^t = x_j^t - \delta$, $y_l^t = x_l^t + \delta$ with $\delta > 0$, then M(Y) > M(X).

We now verify that M_R satisfies Property 5 when W^n is regular and strictly S–concave. The restriction that the transfer does not occur in period one implies that X and Y have the same benchmark structure, so $x_R^b = y_R^b$. Since $\lambda(x^a) = \lambda(y^a)$, y^a is obtained from x^a by a transfer of δ units of income from j to l. The satisfaction of Property 5 by M_R now follows immediately from Theorem 1.2.

An index M is an index of relative income mobility if it is constructed using a completely relatively immobile benchmark. This fact does not mean that M is a relative index. However, if one is concerned with mobility in income shares it seems appropriate to require that the mobility index be a relative index, i.e., an index which is invariant to proportional scalings of income structure.

<u>Property 6</u>

M is a relative index.

If W^n is both regular and homothetic, M_R satisfies Property 6. If $Y = \alpha X$ for some $\alpha > 0$, then $y^a = \alpha x^a$ and $y_R^b = \alpha x_R^b$. Hence if E^n is linearly homogeneous, from (9.3) we have $M_R(Y) = M_R(X)$, which establishes that M_R is a relative index.

Given a regular homothetic aggregate SEF W^n, $\mathcal{M}_R$ contains all the mobility indices which satisfy Properties 1', 2, 3 and 6. If the SEF W^n is also assumed to be strictly S–concave, the corresponding class of mobility indices $\mathcal{M}_R$ exhaust the set of indices which satisfy all the properties introduced in this subsection.

Theorem 9.1

If the SEF $W^n: D^n \to \mathbb{R}^1$ is regular, homothetic and the benchmark structure X^b is X_R^b, then for all $X \in D^{nm}$ a mobility index $M: D^{nm} \to \mathbb{R}^1$ is in $\mathcal{M}_R$ if and only if M satisfies Properties 1', 2, 3 and 6. If in addition W^n is strictly S–concave, then M also satisfies Properties 4 and 5.

Proof

In view of the preceding remarks, it is sufficient to show that Properties 1', 2, 3 and 6 imply M has the form (9.3). By Property 1',

$$M(Y) = g(E^n(x^a), E^n(x_R^b)) \; . \tag{9.7}$$

If (q_1, q_2) is in the domain of g, there must exist an income structure X such that $E^n(x^a) = q_1$ and $E^n(x_R^b) = q_2$. (Given that W^n is regular and the benchmark is X_R^b, the domain of g is D^2.) If $Y = \alpha X$, for some scalar $\alpha > 0$, then $y^a = \alpha x^a$ and $y_R^b = \alpha x_R^b$. Since E^n is linearly homogeneous, $E^n(y^a) = \alpha E^n(x^a)$ and $E^n(y_R^b) = \alpha E^n(x_R^b)$. By Property 6, $M(Y) = M(X)$ so $g(\alpha q_1, \alpha q_2) = g(q_1, q_2)$ for all $\alpha > 0$ and all (q_1, q_2) in the domain of g. Thus, g is homogeneous of degree zero, so M can be rewritten as

$$M(X) = \phi\left(\frac{E^n(x^a)}{E^n(x_R^b)}\right) \; . \tag{9.8}$$

Since $E^n(x) > 0$ for all $x \in D^n$, $\phi(r)$ only needs to be defined for $r > 0$. Property 2 implies ϕ is continuous since E^n is continuous and x^a and x_R^b are continuous in X. Property 1' implies ϕ is increasing, while Property 3 implies $\phi(1) = 0$. ■

Suppose $M \in \mathcal{M}_R$. We now illustrate its performance in two examples.

In the first example, $X(\epsilon) = ((1-\epsilon,1+\epsilon),(1+\epsilon,1-\epsilon))$ where $0 \leqq \epsilon < 1$. The common aggregate profile is $x^a = (2,2)$, while the reference aggregate profiles are $x_R^b(\epsilon) = (2-2\epsilon,2+2\epsilon)$. In an intuitively obvious sense, the extent of mobility depends on ϵ – the larger is ϵ, the greater is the mobility. Since the aggregate SEF is strictly S–concave, $E^2(x_R^b(\epsilon))$ is decreasing in ϵ. Hence by Property 1', $M(X(\epsilon))$ is increasing in ϵ, as desired.

In the second example, $X = ((10,10),(18,2))$ and $Y = ((18,2),(10,10))$. These structures differ only in the sequence of the one–period profiles. For X the income mobility introduces inequality into an egalitarian profile while for Y the inequality in the profile is narrowed by mobility. The second kind of mobility is socially desirable while the first is not. In this example $x^a = y^a = (28,12)$ and the reference aggregate profiles are $x_R^b = (20,20)$ and $y_R^b = (36,4)$. By strict S–concavity of E^n, $E^2(20,20) > E^2(28,12) > E^2(36,4)$. Thus, the argument in the function ϕ found in (9.3) is less than one for X and greater than one for Y, implying $M(X) < 0$ and $M(Y) > 0$.

9.2.3 A Characterisation Theorem

In the preceding discussion we have assumed that a functional form W^n for the SEF defined on the aggregate income profile has been pre–specified and used this functional form to construct the mobility index M_R (or some member of the class $\mathcal{M}_R$). In Chapter 2 (Subsection 2.3.3) we remarked that not only is it possible to determine a functional form for an inequality index given the functional form of an evaluation function, it is also possible to start with a functional form for an inequality index and determine the SEF which would generate the given inequality index. In this subsection we study the analogous problem for indices of relative mobility. Specifically we wish to determine a set of necessary and sufficient conditions on the form of a mobility index to guarantee that there exists an SEF defined on the aggregate income profile which would generate the mobility index by the formula (9.4). In other words, we wish to determine conditions on a mobility index which would enable us to interpret it as an ethical index of relative mobility in the class $\mathcal{M}_R$. If the mobility index can be given such an interpretation, it is also desirable to determine the functional form of underlying evaluation function from knowledge of the functional form of the mobility index. While it is always possible to recover an evalution function from an inequality index, it is often the case that the terms in the formula for the index must be manipulated before it is in the form given by (2.27). The Gini index provides such an example(see Chapter 2, Subsection 2.3.3). With mobility indices, it is not a priori obvious that the formula for the mobility index can be rearranged into the form (9.4), as the unknown evaluation function appears in a ratio form. We show that it is possible to determine the functional form of the underlying evaluation function by constructing an algorithm designed for this purpose.

The discussion in the previous subsection has shown that a mobility index derived from a regular SEF defined on aggregate income profiles using (9.4) must satisfy Properties 1', 2 and 3. However, to use Property 1' as one of the necessary and sufficient conditions would be inappropriate, as this axiomexplicitly assumes that a welfare function exists; a satisfactory set of conditions on M would not involve reference to an SEF. Two new properties which share this characteristic are now introduced. While Properties 1 – 6 are natural restrictions on an ethical index of relative mobility, the two new properties described below do not have the same a priori appeal. However, if a regular aggregate SEF is used to derive M_R, this index necessarily satisfies these additional properties and, consequently, these properties must be imposed on an index M if it is to have the ethical interpretation described above.

The index M_R in (9.4) is the percentage change in the EDE income of the actual aggregate profile compared with what it would be with the immobile benchmark structure. Since E^n is assumed to be regular, $E^n(x) > 0$ for all $x \in D^n$. As a consequence, the largest percentage decrease in the EDE income of the actual aggregate profile compared with what it would be with the immobile benchmark structure is bounded by 100%. (The index M_R has no upper bound.) This restriction on the value of a mobility index is stated as Property 7.

Property 7

For all $X \in D^{nm}$, $M(X) > -1$.

The last property considered requires the introduction of some additional notation. Define

$$S = \{X \in D^{nm} \mid x_i^1 = x_j^1,\ i,j = 1,2, ..., n\} \ . \tag{9.9}$$

The set S consists of all income structures which have completely equal first–period profiles. For all $x \in D^n$, define

$$\Psi(x) = \{X \in D^{nm} \mid X \in S \text{ and } x^a = x\} \ . \tag{9.10}$$

The set $\Psi(x)$ consists of all income structures with equal first–period incomes which have aggregate profiles equal to x. Similarly for all $X \in D^{nm}$, define

$$\Psi'(X) = \{Y \in D^{nm} \mid Y \in S \text{ and } y^a = x^a\} \ . \tag{9.11}$$

The set $\Psi'(X)$ consists of all income structures with equal first–period incomes which have the same aggregate distribution as the structure X. The following theorem shows that $\Psi(x)$ and $\Psi'(X)$ are both non–empty.

<u>Theorem 9.2</u>

(a) For all $x \in D^n$, $\Psi(x)$ is non–empty.
(b) For all $X \in D^{nm}$, $\Psi'(X)$ is non–empty.

<u>Proof</u>

(a) The proof is by construction.
For $x \in D^n$, let $\mu = \min_i \{x_i\} > 0$. Set $x^1 = (\mu \cdot 1^n)/m$. For the remaining periods, let $x_i^k = (\dfrac{1}{m-1}) \cdot (x_i - x_i^1)$. For the income structure X obtained by this algorithm we have $X \in S$ and $x^a = x$.
(b) Part (b) follows immediately from the definition (9.11) and the proof of (a)[7]. ■

---

[7] For $x \in D^n$, if $x_i = 0$ for some i, then the algorithm yields the first period profile $0 \cdot 1^n$, a profile which is not in the domain. Consequently, for such x, $\Psi(x)$ is empty. Thus, strictly speaking, Theorem 9.2 is valid for all those profiles all of whose components are positive. However, this boundary problem is unimportant for the main theorem of this subsection.

One of the major goals in this section is to provide an algorithm which enables us to generate an aggregate SEF which rationalises a given mobility index. Theorem 9.2 and its proof provide a key element in this endeavour. Theorem 9.2(b) says that for any income structure X, there exists an income structure Y with the same aggregate profile as X but which has a first–period profile exhibiting complete equality.

The mobility indices belonging to the class $\mathcal{M}_R$ are normalised so that immobile benchmark structures are assigned zero value. It is convenient to consider an alternative normalisation obtained by setting

$$\bar{M}(X) = M(X) + 1 \tag{9.12}$$

for all $X \in D^{nm}$. If M satisfies Property 3, then $\bar{M}(X) = 1$ for any completely relatively immobile benchmark structure.

Because attention is restricted to mobility indices which compare the actual aggregate profile with the aggregate benchmark profile, all elements of $\Psi'(X)$ which have the same mean first–period income are assigned the same index value. For an income structure X $\in$ S, that is, an income structure with equal first–period incomes, the corresponding benchmark X_R^b is completely relatively immobile, so $\bar{M}(X) = \bar{M}(X)/\bar{M}(X_R^b)$ as $\bar{M}(X_R^b) = 1$. Furthermore, for such X, $X \in \Psi'(X)$, so $\bar{M}(\hat{X}) = \bar{M}(X)$ for all $\hat{X} \in \Psi'(X)$ which have $\lambda(\hat{x}^1) = \lambda(x^1)$. Analogously, $M(\tilde{X}) = \bar{M}(X_R^b)$ for all $\tilde{X} \in \Psi'(X_R^b)$ which have $\lambda(\tilde{x}^1) = \lambda(x^1)$. Consequently, for all $X \in S$,

$$\bar{M}(X) = \frac{\bar{M}(\hat{X})}{\bar{M}(\tilde{X})} \tag{9.13}$$

if $\hat{X} \in \Psi'(X)$, $\tilde{X} \in \Psi'(X_R^b)$ and $\lambda(\hat{x}^1) = \lambda(\tilde{x}^1) = \lambda(x^1)$. Equation (9.13) can be viewed as a decomposition principle. Property 8 requires that a mobility index satisfies (9.13) for all $X \in D^{nm}$, not just for $X \in S$, provided $\hat{x}^1$ and $\tilde{x}^1$ have equal means.

<u>Property 8</u>

For all $X \in D^{nm}$, if $\hat{X} \in \Psi'(X)$, if $\tilde{X} \in \Psi'(X^b)$, and if $\hat{x}^1 = \tilde{x}^1$, then $\bar{M}$ satisfies (9.13).

Property 8 may be of considerable practical benefit in constructing mobility indices.

The income structures $\hat{X}$ and $\tilde{X}$ have equal first–period incomes, making it easier to judge the mobility in the income structure than would be the case for an income structure in $D^{nm}\backslash S$. Property 8 says that the evaluation of the mobility exhibited by a structure X can always be decomposed into evaluations of simpler structures which initially have equal means.

We now demonstrate that Property 8 implies: (i) the normalisation rule, Property 3, and (ii) for all $X \in D^{nm}$,

$$M(X) = h(x^a, x^b) \qquad (9.14)$$

for some function h[8].

<u>Theorem 9.3</u>

Property 8 implies Property 3.

<u>Proof</u>

Since $\lambda(x^a) = \lambda(x^b)$ for all $X \in D^{nm}$, the algorithm used to establish Theorem 9.2 implies that two structures $\hat{X}$ and $\tilde{X}$ can be found to satisfy the antecedent in Property 8 for any $X \in D^{nm}$. If $X = X^b$, $\Psi'(X) = \Psi'(X^b)$ and $\hat{X}$ can be chosen to equal $\tilde{X}$. Doing this implies $\bar{M}(X) = 1$, that is, $M(X) = 0$. ■

<u>Theorem 9.4</u>

Property 8 implies (9.14).

<u>Proof</u>

Consider Y and Z with $y^a = z^a$ and $y^b = z^b$. By construction $\Psi'(Y) = \Psi'(Z)$ and $\Psi'(Y^b) = \Psi'(Z^b)$. Using the observation in the first line of the proof of Theorem 9.3, we can verify the hypothesis of Property 8 for Y and Z with $\hat{Y} = \hat{Z}$ and $\tilde{Y} = \tilde{Z}$. The conclusion now follows from (9.12) and (9.13). ■

We are now in a position to state the main theorem concerning the ethical interpretation of a mobility index.

---

8 Recall that a defining characteristic of an immobile benchmark X^b is $\lambda(x^a) = \lambda(x^b)$.

Theorem 9.5

There exists a regular aggregate SEF $W^n: D^n \longrightarrow \mathbb{R}^1$ which generates the mobility index $M: D^{nm} \longrightarrow \mathbb{R}^1$ by means of (9.4) if and only if M satisfies Properties 2, 7 and 8 with $X^b = X^b_R$. If M satisfies Properties 2, 7 and 8 and $X^b = X^b_R$, then knowledge of the functional form of M is sufficient to determine the functional form of W^n upto an increasing monotone transformation.

Proof

(a) Necessity

Our informal discussion has already established that M must satisfy Properties 2 and 7 if W^n is regular. To show that Property 8 is also satisfied suppose $\hat{X} \in \Psi'(X)$, $\tilde{X} \in \Psi'(X^b_R)$, and $\hat{x}^1 = \tilde{x}^1$. We have

$$\bar{M}(X) = \frac{E^n(x^a)}{E^n(x^b_R)}$$

$$= \frac{E^n(\hat{x}^a)}{E^n(\tilde{x}^a)} \qquad \text{(since } \hat{x}^a = x^a \text{ and } \tilde{x}^a = x^b_R\text{)}$$

$$= \frac{E^n(\hat{x}^a)/\lambda(\hat{x}^b_R)}{E^n(\tilde{x}^a)/\lambda(\tilde{x}^b_R)} \qquad \text{(since } \lambda(x^b_R) = \lambda(\tilde{x}^b_R)\text{)}$$

$$= \frac{E^n(\hat{x}^a)/E^n(\hat{x}^b_R)}{E^n(\tilde{x}^a)/E^n(\tilde{x}^b_R)} \qquad \text{(since } \hat{x}^b_R \text{ and } \tilde{x}^b_R \text{ are on the ray of equality)}$$

$$= \frac{\bar{M}(\hat{X})}{\bar{M}(\tilde{X})} .$$

(b) Sufficiency

To establish the sufficiency part of the theorem we actually construct the SEF, thus also proving the last part of the theorem.

For $x \in D^n$, let X(x) denote the income structure generated by the algorithm introduced in the proof of Theorem 9.2. Define $\Omega: D^n \longrightarrow \mathbb{R}^1$ by

$$\Omega(x) = [M(X(x)) + 1] \cdot \lambda(x) . \tag{9.15}$$

We demonstrate that Ω is a regular EDE income function which generates M by means of (9.4).

First we show that Ω is a regular EDE income function. By Proprty 2, M is continuous. As $X(\cdot)$ and $\lambda(\cdot)$ are continuous as well, Ω is continuous. If x has equal components, X(x) has also equal components and the benchmark corresponding to X(x) is simply X(x). By Property 8, $M(X(x)) = 0$. Using (9.15), $\Omega(x) = \lambda(x)$. Thus, Ω is increasing along the ray of equality and has the appropriate normalisation for an EDE income function. For an arbitrary $x \in D^n$, $\lambda(x) > 0$ and, by Property 7, $M(X(x)) > -1$. Thus, from (9.15), $\Omega(x) > 0$ and the social indifference curve through x intersects the ray of equality at the point $\lambda(x) \cdot 1^n$.

We now show that using Ω as an EDE income function, $M(X) = M_R(X)$ for all $X \in D^{nm}$ i. e., M is generated from Ω by means of (9.4). For an arbitrary $X \in D^{nm}$, determine the correspondending x^a and x_R^b. Let $\hat{X} = X(x^a)$ and $\tilde{X} = X(x^b)$. From (9.15),

$$\frac{\Omega(x^a)}{\Omega(x_R^b)} = \frac{\bar{M}(\hat{X})}{\bar{M}(\tilde{X})} \cdot \frac{\lambda(x^a)}{\lambda(x_R^b)} . \tag{9.16}$$

By the definition of the benchmark, $\lambda(x^a) = \lambda(x_R^b)$, so

$$\frac{\Omega(x^a)}{\Omega(x_R^b)} = \frac{\bar{M}(\hat{X})}{\bar{M}(\tilde{X})} . \tag{9.17}$$

By the construction, $\hat{X} \in \Psi'(X)$, $\tilde{X} \in \Psi'(X_R^b)$, and $\hat{x}^1 = \tilde{x}^1$. Hence by Property 8,

$$\bar{M}(X) = \frac{\bar{M}(\hat{X})}{\bar{M}(\tilde{X})} . \tag{9.18}$$

Substituting (9.18) in (9.17),

$$\Omega(x^a) = [M(X) + 1] \cdot \Omega(X_R^b),$$

which is (9.4) with Ω substituted for E^n amd M substituted for M_R[9]. ■

The basic idea of the algorithm used to construct an SEF W^n (more precisely, an EDE income function E^n) from the functional form of a mobility index M is quite simple, and can be illustrated with a numerical example.

Suppose there are two individuals, two subperiods, the functional form of M is known, and we wish to determine $E^2(x)$ for $x = (14,4)$. From Theorem 9.2, it is known that there exists an income structure X with equal first–period incomes which has x as its aggregate income. Applying the algorithm given in the proof of Theorem 9.2 to construct such a structure, we obtain $X = ((2,2),(12,2))$. Since the functional form of M is given, we know the value of $M((2,2),(12,2))$, say 3. The benchmark aggregate profile corresponding to X is $x_R^b = (9,9)$. This benchmark aggregate profile must have equal components since the structure X has equal first–period incomes. Consequently, the value of $E^2(x_R^b)$ is known since $E^n(\alpha \cdot 1^n) = \alpha$ for all $\alpha > 0$. In this example, $E^2(x_R^b) = E^2(9,9) = 9$. It is this fact which allows us to untangle the ratio of term involving the EDE income functions in (9.4). Since $x = x^a$, substituting the mobility index value of 3 for the left–hand side of (9.4) and substituting 9 for $E^2(x_R^b)$, we obtain the unknown value for $E^2(14,4)$, namely, $E^2(14,4) = (3 + 1) \cdot 9 = 36$.

In Theorem 9.5, the aggregate SEF W^n is only required to be regular. The implications of requiring this function to also be homothetic and/or strictly S–concave are stated in Theorem 9.6.

Theorem 9.6

(a) There exists a regular homothetic aggregate SEF $W^n: D^n \to \mathbb{R}^1$ which gene–

9 For proving sufficiency part of Theorem 9.5, use has been made of the algorithm introduced in the proof of Theorem 9.2. Thus, we have implicitly assumed that all the components of the income vector x are positive. If $x_i = 0$ for some i, the algorithm is used to determine Ω on strictly positive part of D^n and continuity is used to determine the values on the boundary of the domain.

rates the mobility index $M: D^{nm} \rightarrow \mathbb{R}^1$ by means of (9.4) if and only if M satisfies Properties 2, 6, 7 and 8 with $X^b = X^b_R$.

(b) There exists a regular strictly S–concave aggregate SEF $W^n: D^n \rightarrow \mathbb{R}^1$ which generates the mobility index $M: D^{nm} \rightarrow \mathbb{R}^1$ by means of (9.4) if and only if M satisfies Properties 2, 4, 5, 7 and 8 with $X^b = X^b_R$.

<u>Proof</u>

The remarks made in Subsection 9.2.2 establish the necessity part of the proof, so we restrict attention to sufficiency.

(a) Suppose $\hat{x} = \alpha x$ for some scalar $\alpha > 0$. Construct the structures X and $\hat{X}$ according to the algorithm used to prove Theorem 9.2. Thus $\hat{X} = \alpha X$ and $\hat{x}^b_R = \alpha x^b_R$, where $x^b_R = \lambda(X^b_R) \cdot 1^n$. Hence $E^n(\hat{x}^b_R) = \alpha E^n(x^b_R)$. Combined with the assumption that M is a relative index, we obtain from (9.4) that E^n is linearly homogeneous and, by Theorem 2.7, W^n is homothetic.

(b) Suppose $\hat{x}_i = x_i$ for all $i \neq j,l$ $x_j > x_l$, $\hat{x}_j > \hat{x}_l$, $\hat{x}_j = x_j - \delta$ and $\hat{x}_l = x_l + \delta$. We wish to construct structures from x and $\hat{x}$ which have $x^1 = \hat{x}^1$. Note that the algorithm used in the proof of Theorem 9.2 will not achieve this objective if l is the unique recipient of the minimal income in x. To overcome this difficulty we apply the algorithm in the proof of Theorem 9.2 to obtain the structure X from x and define the structure $\hat{X}$ by setting $\hat{x}^1 = x^1$ and letting $\hat{x}^k = (\hat{x} - \hat{x}^1)/(m-1)$ for all $k \geq 2$. Note that $\hat{x}_i - \hat{x}^1_i > 0$ for all i. For all $k \geq 2$, $\hat{x}^k_i = x^k_i$ for $i \neq j, l$, $x^k_j > x^k_l$, $\hat{x}^k_j > \hat{x}^k_l$, $\hat{x}^k_j = x^k_j - (\dfrac{\delta}{m-1})$, and $\hat{x}^k_l = x^k_l + (\dfrac{\delta}{m-1})$. By an application of Property 5 to each $k \geq 2$ separately, we obtain from (9.4) that $E^n(\hat{x}) > E^n(x)$ as $x^a = x$ and $\hat{x}^a = \hat{x}$. Property 4 implies that E^n is symmetric, so by Theorem 1.2, E^n (and hence W^n) is strictly S–concave. ∎

Theorem 9.5 and 9.6 are extremely powerful results. Theorem 9.5 shows that any mobility index M which satisfies Properties 2, 7 and 8 can be thought of as being an index generated by a regular aggregate SEF by means of (9.4). This conclusion is true regardless of whether the mobility index is in fact so constructed. By writing the mobility index explicitly in the form shown in (9.4), Theorems 9.3, 9.4 and 9.5 tell us that the mobility index will <u>automatically</u> possess Property 3 and satisfy (9.14). Furthermore,

Theorem 9.6 informs us that the implicit evaluation function is homothetic if M is a relative index and is strictly S–concave if M satisfies Properties 4 and 5.

9.3 Alternative Concepts of Mobility

In this section we contrast the ethical approach to measuring relative income mobility with the alternative mobility concepts considered by Shorrocks(1978a), Markandya (1982), King(1983) and Chakravarty(1984). Because each of these authors is interested in a different aspect of mobility from the one considered in Section 9.2, not all of the properties of mobility indices considered in Subsection 9.2.2 are appropriate for their indices. However, by contrasting these alternative approaches to the ethical approach, it is hoped that the implications of adopting the mobility indices discussed in Section 9.2 will be more fully appreciated.

9.3.1 Shorrocks' Concept of Mobility

Shorrocks(1978a) is primarily interested in constructing a descriptive index of income mobility, although he does suggest a social welfare interpretation for the measure he proposes. In his study, 'mobility is measured by the extent to which the income distribution is equalised as the accounting period is extended'. Shorrocks works with relative inequality indices and to simplify the exposition it is assumed that they are continuous, strictly S–convex and normalised on [0,1]. Shorrocks' results on descriptive mobility indices hold for a somewhat more general class of inequality indices, but this generality is not an issue for the points we wish to discuss.

Given a particular relative inequality index I, Shorrocks wishes to compare the inequality $I^n(x^a)$ when the accounting period is the complete time interval $[t_0,t_m)$ with the m one–period inequality values $I^n(x^k)$, $k = 1, \dots, m$. Thus, in contrast to the ethical approach, Shorrocks assumes that the functional form for an inequality index is the same for each of the subperiods and for the whole time interval. To make this comparison operational, the one–period measures are combined into a single–measure by taking a weighted sum, where the kth weight $w^k = \lambda(x^k)/\lambda(x^a)$. Formally, Shorrocks' mobility index is the function M_S: $D^{nm} \rightarrow \mathbb{R}^1$ defined by

$$M_S(X) = 1 - \frac{I^n(x^a)}{\sum_{k=1}^{m} w^k I^n(x^k)} . \tag{9.19}$$

Shorrocks demonstrates that M_S lies in the interval [0,1], attaining its minimum value when relative incomes remain constant over time and attaining its maximum value when the aggregate incomes are completely equalised.

Even when used as a descriptive index, Shorrocks' measure can yield unintuitive conclusions. As an illustration, let us consider the first example discussed in Section 9.2.2. In that example we considered the income structure $X(\epsilon) = ((1-\epsilon,1+\epsilon),(1+\epsilon,1-\epsilon))$, concluding that mobility increases with ϵ, a property exhibted by any $M \in \mathcal{M}_R$. The aggregate profile for $X(\epsilon)$ is $x^a = (2,2)$, so $M_S = 1$ (complete mobility) regardless of the value of ϵ. This feature of M_S arises due to the fact that $I^n(x^a)$ may be close to zero either because annual inequalities are very low or because annual inequalities are high but the relative income variations cancel out over time. One would surely only wish to call an income structure mobile in the latter case.

If the inequality index in (9.19) is an AKS index, Shorrocks shows that (9.19) may be rewritten as

$$M_S(X) = 1 - \frac{\lambda(x^a) - E^n(x^a)}{\sum_{k=1}^{m} [\lambda(x^k) - E^n(x^k)]} . \tag{9.20}$$

The numerator of the right–hand term in (9.20) is interpreted to be the 'true welfare loss' per capita while the denominator is the 'apparent welfare loss' per capita. As the numerator never exceeds the denominator, Shorrocks concludes that mobility is <u>always desirable</u>. Furthermore, he argues that if two income structures have the same total income and have vectors of one–period incomes which are permutations of each other, then social welfare is greater for the structure exhibiting the largest mobility.

In the ethical approach mobility could be either socially desirable or socially harmful, depending on how the actual aggregate profile is ranked in comparison with the immobile benchmark profile. Thus, in the example with $X = ((10,10),(18,2))$ and $Y =$

((18,2),(10,10)) we have found $M_R(X) < 0$ and $M_R(Y) > 0$. For Shorrocks' index $M_S(X) = M_S(Y)$ since these structures differ only in the sequence of one period profiles. We believe that the actual time sequence of incomes is important in constructing an ethical index of mobility[10,11].

9.3.2 Markandya's Concept of Mobility

Markandya's analysis is restricted to situations involving two periods. He views mobility 'as something of interest in itself and distinct from changes in equality'. He regards the movement from x^1 to x^2 in the income structure $X = (x^1,x^2)$ as involving, in general, a change in total income, a change in inequality, and mobility in the income profile. He eliminates the first source of change by scaling each period's income profile so that their means are equal. Call this income structure $\hat{X} = (\hat{x}^1,\hat{x}^2)$. To measure 'mobility as distinct from changes in inequality', Markandya introduces a hypothetical income structure $X^M = (x^{M1},x^{M2})$ which involves no change in inequality between two time periods. Specifically, for a relative inequality index I^n defined on one–period incomes he chooses $x^{M1} = \hat{x}^1$ and x^{M2} to be the element closest to $\hat{x}^2$ among all the profiles x which have $I^n(x) = I^n(\hat{x}^1)$ and $\lambda(x) = \lambda(\hat{x}^1)$. Markandya uses the square of the coefficient of variation as the inequality index and measures mobility by the normalised distance between x^{M1} and x^{M2},

$$M_M(X) = \frac{[\sum_{i=1}^{n} (x_i^{M2} - x_i^{M1})^2]^{1/2}}{2[\sum_{i=1}^{n} (x_i^{M1} - 1)^2]^{1/2}} . \tag{9.21}$$

The denominator in (9.21) ensures that the index value lies in the interval [0,1], taking the lower bound if and only if $x^{M1} = x^{M2}$ and the upper bound when x^{M2} is the permutation of x^{M1} obtained by reversing the rank order in the initial profile[12].

---

10 Markandya(1982a) provides further discussion of Shorrocks' index.

11 Using U.S. income data, Shorrocks(1981) provided a numerical illustration of his mobility index.

12 When there are only two people mobility is zero if rank orders do not change and one if they do.

While Markandya often refers to welfare functions it is not clear if he views his mobility index as having ethical significance. Because M_M measures the distance between two profiles, and is thus non–negative, it is not possible to distinguish socially desirable and socially undesirable mobility in this framework. Furthermore, one can easily verify that $M_M(X) = M_M(Y)$ if X and Y differ only in the order of the two time periods[13].

The most interesting feature of Markandya's index is its use of a hypothetical income structure, albeit one quite different from that of ethical index. While in the ethical approach the counterfactual benchmark is a structure exhibiting no mobility, Markandya's structure exhibits no change in inequality between periods.

9.3.3 King's Concept of Mobility

King(1983) is essentially interested in obtaining a normative index which measures changes in the rank orders of income profile. His analysis is conducted in a two–period framework. From the actual income structure $X = (x^1,x^2)$ King, in effect, constructs a hypothetical benchmark structure $X = (\hat{x}^1,\hat{x}^2)$ where $\hat{x}^1 = x^1$ and $\hat{x}_i^2$ is the element in $\{x_1^2, \dots, x_n^2\}$ which person i would obtain if his rank order in the income profile did not change (from x^1). This hypothetical structure is used to define the scaled order statistic $e_i = |\hat{x}_i^2 - x_i^2|/\lambda(x^2)$, i = 1, 2, ..., n.

King's SEF is defined on the final profile x^2 and the vector of scaled order statistics $e = (e_1, e_2, \dots, e_n)$,

$$W^{2n}(x^2,e) \ . \tag{9.22}$$

King assumes that W^{2n} is increasing in all of its arguments. Using (9.22) he determines a 'zero mobility equivalent proportion of income ρ', defined implicitly in

$$W^{2n}(\rho x^2,0\cdot 1^n) = W^{2n}(x^2,e) \ . \tag{9.23}$$

---

13 If some other inequality index I^n is used in place of the squared coefficient of variation, this property of Markandya's index need not hold if $I^n(\hat{x}^1) \neq I^n(\hat{x}^2)$. It continues to hold if $I^n(\hat{x}^1) = I^n(\hat{x}^2)$.

The increasingness of W implies $\rho \geqq 1$, where the lower bound is attained whenever there is no change in rank orders. King's index of mobility is

$$M_K(X) = 1 - \frac{1}{\rho} . \tag{9.24}$$

This index is interpreted to be the 'proportion of total income which, from a position of zero mobility, we would be prepared to sacrifice in order to achieve the degree of mobility we observe'.

To get explicit functional form of the index in (9.24) it is necessary to put some structure on the SEF. King considered the additively separable form of the SEF and constructed a particular index of mobility. For generalising this to an arbitrary SEF, we assume that the SEF in (9.22) be written as

$$W^{2n}(x^2,e) = W^n(x_1^2 \cdot e^{\alpha e_1}, x_2^2 \cdot e^{\alpha e_2}, ..., x_n^2 \cdot e^{\alpha e_n}) \tag{9.25}$$

where $\alpha > 0$ is the immobility aversion parameter[14]. If W^n in (9.25) is the symmetric mean of order r (< 1), then $M_K(X)$ is the particular index constructed by King. It is evident from (9.25) that given any homothetic SEF we have a corresponding index of relative mobility.

A natural extension of the preceding analysis is the construction of absolute mobility indices. For this we assume that the increasing, translatable SEF be written as

$$W^{2n}(x,d) = W^n(x_1 + d_1, ..., x_n + d_n) , \tag{9.26}$$

where $d = (d_1, d_2, ..., d_n)$ and $d_i = \lambda(x^2) \cdot e_i$, i = 1, 2, ..., n.

We now determine c, an equal equivalent income level, defined implicitly by

$$W^n(x + c \cdot 1^n) = W^n(x + d) . \tag{9.27}$$

---

[14] More generally, we can multiply x_i^2 in (9.25) by $f(e_i)$ where f is increasing, continuous and f(0) = 1. Increasingness of f reflects social desirability of mobility, that is, changes in rank orders.

c can be referred to as the zero mobility equivalent absolute income. From policy point of view c is the amount of income, which, if given to each individual, enables the community to reach the level of mobility that exists from the situation of zero mobility at an aggregate cost of nc. Thus, a natural index of absolute mobility is

$$M_A(X) = nc \ . \tag{9.28}$$

M_A is bounded below by zero, where this bound is achieved in the case of zero mobility. Given a translatable SEF, there exists an absolute mobility index of the type (9.28) that measures total cost of mobility.

According to the King concept of mobility, if there is no difference between the rank orders in x^1 and x^2, there is no mobility (since $e_i = 0$). In the ethical approach there can be mobility whenever relative incomes change, even if there are no rank order changes.

Again the most interesting feature of the King indices is their use of a hypothetical benchmark structure. While these indices are based on a benchmark which exhibits no change in rank orders, the ethical indices use a benchmark which exhibits no mobility in relative incomes.

9.4 Concluding Remarks

The innovative feature of the approach adopted in Section 9.2 is the suggestion embodied in Property 1 that an ethical index of income mobility is obtained from a welfare comparison of the actual income structure X with an immobile benchmark structure X^b. However, for the specific indices considered in Section 9.2, this comparison has been operationalised by making the assumptions that the benchmark is a relatively immobile income structure and that the intertemporal evaluation function used to make the comparison is sensitive only to the aggregate income profile. Alternatives to both of these assumptions are possible within the general framework considered in the section. For example, if one is interested in indices of absolute income mobility, it is more appropriate to use a benchmark which preserves income differences through time.

For two–period problems, the assumptions that the intertemporal evaluation function is sensitive to only the aggregate income profile does not appear to be an unreasonable restriction as income profiles in both periods are reflected in the construction of the ethical indices, the first–period profile through its effect on the aggregate benchmark profile x_R^b and the second–period profile through its effect on the actual aggregate profile x^a. With more than two periods, these indices are sensitive to only x^1 and $\sum_{k=2}^{m} x^k$ rather than the whole structure X. Consequently, these indices have properties which to many would seem inappropriate. For example, consider the following two person, three period structures. In the first structure X = ((2,2),(2,2),(2,2)), a structure exhibiting no mobility. In the second, X = ((2,2),(3,1),(1,3)), a structure which also exhibits no mobility for any mobility index derived from an intertemporal evaluation function sensitive only to aggregate profiles. Examples, such as this, provide an important test for the assumption that $\mathscr{W}$ satisfies (9.2).

However, in the light of such examples, it seems worth exploring other ways of operationalising welfare comparison. One such way is suggested by the growing literature on measuring lifetime income and lifetime inequality, a literature which includes contributions by von Weizsäcker(1978), Cowell(1979) and Blewett(1982). In this literature each individual has an intertemporal utility function U^1: $D^m \longrightarrow \mathbb{R}^1$ which is used to evaluate his income stream x_i. An individual may care about the time path of this income receipts because of capital market imperfections or a number of other reasons studied by Cowell. With perfect capital markets these utility functions will depend nontrivially only on the present–value of the income stream. Cowell has suggested a useful way of employing the intertemporal utility functions to construct a summary statistic x_i^r of the income stream x_i, which following Blewett we call representative life time income. Representative lifetime income is defined to be the level of income which if received in each subperiod would yield an income stream judged equivalent to the actual income stream[15]. Formally, it is implicitly defined by

$$U^i(x_i^r \cdot 1^m) = U^i(x_i) . \tag{9.29}$$

Thus, the construction of x_i^r is similar in spirit to the construction of the EDE income. Mild restrictions on U^i ensure that x_i^r exists, in which case x_i^r is an exact index of individual welfare for the same reason as E^n is an exact index of W^n.

[15] A somewhat similar idea is briefly considered in Shorrocks(1978a).

In terms of ethical mobility indices one could use evaluation functions $E^n: D^n \longrightarrow \mathbb{R}^1$ but with vectors of representative lifetime incomes as arguments rather than vectors of aggregate incomes. Letting $x^r = (x^r, x_2^r, \ldots, x_n^r)$ and x^{br} be the vector of representative lifetime incomes for the benchmark structure, Property 1' could be replaced by Property 1''.

Property 1''

For all $X \in D^{nm}$, $M(X) = d(E^n(x^r), E^n(x^{br}))$ for some function d, with d increasing in its first argument and decreasing in its second argument.

No doubt such modifications would considerably alter the specific results obtained here, but this alternative approach does appear structured enough to yield results of interest.

Finally, it may be interesting to note the formal equivalence between the Blackorby – Donaldson relative tax progressivity index in (8.19) and the mobility index M_R in (9.4). However, Blackorby and Donaldson(1984b) did not consider general index of the form (9.3). Moreover, they did not develop results analogous to that presented in Subsection 9.2.3.

Extended Bibliography

Acemoglu, D. and P. J. Lambert(1989): Equiproportionate Growth of Incomes and Fiscal Drag, Bulletin of Economic Research, 41.

Aczél, J. (1966): Lectures on Functional Equations and their Applications, Academic Press, London.

Adelman, I. and A. Levy (1984): Decomposing Theil's Index of Income Inequality into between and within Components, Review of Income and Wealth, 30.

Adelman, I. and A. Levy (1986): Decomposing Theil's Index of Inequality: A Reply, Review of Income and Wealth, 32.

Addo, H. (1973): Trends in International Value Inequality 1969 – 1970: An Empirical Research, Journal of Peace Research, 13.

Aghevli, B. B. and F. Mehran (1981): Optimal Grouping of Income Distribution Data, Journal of the American Statistical Association, 76.

Ahluwalia, M. S. (1978): Rural Poverty and Agricultural Performance in India, Journal of Development Studies, 14.

Aigner, D. J. and A. J. Heins (1967): A Social Welfare View of the Measurement of Income Inequality, Review of Income and Wealth, 13.

Aitchison, J. and J. A. C. Brown (1957): The Lognormal Distribution, Cambridge University Press, London.

Alchin, T. M. (1984): A New Measure of Tax Progressivity, Public Finance, 39.

Alker, H. R. (1965): Mathematics and Politics, Macmillan, New York.

Alker, H. R. (1970): Measuring Inequality, in E. R. Tufte (ed.) The Quantitative Analysis of Social Problems, Addison–Wesley, London.

Allingham, M. G. (1972): The Measurement of Inequality, Journal of Economic Theory, 5.

Allison, P. D. (1978): Measures of Inequality, American Sociological Review, 43.

Amiel, Y. (1981): Some Remarks on Income Inequality, the Gini Index and Paretian Social Welfare Functions, Working Paper No. 17 – 81, Foerder Institute for Economic Research.

Anand, S. (1977): Aspects of Poverty in Malaysia, Review of Income and Wealth, 23.

Anand, S. (1983): Inequality and Poverty in Malaysia, Oxford University Press, London.

Anand, S. and S. M. R. Kanbur (1985): Poverty under the Kuznets Process, Economic Journal, 95.

Apostol, T. (1975): Mathematical Analysis, Addison – Wesley, London.

Arnold, B. C. (1986): A Class of Hyberbolic Lorenz Curves, Sankhyā, The Indian Journal of Statistics, Series B, 48.

Arnold, B. C. and J. A. Villaseñor (1989): Elliptical Lorenz Curves, Journal of Econometrics, 40.

Arrow, K. J. (1951): Social Choice and Indivudual Values, Wiley, New York.

Arrow, K. J. (1963): Social Choice and Indivudual Values (2nd edition), Wiley, New York.

Arrow, K. J. (1971): Essays in the Theory of Risk Bearing, North–Holland, Amsterdam.

Atack, J. and F. Bateman (1979): The Measurement and Trend of Inequality: An Amendment to a Basic Revision, Economics Letters, 4.

Atkinson, A. B. (1969): Poverty in Britain and the Reform of Social Security, Cambridge University Press, London.

Atkinson, A. B. (1970): On the Measurement of Inequality, Journal of Economic Theory, 2. Reprinted in Atkinson (1983).

Atkinson, A. B. (1974): Poverty and Income Inequality in Britain, in D. Wedderburn (ed.), Poverty, Inequality and the Class Structure, Cambridge University Press, London.

Atkinson, A. B. (1980): On Intergenerational Income Mobility in Britain, Journal of Post Keynesian Economics, 3.

Atkinson, A. B. (1980a): Horizontal Equity and the Distribution of Tax Burden, in H. Aaron and M. Boskin (eds.), The Economics of Taxation, The Brookings Institution, Washington, D. C.. Reprinted in Atkinson (1983).

Atkinson, A. B. (1981): The measurement of Economic Mobility, in P. J. Eggelshoven and L. J. van Gemerden (eds.), Inkomensverdeling en Openbare Financien, Het Spectrum, Leiden. Reprinted in Atkinson (1983).

Atkinson, A. B. (1983): Social Justice and Public Policy, MIT Press, Cambridge.

Atkinson, A. B. (1983a): The Economics of Inequality (2nd edition), Oxford University Press, London.

Atkinson, A. B. (1987): On the Measurement of Poverty, Econometrica, 55.

Atkinson, A. B. (1989): Poverty and Social Security, Harvester Wheatsheaf, England.

Atkinson, A. B. and F. Bourguignon (1982): The Comparison of Multi–dimensioned Distributions of Economic Status, Review of Economic Studies, 49. Reprinted in Atkinson (1983).

Atkinson, A. B., F. Bourguignon and C. Morrison (1988): Income Distribution and Wealth Inequalities, European Economic Review, 32.

Atkinson, A. B. and J. E. Stiglitz (1980): Lectures on Public Economics, McGraw–Hill, London.

Atkinson, A. B., C. G. Trinder and A. K. Maynard (1978): Evidence on Intergenerational Income Mobility in Britain, Economics Letters, 1.

Bardhan, P. K. (1970): On the Minimum Level of Living and the Rural Poor, Indian Economic Review, 5.

Bardhan, P. K. (1971): On the Minimum Level of Living and the Rural Poor: A Further Note, Indian Economic Review, 6.

Bardhan, P. K. (1974): On the Incidence of Poverty in Rural India, in Srinivasan and Bardhan (1974).

Barglas, E. (1971): Income Tax and the Distribution of Income: An International Comparison, Public Finance, 26.

Bartels, C. P. A. (1977): Economic Aspects of Regional Welfare, Income Distribution and Unemployment, Martinus Nijhoff, Boston.

Bartels, C. P. A. and P. Nijkamp (1976): An Empirical Welfare Approach to Regional Income Distributions, Socio–Economic Planning Sciences, 10.

Bartholomew, D. J. (1973): Stochastic Models for Social Processes (2nd edition), Wiley, London.

Basmann, R. and G. Rhodes (eds.) (1984): Advances in Econometrics, vol. 3, JAI Press, Greenwich.

Basmann, R. and G. Rhodes (eds.) (1985): Advances in Econometrics, vol.4, JAI Press, Greenwich.

Basmann, R. and D. L. Slottje (1987): A New Index of Income Inequality: The B Measure, Economics Letters, 24.

Basu, K. (1985): Poverty Measurement: A Decomposition of the Normalisation Axiom, Econometrica, 53.

Basu, K. (1987): Axioms for a Fuzzy Measure of Inequality, Mathematical Social Sciences, 14.

Batchelder, A. B. (1971): The Economics of Poverty, Wiley, New York.

Bawa, V. (1976): Optimal Rules for Ordering Uncertain Prospects, Journal of Financial Economics, 2.

Beach, C. M. and R. Davidson (1983): Distribution Free Statistical Inference with Lorenz Curves and Income Shares, Review of Economic Studies, 50.

Beach, C. M. and S. F. Kaliski (1986): Lorenz Curve Inference with Sample Weights: An Application to the Distribution of Unemployment Experience, Applied Statistics, 35.

Beach, C. M. and J. Richmond (1985): Joint Confidence Intervals for Income Shares and Lorenz Curves, International Economic Review, 26.

Bentzel, R. (1970): The Social Significance of Income Distribution Statistics, Review of Income and Wealth, 16.

Berge, C. (1961): Topological Spaces, Oliver and Boyd, Edinburgh.

Bergson, A. (1938): A Reformulation of Certain Aspects of Welfare Economics, Quarterly Journal of Economics, 52.

Berrebi, Z. M. and J. Silber (1981): Weighting Income Ranks and Levels: A Multiple –Parameter Generalisation for Absolute and Relative Indices, Economics Letters, 7.

Berrebi, Z. M. and J. Silber (1983): On an Absolute Measure of Distributional Change, European Economic Review, 22.

Berrebi, Z. M. and J. Silber (1985): The Gini Coefficient and Negative Income: A Comment, Oxford Economic Papers, 37.

Berrebi, Z. M. and J. Silber (1985a): Income Inequality Indices and Deprivation: A Generalization, Quarterly Journal of Economics, 100.

Berrebi, Z. M. and J. Silber (1987): Dispersion, Asymmetry and the Gini Index of Inequality, International Economic Review, 28.

Berrebi, Z. M. and J. Silber (1987a): Interquantile Difference, Income Inequality Measurement and the Gini Concentration Index, Mathematical Social Sciences, 13.

Berrebi, Z. M. and J. Silber (1987b): Regional Differences and the Components of Growth and Inequality Change, Economics Letters, 25.

Besley, T. J. and S. M. R. Kanbur (1988): Food Subsidies and Poverty Alleviation, Economic Journal, 98.

Besley, T. J. and I. P. Preston (1988): Invariance and the Axiomatics of Income Tax Progression, Bulletin of Economic Research, 40.

Bhattacharya, N. and B. Mahalanobis (1967): Regional Disparities in Household Consumption in India, Journal of the American Statistical Association, 62.

Bhatty, I. Z. (1974): Inequality and Poverty in Rural India, in Srinivasan and Bardhan (1974).

Birchenhall, C. R. and P. Grout (1979): On Equal Plans with an Infinite Horizon, Journal of Economic Theory, 21.

Black, D. (1958): The Theory of Committees and Elections, Cambridge University Press, London.

Blackburn, M. L. (1989): Interpreting the Magnitude of Changes in Measures of Income Inequality, Journal of Econometrics, 42.

Blackorby, C. and D. Donaldson (1977): Utility versus Equity: Some Plausible Quasi –Orderings, Journal of Public Economics, 7.

Blackorby, C. and D. Donaldson (1978): Measures of Relative Equality and their Meaning in terms of Social Welfare, Journal of Economic Theory, 18.

Blackorby, C. and D. Donaldson (1980): A Theoretical Treatment of Indices of Absolute

Inequality, International Economic Review, 21.

Blackorby, C. and D. Donaldson (1980a): Ethical Indices for the Measurement of Poverty, Econometrica, 48.

Blackorby, C. and D. Donaldson (1982): Ratio–Scale and Translation–Scale Full Inter–personal Comparability without Domain Restrictions: Admissible Social –Evaluation Functions, International Economic Review, 23.

Blackorby, C. and D. Donaldson (1984): Ethically Significant Ordinal Indexes of Relative Inequality, in Basmann and Rhodes (1984).

Blackorby, C. and D. Donaldson (1984a): Social Criteria for Evaluating Population Change, Journal of Public Economics,25.

Blackorby, C. and D. Donaldson (1984b): Ethical Social Index Numbers and the Measurement of Effective Tax/Benefit Progressivity, Canadian Journal of Economics, 17.

Blackorby, C., D. Donaldson and M. Auersperg(1981): A New Procedure for the Measurement of Inequality within and among Population Subgroups, Canadian Journal of Economics, 14.

Blackorby, C., D. Donaldson and J. A. Weymark (1984): Social Choice Theory with Interpersonal Utility Comparisons: A Diagrammatic Introduction, International Economic Review, 25.

Blackorby, C., D. Primont and R. R. Russell (1978): Duality, Separability and Functional Structure: Theory and Economic Applications, North–Holland, Amsterdam.

Blau, P. M. (1977): Inequality and Heterogeneity: A Primitive Theory of Social Structure, Free Press, New York.

Blewett, E. (1982): Measuring Life Cycle Inequality, Ph. D. Dissertation, Department of Economics, University of British Columbia, Canada.

Blitz, R. C. and J. A. Brittain(1964): An Extension of the Lorenz Diagram to the Correlation of Two Variables, Metron, 23.

Boadway, R. and N. Bruce (1984): Welfare Economics, Basil Blackwell, Oxford.

Booth, C. (1889): Life and Labour of the People in London, London.

Bossert, W. (1989): A Note on Intermediate Inequality Indices which are Quasilinear Means, Methods of Operations Research (forthcoming).

Bossert, W. (1989a): An Axiomatisation of the Single–Series Ginis, Journal of Economic Theory (forthcoming).

Bossert, W. (1989b): Population Replications and Ethical Poverty Measurement, Discussion Paper Number 348, University of Karlsruhe.

Bossert, W. and A. Pfingsten (1989): Intermediate Inequality: Concepts, Indices and

Welfare Implications, Mathematical Social Sciences (forthcoming).
Boudon, R. (1973): Mathematical Structures of Social Mobility, North–Holland, Amsterdam.
Bourguignon, F. (1979): Decomposable Income Inequality Measures, Econometrica, 47.
Bourguignon, F. (1989): Family Size and Social Utility: Income Distribution Dominance Criteria, Journal of Econometrics, 42.
Bowley, A. L. (1937): Elements of Statistics, P. S. King, New York.
Bracewell, B. (1977): Measurement of Tax Progressivity: A Comment, Economic Journal, 89.
Braulke, M. (1983): An Approximation to the Gini Coefficient for Population Based on Sparse Information for Subgroups, Journal of Development Economics.
Braulke, M. (1988): How to Retrieve Lorenz Curve from Sparse Data?, in Eichhorn (1988).
Brennan, G. (1971): Horizontal Equity: An Extension of an Extension, Public Finance, 26.
Bridges, B. (1984): Post–Fisc Distribution of Income: Comment, Public Finance Quarterly, 12.
Brittain, J. A. (1962): Interpolation of Frequency Distributions of Aggregated Variables and Estimation of the Gini Concentration Measure, Metron, 22.
Bruno, M. (1974): Economic Consequences of Educational Policies, Paper Presented at the I.E.A. Conference on the Economics of Public Services, Torino.
Bruno, M. and J. Habib (1976): Taxes, Family Grants and Redistribution, Journal of Public Economics, 5.
Buchanan, J. M. (1965): An Economic Theory of Clubs, Economica, 32.
Buchholz, W., W. F. Richter and J. Schwaiger (1988): Distributional Implications of Equal Sacrifice Rules, Social Choice and Welfare, 5.
Bürk, R. and W. Gehrig (1978): Indices of Income Inequality and Societal Income, in W. Eichhorn, R. Henn, O. Opitz and R. W. Shephard (eds.), Theory and Applications of Economic Indices, Physica–Verlag, Würzburg.
Butler, R. J. and J. B. McDonald (1987): Interdistributional Income Inequality, Journal of Business and Economic Statistics, 5.
Butler, R. J. and J. B. McDonald (1989): Using Incomplete Moments to Measure Inequality, Journal of Econometrics, 42.
Cannan, E. (1930): Elementary Political Economy, London.
Cassel, G. (1901): The Theory of Progressive Taxation, Economic Journal, 11.
Chakravarty, S. R. (1981): Two Results on Theil's Entropy Measure of Inequality, in J. K. Ghosh and J. Roy (eds.), Statistics: Applications and New Directions,

Statistical Publishing Society, Calcutta.

Chakravarty, S. R. (1982): An Axiomatisation of the Entropy Measure of Inequality, Sankhyā, The Indian Journal of Statistics, Series B, 44.

Chakravarty, S. R. (1983): Ethically Flexible Measures of Poverty, Canadian Journal of Economics, 16.

Chakravarty, S. R. (1983a): A New Index of Poverty, Mathematical Social Sciences, 6.

Chakravarty, S. R. (1983b): Measures of Poverty Based on the Representative Income Gap, Sankhyā, The Indian Journal of Statistics, Series B, 45.

Chakravarty, S. R. (1984): Normative Indices for Measuring Social Mobility, Economics Letters, 15.

Chakravarty, S. R. (1985): Normative Indices for the Measurement of Horizontal Inequity, Journal of Quantitative Economics, 1.

Chakravarty, S. R. (1988): Extended Gini Indices of Inequality, International Economic Review, 29.

Chakravarty, S. R. (1989): On Quasi–Orderings of Income Profiles, Methods of Operations Research (forthcoming).

Chakravarty, S. R. and A. B. Chakraborty (1984): On Indices of Relative Deprivation, Economics Letters, 14.

Chakravarty, S. R. and B. Dutta (1987): A Note on Measures of Distance between Income Distributions, Journal of Economic Theory, 41.

Chakravarty, S. R., B. Dutta and J. A. Weymark (1985): Ethical Indices of Income Mobility, Social Choice and Welfare, 2.

Champernowne, D. G. (1952): The Graduation of Income Distributions, Econometrica, 20.

Champernowne, D. G. (1974): A Comparison of Measures of Inequality of Income Distribution, Economic Journal, 84.

Chatterjee, G. S. and N. Bhattacharya (1974): Between States Variation in Consumer Prices and Per Capita Household Consumption in Rural India, in Srinivasan and Bardhan (1974).

Chen, C., T. Tsaur and T. Rhai (1982): The Gini Coefficient and Negative Income, Oxford Economic Papers, 34.

Chen, C., T. Tsaur and T. Rhai (1985): The Gini Coefficient and Negative Income: A Reply, Oxford Economic Papers, 37.

Chew, S. H. (1983): A Generalisation of the Quasilinear Mean with Applications to the Measurement of Income Inequality and Decision Theory Resolving the Allias Paradox, Econometrica, 51.

Chew, S. H. and L. G. Epstein (1987): Generalised and Implicit Gini Indices,

Department of Economics, University of Toronto.

Chew, S. H., L. G. Epstein and U. Segal (1987): Invariant Mean Values and Measures of Income Inequality, Department of Economics, University of Toronto.

Chipman, J. S. (1974): The Welfare Ranking of Pareto Distributions, Journal of Economic Theory, 9.

Chipman, J. S. (1985): The Theory and Measurement of Income Distribution, in Basmann and Rhodes (1985).

Clark, S., R. Hemming and D. Ulph (1981): On Indices for the Measurement of Poverty, Economic Journal, 91.

Cowell, F. A. (1977): Measuring Inequality, Phillip Allan, Oxford.

Cowell, F. A. (1979): The Definition of Lifetime Income, Discussion Paper No. 566–79, Institute for Research on Poverty, University of Wisconsin.

Cowell, F. A. (1980): On the Structure of Additive Inequality Measures, Review of Economic Studies, 47.

Cowell, F. A. (1980a): Generalised Entropy and the Measurement of Distributional Change, European Economic Review, 13.

Cowell, F. A. (1985): Multidimensional Decomposition of Theil's Index of Inequality, Review of Income and Wealth, 31.

Cowell, F. A. (1985a): Measures of Distributional Change: An Axiomatic Approach, Review of Economic Studies, 52.

Cowell, F. A. (1985b): 'A Fair Suck of the Sauce Bottle' or, What Do You Mean by Inequality?, Economic Record, 61.

Cowell, F. A. (1988): Inequality Decomposition: Three Bad Measures, Bulletin of Economic Research, 40.

Cowell, F. A. (1988a): Poverty Measures, Inequality and Decomposability, in D. Bös, M. Rose and C. Seidl (eds.) Welfare Efficiency in Public Economics, Springer–Verlag, Heidelberg.

Cowell, F. A. (1989): Sampling Variance and Decomposable Inequality Measures, Journal of Econometrics, 42.

Cowell, F. A. and K. Kuga (1981): Inequality Measurement: An Axiomatic Approach, European Economic Review, 15.

Cowell, F. A. and K. Kuga (1981a): Additivity and the Entropy Concept: An Axiomatic Approach to Inequality Measurement, Journal of Economic Theory, 25.

Cowell, F. A. and F. Mehta(1982): The Estimation and Interpolation of Inequality Measures, Review of Economic Studies, 49.

Creedy, J. (1977): The Principle of Transfers and the Variance of Logarithms, Oxford Bulletin of Economics and Statistics, 39.

Dagum, C. (1978): A Measure of Inequality between Income Distributions, Economie Appliqueé, 31.

Dagum, C. (1980): Inequality Measures between Income Distributions with Applications, Econometrica, 48.

Dagum, C. (1980a): The Generation and Distribution of Income, the Lorenz Curve and the Gini Ratio, Economic Appliquée, 33.

Dagum, C. (1985): Analysis of Income Distribution and Inequality by Education and Sex in Canada, in Basmann and Rhodes (1985).

Dalton, H. (1920): The Measurement of Inequality of Incomes, Economic Journal, 30.

Dalton, H. (1920a): The Inequality of Incomes, Routledge, London.

Dalton, H. (1922): Principles of Public Finance, Routledge, London.

Dandekar, V. M. and N. Rath (1971): Poverty in India, Indian School of Political Economy, Poona.

Danziger, S., R. Haveman and E. Smolensky (1977): The Measurement and Trend of Inequality: Comment, American Economic Review, 67.

Dardanoni, V. and P. J. Lambert(1988): Welfare Rankings of Income Distributions: A Role for the Variance and Some Insights for Tax Reform, Social Choice and Welfare, 5.

Das, T. and A. Parikh (1981): Decomposition of Atkinson's Measure of Inequality, Australian Economic Papers, 20.

Das, T. and A. Parikh (1982): Decomposition of Inequality Measures and a Comparative Analysis, Empirical Economics, 7.

Dasgupta, P., A. K. Sen and D. Starrett (1973): Notes on the Measurement of Ine– quality, Journal of Economic Theory, 6.

D'Aspremont, C. and L. Gevers (1977): Equity and the Informational Basis of Collective Choice, Review of Economic Studies, 44.

David, H. A. (1968): Gini's Mean Difference Rediscovered, Biometrika, 55.

Davies, D. (1980): Measurement of Tax Progressivity: Comment, American Economic Review, 70.

Davies, J. B. (1982): The Relative Impact of Inheritance and Other Factors of Economic Inequality, Quarterly Journal of Economics, 97.

Davies, J. B. (1986): Does Redistribution Reduce Inequality?, Journal of Labor Economics, 7.

Davies, J. B. and A. F. Shorrocks (1989): Optimal Grouping of Income and Wealth Data, Journal of Econometrics, 42.

Desai, M. and A. Shah (1985): An Econometric Approach to the Measurement of Poverty, Welfare State Program Discussion Paper No. 5, London School of

Economics.

Donaldson, D. and J. A. Weymark (1980): A Single–Parameter Generalisation of the Gini Indices of Inequality, Journal of Economic Theory, 22.

Donaldson, D. and J. A. Weymark (1983): Ethically Flexible Gini Indices for Income Distributions in the Continuum, Journal of Economic Theory, 29.

Donaldson, D. and J. A. Weymark (1986): Properties of Fixed Population Poverty Indices, International Economic Review, 27.

Dorfman, R. (1979): A Formula for the Gini Coefficient, Review of Economics and Statistics, 61.

Duesenberry, J. S. (1949): Income, Saving and the Theory of Consumer Behavior, Hardvard University Press, Cambridge.

Dutta, B. (1978): On Poverty in India, Indian Economic Review, 13.

Dutta, B. and J. M. Esteban (1988): Social Welfare and Inequality, Presented at the European Meating of the Econometric Society, Bologna.

Ebert, U. (1984): Measures of Distance between Income Distributions, Journal of Economic Theory, 32.

Ebert, U. (1987): Size and Distribution of Incomes as Determinants of Social Welfare, Journal of Economic Theory, 41.

Ebert, U. (1987a): Global Tax Progressivity, Discussion Paper Number A–109, University of Bonn.

Ebert, U. (1988): On the Decomposition of Inequality: Partitions into Non–over–lapping Subgroups, in Eichhorn (1988).

Ebert, U. (1988a): Measurement of Inequality: An Attempt at Unification and Generalisation, Social Choice and Welfare, 5.

Ebert, U. (1988b): On a Family of Aggregate Compromise Inequality Measures, International Economic Review, 29.

Eichhorn, W. (1978): Functional Equations in Economics, Addison–Wesley, London.

Eichhorn, W. (1983): Tax Progression and Decrease of Income Inequality, in E. F. Beckenbach and W. Walter (eds.), General Inequalities 3, Birkhauser–Verlag, Boston.

Eichhorn, W. (1984): Remarks on Progressive Income Taxation: Inequalities in the Theory of Economic Inequality, in W. Walter (ed.), General Inequalities 4, Birkhauser–Verlag, Boston.

Eichhorn, W. (ed.) (1988): Measurement in Economics, Physica–Verlag, New York.

Eichhorn, W. (1988a): On a Class of Inequality Measures, Social Coice and Welfare, 5.

Eichhorn, W. and H. Funke (1983): A Characterisation of the Proportional Income Tax, in G. Hammer and D. Pallaschke (eds.), Selected Topics in Operations Research

and Mathematical Economics, Springer–Verlag, New York.
Eichhorn, W., H. Funke and W. Gleissner (1983): Income Tax Rate: Properties and Implications, Mimeographed, University of Karlsruhe.
Eichhorn, W., H. Funke and W. F. Richter (1984): Tax Progression and Inequality of Income Distribution, Journal of Mathematical Economics, 13.
Eichhorn, W. and W. Gehrig (1981): Generalised Convexity and the Measurement of Inequality, in S. Schaible and W. P. Ziemba (eds.) Generalised Concavity in Optimisation and Economics, Academic Press, New York.
Eichhorn, W. and W. Gehrig (1982): Measurement of Inequality in Economics, in B. Korte (ed.), Modern Applied Mathematics, North–Holland, Amsterdam.
Eltetö, O. and E. Frigyes (1968): New Inequality Measures as Efficient Tools for Causal Analysis and Planning, Econometrica, 36.
Epstein, L. G. (1983): Ethical Indices of Equality and Unpredictability, Department of Economics, University of Toronto.
Esberger, S. E. and S. Malmquist (1972): A Statistical Study of the Development of Incomes, Statistiska Centralbyrån Och Bostadsstyrelsen, Stockholm.
Esteban, J. M. (1976): Social Welfare Functions and Inequality Measures, Universitat Autonoma de Barcelona, Spain.
Fei, J. C. H. (1981): Equity Oriented Fiscal Programs, Econometrica, 49.
Fei, J. C. H., G. Ranis and S. W. Y. Kuo (1978): Growth and the Family Distribution of Income by Factor Components, Quarterly Journal of Economics, 92.
Fei, J. C. H., G. Ranis and S. W. Y. Kuo (1979): Growth with Equity: The Taiwan Case, Oxford University Press, London.
Feldstein, M. (1976): On the Theory of Tax Reform, Journal of Public Economics, 6.
Fellman, J. (1976): The Effect of Transformation on Lorenz Curves, Econometrica, 44.
Fields, G. S (1979): Income Inequality in Urban Columbia: A Decomposition Analysis, Review of Income and Wealth, 25.
Fields, G. S. (1979a): Decomposing LDC Inequality, Oxford Economic Papers, 31.
Fields, G. S. (1980): Poverty, Inequality and Development, Cambridge University Press, London.
Fields, G. S. and J. C. S. Fei (1978): On Inequality Comparisons, Econometrica, 46.
Fine, B. (1985): A Note on the Measurement of Inequality and Interpersonal Comparability, Social Choice and Welfare, 1.
Fine, B. and K. Fine (1974): Social Choice and Individual Ranking, Review of Economic Studies, 41.
Fishburn, P. C. (1973): The Theory of Social Choice, Princeton University Press, Princeton.

Fishburn, P. C. (1979): Evaluative Comparisons of Distributions of a Social Variable, Social Indicators Research, 6.

Fishburn, P. C. (1980): Continua of Stochastic Dominance Relations for Unbounded Probability Distributions, Journal of Mathematical Economics, 7.

Fishburn, P. C. (1982): Moment–Preserving Shifts and Stochastic Dominance, Mathematics of Operations Research, 7.

Fishburn, P. C. and R. D. Willig (1984): Transfer Principles in Income Distribution, Journal of Public Economics, 25.

Fisk, P. R. (1961): The Graduation of Income Distributions, Econometrica, 29.

Formby, J. P. and T. G. Seaks (1980): Paglin's Gini Measure of Inequality: A Modification, American Economic Review, 70.

Formby, J. P., T. G. Seaks and W. J. Smith (1981): A Comparison of Two New Measures of Tax Progressivity, Economic Journal, 91.

Formby, J. P., T. G. Seaks and W. J. Smith (1984): Difficulties in the Measurement and Comparison of Tax Progressivity, Public Finance, 39.

Formby, J. P., T. G. Seaks and W. J. Smith (1989): On the Measurement and Trend of Inequality: A Reconsideration, American Economic Review, 79.

Formby, J. P., T. G. Seaks and P. D. Thistle (1987): Difficulties in the Measurement of Tax Progressivity: A Further Analysis, Public Finance, 42.

Formby, J. P. and W. J. Smith (1986): Income Inequality across Nations over Time: Comment, Southern Economic Journal, 53.

Formby, J. P., W. G. Smith and D. Skyes (1986): Income Distribution and Tax Progressivity: A Re–consideration, Canadian Journal of Economics, 19.

Formby, J. P., W. G. Smith and D. Skyes (1986a): Intersecting Tax Concentration Curves and the Measurement of Tax Progressivity, National Tax Journal, 39.

Formby, J. P. and D. Skyes (1984): State Income Tax Progressivity, Public Finance Quarterly, 12.

Foster, J. E. (1983): An Axiomatic Characterisation of the Theil Measure of Income Inequality, Journal of Economic Theory, 31.

Foster, J. E. (1984): On Economic Poverty: A Survey of Aggregate Measures, in Basmann and Rhodes (1984).

Foster, J. E. (1985): Inequality Measurement, in H. P. Young (ed.), Fair Allocation, American Mathematical Society, Providence.

Foster, J. E., J. Greer and E. Thorbecke (1984): A Class of Decomposable Poverty Measures, Econometrica, 52.

Foster, J. E. and A. F. Shorrocks (1988): Poverty Orderings, Econometrica, 56.

Foster, J. E. and A. F. Shorrocks (1988a): Poverty Orderings and Welfare Dominance,

Social Choice and Welfare, 5.

Foster, J. E. and A. F. Shorrocks (1988b): Inequality and Poverty Orderings, European Economic Review, 32.

Foster, J. E. and A. F. Shorrocks (1988c): Subgroup Consistent Poverty Indices, Presented at the European Meeting of the Econometric Society, Bologna.

Fuller, M. (1979): The Estimation of Gini Coefficients from Grouped Data: Upper and Lower Bounds, Economics Letters, 3.

Gail, M. H. and J. L. Gastwirth (1978): A Scale–Free Goodness–of–Fit Test for the Exponential Distribution Based on the Lorenz Curve, Journal of the American Statistical Association, 73.

Gardenfors, P. (1974): Positional Voting Functions, Theory and Decision, 4.

Gastwirth, J. L. (1971): Robust Estimation of the Gini Index of Inequality, Bulletin of the International Statistical Institute, 44.

Gastwirth, J. L. (1971a): A General Definition of the Lorenz Curve, Econometrica, 39.

Gastwirth, J. L. (1972): The Estimation of the Lorenz Curve and the Gini Index, Review of Economics and Statistics, 54.

Gastwirth, J. L. (1974): A New Index of Income Inequality, Bulletin of the International Statistical Institute, Book I,45.

Gastwirth, J. L. (1974a): Large Sample Theory of Some Measures of Income Inequality, Econometrica, 42.

Gastwirth, J. L. (1975): The Estimation of a Family of Measures of Economic Inequality, Journal of Econometrics, 3.

Gastwirth, J. L. (1975a): Statistical Measures of Earnings Differentials, The American Statistician, 29.

Gastwirth, J. L., and M. Glauberman (1976): The Interpolation of the Lorenz Curve and the Gini Index from Grouped Data, Econometrica, 44.

Gastwirth, J. L., T. K. Nayak and A. M. Krieger (1986): Large Sample Theory for the Bounds on the Gini and Related Indices of Inequality Estimated from Grouped Data, Journal of Business and Economic Statistics, 4.

Gastwirth, J. L., T. K. Nayak and J. L. Wang (1989): Statistical Properties of Measures of Between–Group Income Differentials, Journal of Econometrics, 42.

Gevers, L. (1979): On Interpersonal Comparability and Social Welfare Orderings, Econometrica, 47.

Gibrat, R. (1931): Les Inegalités Économiques, Libraire du Recueil Sirey, Paris.

Gillespie, W. I. (1976): On the Redistribution of Income in Canada, Canadian Tax Journal, 24.

Gini, C. (1912): Variabilità e Mutabilità, Bologna.

Gini, C. (1921): Measurement of Inequality of Incomes, Economic Journal, 31.

Gini, C. (1936): On the Measure of Concentration with Especial Reference to Income and Wealth, Cowles Commission.

Glasser, G. J. (1961):Relationship between the Mean Difference and Other Measures of Variation, Metron, 21.

Glasser, G. J. (1962): Variance Formulas for the Mean Difference and Coefficient of Concentration, Journal of the American Statistical Association, 57.

Goedhart, T., V. Halberstadt, A. Kapteyn and B. M. S. van Praag (1977): The Poverty Line: Concept and Measurement, Journal of Human Resources, 12.

Graaff, J. de V. (1957): Theoretical Welfare Economics, Cambridge University Press, London.

Graaff, J. de V. (1977): Equity and Efficiency as Components of the General Welfare, South African Journal of Economics, 45.

Gravy, G. (1952): Inequality of Income: Causes and Measurement, in Studies in Income and Wealth, vol. 15: Eight Papers on the Size Distribution of Income, NBER, New York.

Greer, J. and E. Thorbecke (1986): Pattern of Food Consumption and Poverty in Kenya and Effects of Food Prices, Journal of Development Economics, 24.

Guerrero, V. M. (1987): A Note on the Estimation of Atkinson's Index of Inequality, Economics Letters, 25

Gupta, M. R. (1984): Functional Form for Estimating the Lorenz Curve, Econometrica, 52.

Habib, J. (1979): Horizontal Equity with respect to Family Size, Public Finance Quarterly, 7.

Hader, J. and W. Russell (1969): Rules for Ordering Uncertain Prospects, American Economic Review, 59.

Hader, J. and W. Russell (1974): Stochastic Dominance in Choice under Uncertainty, in M. S. Balch, D. L. McFadden and S. Y. Wu (eds.), Essays on Economic Behaviour Under Uncertainty, North–Holland, Amsterdam.

Hagenaars, A. (1986): Perception of Poverty, North–Holland, Amsterdam.

Hagenaars, A. (1987): A Class of Poverty Indices, International Economic Review, 28.

Hagenaars, A. and B. M. S. van Praag (1985): A Synthesis of Poverty Line Definitions, Review of Income and Wealth, 31.

Hagerbaumer, J. B. (1977): The Gini Concentration Ratio and the Minor Concentration Ratio: A Two Parameter Index of Inequality, Review of Economics and Statistics, 59.

Hainsworth, G. B. (1964): The Lorenz Curve as a General Tool of Economic Analysis,

Economic Record, 40.
Hamada, K. (1973): A Simple Majority Rule on the Distribution of Income, Journal of Economic Theory, 6.
Hamada, K. and N. Takayama (1977): Censored Income Distributions and the Measurement of Poverty, Bulletin of the International Statistical Institute, Book I, 47.
Hammond, P. J. (1975): A Note on Extreme Inequality Aversion, Journal of Economic Theory, 11.
Hammond, P. J. (1976): Equity, Arrow's Conditions and Rawls' Difference Principle, Econometrica, 44.
Hammond, P. J. (1976a): Why Ethical Indices of Inequality Need Interpersonal Comparisons?, Theory and Decision, 7.
Hammond, P. J. (1977): Dual Interpersonal Comparisons of Utility and the Welfare Economics of Income Distribution, Journal of Public Economics, 7.
Hammond, P. J. (1979): Equity in Two–Person Situations: Some Consequences, Econometrica, 47.
Hanoch, G. and H. Levy (1969): The Efficiency Analysis of Choices Involving Risk, Review of Economic Studies, 36.
Hansson, B. (1973): The Independence Condition in the Theory of Social Choice, Theory and Decision, 4.
Hansson, B. (1977): The Measurement of Social Inequality, in R. Butts and J. Hintikka (eds.), Foundational Problems in the Special Sciences, Reidel, Boston.
Hardy, G. H., J. Littlewood and G. Polya (1934): Inequalities, Cambridge University Press, London.
Harrison, A. J. (1974): Inequality of Income and the Champernowne Distribution, in M. Parkin and A. R. Nobay (eds.), Current Economic Problems, Cambridge University Press, London.
Hart, P.E. (1975): Moment Distribution in Economics: An Exposition, Journal of the Royal Statistical Society, Series A, 138.
Hart, P.E. (1976): The Comparative Statics and Dynamics of Income Distribution, Journal of the Royal Statistical Society, Series A, 139.
Hart, P.E. (1981): The Statics and Dynamics of Income Distributions; A Survey,in Klevmarken and Lybeck (1981).
Hemming, R. and M.J. Keen (1983): Single–Crossing Conditions in Comparisons of Tax Progressivity, Journal of Public Economics, 20.
Hettich, W. (1979): A Theory of Partial Tax Reform, Canadian Journal of Economics, 12.

Hey, J. D. and P. J. Lambert (1980): Relative Deprivation and the Gini Coefficient: Comment, Quarterly Journal of Economics, 95.

Hirschman, A. (1973): The Changing Tolerance of Income Inequality in the Course of Economic Development, with a Mathematical Appendix by M. Rothschild, Quarterly Journal of Economics, 87.

Hutton, J. P. and P. J. Lambert (1979): Income Tax Progressivity and Revenue Growth, Economics Letters, 3.

Hutton, J. P. and P. J. Lambert (1980): Evaluating Income Tax Revenue Elasticities, Economic Journal, 90.

Hutton, J. P. and P. J. Lambert (1982): Modelling the Effects of Income Growth and Discretionary Change on the Sensitivity of U.K. Income Tax Revenue, Economic Journal, 92.

Hutton, J. P. and P. J. Lambert (1982a): Simulating the Revenue Elasticity of an Individual Income Tax, Economics Letters, 9.

Iritani, J. and K. Kuga (1983): The Duality between the Lorenz Curve and the Income Distribution Functions, Economic Studies Quarterly, 34.

Iyengar, N. S. (1960): On the Standard Error of the Lorenz Concentration Ratio, Sankhyā, The Indian Journal of Statistics, 22.

Jakobsson, U. (1976): On the Measurement of Degree of Progression, Journal of Public Economics, 5.

Jasso, G. (1979): On Gini's Mean Difference and Gini's Index of Concentration, American Sociological Review, 44.

Jasso, G. (1982): Measuring Inequality: Using the Geometric Mean Arithmetic Mean Ratio, Sociological Methods and Research, 10.

Jean, W. H. and B. P. Helms (1983): Geometric Mean Approximations, Journal of Financial and Quantitative Analysis, 18.

Jencks, C. (1973): Inequality, Allen Lane, London.

Jenkins, S. (1988): Calculating Income Distribution Indices from Micro Data, National Tax Journal, 41.

Jenkins, S. (1988a): Reranking and the Analysis of Income Redistribution, Scottish Journal of Political Economy, 35.

Jenkins, S. (1989): The Measurement of Economic Inequality, in L. Osberg (ed.), Readings on Economic Inequality, Sharpe, New York.

Jenkins, S. and M. O'Higgins (1989): Inequality Analysis Using 'Norm Income', or was Paglin onto Something after all?, Review of Income and Wealth (forthcoming).

Johnson, S. and T. Mayer (1962): An Extension of Sidgwick's Equity Theorem, Quarterly Journal of Economics, 76.

Johnson, W. R. (1977): The Measurement and Trend of Inequality: Comment, American Economic Review, 67.

Jorgenson, D. W. and D. T. Slesnick (1984): Inequality in the Distribution of Individual Welfare, in Basmann and Rhodes (1984).

Jorgenson, D. W. and D. T. Slesnick (1984a): Aggregate Consumer Behavior and the Measurement of Inequality, Review of Economic Studies, 51.

Jorgenson, D. W. and D. T. Slesnick (1985): Efficiency versus Equity in Natural Gas Price Regulation, Journal of Econometrics, 30.

Kakwani, N. C. (1974): A Note on the Efficient Estimation of the New Measures of Income Inequality, Econometrica, 42.

Kakwani, N. C. (1976): On the Estimation of Income Inequality Measures from Grouped Observations, Review of Economic Studies, 43.

Kakwani, N. C. (1977): Applications of Lorenz Curve in Economic Analysis, Econometrica, 45.

Kakwani, N. C. (1977a): Measurement of Poverty and Negative Income Tax, Australian Economic Papers, 16.

Kakwani, N. C. (1977b): Measurement of Tax Progressivity: An International Comparison, Economic Journal, 87.

Kakwani, N. C. (1979): Measurement of Tax Progressivity: A Reply, Economic Journal, 89.

Kakwani, N. C. (1980): Income Inequality and Poverty: Methods of Estimation and Policy Applications, Oxford University Press, London.

Kakwani, N. C. (1980a): Functional Forms For Estimating the Lorenz Curve: A Reply, Econometrica, 48.

Kakwani, N. C. (1980b): On a Class of Poverty Measures, Econometrica, 48.

Kakwani, N. C. (1981): Welfare Measures: An International Comparison, Journal of Development Economics, 8.

Kakwani, N. C. (1981a): Note on a New Measure of Poverty, Econometrica, 49.

Kakwani, N. C. (1984): Welfare Ranking of Income Distributions, in Basmann and Rhodes (1984):

Kakwani, N. C. (1984a): On the Measurement of Tax Progressivity and Redistributive Effect of Taxes with Applications to Horizontal and Vertical Equity, in Basmann and Rhodes (1984).

Kakwani, N. C. (1984b): Issues in Measuring Poverty, in Basmann and Rhodes (1984).

Kakwani, N. C. (1985): Measurement of Welfare with Applications to Australia, Journal of Development Economics, 18.

Kakwani, N. C. (1986): Analysing Redistribution Policies: A Study Using Australian

Data, Cambridge University Press, London.

Kakwani, N. C. (1986a): Decomposition of Normalisation Axiom in the Measurement of Poverty: A Comment, WIDER Working Paper No. 3/1986.

Kakwani, N. C. (1987): Measures of Tax Progressivity and Redistributive Effect: A Comment, Public Finance, 42.

Kakwani, N. C. (1987a): Inequality of Income Derived from Survey Data during Inflationary Period, Economics Letters, 23.

Kakwani, N. C. (1988): Income Inequality, Welfare and Poverty in a Developing Economy with Applications to Sri Lanka, Social Choice and Welfare, 5.

Kakwani, N. C. (1989): On Measuring Undernutrition, Oxford Economic Papers, 41.

Kakwani, N. C. and N. Podder (1973): On the Estimation of Lorenz Curves from Grouped Observations, International Economic Review, 14.

Kakwani, N. C. and N. Podder (1976): Efficient Estimation of the Lorenz Curve and Associated Inequality Measures from Grouped Observations, Econometrica, 44.

Kamat, A. R. (1953): The Third Moment of Gini's Mean Difference, Biometrika, 40.

Kanbur, S. M. R. (1979): Of Risk Taking and Personal Distribution of Income, Journal of Political Economy, 87.

Kanbur, S. M. R. (1984): The Measurement and Decomposition of Inequality and Poverty, in F. van der Ploeg (ed.), Mathematical Methods in Economics, Wiley, New York.

Kanbur, S. M. R. (1986): Budgetary Rules for Poverty Alleviation Policies, Institute for Economic Studies, University of Stockholm.

Kanbur, S. M. R. (1987): Transfers, Targeting and Poverty, Economic Policy, 4.

Kanbur, S. M. R. and M. Keen (1988): Poverty, Incentives and Linear Income Taxation, Department of Economics, University of Essex.

Kanbur, S. M. R. and J. E. Stiglitz (1982): Mobility and Inequality: A Utilitarian Analysis, Economic Theory Discussion Paper No. 57, Department of Applied Economics, University of Cambridge.

Kanbur, S. M. R. and J. E. Stiglitz (1986): Intergenerational Mobility and Dynastic Inequality, Presented at the 'Seminar on Distributive Justice and Inequality', Institute for Advanced Study, Berlin.

Kanbur, S. M. R. and J. Stromberg (1988): Income Transitions and Income Distribution Dominance, Journal of Economic Theory, 45.

Kats, A. (1972): On the Social Welfare Function and the Parameters of Income Distribution, Journal of Economic Theory, 5.

Kay, J. A. and C. N. Morris (1984): The Gross Earnings Deflator, Economic Journal, 94.

Khetan, C. and S. Podder (1976): Measurement of Income Tax Progression in a Growing

Economy: The Canadian Experience, Canadian Journal of Economics, 4.
Kiefer, D. W. (1985): Distributional Tax Progressivity Measurement, National Tax Journal, 37.
Kienzle, E. C. (1980): Measurement of Tax Progressivity: Comment, American Economic Review, 70.
Kienzle, E. C. (1981): Measurement of the Progressivity of Public Expenditures and Net Fiscal Incidence, Southern Economic Journal, 48.
Kienzle, E. C. (1982): Post–Fisc Distributions of Income: Measuring Progressivity with Application to the United States, Public Finance Quarterly, 10.
Kilpatrick, R. W. (1973): The Income Elasticity of the Poverty Line, Review of Economics and Statistics, 55.
King, M. A. (1983): An Index of Inequality: With Applications to Horizontal Equity and Social Mobility, Econometrica, 51.
Klevmarken, A. and J. A. Lybeck (eds.) (1981): The Statics and Dynamics of Income, Clevedon, Tieto.
Kolm, S. C. (1969): The Optimal Production of Social Justice, in J. Margolis and H. Guitton (eds.), Public Economics, Macmillan, London.
Kolm, S. C. (1976): Unequal Inequalities I, Journal of Economic Theory, 12.
Kolm, S. C. (1976a): Unequal Inequalities II, Journal of Economic Theory, 13.
Kolm, S. C. (1979): Multidimensional Egalitarianisms, Quarterly Journal of Economics, 91.
Kondor, Y. (1971): An Old–New Measure of Income Inequality, Econometrica, 39.
Kondor, Y. (1975): Value Judgements Implied by the Use of Various Measures of Income Inequality, Review of Income and Wealth, 21.
Kondor, Y. (1975a): The Gini Coefficient of Concentration and the Kuznets Measure of Inequality: A Note, Review of Income and Wealth, 21.
Koo, A. Y. C., N. T. Quan and R. Rasche (1981): Identification of the Lorenz Curve by Lorenz Coefficient, Weltwirtschaftliches Archiv, 117.
Koo, A. Y. C., N. T. Quan and R. Rasche (1983): Identification of the Lorenz Curve by Lorenz Coefficient: A Reply, Weltwirtschaftliches Archiv, 119.
Krelle, W. and A. F. Shorrocks (eds.) (1978): Personal Income Distribution, North–Holland, Amsterdam.
Krieger, A. M. (1979): Bounding Moments, the Gini Index and the Lorenz Curve from Grouped Data for Unimodal Density Functions, Journal of the American Statistical Association, 74.
Kuga, K. (1979): Comparison of Inequality Measures: A Monte Carlo Study, Economic Studies Quarterly, 30.

Kuga, K. (1980): Gini Index and the Generalised Entropy Class: Further Results and A Vindication, Economic Studies Quarterly, 31.

Kundu, A. and T. E. Smith (1983): An Impossibitlity Theorem for Poverty Indices, International Economic Review, 24.

Kurabayashi, Y. and A. Yatsuka (1977): Redistribution of Income and Measures of Income Inequality, in T. Fuji and R. Sato (eds.), Resource Allocation and Division of Space, Springer–Verlag, New York.

Kurien, C. J. (1977): The Measurement and Trend of Inequality: Comment, American Economic Review, 67.

Kuznets, S. (1955): Economic Growth and Income Inequality, American Economic Review, 45.

Kuznets, S. (1963): Quantitative Aspects of the Economic Growth of Nations: VIII, Distribution of Income by Size, Economic Development and Cultural Change, 11.

Kwong, S. (1981): Price Sensitive Inequality Measurement, Ph. D. Dissertation, Economics Department, University of British Columbia, Canada.

Lal, D. (1976): Agricultural Growth, Real Wages and the Rural Poor in India, Economic and Political Weakly, 11.

Lambert, P. J. (1980): Inequality and Social Choice, Theory and Decision, 12.

Lambert, P. J. (1984): Non–equiproportionate Income Growth, Inequality and the Income Tax, Public Finance, 39.

Lambert, P. J. (1985): Social Welfare and the Gini Coefficient Revisited, Mathematical Social Sciences, 9.

Lambert, P. J. (1985a): The Redistributive Effect of Taxes and Benefits, Scottish Journal of Political Economy, 32.

Lambert, P. J. (1985b): Endogenizing the Income Distribution: the Redistributive Effect, and Laffer Effects of a Progressive Tax Benefit System, European Journal of Political Economy, 1.

Lambert, P. J. (1988): Net Fiscal Incidence Progressivity: Some Approaches to Measurement, in W. Eichhorn (1988).

Lambert, P. J. (1989): The Distribution and Redistribution of Income: A Mathematical Analysis, Basil Blackwell, Oxford.

Lambert, P. J. and W. Pfähler (1987): Intersecting Tax Concentration Curves and the Measurement of Tax Progressivity: A Rejoinder, National Tax Journal, 40.

Lambert, P. J. and W. Pfähler (1988): On Aggregate Measures of the Net Redistributive Impact of Taxation and Government Expenditure, Public Finance Quarterly, 16.

Lambert, P. J. and A. Weale (1981): Equality, Risk–Aversion and Contraction Social Choice, Theory and Decision, 13.

Latham, R. (1988): Lorenz Dominating Income Tax Functions, International Economic Review, 29.

Layard, R. and A. Zabalza (1979): Family Income Distribution: Explanation and Policies, Journal of Political Economy, 89.

Le Breton, M. (1983): Arrowian and Topological Aggregation of Differentiable Inequality Pre–orders, Mimeographed, Université de Rennes.

Le Breton, M. (1984): Smooth Inequality Indices and Approximation Theorems, Mimeographed, Université de Rennes.

Le Breton, M. (1984a): Social Choice Issues in Inequality Theory, Mimeographed, Université de Rennes.

Le Breton, M. (1986): Theoretical Foudations of Inequality Measurement in Large Populations, Mimeographed, Université de Rennes.

Le Breton, M. (1986a): Inequality, Poverty Measurement and Welfare Dominance: An Attempt at Unification, Mimeographed, Université de Rennes.

Le Breton, M. and A. Trannoy (1987): Measures of Inequality as an Aggregation of Individual Preferences about Income Distribution: The Arrowian Case, Journal of Economic Theory, 41.

Le Breton, M., A. Trannoy and R. J. Uriarte (1985): Topological Aggregation of Inequality Pre–orders, Social Choice and Welfare, 2.

Lerman, R. I. and S. Yitzhaki (1984): A Note on the Calculation and Interpretation of the Gini Index, Economics Letters, 15.

Lerman, R. I. and S. Yitzhaki (1985): Income Inequality Effects by Income Source: A New Approach and Applications to the U.S.A., Review of Economics and Statistics, 67.

Lerman, R. I. and S. Yitzhaki(1989): Improving the Accuracy of Estimates of Gini Coefficients, Journal of Econometrics, 42.

Levine, D. B. and N. M. Singer (1970): The Mathematical Relation between the Income Density Function and the Measurement of Income Inequality, Econometrica, 38.

Lewis, G. W. and D. Ulph (1988): Poverty, Inequality and Welfare, Economic Journal, 98.

Liu, P. W. (1984): A Note on Two Summary Measures of Tax Progressivity, Public Finance, 39.

Liu, P. W. (1985): Lorenz Domination and Global Tax Progressivity, Canadian Journal of Economics, 18.

Liu, P. W. (1986): Lorenz Domination and Global Tax Progressivity: A Reply, Canadian Journal of Economics, 19.

Liu, P. W. (1987): Measuring Tax Progressivity as Weighted Deviations From Pro–

portional Tax: A Comment, Public Finance, 42.

Loizides, I. (1988): The Decomposition of Progressivity Indices with Applications to the Greek Taxation System, Public Finance, 43.

Lomnicki, Z. A. (1952): The Standard Error of Gini's Mean Difference, Annals of Mathematical Statistics, 23.

Lorenz, M. O. (1905): Methods of Measuring Concentration of Wealth, Journal of the American Statistical Association, 9.

Love, R. and M. C. Wolfson (1976): Income Inequality: Statistical Methodology and Canadian Illustrations, Statistics Canada, Ottawa.

Lydall, H. F. (1959): The Long–Term Trend in the Size Distribution of Income, Journal of the Royal Statistical Society, Series A, 122.

Maasoumi, E. (1986): The Measurement and Decomposition of Multidimensional Inequality, Econometrica, 54.

Maasoumi, E. (1989): Continuously Distributed Attributes and Measures of Multivariate Inequality, Journal of Econometrics, 42.

Maasoumi, E. and J. H. Jeong (1985): The Trend and the Measurement of World Inequality, Economics Letters, 19.

Maasoumi, E. and H. Theil (1979): The Effect of the Shape of the Income Distribution on Two Inequality Measures, Economics Letters, 4.

Maasoumi, E. and S. Zandvakili (1986): A Class of Generalised Measures of Mobility with Applications, Economics Letters, 22.

Madden, P. (1986): Concavity and Optimisation in Microeconomics, Basil Blackwell, Oxford.

Mahalanobis, P. C. (1960): A Method of Fractile Graphical Analysis, Econometrica, 28.

Mandelbrot, B. (1960): The Pareto–Levy Law and the Distribution of Income, International Economic Review, 1.

Mangahas, M (1975): Income Inequality in the Philippines: A Decomposition Analysis, Income Distribution and Employment Program, ILO, Geneva.

Mangahas, M. and E. Gamboa (1976): A Note on Decomposition of the Gini Ratio by Family and by Type of Income, Philippine Review of Business and Economics, 13.

Markandya, A. (1982): The Measurement of Earnings Mobility among Occupational Groups, Scottish Journal of Political Economy, 29.

Markandya, A. (1982a): Intergenerational Exchange Mobility and Economic Welfare, European Economic Review, 17.

Markandya, A. (1984): The Welfare Measurement of Changes in Economic Mobility, Economica, 51.

Marshall, A. W. and I. Olkin (1979): Inequalities: Theory of Majorization and Its Applications, Academic Press, New York.

Martic, L. (1970): A Geometrical Note on New Income Inequality Measures, Econometrica, 38.

McCabe, J. L. (1974): Distribution of Labour Income in Urban Zaire, Review of Income and Wealth, 20.

McDonald, J. B. and B. C. Jensen (1979): An Analysis of Alternative Measures of Income Inequality Based on the Gamma Distribution Function, Journal of the American Statistical Association, 74.

Mehran, F. (1975): A Statistical Analysis on Income Inequality Based on a Decomposition of the Gini Index, Bulletion of the International Statistical Institute.

Mehran, F. (1975a): Bounds on the Gini Index Based on Observed Points on the Lorenz Curve, Journal of the American Statistical Association, 70.

Mehran, F. (1976): Linear Measures of Income Inequality, Econometrica, 44.

Mendershausen, H. (1946): Changes in Income Distribution during the Great Depression, NBER, New York.

Michal, J. M. (1978): Size–Distribution of Households Incomes and Earnings in Developed Socialist Countries; with a Proposed Marginal Utility–Weighted Gini Coefficient, in Krelle and Shorrocks (1978).

Mill, J. S. (1848): Principles of Political Economy, W. J. Ashley (ed.), (1917), Longmans Green, London.

Minarik, J. J. (1977): The Measurement and Trend of Inequality: Comment, American Economic Review, 67.

Minhas, B. S. (1970): Rural Poverty, Land Distribution and Development, Indian Economic Review, 5.

Minhas, B. S. (1971): Rural Poverty and Minimum Level of Living, Indian Economic Review, 6.

Mookherjee, D. and A. F. Shorrocks (1982): A Decomposition Analysis of the Trend in U.K. Income Inequality, Economic Journal, 92.

Morris, C. N. and I. P. Preston (1986): Inequality, Poverty and the Redistribution of Income, Bulletin of Economic Research, 38.

Moyes, P. (1987): A New Concept of Lorenz Domination, Economics Letters, 23.

Moyes, P. (1988): A Note on Minimally Progressive Taxation and Absolute Inequality, Social Choice and Welfare, 5.

Moyes, P. (1988a): Progressive Taxation and After Tax Welfare, Mimeographed, Université de Bordeaux.

Moyes, P. (1989): Some Classes of Functions that Preserve the Inequality and Welfare Orderings of Income Distributions, Journal of Economic Theory (forthcoming).

Moyes, P. (1989a): Equiproportionate Growth of Incomes and After–Tax Inequality, Bulletin of Economic Research, 41.

Muellbauer, J. (1974): Inequality Measures, Prices and Household Composition, Review of Economic Studies, 41.

Muellbauer, J. (1974a): Prices and Inequality: the United Kingdom Experience, Economic Journal, 84.

Mukherjee, M., N. Bhattacharya and G. S. Chatterjee (1972): Poverty in India: Measurement and Amelioration, Commerce, 125.

Murray, D. (1978): Extreme Values of the Gini Coefficient Calculated from Grouped Data, Economics Letters, 1.

Murray, D. (1979): Changes in Income Inequality: Australia, 1968–69 to 1973–74, Review of Income and Wealth, 25.

Musgrave, R. (1976): ET, OT and SBT, Journal of Public Economics, 6.

Musgrave, R. and T. Thin (1948): Income Tax Progression, 1929–48, Journal of Political Economy, 56.

Nair, U. S. (1936): The Standard Error of Gini's Mean Difference, Biometrika, 28.

Nelson, E. R. (1977): The Measurement and Trend of Inequality: Comment, American Economic Review, 67.

Newbery, D. M. G. (1970): A Theorem on the Measurement of Inequality, Journal of Economic Theory, 2.

Nozick, R. (1974): Anarchy, State and Utopia, Basic Books, New York.

Nygård, F. and A. Sandström (1982): Measuring Income Inequality, Almqvist and Wicksell Inrenational, Stockholm.

Nygård, F. and A. Sandström (1985): Estimating Gini and Entropy Inequality Parameters, Journal of Official Statistics, 1.

Nygård, F. and A. Sandström (1989): Income Inequality Measures Based on Sample Surveys, Journal of Econometrics, 42.

Ohja, P. D. (1970): A Configuration of Indian Poverty, Reserve Bank of India Bulletin, 24.

Orshansky, M. (1965): Counting the Poor: Another Look at the Poverty Profile, Social Security Bulletin, 28.

Osmany, S. R. (1978): On the Normative Measurement of Inequality, Bangladesh Development Studies, 6.

Osmany, S. R. (1982): Economic Inequality and Group Welfare: A Theory of Comparison with Application to Bangladesh, Clarendon, Oxford.

Paglin, M. (1975): The Measurement and Trend of Inequality: A Basic Revision, American Economic Review, 65.

Paglin, M. (1977): The Measurement and Trend of Inequality: Reply, American Economic Review, 67.

Paglin, M. (1979): The Measurement of Inequality: Reply, American Economic Review, 69.

Paglin, M. (1989): On the Measurement and Trend of Inequality: Reply, American Economic Review, 79.

Pakes, A. G. (1981): On Income Distributions and their Lorenz Curves, Department of Mathematics, University of Western Australia.

Pal, P., S. R. Chakravarty and N. Bhattacharya (1986): Poverty in Rural India: A Decomposition Analysis, Indian Economic Review, 21.

Pareto, V. (1897): Cours d'Économique Politique, Vol. II, F. Rouge, Lausanne.

Parikh, A. and T. Das (1982): Inequality Index with Differences in Inequality Aversion for Income and Population Groups, Riv. Int. Sci. Eco. Com., 30.

Pattanaik, P. K. (1971): Voting and Collective Choice, Cambridge University Press, London.

Pearson, K. (ed.) (1934): Tables of the Incomplete Beta Function, Biometrika Trustees, London.

Pechman, J. A. and B. Okner (1970): Who Bears the Tax Burden?, Brookings Institution, Washington, D. C..

Petersen, H. (1979): Effects of Growing Incomes on Classified Income Distributions, the Derived Lorenz Curves and Gini Indices, Econometrica, 47.

Pfähler, W. (1984): Linear Income Tax Cuts: Distributional Effects, Social Preferences and Revenue Elasticities, Journal of Public Economics, 24.

Pfähler, W. (1985): Relative Concentration Curve: Functional Form and Measures of Non–proportionality, Bulletin of Economic Research, 37.

Pfähler, W. (1987): Redistributive Effect of Tax Progressivity: Evaluating a General Class of Aggregate Measures, Public Finance, 42.

Pfähler, W. (1987a): Redistributive Effect of Tax Progressivity: A Reply, Public Finance, 42.

Pfähler, W. (1988): Distributional Equity and Measurement of Tax Progressivity, in W. Eichhorn (1988).

Pfähler, W. (1989): Redistributive Effect of Income Taxation: Decomposing Tax Base and Tax Rates Effects, Bulletin of Economic Research, (forthcoming).

Pfingsten, A. (1986): Distributionally Neutral Tax Changes for Different Inequality Concepts, Journal of Public Economics, 30.

Pfingsten, A. (1986a): The Measurement of Tax Progression, Studies in Contemporary Economics (20), Springer–Verlag, Heidelberg, New York.

Pfingsten, A. (1987): Axiomatically Based Local Measures of Tax Progression, Bulletin of Economic Research, 39.

Pfingsten, A. (1988): Measurement of Tax Progression: An Axiomatic Approach, in W. Eichhorn (1988).

Pfingsten, A. (1988a): Progressive Taxation and Redistributive Taxation: Different Labels for the Same Product?, Social Choice and Welfare, 5.

Pfingsten, A. (1988b): Empirical Investigation of Inequality Concepts: A Method and First Result, Presented at the 1988 Meeting of the European Economic Association, Bologna.

Pfingsten, A. (1988c): Surplus Sharing Methods, Presented at the European Meeting of the Econometric Society, Bologna.

Pfingsten, A. (1989): New Concepts of Lorenz Domination and Risk Aversion, Methods of Operations Research (forthcoming).

Pigou, A. C. (1912): Wealth and Welfare, Macmillan, London.

Plotnick, R. (1980): A Comment on Measuring Horizontal Inequity, Quarterly Journal of Economics, 94.

Plotnick, R. (1981): A Measure of Horizontal Inequity, Review of Economics and Statistics, 63.

Plotnick, R. (1982): The Concept and Measurement of Horizontal Inequity, Journal of Public Economics, 17.

Plotnick, R. (1985): A Comparison of Measures of Horizontal Inequity, in M. David and T. Smeeding (eds.), Horizontal Equity, Uncertainty and Economic Well–Being, The University of Chicago Press, Illinois.

Pollak, R. A. (1971): Additive Utility Functions and Linear Engel Curves, Review of Economic Studies, 38.

Pratt, J. W. (1964): Risk Aversion in Small and Large, Econometrica, 32.

Pyatt, G. (1976): On the Interpretation and Disaggregation of Gini Coefficients, Economic Journal, 86.

Pyatt, G. (1985): An Axiomatic Approach to the Gini Coefficient and Measurement of Welfare, in Basmann and Rhodes (1985).

Pyatt, G. (1987): Measuring Welfare, Poverty and Inequality, Economic Journal, 97.

Pyatt, G., C. Chen and J. C. H. Fei (1980): The Distribution of Income by Factor Components, Quarterly Journal of Economics, 95.

Rainwater, L. (1974): What Money Buys: Inequality and the Social Meaning of Income, Basic Books , New York.

Ramasubban, T. A. (1958): The Mean Difference and the Mean Deviation of Some Discontinuous Distributions, Biometrika, 45.

Ramasubban, T. A. (1959): The Generalised Mean Difference of the Binomial and Poisson Distributions, Biometrika 46.

Ranadive, K. R. (1965): The Equality of Incomes in India, Oxford Bulletin of Economics and Statistics, 27.

Rao, C. R. (1969): Linear Statistical Inference and Its Applications, Wiley, New York.

Rao, V. M. (1969): Two Decompositions of Concentration Ratio, Journal of the Royal Statistical Society, Series A, 132.

Rasche, R. H., J. Gaffney, A. Y. C. Koo and N. Obst (1980): Functional Forms for Estimating the Lorenz Curve, Econometrica, 48.

Rawls, J. (1971): A Theory of Justice, Harvard University Press, Cambridge.

Rein, M. (1968): Problems in the Definition and Measurement of Poverty, in L. A. Ferman, J. L. Kornbluth and A. Haber (eds.), Poverty in America, The University of Michigan Press, Ann Arbor.

Reynolds, M. and E. Smolensky (1977): Public Expenditures, Taxes and the Distribution of Income: The United States 1950, 1961, 1970, Academic Press, New York.

Richter, W. F. and J. F. Hampe (1981): On Income Tax Functions, Mimeographed, University of Bielefeld.

Richter, W. F. and J. F. Hampe (1984): Measuring the Gain from Splitting Under Income Taxation, Methods of Operations Research, 51.

Riese, M. (1987): An Extension of the Lorenz Diagram with Special Reference to Survival Analysis, Oxford Bulletin of Economics and Statistics, 49.

Riffault, H. and J. R. Rabier (1977): The Perception of Poverty in Europe, Commission of the European Communities, Brussels.

Roberts, K. W. S. (1980): Possibility Theorems with Interpersonally Comparable Welfare Levels, Review of Economic Studies, 47.

Roberts, K. W. S. (1980a): Interpersonal Comparability and Social Choice Theory, Review of Economic Studies, 47.

Rosen, H. S. (1978): An Approach to the Study of Income, Utility and Horizontal Equity, Quarterly Journal of Economics, 92.

Rosenbluth, G. (1951): Note on Mr. Schutz's Measure of Income Inequality, American Economic Review, 41.

Rothschild, M. and J. E. Stiglitz (1970): Increasing Risk: I, A Definition, Journal of Economic Theory, 2.

Rothschild, M. and J. E. Stiglitz (1973): Some Further Results on the Measurement of Inequality, Journal of Economic Theory, 6.

Rowntree, B. S. (1901): Poverty: A Study of Town Life, Macmillan, London.

Rudin, W. (1976): Principles of Mathematical Analysis, McGraw–Hill Kogakusha, London.

Rudra, A. (1974): Minimum Level of Living: A Statistical Examination, in Srinivasan and Bardhan (1974).

Runciman, W. G. (1966): Relative Deprivation and Social Justice, Routledge, London.

Russell, R. R. (1985): Decomposable Inequality Measures, Review of Economic Studies, 52.

Russett, B. M. (1964): Inequality and Instability, the Relation of Land Tenure to Politics, World Politics, 16.

Sadka, E. (1976): Social Welfare and Income Distribution, Econometrica, 44.

Sadka, E. (1976a): On Progressive Income Taxation, American Economic Review, 66.

Salem, A. B. Z. and T. D. Mount (1974): A Convenient Descriptive Model of Income Distribution: The Gamma Density, Econometrica, 42.

Samuelson, P. A. (1947): Foundations of Economic Analysis, Harvard University Press, Cambridge.

Samuelson, P. A. (1972): A Fallcy in the Interpretation of Pareto's Law of Alleged Constancy of Income Distribution, in R. C. Merton (ed.), Collected Scientific Papers of P. A. Samuelson, vol. 3, M.I.T. Press, Cambridge.

Samuelson, P. A. (1980): Economics (11th edition), McGraw–Hill, Tokyo.

Sandström, A. (1982): Estimating the Gini Coefficient, Research Report No. 18, Department of Statistics, University of Stockholm.

Sandström, A. (1983): Estimating Income Inequality: Large Sample Inference in Finite Populations, Research Report No. 5, Department of Statistics, University of Stockholm.79.

Sandström, A., J. H. Wretman and B. Walden (1985): Variance Estimators of the Gini Coefficient: Simple Random Sample, Metron, 43.

Sandström, A., J. H. Wretman and B. Walden (1988): Variance Estimators of the Gini Coefficient: Probability Sampling, Journal of Business and Economic Statistics, 6.

Saposnik, R. (1981): Rank Dominance in Income Distributions, Public Choice.

Saposnik, R. (1983): On Evaluating Income Distributions: Rank Dominance, the Suppes –Sen Grading Principle of Justice and Pareto Optimality, Public Choice.

Satchell, S. E. (1987): Source and Subgroup Decomposition Inequalities for the Lorenz Curve, International Economic Review, 28.

Schutz, R. R. (1951): On the Measurement of Income Inequality, American Economic Review, 41.

Schwartz, J. and C. Winship (1979): The Welfare Approach to Measuring Inequality, in

K. F. Schuessler (ed.) Sociological Methods 1980, Jossey– Bass, San Francisco.

Seidl, C. (1988): Poverty Measurement: A Survey, in: see Cowell(1988a).

Seiver, D. A. (1979): A Note on the Measurement of Income Inequality with Interval Data, Review of Income and Wealth, 25.

Sen, A. K. (1970): Collective Choice and Social Welfare, Holden – Day, San Francisco.

Sen, A. K. (1973): On Economic Inequality, Oxford University Press, London.

Sen, A. K. (1974): Information Bases of Alternative Welfare Approaches, Journal of Public Economics, 3.

Sen, A. K. (1976): Welfare Inequalities and Rawlsian Axiomatics, Theory and Decision, 7.

Sen, A. K. (1976a): Poverty: An Ordinal Approach to Measurement, Econometrica, 44. Reprinted in Sen (1982).

Sen, A. K. (1976b): Real National Income, Review of Economic Studies, 43. Reprinted in Sen (1982).

Sen, A. K. (1977): Social Choice Theory: A Re–examination, Econometrica, 45. Reprinted in Sen (1982).

Sen, A. K. (1977a): On Weights and Measures: Informational Constraints in Social Welfare Analysis, Econometrica, 45. Reprinted in Sen (1982).

Sen, A. K. (1978): Ethical Measurement of Inequality: Some Difficulties, in Krelle and Shorrocks (1978). Reprinted in Sen (1982).

Sen, A. K. (1979): Personal Utilities and Public Judgements: Or What's Wrong With Welfare Economics?, Economic Journal, 89. Reprinted in Sen (1982).

Sen, A. K. (1979a): Issues in the Measurement of Poverty, Scandinavian Journal of Economics, 81.

Sen, A. K. (1979b): The Welfare Basis of Real Income Comparisons: A Survey, Journal of Economic Literature, 17.

Sen, A. K. (1981): Poverty and Famines: An Essay on Entitlement and Deprivation, Oxford University Press, London.

Sen, A. K. (1982): Choice, Welfare and Measurement, Basil Blackwell, Oxford.

Sen, A. K. (1983): Poor, Relatively Speaking, Oxford Economic Papers, 35.

Sen, A. K. (1986): Social Choice Theory, in K. J. Arrow and M. D. Intrilligator (eds.), Handbook of Mathematical Economics, vol. 3, North–Holland, Amsterdam.

Sen, A. K. (1986a): Commodities and Capabilities, Oxford University Press, London.

Sen, A. K. (1987): The Standard of Living, Cambridge University Press, London.

Sen, A. K. (1988): On Ethics and Economics, Basil Blackwell, Oxford.

Sen, P. K. (1986): The Gini Coefficient and Poverty Indexes: Some Reconciliations, Journal of the American Statistical Association, 81.

Sen, P. K. (1988): The Harmonic Gini Coefficient and Affluence Indexes, Mathematical Social Sciences, 16.

Sendler, W. (1979): On Statistical Inference in Concentration Measurement, Metrika, 26.

Shalit, H. (1985): Calculating the Gini Index of Inequality for Individual Data, Oxford Bulletin of Economics and Statistics, 47.

Shalit, H. and S. Yitzhaki (1984): Mean–Gini, Portfolio Theory, and the Pricing of Risky Assets, Journal of Finance, 39.

Sheshinski, E. (1972): Relation between a Social Welfare Function and the Gini Index of Income Inequality, Journal of Economic Theory, 4.

Sheshinski, E. and Y. Weiss (1982): Inequality within and between Families, Journal of Political Economy, 90.

Shorrocks, A. F. (1978): The Measurement of Mobility, Econometrica, 46.

Shorrocks, A. F. (1978a): Income Inequality and Income Mobility, Journal of Economic Theory, 19.

Shorrocks, A. F. (1980): The Class of Additively Decomposable Inequality Measures, Econometrica, 48.

Shorrocks, A. F. (1981): Income Stability in the United States, in Klevmarken and Lybeck (1981).

Shorrocks, A. F. (1982): Inequality Decomposition by Factor Components, Econometrica, 50.

Shorrocks, A. F. (1982a): On the Distance between Income Distributions, Econometrica, 50.

Shorrocks, A. F. (1983): Ranking Income Distributions, Economica, 50.

Shorrocks, A. F. (1983a): The Impact of Income Components on the Distribution of Family Incomes, Quarterly Journal of Economics, 97.

Shorrocks, A. F. (1984): Inequality Decomposition by Population Subgroups, Econometrica, 52.

Shorrocks, A. F. (1988): Aggregation Issues in Inequality Measurement, in Eichhorn (1988).

Shorrocks, A. F. and J. E. Foster (1987): Transfer Sensitive Inequality Measures, Review of Economic Studies, 54.

Silber, J. (1988): Growth, Inequality Change, Permutations and the Measurement of Change, Department of Economics, Bar–Ilan University.

Silber, J. (1988a): Income Distribution, Tax Structure and the Measurement of Tax Progressivity, Department of Economics, Bar–Ilan University.

Silber, J. (1989): Factor Components, Population Subgroups and the Computation of the

Gini Index of Inequality, Review of Economics and Statistics, 71.
Silber, J. and Z. M. Berrebi (1988): Distance Functions and the Comparison of Development Levels, Economics Letters, 27.
Slesnick, D. T. (1986): Welfare Distributional Change and the Measurement of Social Mobility, Review of Economics and Statistics, 68.
Slesnick, D. T. (1986a): The Measurement of Effective Commodity Tax Progressivity, Review of Economics and Statistics, 68.
Slesnick, D. T. (1989): Specific Egalitarianism and Total Welfare Inequality: A Decomposition Analysis, Review of Economics and Statistics, 71.
Slitor, R. E. (1948): The Measurement of Tax Progressivity and Built–in Flexibility, Quarterly Journal of Economics, 62.
Slottje, D. J. (1984): A Measure of Income Inequality Based upon the Beta Distribution of the Second Kind, Economics Letters, 15.
Slottje, D. J. (1987): Relative Price Changes and Inequality in the Size Distribution of Various Components of Income: A Multidimensional Approach, Journal of Business and Economic Statistics, 5.
Slottje, D. J. (1988): The Structure of Earnings and the Measurement of Income Inequality in the U.S., Kluwer Nijhoff, Amsterdam (forthcoming).
Slottje, D. J., R. Basmann and M. Nieswiadomy (1989): On the Empirical Relationship between Well–known Inequality Measures, Journal of Econometrics, 42.
Snowbarger, M. and J. Kirk (1973): A Cross–Sectional Model of Built–in Flexibility, 1954 – 1969, National Tax Journal, 26.
Soltow, L. (1960): The Distribution of Income Related to Changes in the Distribution of Education, Age and Occupation, Review of Economics and Statistics, 42.
Srinivasan, T. N. (1977): Poverty: Some Measurement Problems, Bulletin of the International Statistical Institute, Book I, 47.
Srinivasan, T. N. and P. K. Bardhan (eds.) (1974): Poverty and Income Distribution in India, Statistical Publishing Society, Calcutta.
Stark, D., J. E. Taylor and S. Yitzhaki (1986): Remittances and Inequality, Economic Journal, 96.
Stark, D. and S. Yitzhaki (1988): The Migration Response to Relative Deprivation, Journal of Population Economics, 1.
Stark, D. and S. Yitzhaki(1988a):Merging Populations, Stochastic Dominance and Lorenz Curves, Journal of Population Economics, 1.
Stark, T. (1972): The Distribution of Personal Incomes in the United Kingdom 1949 – 1963, Cambridge University Press, London.
Stehling, F. (1978): Indices of Preference Inequality and the Construction of Social

Preference Relations, in: see Bürk and Gehrig (1978).

Stiglitz, J. E. (1982): Utilitarianism and Horizontal Equity: The Case for Random Taxation, Journal of Public Economics, 18.

Strauss, R. and M. Berliant (1979): The Vertical and Horizontal Equity of Recent Tax Reform and Reduction Proposals, Unpublished.

Stuart, A. (1954): The Correlation between Variate–values and Ranks in Samples from a Continuous Distribution, British Journal of Statistical Psychology.

Subramanian, S. (1987): On a Simple Transfer–Sensitive Index of Inequality, Economics Letters, 23.

Suits, D. B. (1977): Measurement of Tax Progressivity, American Economic Review, 67.

Suits, D. B. (1980): Measurement of Tax Progressivity: Reply, American Economic Review, 70.

Suppes, P. (1977): The Distributive Justice of Income Inequality, in H. W. Gottinger and W. Leinfellner (eds.), Decision Theory and Social Ethics, Reidel, Boston.

Suppes, P. (1988): Lorenz Curves for Various Processes: A Pluralistic Approach to Equity, Social Choice and Welfare, 5.

Szal, R. and S. Robinson (1977): Measuring Income Inequality, in C. R. Frank and R. C. Webb (eds.) Income Distribution in Less Developed Countries, Brookings Institution, Washington, D.C..

Taguchi, T. (1967): On Some Properties of Concentration Curve and its Applications, Metron, 26.

Taguchi, T. (1968): Concentration Curve Methods and Structures of Skew Populations, Annals of the Institute of Statistical Mathematics, 20.

Takayama, N. (1979): Poverty, Income Inequality and their Measures: Professor Sen's Axiomatic Approach Reconsidered, Econometrica, 47.

Taussig, F. W. (1939): Principles of Economics (4th edition), Macmillan, New York.

Testfatsion, L. (1976): Stochastic Dominance and the Maximisation of Expected Utility, Review of Economic Studies, 43.

Theil, H. (1967): Economics and Information Theory, North–Holland, Amsterdam.

Theil, H. (1972): Statistical Decomposition Analysis, North–Holland, Amsterdam.

Theil, H. (1979): The Measurement of Inequality by Component of Incomes, Economics Letters, 2.

Theil, H. (1989): The Development of International Inequality, Journal of Econometrics, 42.

Thistle, P. D. (1988): Uniform Progressivity, Residual Progression and Single–Crossing, Journal of Public Economics, 37.

Thistle, P. D. (1989): Ranking Distributions with Generalised Lorenz Curves, Southern

Economic Journal, 56.

Thistle, P. D. (1989a): Duality between Generalised Lorenz Curves and Distribution Functions, Economic Studies Quarterly (forthcoming).

Thon, D. (1979): On Measuring Poverty, Review of Income and Welath, 25.

Thon, D. (1981): Income Inequality and Poverty: Some Problems, Review of Income and Wealth, 27.

Thon, D. (1982): An Axiomatisation of the Gini Coefficient, Mathematical Social Sciences, 2.

Thon, D. (1983): A Note on a Troublesome Axiom for Poverty Indices, Economic Journal, 93.

Thon, D. (1983a): A Poverty Measure, Indian Economic Journal, 30.

Thon, D. (1983b): Lorenz Curve and Lorenz Coefficient: A Sceptical Note, Weltwirtschaftliches Archiv, 119.

Thon, D. (1985): A Note on Taxation, Incentives and Risk Sharing, Operations Research Letters, 3.

Thon, D. (1987): Redistributive Properties of Progressive Taxation, Mathematical Social Sciences, 14.

Thurow, L. (1971): The Income Distribution as a Pure Public Good, Quarterly Journal of Economics, 85.

Tinbergen, J. (1975): Income Distribution: Analysis and Policies, North–Holland, Amsterdam.

Tinbergen, J. (1975a): Income Differences: Recent Research, North–Holland, Amsterdam.

Todaro, M. P. (1969): A Model of Labor Migration and Urban Unemployment in Less Developed Countries, American Economic Review, 59.

Townsend, P. (1979): Poverty in the United Kingdom, Allen Lane, London.

Toyoda, T. (1980): Decomposability of Inequality Measures, Economic Studies Quarterly, 31.

Trannoy, A. (1986): On Thon's Axiomatisation of the Gini Index, Mathematical Social Sciences, 11.

Trannoy, A. (1989): An Axiomatisation of Inequality Indices by Principle of Transfers, Presented at the European Meeting of the Econometric Society, Munich.

Ulph, D. (1978): On Labor Supply and the Measurement of Inequality, Journal of Economic Theory, 19.

United Nations Economic Comission for Europe (1957): Economic Survey of Europe in 1956, Geneva.

Vaidyanathan, A. (1974): Some Aspects of Inequalities in Living Standards in Rural

India, in Srinivasan and Bardhan (1974).
van Praag, B. M. S. (1977): The Perception of Welfare Inequality, European Economic Review, 10.
van Praag, B. M. S. (1978): The Perception of Income Inequality, in Krelle and Shorrocks (1978).
van Praag, B. M. S., T. Goedhart and A. Kapteyn (1980): The Poverty Line: A Pilot Survey in Europe, Review of Economics and Statistics, 62.
van Praag, B. M. S., A. Hagenaars and W. V. Eck (1983): The Influence of Classification and Observation Errors on the Measurement of Income Inequality, Econometrica, 51.
Vaughan, R. (1987): Welfare Approaches to the Measurement of Poverty, Economic Journal, 97.
von Weizsäcker, C. C. (1978): Annual Income, Life Time Income and Other Income Concepts in Measuring Income Distribution, in Krelle and Shorrocks (1978).
Watts, H. W. (1968): An Economic Definition of Poverty, in D. P. Moynihan (ed.), On Understanding Poverty, Basic Books, New York.
Weinhardt, C. (1987): On Inequality Measurement when Population Sizes Differ, Methods of Operations Research (forthcoming).
Weinhardt, C. (1988): Currency Independence in Inequality Measurement, Methods of Operations Research (forthcoming).
Weinhardt, C. (1989): The Trade–off between Real Equity and Real Efficiency in Welfare Measurement Theory, Mimeographed, University of Karlsruhe.
Wertz, K. L. (1979): The Measurement and Trend of Income Inequality: Comment, American Economic Review, 69.
Weymark, J. A. (1981): Generalised Gini Inequality Indices, Mathematical Social Sciences, 1.
White, M. and A. White (1965): Horizontal Inequality in the Federal Income Tax Treatment of Homeowners and Tenants, National Tax Journal, 18.
Wiles, P. J. D. (1974): Income Distribution, East and West, North–Holland, Amsterdam.
Williamson, J. G. (1977): Strategic Wage Goods, Prices and Inequality, American Economic Review, 67.
Wold, H. (1935): A Study on the Mean Difference, Concentration Curves and Concentration Ratio, Metron, 12.
Yaari, M. E. (1987): The Dual Theory of Choice under Risk: Risk Aversion without Diminishing Marginal Utility, Econometrica, 55.
Yaari, M. E. (1988): A Controversial Proposal Concerning Inequality Measurement,

Journal of Economic Theory, 44.
Yitzhaki, S. (1979): Relative Deprivation and the Gini Coefficient, Quarterly Journal of Economics, 93.
Yitzhaki, S. (1980): Relative Deprivation and the Gini Coefficient: Reply, Quarterly Journal of economics, 95.
Yitzhaki, S. (1982): Stochastic Dominance, Mean Variance and Gini's Mean Difference, American Economic Review, 72.
Yitzhaki, S. (1982a): Relative Deprivation and Economic Welfare, European Economic Review, 17.
Yitzhaki, S. (1983): On an Extension of the Gini Inequality Index, International Economic Review, 24.
Yitzhaki, S. (1989): Economic Distance and Overlapping of Distributions, Mimeographed, Department of Economics, Hebrew University.
Yitzhaki, S. and R. I. Lerman (1988): Income Stratification and Income Inequality, Mimeographed, Department of Economics, Hebrew University.
Yntema, D. B. (1933): Measures of Inequality in the Personal Distribution of Wealth and Income, Journal of the American Statistical Association, 28.
Yoshida, T. (1977): The Necessary and Sufficient Condition for Additive Separability of Income Inequality Measures, Economic Studies Quarterly, 28.
Yoshida, T. (1983): The Lorenz Partial Ordering and Lerner's Probabilistic Egalitarianism, Economic Studies Quarterly, 34.
Young, A. A. (1917): Do the Statistics of the Concentration of Wealth in the United States Mean What they are Commonly Supposed to Mean?, Journal of the American Statistical Association, 15.
Young, H. P. (1987): Progressive Taxation and the Equal Sacrifice Principle, Journal of Public Economics, 32.
Young, H. P. (1987a): On Dividing an Amount According to Individual Claims or Liabilities, Mathematics of Operations Research, 12.
Young, H. P. (1988): Equal Sacrifice in Taxation, in W. Eichhorn (1988).
Young, H. P. (1988a): Distributive Justice in Taxation, Journal of Economic Theory, 44.
Zagier, D. (1983): Inequalities for the Gini Coefficient of the Composite Population, Journal of Mathematical Economics, 12.

Subject Index

[Page references for definitions and explanations only]

MIX
Papier aus verantwortungsvollen Quellen
Paper from responsible sources
FSC® C105338

If you have any concerns about our products,
you can contact us on
ProductSafety@springernature.com

In case Publisher is established outside the EU,
the EU authorized representative is:
Springer Nature Customer Service Center GmbH
Europaplatz 3, 69115 Heidelberg, Germany

Printed by Libri Plureos GmbH
in Hamburg, Germany